PRAISE FOR *CHALLENGING THE FANTASY BOND*

Challenging the Fantasy Bond is a triumph of contemporary depth psychology. From the formation of human personality to the formation of the culture and spiritual ethos out of which it arises, this book is essential reading for anyone concerned about a deeply gratifying life.

—KIRK J. SCHNEIDER, PHD, AUTHOR OF *THE POLARIZED MIND: WHY IT'S KILLING US AND WHAT WE CAN DO ABOUT IT* AND *THE DEPOLARIZING OF AMERICA: A GUIDEBOOK FOR SOCIAL HEALING*

This lucid and engaging account of the *fantasy bond* and *voice therapy* is fortified by empirical research from clinical, social psychological, and cognitive neuroscience. Profound and provocative, it's a must-read for academics, clinicians, and anyone interested in enhancing personal growth and fostering social progress.

—SHELDON SOLOMON, PHD, SOCIAL PSYCHOLOGIST; PROFESSOR, SKIDMORE COLLEGE, SARATOGA SPRINGS, NY, UNITED STATES; COAUTHOR OF *THE WORM AT THE CORE: ON THE ROLE OF DEATH IN LIFE*

Here is an original guidebook on the process of therapeutic change. Detailing a substantial theory developed and refined over the last 60 years, this is essential reading for those who value in-depth work in psychotherapy.

From the Foreword to *The Fantasy Bond: Structure of Psychological Defenses* (1985)

Firestone's therapy is based on love—genuine love in action, compassionate, forbearing, non-intrusive, skilful in the nitty gritty of psychotherapeutic professional practice.

CHALLENGING
the
FANTASY
BOND

CHALLENGING

the

FANTASY
BOND

A Search for Personal Identity and Freedom

ROBERT W. FIRESTONE

In Collaboration With Tamsen Firestone and Joyce Catlett

 AMERICAN PSYCHOLOGICAL ASSOCIATION

Published by
American Psychological Association
750 First Street, NE
Washington, DC 20002
https://www.apa.org

Order Department
https://www.apa.org/pubs/books
order@apa.org

In the U.K., Europe, Africa, and the Middle East, copies may be ordered from Eurospan
https://www.eurospanbookstore.com/apa
info@eurospangroup.com

Typeset in Charter and Interstate by Circle Graphics, Inc., Reisterstown, MD

Printer: Gasch Printing, Odenton, MD
Cover Designer: Mark Karis

Library of Congress Cataloging-in-Publication Data

Names: Firestone, Robert, author.
Title: Challenging the fantasy bond : a search for personal identity and freedom / Robert W. Firestone.
Description: Washington, DC : American Psychological Association, [2022] | Includes bibliographical references and index.
Identifiers: LCCN 2021030431 (print) | LCCN 2021030432 (ebook) | ISBN 9781433835810 (paperback) | ISBN 9781433835827 (ebook)
Subjects: LCSH: Fantasy. | Defense mechanisms (Psychology) | Denial (Psychology) | Separation (Psychology)
Classification: LCC BF175.5.F36 F567 2022 (print) | LCC BF175.5.F36 (ebook) | DDC 154.3--dc23
LC record available at https://lccn.loc.gov/2021030431
LC ebook record available at https://lccn.loc.gov/2021030432

https://doi.org/10.1037/0000268-000

Printed in the United States of America

10 9 8 7 6 5 4 3 2 1

To Barry Langberg,
true friend and compatriot.

Contents

Foreword

It's an honor to contribute a foreword to this comprehensive book by Robert W. Firestone, a brilliant psychologist who has led an amazingly long, creative, and productive life as a clinician, researcher, and writer. As he mentions when describing his personal and professional history, he completed his doctoral dissertation in 1957, based on experiences with schizophrenic patients, and has since worked with a diverse array of "neurotic" and "normal" children, adults, couples, and families. This means he has been developing, testing, and perfecting his ideas for over 60 years! During that time, in addition to working with hundreds of clients, he has studied a large longitudinal sample of "normal" (i.e., normally troubled) American individuals and their families and has helped to create a unique institution in Santa Barbara, California: The Glendon Association, which produces excellent books, videos, and webinars related to his work.

Many of the Glendon webinars are conducted by one of Robert's daughters, Lisa Firestone, who is also a clinical psychologist. She and Robert coauthored a chapter in one of our edited volumes, *Meaning, Mortality, and Choice*, and we have spoken with Lisa, along with her and Robert's colleague and coauthor, Joyce Catlett, in webinars and at various professional conferences over the years. We know them well, have been influenced by their work, and are now pleased to see that some of our work has influenced them and this new book.

Robert W. Firestone's separation theory, in name and content, is in some respects a complement to John Bowlby's attachment theory, the focus of our own research. Firestone analyzes what he calls a "fantasy bond" that can develop in close relationships (e.g., between a child and parent, between marital partners, between a religious individual and God, between group members and their groups and group leaders). This kind of bond (a word, in this case, meant to evoke "bondage") is created as a defense against anxiety related to separation, aloneness, and—ultimately—death. It's an aspect of what we would call insecure attachment and is, early in life, a result of non-optimal parenting.

While providing a degree of comfort, fantasy bonds interfere with the novelty, vitality, and complexity of authentic human relationships and with mature individuation. When challenged or threatened, the bonds are defensively clung to. (They are what Buddhists call "attachments"—a goal of Buddhist practice being a state of "nonattachment.") Firestone analyzes the psychological costs of fantasy bonds (e.g., rigidity, withdrawal, self-preoccupation, projection, sexual difficulties, health problems) in illuminating detail and explains the costs (psychological pain) and gains of successfully severing or deconstructing the bonds. His account is clear, beautifully organized, personally revealing, and leavened with engaging and enlightening case examples.

The terms "bond," "bonding," "attachment," "secure" and "insecure attachment," and "nonattachment" can be confusing. When most contemporary writers use the term "attachment bond," they intend it to be positive, but when Firestone writes about "fantasy bonds," he intends the word "bond" to be negative. Within attachment theory, attachment is viewed as a natural process that can have positive effects, including supporting a person in ways that increase his or her strengths and skills, contributing to an increased capacity for individuality and autonomy. But attachment can also occur within the context of a dysfunctional relationship, leading to greater insecurity (of an anxious, avoidant, or disorganized/disoriented quality). The ideal adult outcome, according to attachment theory, is a person who is secure enough in relationships to be able to do without dysfunctional defenses and act and communicate authentically in ways that benefit both self and others. But the theory still views adults as potentially positively "attached" in their relationships.

Bowlby's conception of attachment was based partly on an evolutionary biological analysis of the function of infant–mother attachment in the lives of humans and nonhuman primates and in emotional attachments between marital partners. Being trained as a psychoanalyst, Bowlby incorporated his ideas about primate attachment, separation anxiety, and grief into a version of psychoanalytic theory that included the usual Freudian desires, passions, conflicts, and defenses. But besides characterizing the infant–mother bond in Darwinian and psychoanalytic terms, Bowlby also incorporated ideas from then-emerging cognitive and cognitive developmental theories. He hypothesized that early experiences with parents, as well as later close relationships, including those with a therapist, contribute to conscious and unconscious "internal working models" of self and relationship partners. Aspects of working models have now been measured in numerous ways by attachment researchers—via dreams, fantasies, projective tests, laboratory priming experiments, questionnaires, and interviews.

Firestone has developed another fascinating and important method for revealing the nature of conscious and unconscious working models: voice therapy. When a therapy client is asked to give literal voice to the kinds of internal criticisms, worries, and uncertainties that all of us experience from time to time—criticisms that cause shame, guilt, frustration, and feelings of inadequacy—the surprised client may suddenly experience and express power-ful, painful emotions. (There are helpful examples of these reactions in the present book and in several instructive and emotionally moving Glendon videos.) Firestone calls this process "feeling release therapy," originally based in part on Arthur Janov's primal scream therapy. Several useful things can happen when a person engages in voice therapy: (a) he or she may realize that the externalized voice ("You're the stupid one, you're the ugly one," etc.) is the voice of a parent or other important attachment figure; (b) memories or exam-ples of being treated this way, often years or decades earlier, become vividly available to consciousness; and (c) with the help of the therapist, a person can look at this aspect of his or her working models from a new, more mature perspective and consider ways to counteract or change them. The resulting insights and freedom from the tension associated with defending against the critical voices play an important part in the therapeutic process.

Because we are academic researchers rather than clinicians, we have con-ducted theory-based studies, using standardized measures and procedures, to test specific hypotheses. The results are usually stated in general, statistical terms. For example, people who score relatively high on measures of attach-ment anxiety tend to be overly vigilant about their romantic partners' where-abouts, phone calls, interest in possible alternative partners, etc. People who score relatively high on measures of attachment-related avoidance eschew self-disclosure in a laboratory get-acquainted exercise.

The beauty of the "voice" technique is that it reveals an individual's unique pattern of "anti-self" attacks. Having encountered and studied many forms of fantasy bonds and self-attacks, Firestone is able to conceptualize and generalize about them, but at the same time, in his clinical work with individuals, he adjusts his approach to fit each unique client. His insight into individual cases is something we, as academic generalizers, don't convey with general terms like "negative working models of self and others."

In Firestone's studies of and clinical interactions with a large group of families, he was able to see how a parent's unique inner voices and working models, often hidden from consciousness and self-examination by strong defenses, can be passed on to the parent's children. One woman externalized a voice toward herself that said, "You were never supposed to have been born; no one wanted you." Amazingly, her daughter later enacted a similar voice, which she said didn't literally duplicate something her mother said aloud, but did express the way the mother's behavior made her feel. Such occasions provide special opportunities to work clinically with both mother and daughter.

Because of the long period over which Firestone's work has developed, it incorporates a number of theoretical and empirical traditions from different decades. In the beginning, he was influenced by a combination of ideas and techniques from classical and existential psychoanalysis, as well as radical "anti-psychiatrists" (e.g., R. D. Laing) and Marxist-influenced psychoanalysts (e.g., Herbert Marcuse). There was, and still is, in Firestone's theorizing a strong sense of the importance of liberation from restrictive social and psychological constraints (liberation being conceptualized as the breaking of fantasy bonds). This is rather different from the tenor of Bowlby's attachment theory and therapy, which suggests altering dysfunctional working models in the direction of greater security but not (at least not explicitly) achieving liberation from constraints. There's also an echo in Firestone's writing of early humanistic psychologists (e.g., Carl Rogers, Abraham Maslow), who suggested that a fully functioning and maturely autonomous person can get free from parental "conditions of worth" and achieve a state of unconstrained creativity and self-actualization. Beyond those early roots of Firestone's theory are several new elements: recent discoveries in clinical and social neuroscience (e.g., mirror neurons being one means of unconsciously incorporating parental behavior and speech), developmental and adult attachment research, and research on death anxiety inspired by terror management theory. The range of ideas and clinical problems addressed by Firestone, as well as his clear expression of personal values, make the book philosophical as well as scientific in a way not often seen in contemporary research-oriented psychological writings. The book can be read productively and with great interest by a general audience as well as professional researchers and clinicians.

The important issues of death and death anxiety (the "terror" aroused by the ultimate, mysterious, uncontrollable, and unavoidable separation) are covered by Firestone in several ways, including from an existential perspective, a review of terror management theory and research, and a knowledge of research on suicidal tendencies and "microsuicidal" behaviors. (Finding ways to provide effective therapy for suicidal clients has been one important aim of The Glendon Association.) Firestone also deals with the human tendency to cling to restrictive religious ideas and commandments, and to become blindly enmeshed in powerful, domineering organizations and social movements. In many organizational contexts, a person may defend against feelings of separateness, vulnerability, and insignificance by developing a fantasy bond with someone or something larger than self, which often creates a temptation to merge uncritically into an ingroup and viciously attack outgroups. (One common reaction to critical inner voices is projection, leading a person to strike out in anger against supposed external enemies.)

In short, in this impressive book, based on a long lifetime of careful observation and thinking, Firestone deals with all levels of psychological and sociological analysis from brain to child–parent relationships, adult sexual relationships, group membership, and collective aggression. His comprehensive and profound theorizing is something rarely encountered in this era of quick drug or behavioral therapy and small, focused empirical studies. It has been energizing and intellectually productive for us to grapple with and discuss Firestone's manuscript. All of us can enjoy and benefit from Firestone's deep insights into our problems and various means by which to improve ourselves and our relationships.

Phillip R. Shaver, PhD
Distinguished Professor of Psychology Emeritus
University of California, Davis

Mario Mikulincer, PhD
Professor of Psychology
Baruch Ivcher School of Psychology
Interdisciplinary Center (IDC) Herzliya
Herzliya, Israel

Acknowledgments

I want to express my appreciation to Tamsen Firestone and Jo Barrington for their dedicated involvement in producing this update, *Challenging the Fantasy Bond.* I am also grateful to Lisa Firestone, who, with her experience as a psychotherapist and her extensive knowledge in the field of psychology, has helped in updating this volume.

I thank Susan Short for her editing skills, Maria D. Vazquez for assembling a comprehensive new reference list, and Myah Mashhadialireza for helping with this task. I am appreciative to Frank Tobe for compiling and formatting the manuscript in preparation for publication, as well as for founding The Glendon Association. I extend my gratitude to the staff of The Glendon Association for supporting and promoting my work, especially Jina Carvalho, Director of Communications. I am also thankful to Nina, Carolyn, Lena, and Sara Firestone for their long-term involvement in PsychAlive.com, a website devoted to "psychology for everyday life."

My appreciation goes to Emily Ekle, editorial acquisitions director, academic and professional books, at American Psychological Association Books, for asking me to update my original work so that it would reflect the development of my theory and methodology over the last 35 years. I thank Susan Reynolds, acquisition editor, Judy Barnes, development editor, and Erin O'Brien, copy editor, for their encouragement and suggestions regarding the mechanics of producing a completely revised edition of an established work.

I extend my special thanks to Phillip R. Shaver and Mario Mikulincer for their acknowledgment of my work, their contribution to the field, and their generosity in writing the foreword for this book. I would also like to express my gratitude to each person who has contributed their personal experiences to this book, thereby opening a window to the core dynamics affecting individuals, relationships, family life, and society at large.

Finally, I would like to express my deep appreciation to my longtime dear friend and fellow author, Joyce Catlett, with whom I wrote the original *Fantasy Bond* in 1985. We have collaborated on 16 books and countless journal articles since writing our first book in 1981. Joyce, I have valued sharing this long and remarkable journey with you.

CHALLENGING
the
FANTASY
BOND

INTRODUCTION

The early version of my theoretical approach set forth in *The Fantasy Bond* was intended primarily for psychologists, psychiatrists, and others in the mental health field. However, it has come to be sought after by lay readers as well, many of whom commented on the book's profound impact on their lives. In addition, the core concepts involved in this work have proven to be valid since the original publication in 1985. This, combined with the continuing demand from psychotherapists and other mental health professionals who recommended *The Fantasy Bond* to their clients as an adjunct to their therapy, made me feel it necessary to update the book and to place the original concepts in the broader context of my overall theoretical approach, separation theory.

This new volume, *Challenging the Fantasy Bond: A Search for Personal Identity and Freedom*, reflects a more thorough look at the destructive manifestations of the fantasy bond and its negative impact on the individual, partners in intimate relationships, families, and the larger society. It emphasizes the exposure of fantasy bonds, manifested externally in the form of imagined connections and internally in the form of a disparaging critical

https://doi.org/10.1037/0000268-001
Challenging the Fantasy Bond: A Search for Personal Identity and Freedom, by R. W. Firestone

inner voice. Dissolution of the fantasy bond and movement toward separation and individuation are essential for the pursuit of one's destiny as a fully autonomous human being.

The book describes how the fantasy bond acts as a primary psychological defense, partially alleviating anxiety and offering a false sense of security and safety. This revised publication stresses how this illusion of merged identity acts as a buffer against death anxiety, illustrating how this contributes to distortion and maladaptation in personal relationships and other aspects of life. On a societal level, the feelings of security achieved by identifying with a specific group or cause provide individuals with a sense of belonging, while at the same time, the fantasy of fusion predisposes alienation and fear of those who have different beliefs and worldviews.

In this updated text, I describe my expanded investigations into the dynamics of the critical inner voice, which supports both the fantasy bond and a generally defensive style of living. I explain how hurtful, hostile, and rejecting parental attitudes are incorporated into the child's negative self-concept. This is the origin of a basic division of the mind that exists within each person, which can be conceived of as a fundamental split between the self and the anti-self. This concept clarifies how children, and later adults, become divided between maintaining a positive regard for themselves and others, as well as an angry, critical, alien view that has a damaging effect on their lives.

New case histories illustrate and elaborate the dynamics involved in the underlying forces at work between the fantasy bond and the critical inner voice. The book offers a fresh look into the relationship between the voice and self-destructive behavior, suicide, and acts of violence and describes the development of assessment tools for identifying at-risk individuals. *Challenging the Fantasy Bond* also presents the latest version of voice therapy, which has proven to be effective in identifying and counteracting both self-destructive attitudes and behavior and cynical, hostile attitudes toward others (Doucette-Gates et al., 1999; L. Firestone, 2004; R. W. Firestone, 1992, 2021; Leonard, 1967 [cited in R. W. Firestone & Firestone, 2002]; Lester, 2004; Schneidman, 1985 [cited in R. W. Firestone & Firestone, 2002]). It explains how the methods have been used to help clients differentiate from enmeshed family systems.

In the intervening years since *The Fantasy Bond* was published in 1985, I have become familiar with key findings from the neurosciences, attachment theory, and terror management theory that validate many aspects of my theory. In addition, I have had the opportunity to gather further data and insights from individuals in both clinical and nonclinical populations that have contributed significantly to my understanding of human behavior. These developments have further convinced me of the value of revising *The Fantasy Bond* to include the evolution in my own thinking, as well as corroborative research in related disciplines.

This edition is especially timely because it identifies significant psychological and social factors, based on people's defensive responses to existential fears, that contribute to malignant prejudice, warfare, terrorism, and ethnic cleansing. Developing an understanding of the role played by the fantasy bond as a powerful defense against death anxiety that ultimately leads to polarization and divisiveness between groups and nations may well be essential to human existence.

ORGANIZATION OF THE BOOK

Challenging the Fantasy Bond is divided into five sections. Part I, Introduction to the Fantasy Bond, describes the basic tenets of my theoretical approach, the fantasy bond, and the voice process. Chapter 1 delineates factors in early childhood that predispose the development of these core defenses, which significantly limit one's adult life. Chapter 2 explores the distinctive negative effects that the fantasy bond has on couple relationships, family life, and child-rearing practices.[1]

Part II, Dimensions of the Fantasy Bond, provides an in-depth analysis of the major components of the fantasy bond. Chapter 3 describes the idealization of parents and family, a dimension of the fantasy bond stemming from the infant's extreme and prolonged dependence on parental figures. Chapter 4 explains how the negative self-concept develops concomitantly with the idealized image of the parent, leading to the division in the psyche described earlier between the self and the anti-self. Chapter 5 shows how the processes of projection and incorporation help maintain the child's imagined merger with the idealized parent—that is, the projection of the parent's negative traits onto other people and the incorporation of these undesirable traits into the self.

Each chapter in Part III, Behavioral Manifestations of the Fantasy Bond, deals with specific behaviors and lifestyles that represent an adaptation to deficiencies and painful experiences in one's early environment. These defenses include inwardness and a progressive loss of feeling; withholding,

---

[1]The names, places, and other identifying facts in the case examples have been fictionalized, and no similarity to any persons, living or dead, is intended.

a holding back or withdrawal of emotional and behavioral responses from others; self-nourishing habit patterns and addiction; regressive trends associated with the process of individuation, which can be precipitated by both positive and negative events; and an analysis of the dynamics underlying problems in sexual relating.

In Part IV, Implications for Psychotherapy, Chapter 11 outlines my overall approach to psychotherapy, which is multidimensional and represents a synthesis of psychoanalytic techniques, feeling release therapy, and voice therapy. Chapter 12 delineates the steps in voice therapy, a cognitive–affective–behavioral methodology, that helps people emancipate themselves from imagined connections with parents, identify and overcome destructive internalized voices, and embrace more life-affirming ways of meeting their needs and pursuing their goals in life.

Part V discusses theoretical issues that are brought to the fore when the pervasive influence of the fantasy bond is understood. Chapter 13 describes myriad psychological defenses against death anxiety that, although providing a modicum of comfort, have serious negative consequences for individuals, their relationships, and society at large. Chapter 14 examines the impact of the individual on society and of society back on the individual. It addresses conformity, social pressure, and the subject of human rights. The final chapter of *Challenging the Fantasy Bond* explores polarization and the psychodynamics of aggression, prejudice, and ethnic strife.

CONCLUSION

As I see it, each person is born with a variety of propensities that are essentially human. The basic qualities of our unique heritage are the ability to love and feel compassion for ourselves and others, the capacity for abstract reasoning and creativity, the capability to set goals and develop strategies to accomplish them, the awareness of our mortality and other existential concerns, the desire to search for meaning and social affiliation, and the opportunity to experience the sacredness and mystery of life. Whenever any of these qualities is damaged, we lose a part of ourselves that is vital. Working through and growing beyond destructive aspects of the fantasy bond and other self-limiting psychological defenses allow individuals to develop their independence and autonomy, achieve greater freedom and satisfaction in life, and ultimately help people fulfill their human potential.

PART I INTRODUCTION TO
THE FANTASY BOND

1

THE FANTASY BOND AND SEPARATION THEORY

We live in a fantasy world, a world of illusion.
The great task in life is to find reality.

—Iris Murdoch

The fantasy bond, a major tenet of my theoretical approach, separation theory, explains how children defend themselves from interpersonal pain and existential angst by forming an illusion of connection, fusion, or merged identity originally with the parent or primary caregiver. As individuals develop, the fantasy process is extended to family members, romantic partners, authority figures, and social groups. While the imagined connection offers a temporary respite from stress, separation anxiety, and death fears, it tends to be maladaptive in life and interferes with a person's movement toward individuation and autonomy (R. W. Firestone, 1984, 1985).

When misattunement, neglect, or mistreatment threaten the security of the child's attachment to their primary caregiver, they attempt to deny the stressful situation and maintain an idealized conception of that person. At the same time, they internalize an image of themselves as worthless or bad,

https://doi.org/10.1037/0000268-002
Challenging the Fantasy Bond: A Search for Personal Identity and Freedom,
by R. W. Firestone

thereby developing a negative self-concept. The fantasy bond represents both the original imagined connection with one's parents or primary caregiver formed in childhood and the adult's repetitive efforts to seek security in forming fantasized connections in new relationships. Elements of the fantasy bond are manifested in group identification and religious and ideological alliances, as well as political affiliations, often leading to elitism and exclusivity and eventually to prejudice and ethnic strife. Anger and resentment are directed toward people with different beliefs and customs from one's own because they threaten one's fantasy solutions (R. W. Firestone, 1994, 1996, 1997a).

The fantasy bond is a unifying psychological concept that explains how human beings seek comfort and security in fantasies of fusion that insulate them from the emotional pain and the tragic awareness of death's inevitability. Yet, it tends to lead to an inward, protective style of living in which an individual seeks satisfaction more in fantasy than in the real world. It involves reliving rather than living, choosing bondage over freedom, the old over the new, the past over the now (R. W. Firestone, 1985). It initiates the attempt to recreate a parent or parents in other persons or institutions. It causes the abrogation of real power in exchange for childish manipulations. It instigates the avoidance of genuine friendship, free choice, and love in favor of illusion and a false sense of safety.

Over the past 5 decades, I have continued to develop and refine my theoretical ideas. I refer to my theory as separation theory because human life can be conceived of as a series of significant weaning experiences beginning with birth and ending with death, the ultimate separation. My theory points out how psychological defenses operate to relieve the anxiety related to separation experiences but at the same time restrict one's personal fulfillment, freedom, and self-actualization. In this book, I endeavor to place the fantasy bond, along with other fundamental concepts from current theoretical thought, in the context of separation theory.

SEPARATION THEORY

My approach integrates psychodynamic and existential systems of thought in explaining how early trauma leads to defense formation and how these original defenses are reinforced as the developing child becomes aware of their mortality. It emphasizes the major impact of death awareness on early personality development, as well as its continued influence on human beings throughout life (R. W. Firestone, 1994, 1997a, 2019; R. W. Firestone & Firestone, 2012).

Psychoanalytic theory stresses the importance of unconscious motivation, explains how interpersonal trauma leads to the formation of defenses, identifies conflict and competition within the family system, and explains how resistance and transference enter into the therapeutic process (S. Freud, 1953). However, it fails to deal effectively with the role that death awareness and existential anxiety play in life and the powerful impact these phenomena bring to bear on the continuing development of the individual.

Existential psychology emphasizes the importance of death anxiety and death awareness on the personality, as well as on other issues of being, such as individuation, autonomy, and the pursuit of transcendent goals (Bugental, 1976; Frankl, 1963; Kierkegaard, 1954; Maslow, 1971; May, 1983; Schneider, 2004; Yalom, 1980). However, it largely neglects to address the dynamic psychoanalytic conception of defense formation, competition, and family dynamics. It is my opinion that neither approach is sufficient; both are necessary for a complete understanding of human behavior.

Separation theory is akin to the theories of Rank (1936/1972), Sullivan (1953), Fairbairn (1952), and Guntrip (1969). It underscores the polarity within a person between self-affirming, goal-directed tendencies and defensive, self-defeating processes (R. W. Firestone, 1997a). Separation theory is a comprehensive conceptual model that explains defense formation as a response to both interpersonal and existential trauma. It acknowledges the effect of death awareness on human life and describes both individual and societal defenses against death anxiety.

Separation theory also shares a close kinship with attachment theory. Attachment theory systematically illustrates a variety of psychological adaptations related to the degree of distress people experience early in life. Both theories recognize that children are born into an imperfect world and develop survival mechanisms to cope and adapt and that later these same defensive adaptations limit and hurt individuals in their natural development. While separation theory and attachment theory are dynamic and closely related, separation theory emphasizes the effects of existential fears on the developing child.

THE FANTASY BOND

To some degree, all children suffer from the pain and frustration of not having their needs adequately met in early childhood. Human beings are born into an inherently flawed situation because they are totally reliant on their parents for physical and emotional survival over a prolonged period. Unfortunately, it is not possible for even the most sensitive parents to be perfectly attuned to their offspring. Therefore, it is unfeasible, even under the best circumstances, that all of a child's needs will be fully met at all times (Tronick, 2007; Note 1).

When the infant experiences a distressing event or overwhelming feelings of aloneness or rejection, they attempt to cope with the excessive frustration, separation anxiety, and personal trauma by using their emerging powers of imagination to create an internal image of being fused with the parent or significant caregiver. This imagined connection becomes the original fantasy bond and, together with rudimentary self-nurturing, self-soothing behaviors, acts as a self-parenting process that leads to an illusory feeling of safety and self-sufficiency.

It is necessary to differentiate this specific use of the word *bond* from its other uses in psychological and popular literature. It does not refer to *bond* as in *bonding* (parent–infant attachment) in a positive sense, nor does it refer to a relationship that includes loyalty, devotion, and genuine love. The concept of the fantasy bond uses *bond* in the sense of bondage or limitation of freedom.

The *fantasy bond* refers to an imaginary connection or illusion of fusion with the parent that offers relief from emotional distress (Note 2). It involves an idealization of the parental figure and a corresponding negative image of self. To some extent, it minimizes and denies the reality of parental abuses. This process predisposes the child's incorporation of critical and destructive parental attitudes. These attitudes are often internalized during the parents' worst moments, when they are most punitive and are perceived by the child as the most threatening.

In romantic relationships, people tend to recreate the original fantasy bond within the dynamics that develop within the couple. As a relationship progresses and becomes more meaningful, the personal attachment threatens to penetrate basic defenses and disrupt the emotional balance each person has carefully constructed. Conflict often develops between partners as they strive to preserve their defenses while simultaneously trying to remain close.

When feelings of anxiety and insecurity inherent in being vulnerable and undefended arise in the relationship, partners unconsciously try to merge and form an imaginary unit. Gradually they substitute a fantasy of love for genuine affection and closeness. The fantasy bond within the couple acts as a core defense alleviating anxiety and offering a false sense of security and safety. To the extent that couples form this bond, they tend to become emotionally cut off from their real feelings and insensitive to those of their partner. At the same time that the partners are avoiding intimacy, they are generally forming destructive dependency ties with one another (R. W. Firestone & Catlett, 1999).

Originally, the infant uses the fantasy bond to defend against feeling helpless, frightened, and alone. Later, when the child becomes aware of death, the fantasy of fusion is used to defend against the fear, anxiety, and desperation caused by this existential crisis. The imagination of fusion in couple relationships also functions as a defense against death anxiety. On a societal level, the fear of death reinforces a tendency to unconsciously merge with a group or cause (R. W. Firestone, 1994).

Once a fantasy bond is established, considerable anxiety is experienced when the imaginary connection is threatened. Both children and adults unconsciously defend the fantasy bond against any persons or events that may challenge or contradict it.

Determining Factors of the Fantasy Bond

The protracted dependence of the human infant on its parents for physical and psychological survival provides the original condition for the creation of defenses. The fantasy bond is formed during this critical growth period when children are the most vulnerable to inputs from the environment. According to researchers in the field of interpersonal neurobiology, development of an infant's mind is almost completely dependent on stimuli from the people in the immediate surroundings, especially during the first 2 years of life (Cozolino, 2006; Schore, 2003, 2005, 2009, 2019; D. J. Siegel, 1999, 2012, 2020; D. J. Siegel & Hartzell, 2003; Note 3). The infant, lacking any sense of time, knows only the intensity of the moment and suffers intolerable fear and emotional pain when faced with frustration and separation anxiety (Winnicott, 1958; Note 4).

For the infant, the imagined connection with the parent provides partial gratification of their emotional needs and physical hunger, relieves their anxiety, and soothes their distress (Note 5). In other words, the fantasy bond serves as a substitute for love and care when it is missing in the early environment. The more emotional and physical deprivation that the infant experiences, the more dependency they will have on the illusion of fusion. An infant who feels empty and starved emotionally increasingly relies on self-nurturing fantasies and self-soothing behaviors (e.g., thumb sucking, rocking) for gratification, and indeed, this process offers some degree of relief.

Psychological defenses, including the fantasy bond, are strongly reinforced as children become aware of death, usually between the ages of 3 and 7 (Anthony, 1973; Hoffman & Strauss, 1985; Kastenbaum, 2000). Initially, they realize that their parents will die. They become afraid and grieve the possible loss of their parents but still retain some semblance of security. Later, children become aware that they themselves will die. This traumatic discovery demolishes their illusion of self-sufficiency and omnipotence. The world that they once believed to be permanent is turned on its head by their realization that everyone, even they, must eventually die. On an unconscious level, they attempt to deny the certainty of their finite existence. Often, children regress to a stage of development before they were aware of death and, in the process, strengthen the fantasy bond (R. W. Firestone, 1994; R. W. Firestone & Catlett, 2009a).

After children learn about death, the fantasy bond becomes their core defense against death anxiety. Even though defenses are instituted to block death awareness from consciousness, children's trauma is preserved in the unconscious, much as it was originally experienced. This terror is partially relieved by maintaining, on some level, a magical belief or fantasy that they will never die. Nevertheless, the suppressed fear of death continues to exert an influence on the life of the developing child and later on the adult.

Throughout the life span, although defenses against death anxiety may provide some relief, they also tend to be self-limiting and maladaptive. The fear of death continues to reinforce the defenses that people formed early on. In an unconscious effort to avoid this anxiety, most people ration their aliveness and spontaneity, restricting their freedom or carefully doling out positive or potentially fulfilling experiences to themselves. Nevertheless, when there is an increase in death awareness or an indirect reminder of death, their primitive fear reactions frequently reemerge. Defenses against death awareness rarely succeed in completely eliminating existential fear (R. W. Firestone & Catlett, 2009a).

Pseudo-Independence and the Process of Incorporation

The fantasy bond and its illusion of connection with an all-powerful parent lead to a posture of pseudo-independence in the developing child: "I don't need anyone; I can take care of myself." By denying their needs and wants from other people and, in effect, parenting themselves, children strive to operate as a complete, self-sufficient system. The more pain and suffering a child experiences, the greater the necessity to incorporate the parent and the accompanying self-parenting process.

To feel safe, the child must maintain an idealized image of a parent who is loving, nurturing, and invincible. Recognition of real shortcomings in the parent would threaten to destroy the fantasy bond and the imagined self-sufficiency it provides. If children were to find fault with their parents and see them as lacking, their situation would truly be hopeless. To defend against the realization that their parents are inadequate or even threatening, children deny their parents' limitations and failings and instead conceive of themselves as bad or unlovable.

Children develop an internal split and come to view themselves as a combination of the good, omnipotent parent and the bad, needy child. The more they retain the division of this dualistic notion, the more dysfunctional their actual relations are with others. The more pseudo-independent and reliant on fantasy children are, the more dependent and helpless they become in the real world and the more they feel the need to be taken care of (R. W. Firestone, 1997a, 1997b).

When children imagine themselves as one with their parent to protect against the feelings of hurt, pain, and rejection from that parent, they also incorporate the parental attitudes and behaviors that are causing them distress. In this manifestation of the fantasy bond, children parent themselves in the same destructive ways their parents did.

THE SELF AND THE ANTI-SELF

Children's total dependency on their parents for survival underscores their need to preserve the fantasy bond; thus, when they are criticized or rejected by the parent, they are prone to side with that parent and take on a negative view of themselves. As a result, they are divided between a positive regard for themselves and an alien, hostile view that has a destructive effect on their lives. This division within the personality can be conceptualized as comprising the self and the anti-self systems (R. W. Firestone, 1997b).

The *self system* consists of individuals' unique characteristics, including their biological, temperamental, and genetic traits, the synchronistic identification with parents' affirmative qualities and strivings, and the ongoing effects of experience and education. Parents' lively attitudes, positive values, and active pursuit of life are easily assimilated into the self system through the process of identification and imitation and become part of the child's developing personality (R. W. Firestone, 1997b).

In contrast, the *anti-self system* is made up of assimilated negative parental points of view that become a discordant and incompatible aspect of the personality (R. W. Firestone, 1997b). During times when a parent acts uncharacteristically out of control and appears to be frightening and threatening to their child, children defend themselves by identifying with that parent, partially relieving their fear and further exacerbating the essential division within their personality. For example, irritability or anger on the part of parents, particularly when disciplining their children, may be felt as threatening and cause tremendous fear to the child. In situations where there are deficiencies in the parental environment or where parents are punitive or abusive, children cease to identify themselves as the helpless victim and instead assume the characteristics of the powerful, hurtful, or punishing parent. This maneuver of splitting from the self partially alleviates the child's terror. However, in the process, children take on not only the animosity and aggression directed toward them but also the guilt, fear, and, indeed, total complex of the parent's defensive adaptation (R. W. Firestone, 1997b). In identifying with the aggressor, the child fragments into the self and the anti-self. Rather than suffer this fracture, many children side with this internal enemy (Note 6).

To the extent that people are possessed by this alien aspect of their personality, they exist as divided selves. Depending on which element is ascendant at any one moment—self or anti-self—an entirely different point of view will be manifested (R. W. Firestone, 1997b; Note 7).

THE CRITICAL INNER VOICE

The critical inner voice represents the language of the internalized parental anti-self system described earlier. It functions as a secondary defense that supports the fantasy bond and the self-parenting, inward behavior patterns that accompany it. The voice comprises a series of negative thoughts that criticize and punish a person, oppose the process of self-realization, and predispose negative, cynical, and hostile attitudes toward self and others. These thoughts range from minor criticisms to major attacks and foster soothing habit patterns, isolation, and a destructive lifestyle (R. W. Firestone, 1986, 1987).

Critical attitudes and destructive internal voices are incorporated either through parents' verbally assigned negative labels to their children or generalizations and assumptions that children made about themselves based on the type of mistreatment they encountered. Subsequently, what people tell themselves about their experiences contributes more to their personal misery than do the actual problems and negative events in their lives. Individuals carry this abusive voice with them throughout their lifetime, restricting and punishing themselves and eventually repeating similar abuses with their own children (R. W. Firestone, 1990a).

The Critical Inner Voice and the Fantasy Bond

The voice directly supports the defensive manifestations of the fantasy bond: the attitude of pseudo-independence and the incorporation of negative parental attitudes and behaviors. The voice encourages self-protective, self-nurturing thoughts and behaviors, as well as self-hating, self-punitive attitudes and self-destructive actions (Note 8).

Voices that are self-nurturing simultaneously discourage wanting and interpersonal interactions while encouraging pseudo-independence. They are destructive in that they support a defensive adaptation of self-denial and self-sufficiency. They have overtones similar to those of an overprotective parent, coddling, directing, praising, and controlling in a way that ostensibly has the person's best interests at heart. In reality, these voices make a person more fearful and dependent. They also offer a false build-up, thereby setting the stage for subsequent self-attacks, as well as hostile and/or aggressive attitudes toward others, when the person inevitably fails to live up to the aggrandized image.

The self-punishing aspect of the voice process acts as a malevolent and disapproving parent who directs, criticizes, and punishes the person. The voice communicates the message that the person is unlovable and worthless. In this way, it preserves the initial image of the bad child. Voice attacks may or may not be the specific criticisms or abuses that the parents expressed; however, the style of attack and the underlying hostility are representative of the parents' negative feelings toward the child. Children are attuned to their parents' feelings and incorporate the emotions that lie behind their statements. The critical inner voice serves to protect the fantasy bond by interpreting reality in such a way as to uphold the original parental misconceptions of the child (R. W. Firestone, 1985, 1988, 1997a).

Voice Therapy Methodology

A technique that I designed and termed *voice therapy* helps people to identify faulty programming both from their family of origin and from society; gain insight into the relationship between these factors and negative internal voices; modify their hostile, critical attitudes, toxic personality traits, and hurtful behaviors accordingly; and, last, formulate their own ideals and values rather than automatically adopting those of others. Through this process, people are able to emancipate themselves from imagined connections with parents, challenge self-destructive manifestations of early imprinting, and learn to embrace more life-affirming ways of satisfying their needs and pursuing their goals.

Voice therapy methodology encompasses five steps: (a) identifying and verbalizing hostile thoughts and attitudes toward one's self and/or others and releasing the accompanying affect, (b) discussing insights from verbalizing the voice, (c) confronting and answering back to the attacks on self and others from one's own point of view, (d) understanding the impact of voice attacks on present-day behavior and formulating therapeutic goals, and (e) challenging the negative traits and reactions promoted by the voice by collaborating with the therapist in the planning and implementation of corrective behaviors (R. W. Firestone, 2018).

Voice therapy involves being able to process anger and deep sadness without resorting to defensive maneuvers. When people are open to their emotions and are able to tolerate irrational, angry, competitive, or other "unacceptable" feelings, they are less compelled to act these out toward themselves or others. Remaining vulnerable and undefended not only allows people to avoid neuroses and live fuller lives but also leads to a more positive and humane approach to others. In recognizing and gradually relinquishing the authority of the voice as an antifeeling, antilife regulatory mechanism, people gain a sense of their personal power and feel far less victimized by other people or situations.

DIFFERENTIATION

Separation theory has significant implications for psychotherapy in that it places a strong emphasis on individuation and differentiation from the conditioning that occurred in the family of origin. The ultimate goal of psychotherapy is to help people overcome their personal limitations and to maintain a healthy balance between feeling and rationality that reflects their basic humanness and supports the development of their true self. Separation theory focuses on identifying and breaking with negative parental introjects and addictive attachments and moving toward autonomy and independence.

Most people are largely unaware of the extent to which they are reliving rather than living their lives. They fail to fully recognize how their lives are divided and negatively affected by what their critical inner voices tell them about themselves and the world in general. Indeed, many find it difficult to tolerate the kind of life they say they want because expanding their boundaries and finding love or warmth revive the pain and emptiness of past hurts. They find it difficult to differentiate from the familiar, albeit negative, image of themselves because to think of themselves as genuinely good or kind or generous could rekindle feelings of repressed sadness. They are averse to reawakening primitive feelings left over from childhood and, in numbing themselves to these negative emotions, they block out positive emotions as well. If they were to embrace their true feelings and experience them fully, they would have to recognize their own innocence and feel their vulnerability. They would become aware that they were hurt or rejected through no fault of their own.

For people to pursue their own destiny, they must differentiate from the destructive aspects of their early programming and cultivate significant characteristics of their unique identities (Bowen, 1978; Kerr & Bowen, 1988). In the process of differentiating, they must contend with and challenge fantasy bonds and develop a realistic perspective of themselves and their formative influences (R. W. Firestone et al., 2012). Differentiation makes it possible for people to become more independent, function primarily in the adult mode, live with integrity, and potentially embrace a more inclusive worldview.

RESEARCH THAT VALIDATES SEPARATION THEORY

In recent years, there have been research findings from attachment theory, the neurosciences, and terror management theory that support and validate key concepts of separation theory.

Findings From Attachment Theory

Attachment theory is based on Bowlby's (1973, 1980) concept of an evolutionarily determined attachment behavioral system. When the attachment system is activated—that is, when infants are distressed or afraid—they seek proximity to the parent or primary caregiver for a sense of safety, security, soothing, and being seen in relation to their wants and needs. In situations where caregivers fail to respond to the infant's distress, respond inconsistently, or are largely misattuned, infants adapt by developing specific strategies to get their needs met. They attempt to deactivate the awareness of their wants and needs (avoidant attachment) or intensify the expression of their needs (anxious attachment), depending on their parent's characteristic way of responding or not responding because of their own unresolved issues of trauma and loss (Ainsworth et al., 1978).

There are certain commonalities between separation theory and attachment theory. Both address the process of defense formation—that is, the adaptations that children make to survive psychologically in the environment into which they are born. As Laczkovics et al. (2018) observed, there is "compelling evidence that attachment style is an important determinant of the type of defense mechanism utilized by the individual to maintain psychological stability" (Abstract). Both separation theory and attachment theory focus on relational, two-person, or dyadic phenomena in exploring children's reactions to separation, loss, and other trauma (Lyons-Ruth, 2003; Note 9).

Attachment researchers have observed that when the parent is unresponsive for any reason, infants experience painful feelings of shame because they sense they are unimportant in that when they express their needs, nothing happens. They attempt to "downregulate" their emotions and shut down or put below their level of awareness their basic wants and needs to avoid being repeatedly subjected to unbearable feelings of shame. Due to their overriding need for safety, however, they cannot afford to see the parent as weak or unable to meet their needs; instead, they see themselves as not having needs, as being able to take care of themselves. By adopting an avoidant attachment strategy, these children feel self-sufficient, imagine they need nothing from anyone, and see others who express their needs as childish and dependent.

In a similar vein, it is my hypothesis that in forming a fantasy bond, children tend to idealize their parents and develop a negative self-concept, a sense of being unlovable or undeserving of love. The posture of complete self-sufficiency manifested by these children, as depicted in attachment literature, is also closely related to my description of the sense of pseudo-independence that children achieve in forming a fantasy bond.

If a parent is inconsistent, intrusive, or, as I have described in my work, "emotionally hungry," the infant intensifies its efforts to gain proximity to that attachment figure. The child turns up the volume, so to speak, and remains hyperfocused on the parent, hoping to eventually elicit a response. These infants become anxiously attached to the parent, exhibiting clinging behavior and desperately trying to get their needs met, while at other times, they push away or try to avoid the parent who is intrusive or emotionally hungry. These children are rarely relaxed or satisfied because they are unable to be soothed.

Most concerning are situations in which a parent is either terrifying or terrified when the infant approaches them for comfort. In these cases, the infant exists in a situation of fear with no resolution—essentially a double bind: The person to whom they would naturally turn for safety, security, and soothing is terrifying or terrified of them (Main, Goldwyn, & Hesse, 1985). Because the parent is unpredictable and alarming, there is no organized strategy for infants to adopt to have their needs met. These infants would be described as having a disorganized attachment to a specific parent. The outcome for these children can be observed in their inability to regulate their emotions in healthy ways.

Children develop "internal working models" consisting of cognitive schema or scripts related to their expectations and beliefs regarding the possibility of having their needs sensitively responded to in a new relationship. Insecure (avoidant and anxious) attachment patterns are strongly influenced by these working models and persist over time, particularly if the environment remains relatively constant. According to Bowlby (1973, 1980), these patterns tend to continue into adulthood, mediated by internal working models with beliefs and expectations regarding the availability and reliability of future relationship partners (Note 10).

There are a number of similarities between the concept of the voice and the idea of negative internal working models in terms of their predisposing factors (Bretherton & Munholland, 2016). Both concepts refer to, or include, negative views of the self, distrust of others, and expectations of rejection, which are hypothesized to originate in early experiences with misattuned, inconsistent, or emotionally unavailable parents.

The voice can be conceptualized as the "language" of the cognitive schema or scripts that make up negative internal working models. In a previous work (R. W. Firestone, 1990b), I proposed that the voice represents an unconscious or partly conscious mechanism that is primarily responsible for the transmission of negative parental traits, behaviors, and defenses through successive generations. Other attachment researchers (Bretherton & Munholland, 2016; Shaver & Clark, 1994) have found that negative internal working models have a detrimental effect on the way partners relate to one another in an intimate relationship. Similarly, I have shown how the voice induces people to maintain the negative identity incorporated during early personal interactions in their new affiliations.

Findings From Interpersonal Neurobiology

Findings from research in the neurosciences and interpersonal neurobiology have illuminated physiological changes that take place in the brain when a person suffers trauma or unusual stress (Note 11). It has become increasingly clear from brain imaging studies that painful experiences occurring during infancy and early childhood lay down neural pathways in the developing brain, often before children are capable of formulating words to describe what they are experiencing (Cozolino, 2014, 2020; Schore, 2009, 2011, 2019; D. J. Siegel, 2020). Researchers have pinpointed mirror neurons in the brain that enable infants to recognize and adapt to their parent's feeling state and intentions (Iacoboni, 2009). During misattuned or otherwise frightening interactions with a parent, these specialized brain cells enable an infant to detect the parent's emotional state and intentions, but they also result in the infant internalizing or taking on the parent's negative attitudes and state of mind at that moment in time. According to Badenoch (2008), "With the discovery and exploration of *mirror neurons* in the last decade, we are becoming aware of how we constantly embed within ourselves the intentional and feeling states of those with whom we are engaged" (p. 37).

Separation theory provides a psychological understanding of the physiological processes uncovered by researchers in the field of interpersonal neurobiology. The data from voice therapy research support their observation of how, under conditions of stress, children adapt by identifying with the damaging parent or perpetrator and incorporate into themselves the critical or hostile attitudes that are being directed toward them (Note 12).

Findings From Terror Management Research

In my theoretical approach to existential issues, I describe a wide range of psychological defenses against death anxiety and show how the defensive denial of death, while providing a modicum of comfort, also leads to serious negative consequences. A primitive survival strategy of human beings is to seek safety in numbers, to gain protection from predators by seeking the cover of a group. On a societal level, when death anxiety is aroused, frightened individuals attempt to merge their identities with that of the group by conforming to its beliefs or worldviews. This illusory fusion provides them with a feeling of immortality and invulnerability. They feel threatened and become hostile and aggressive when these defenses are disrupted by people with different attitudes and customs (R. W. Firestone, 1996; R. W. Firestone & Catlett, 2009a, 2009b).

These hypotheses have been validated by extensive empirical studies conducted by terror management theorists and researchers. Their findings have demonstrated that when death awareness is experimentally heightened, people increasingly rely on defense mechanisms (Solomon et al., 2004, 2015). More specifically, reminders of death trigger people to reaffirm the aspects of their culture or religious beliefs that imbue them with a sense of immortality and direct hostility toward individuals and groups holding conflicting views or beliefs.

Both theories recognize that people have defensive reactions to death anxiety and that individual defenses are combined with those of others to form a significant aspect of culture. In turn, these socially validated mores, rituals, and institutions continually reinforce the defenses each member employs to protect against the fear of death (R. W. Firestone, 1985, 1994, 1996; R. W. Firestone & Catlett, 2009a, 2009b). Group identification based on the fantasy bond leads to a sense of superiority of one group over others. This partially explains why people with their own particular set of customs, belief systems, and religious practices are often polarized against those who manifest different ways of living and viewing the world.

Once a fantasy bond is formed, any eventualities that threaten it cause anxiety and arouse aggression. This core element is a contributory factor in prejudice, ethnic strife, genocide, and religious wars and is therefore relevant to both understanding and changing the destructive orientation of humankind. Hopefully, insight into the dynamics of the fantasy bond could lead to a more inclusive worldview that inspires people to value life and humanitarian ideals for everyone (R. W. Firestone & Catlett, 2009a).

CONCLUSION

This chapter has described the development of separation theory and articulated its basic tenets—in particular, the fantasy bond and the voice process. The fantasy bond is a unifying psychological concept that explains how human beings seek comfort and security in fantasies of fusion that insulate them from emotional pain and the tragic awareness of death's inevitability.

The voice process explains how the traumatic elements of one's childhood are internalized, creating an ongoing division in the personality between the self and the anti-self. Left unchallenged, the anti-self operates as an extensive alien viewpoint that negatively impacts people throughout their lives. This unconscious or partly conscious mechanism is responsible for the transmission of destructive parental qualities, behaviors, and patterns of defense through successive generations (R. W. Firestone, 1990b).

Understanding the dynamics of the fantasy bond and voice process has strong implications for identifying damaging behaviors and flawed programming in the family and society. Developing insight into the relationship between defenses and aggressive responses and offering a method for counteracting these destructive trends constitute a challenge to what some consider to be humankind's basically violent nature.

It has been my clinical experience that individuals can challenge their defenses, alter their self-concept in a favorable direction, and develop a more realistic view of themselves and their parents. This frees them to pursue more goal-directed lives, achieve better, more rewarding personal relationships and enhances their sense of happiness and well-being. In addition to furthering their personal development, it also increases their understanding of and compassion toward others; this involves learning to be human in the best sense.

2 THE FANTASY BOND IN THE COUPLE AND FAMILY

Let there be spaces in your togetherness . . .
Love one another but make not a bond of love . . .
Give your hearts, but not into each other's keeping.

—Khalil Gibran, *The Prophet*

By the time most people reach adulthood, they have solidified their defenses and exist in a psychological equilibrium that they do not wish to disturb. Remnants of the original fantasy bond persist and are manifested in self-protective, self-nurturing, self-critical, and self-destructive behaviors, attitudes, and habits that keep them self-contained and contribute in part to an illusion of self-sufficiency. While this self-protective orientation has a negative impact on a person's overall adjustment, it particularly affects the ability to form and sustain a love relationship.

Most adults have some fear of intimacy, but at the same time, they are terrified of being alone. Their solution to this dilemma is to form a fantasy bond with their partner. The fantasy of love and attachment allows them to maintain emotional distance while simultaneously assuaging loneliness.

https://doi.org/10.1037/0000268-003
Challenging the Fantasy Bond: A Search for Personal Identity and Freedom,
by R. W. Firestone

Within a couple, symbols of togetherness and images of love strengthen the fantasy bond, whereas genuine experiences of love and intimacy may intrude on the imaginary connection. Many people sustain an illusion of love and unity while behaving toward their partners in ways that are insensitive, overly critical, hostile, or disrespectful. Even when this type of relationship lasts, each person's individuality, independence, and overall sense of well-being are often seriously compromised (R. W. Firestone & Catlett, 1999).

The fantasy bond is the antithesis of a healthy personal relationship in which people are free to express true feelings and desires. The imagined connection perpetuates feelings of distrust, self-hating thought processes, and a tendency to engage in distancing behavior. In this type of destructive coupling, people surrender their unique point of view for a mirage of safety and a fantasy of eternal love. Fantasy bonds exist, to varying degrees, in a majority of couple relationships and are discernible in most families (R. W. Firestone, 1987, 1990b).

DETERMINING FACTORS OF THE FANTASY BOND IN THE COUPLE

People are most likely to form romantic attachments at a time when they are open, outward and less defended, and willing to reach out to others and risk more of themselves emotionally. In the new love relationship, the person exists for a while in a vulnerable state in which they feel exhilarated and spontaneous in their personal interactions.

Because of this, being in love is exciting but often frightening at the same time. As a relationship evolves and becomes more meaningful and intimate, it threatens to disrupt each individual's emotional homeostasis by penetrating basic defenses. The level of emotional exposure arouses fears of loss or abandonment and a dread of being rejected. The depth of loving feelings evokes poignancy and sadness in the partners, especially when the affection and companionship in the new relationship stand in stark contrast to a lack of love in their early lives.

Sooner or later, these reactions become so disconcerting that people unknowingly attempt to erase this difference. Partners gradually retreat from feeling close and begin to give up the most valued parts of their relationship. Conflict develops between them as they attempt to maintain the defenses and fantasies of love that have helped sustain them since childhood while at the same time trying to hold onto their initial feelings of genuine love and affection. The two conditions tend to be mutually exclusive (A. Freud, 1966; Person, 1996, 2006; Person & Klar, 1994; Note 1). As Anna Freud

(1966) asserted, "It is certain that in adult life gratification through fantasy is no longer harmless. Fantasy and reality become incompatible: it must be one or the other" (p. 81) and Eric Hoffer (1955/2006) affirmed, "We do not really feel grateful to those who make our dreams come true, they ruin our dreams" (p. 97).

It becomes difficult for members of a couple to sustain loving feelings toward their partner or to feel that they themselves are lovable once they have defended themselves. Friendly and respectful feelings begin to deteriorate. In a relatively short time, one or both partners often unconsciously forfeit companionship and love to preserve their respective defenses. As the relationship declines, they gradually substitute a fantasy of love in place of kind, respectful, and loving interactions, preferring symbols of love over its reality.

As the fantasy bond in the relationship solidifies, symptoms of the destructive connection begin to appear more frequently. For example, partners who once spent hours talking to each other begin to be less communicative. They make less eye contact and stop noticing what the other person is feeling. They become less personal and honest in their interactions. A sense of obligation or reliance on routine replaces the desire to be together. They begin to act according to roles, behaving more like half of a couple or like a "boyfriend," "girlfriend," "partner," or "spouse," rather than as a separate person who is in a relationship with another, absent any role. Typically, one or both partners begin to hold back their affectionate and sexual responses. Their original attraction for each other tends to diminish, and their sex life becomes more predictable.

Symptoms of a bond often appear following a commitment that originally reflected the partners' real feelings for each other. This commitment may be to living together, marriage, or starting a family. These milestones are often mistakenly taken to be a guarantee of continued love and security—an external validation of the fantasy bond. The sense of belonging to another person, of having proprietary rights over the other, of being loved forever after offers a reassurance, albeit an illusion, that is difficult to resist.

Given the nature of love—a feeling that is dependent on a wide range of circumstances and that can fluctuate from weak to strong—pledges of absolute, eternal love are unrealistic. Partners tend to react negatively when they attempt to nail down each other's feelings or make promises that they will always feel loving toward each other. However, a mutual commitment that respects each person's individuality and expresses a desire to be associated with the other throughout life can be a positive expression of deep feeling rather than an attempt to find ultimate security.

More often than not, both members of a couple are resistant to recognizing the fantasy bond and its destructive effect on their relationship. They surrender themselves as autonomous individuals to be able to hold on to their imagination of fusion, as though they were clinging to real people.

> Mateo and Victoria had been married for 15 years, but their relationship had deteriorated considerably in the last 5. They were spending more and more time apart, with Victoria spending most of her free time with her girlfriends. When the couple was together, the tension between them was apparent.
>
> Victoria spoke openly about her unhappiness in their relationship. With her close friends, she expressed her dissatisfaction with their sexual relationship. She disclosed that she felt very little when she and Mateo were sexual and had to fantasize to get excited. She even wondered how it would be to explore her sexuality with another partner.
>
> Mateo complained about Victoria's increasing absences. He felt rejected by her. He also objected to her moodiness, which she acted out freely with him. He disliked that she was away, even though when she was home, he did not feel close to her, and she seemed unhappy and irritable.
>
> When Victoria eventually left Mateo, their friends were not surprised. Everyone who knew them thought their split was long overdue. However, Mateo was devastated. He felt completely blindsided by Victoria's rejection. His friends and family were shocked when he said that he had not seen it coming. When they pointed out how unhappy he and Victoria had been with each other, Mateo said, "We did have a few minor problems, but basically we were in love."
>
> Mateo's idealization of Victoria, and his fantasy bond with her, enabled him to ignore the reality of how their relationship had become unsatisfying and hurtful. Over the following year, even though Mateo began to feel livelier and more engaged in his life than he had in a long time, he continued to grieve for the loss of what he imagined their relationship to have been.

In my therapy practice, I have seen many couples who manifest this type of dynamic. In a conjoint session, a husband might complain about his wife ("She's always distracted," "She won't discipline the kids," "She doesn't want to make love"). The wife, in turn, might enumerate her husband's faults ("He always watches sports," "He indulges the kids," "He doesn't open up and talk personally"). The accumulation of years of criticisms and frustrations is revealed. When I ask, "Why are you two together?" their answer is often indignant: "Because we love each other!" However, it is difficult for me to see the love in some of these battle-scarred couples. The respect, concern, and caring that existed at one time are now barely visible.

Characteristics of the Fantasy Bond in the Couple

People who have formed a bond in their romantic relationship tend to idealize their partner much like they do their family of origin. Often, they come to prefer an inward style of existence, with a minimum of authentic relating. In addition, each partner unconsciously attempts to regulate the flow of love and affection, both the amount of love they express and the amount of gratification they are willing to receive. By holding back qualities that are most admired or valued by the partner in this manner, they can unwittingly diminish their partner's love, even turning it into anger or hatred. By moderating the partner's loving feelings in these ways, they maintain a more comfortable distance while keeping their defenses intact. Through withholding and manipulation, each partner is able to control and limit the other's positive feelings.

The transition from real love to a fantasy of love is subtle and hard to detect. The fantasy bond can be inferred from certain types of behavior that demonstrate that the partners have moved away from actively relating and expressing love to one another. The changes described next often indicate that a fantasy bond has formed within a couple.

Form Replaces Substance

Couples caught up in a fantasy bond typically focus on form over substance. That is, they place more value on symbols of their union than on maintaining actual intimacy in real time. They put great importance on honoring established routines, rituals, and traditions, such as birthdays, holidays, fixed date nights, and regular vacations. As long as these symbolic activities are maintained, the fantasy of love is upheld, regardless of whether or not it is emotionally close and loving between the couple. Both people begin operating more from habit and a sense of obligation than from choice.

At the same time, any event that arouses an awareness of separateness threatens partners' fantasies of fusion and precipitates anxiety. Sensing this threat on some level, most couples negotiate agreements regarding a wide range of rules and implicit contracts to reassure themselves that they are still in love. When analyzed, these arrangements can be seen to represent the "form" of a relationship; they include unspoken rules governing conventional and obligatory behaviors that replace partners' spontaneous acts of generosity and kindness that characterized the early phases of their relationship (R. W. Firestone et al., 2006; Kipnis, 2003; Note 2).

Individuality Is Sacrificed

As the fantasy bond becomes stronger, both partners sacrifice their individuality to maintain the illusion of being joined. They gradually assume an attitude of ownership over each other, with less concern for the partner as a separate entity. Eventually, each of them effectively disappears as a distinct human being.

As partners forfeit their independence, they become increasingly code-pendent rather than interdependent. Both are weakened as individuals and lose sight of the reality that they are each capable of functioning auton-omously. Operating as half of a whole rather than as a complete person slowly takes its toll. When the individuals in a couple stop regarding them-selves and their partner as separate beings, they are less able to see each other clearly. They become blind not only to the positive traits in the other but also to the other's negative or self-destructive qualities. With this limita-tion, they are no longer able to offer empathy and compassion and cannot be true friends to one another.

Equality Is Compromised

As partners give up their autonomy, the equality between them erodes. When they stop interacting as two separate people, their relationship tends to become unbalanced and unequal. Often, one person takes on the role of parent while the other assumes the role of child. In areas where one partner is weaker or less accomplished than the other, it is tempting for that partner to lean on the other and become progressively more dependent. This type of dependency further undermines people, and they become increasingly dysfunctional. If one partner is stronger or more capable in general, there is a tendency for that partner to take over and assume control in many areas of the relationship. The authoritarian role disregards this partner's vulnera-bility and disrespects the other's capability. These polarizing postures do not only foster inequality and upset the balance in a relationship but they are also fundamentally dishonest because neither partner is a parent or a child; they are both simply adults (Willi, 1982; Note 3).

Sexuality Wanes

By and large, the fantasy bond has a detrimental impact on sexual relating. Form and routine gradually replace lively and spontaneous sexual inter-actions. Each partner begins to relate as a mere extension of the other—an appendage—and thus becomes less appealing to the other. Inequality between partners fosters hostility and resentment that typically permeate the couple's overall sexual relating. Consequently, the partners are intimate less and less frequently, often moving toward a sexless relationship.

Physical intimacy can disrupt the illusion of connection provided by the fantasy bond. The sex act is a real but temporary physical connection or union followed by a distinct separation. Similarly, moments that are emo-tionally personal and intimate, with close and affectionate contact, always come to an end, at least for a time, as the partners move on with their everyday lives. Each of these transactions has an ending and necessitates a letting go. For these reasons, authentic love and sexual intimacy can challenge the fantasy of connection and arouse an acute awareness of aloneness (R. W. Firestone, 1984, 1987; R. W. Firestone & Catlett, 1999; R. W. Firestone et al., 2006; Perel, 2006; Schnarch, 1991; Note 4).

Communication Breaks Down

Formation of the fantasy bond usually leads to a breakdown in communication within a couple. When the partners' life together becomes more focused on the superficial aspects of their relationship, their conversation also becomes shallower and more practical. When they engage in behavior that is routine and predictable, they tend to seek comfort in discussing the same narrow range of topics. When the partners come to relate more as a unit, they often invade each other's boundaries. They may even speak for each other. Each may become dismissive and impatient when the other talks or may not listen at all. When partners no longer see the other as who they are, they lose the ability to communicate the way they would with anyone else. Instead, they relate with less compassion, empathy, interest, and understanding.

In time, the fantasy bond becomes a pact of mutual protection wherein each partner implicitly agrees to honor the other's defenses. Each avoids confronting their partner's self-destructive habits and behaviors, though these behaviors may cause great concern and worry. Each wards off the other's deep feelings so that neither has to experience the sadness inherent in the caring and tenderness shared within an intimate relationship.

Dynamics of the Fantasy Bond in the Couple

Most adults have unconsciously established a psychological equilibrium to contend with the basic conflict between reliance on an internal fantasy process for gratification and seeking satisfaction in the external world. This balance is threatened when their incorporated negative identity is disrupted by being valued or loved by someone significant to them in their adult life. Anxiety is aroused when the balance shifts away from being self-contained, and they begin to turn to another person for love and fulfillment. As noted by R. D. Laing (1960/1969), this shift in relating from the intrapersonal to the interpersonal can leave partners feeling unstable and insecure, and they often react by retreating to a more familiar, less personal style of relating that replicates the dynamics in their family of origin.

The concept of the fantasy bond when applied to a couple relationship demonstrates people's compulsion to relive the past with new persons. The illusory connections they form invariably lead to a reenactment of defensive styles of relating developed in childhood. In essence, people transform the dynamics in their new relationship to more closely correspond to those present in the early environment in which their defenses were established. This process of reverting to outmoded patterns of relating interferes with the establishment of secure and satisfying adult relationships.

The processes of selection, distortion, and provocation enable partners to preserve their introjected parent, or voice, and relive the emotional climate of their childhoods in their current relationships.

Selection

Selection is a defensive mechanism whereby individuals choose partners who are similar in appearance, behavior, and defenses to one or another member of their family of origin. People are resistant to forming a relationship with someone who behaves toward them in a manner that is qualitatively different from the type of treatment they received as children. They are drawn to a person whose style of relating feels comfortable and familiar. In essence, they select a partner who fits in with their own defenses. Often, people come to hate the very traits in their partner that they were originally drawn to (Pines, 1999). This explains the irony of the fact that the people to whom one is most attracted are often not necessarily those who are good for one's overall development (Mikulincer & Shaver, 2016; Note 5).

Distortion

When people select a partner whose manner of relating is unfamiliar to them, particularly one who loves and values them in a way that is essentially different from what they are used to, they tend to distort that person to recreate conditions that are more familiar. They often misperceive their partner as more similar to a parent or family member than they actually are. This often involves exaggerating their partner's faults. Clearly, this process is hurtful and leads to escalating cycles of blame and counter-blame and to developing grudges on both sides that are difficult to resolve. As a result, much individuality and closeness are lost.

> Kara and Peter had been in a long-term relationship when Kara was diagnosed with an illness that would impact her life for several years. They were told that her recovery would be slow and she would be unable to work. Peter was deeply pained for Kara, especially because he knew how much she valued her independence and how ambitious she was. Peter was particularly loving and supportive toward her during this time.
>
> Kara began to struggle in their relationship. At times, she thought that Peter was critical of her or annoyed with her. On occasion, she misread him

and imagined that he was angry with her. When she felt ill, she assumed that he wanted to get rid of her. Peter felt misunderstood and confused by Kara's reactions to him.

Kara sought therapy to help her come to terms with her illness and the impact it was having on their relationship. As she explored her childhood, her reactions began to make sense to her. She described how her mother was typically aloof and remote. When she was a baby, her mother had hired a nanny because she did not like changing diapers. Kara recounted how her mother had been especially rejecting and disengaged whenever Kara was sick. Kara realized that she had been misperceiving Peter as reacting to her as her mother had. She was pained when she understood this connection, both for herself as a child and for her relationship with Peter. She began to be able to sense when she was distorting him and used what she was learning in therapy, especially insights like this, to help her see Peter more clearly at those times.

Not all distortions are negative. Positive as well as negative qualities from the past are assigned to significant people in a person's current life. However, both types of distortion of reality are maladaptive. Any misconception, whether an exaggeration of admirable traits or undesirable qualities, causes problems in relating. People want to be seen for who they are. Being misperceived by one's partner is hurtful and arouses angry responses.

Provocation

When the two previous methods fail to reproduce past relationship dynamics adequately, people resort to provocative behavior that establishes distance from their partner and helps maintain the safety of their original defensive solution. Provocation involves the manipulation of a loved one to elicit familiar parental responses. People may accomplish this with overt behavior that incites angry, critical, or harsh reactions from their partner. They often engage in covert and passive–aggressive behavior, such as forgetfulness and insensitivity, that causes frustration, confusion, and even rage. They may hold back affectionate, loving, and sexual responses that were especially appealing to their partner. Eventually, their partner may be provoked out of their usual point of view and actually verbalize the person's exact self-attacks. Most people are unaware that their actions are inducing aggression, hostility, or withdrawal in their partner. They feel innocent because instead of recognizing that their own behaviors have changed, they perceive only that their partner is changing. Meanwhile, one's partner can ultimately be provoked to no longer love or even like them.

Patrick and Nathan met and fell in love in their late 20s. They had much in common: similar jobs, many of the same friends, and similar senses of humor. They both valued the equality in their relationship and the respect they felt for one another. This was especially true for Nathan, whose father had been overbearing and domineering. As Nathan was growing up, his father had taken control of his life, making all of the decisions and overriding Nathan's choices. Nathan resented the overinvolvement and rebelled against it as a teen.

Nathan and Patrick enjoyed the process of building a life together and sharing in the decisions involved: looking for an apartment, picking out furniture, and so forth. However, as they settled into living with one another, Nathan became indecisive and tentative about his opinions, and he began to turn to Patrick to make the decisions for them. Patrick gradually took on a more dominant role in their relationship. Nathan came to resent Patrick's assertiveness and the inequality developing between them. And, as he had with his father, he began to react as a rebellious adolescent.

Most people are largely unaware of the underlying dynamic that brings about this shift. Before they develop a conscious awareness of their anxiety, they begin to act in a manner that alters the situation. The most tender, sensitive moments in an intimate relationship are often followed by both partners pulling back to a less vulnerable, more defended place. Many relationships fail because each person incites responses in the other, which allows them to maintain a safe distance and create a familiar, albeit ungratifying, emotional environment.

Critical Inner Voices That Support the Fantasy Bond in Couples

As described in Chapter 1, the critical inner voice supports the fantasy bond by encouraging and upholding a person's retreat into an inward, self-parenting existence. This destructive thought process, which is directed both toward the self and the significant other, predisposes alienation in intimate relationships (R. W. Firestone, 1990c). The voice attacks love relationships on many fronts, not only attacking the person directly but also attacking their partner, the relationship, and even love in general. For example, in regard to oneself, the voice can try to stifle enthusiasm and feed insecurity: "Don't get so excited; you look ridiculous" or "Don't ask them out; they're not really into you."

Just as people have a split view of themselves, they also possess opposing views of the people who are significant to them. One view is compassionate and loving, while the other, which represents the anti-self, promotes the negative side of the split and is critical and cynical of one's partner: "He's so passive. You're with such a loser" or "They're just using you. When they meet someone better, they'll be done with you" or "She's not good enough for you" and the reverse, "You're not good enough for her."

The critical inner voice tries to sabotage love by attacking a person's relationship: "You're too dependent on each other" or "This relationship is never going to last." It also makes negative generalizations about love and relationships: "You can't trust anybody" or "People are fundamentally dishonest—it's just human nature." It also generalizes about gender stereotypes: "Men don't have feelings—all they care about is sex" or "Women are irrational and overemotional."

When members of a couple are "listening" to the dictates of their respective voices, their perspective is filtered through a biased, alien point of view that distorts their partner's real image. Both parties ward off loving responses, using rationalizations generated by the voice to justify their anger or distancing behavior. Partners unknowingly project their specific self-attacks onto one another and, as a result, respond inappropriately, as though they were truly being victimized or criticized.

This projection is an unconscious attempt to disown one's self-attacks in an effort to diminish internal feelings of anxiety and self-hatred. Often, it is less painful to defend one's self against outside attack than to experience the torment and sense of division inherent in recognizing the enemy within. By externalizing the voice, people are also able to deny negative experiences they encountered in their family of origin by displacing them onto their current relationship (Note 6).

DETERMINING FACTORS OF THE FANTASY BOND IN THE FAMILY

Just as the defenses that people formed in childhood hinder them from being able to experience love and intimacy fully in their adult relationships, these same defenses interfere with their ability to respond with sensitivity and attunement to their children. The child's reliance on the parents and their openness to them threaten the parents' self-protective state. Their psychological equilibrium is disturbed by their child's emotional and physical needs, as well as by the spontaneous expressions of love and affection their child directs toward them.

In forming a bond, a couple is under pressure to prevent any rupture in their image of being connected or belonging to each other. This illusion can be disturbed by the intrusion of a spontaneous, lively, loving, and affectionate child (Bowen, 1978; Kerr & Bowen, 1988; Note 7). Parents' efforts to defend themselves against the possible disruption their child may cause to their fantasy bond begin early in their child's life.

The infant is immediately drawn into the parents' world of illusion and pretense. To maintain their unreal ties, couples in a fantasy bond limit genuine emotional exchanges, and this subsequently numbs the aliveness of their children. Despite parents' concern with protecting and preserving the physical life of their offspring, they inadvertently damage the child's spirit.

Children are diverted from their natural inclination to respond lovingly to their parents. Instead, the child becomes self-protective and progressively more dependent on an illusion of being connected to them. Eventually, children become part of their parents' fantasy world. Their distress is eased to some degree as they incorporate the parents' inward lifestyle and learn to adopt their parents' specific defensive maneuvers as a coping strategy. Within the family bond, the tendency of the child to idealize their parents extends to each family member and to an illusion of family love and superiority in general. They tend to subscribe to their family's beliefs and rarely consider deviating from the shared point of view.

The common practice of defining family members in narrow terms supports the imagined connection between parents and children. Children are often categorized and given labels by their parents—labels that they carry into adulthood, often without ever challenging their accuracy. Being known as the "quiet one," "the pretty one," "the wild one," "the smart one" limits a person's sense of self. These evaluations and judgmental characterizations, positive or negative, accurate or inaccurate, are damaging because they suggest that people have static, unchanging identities. They reflect a deterministic view of human beings that militates against change and individual responsibility. In effect, defining and affixing labels provides an artificially stable identity to family members, which contributes to a false sense of security and belonging.

Emotional Hunger Versus Love

Emotional hunger is often manifested in the fantasy bond within the family. Emotional hunger is not love, though people often confuse the two. It is a primitive condition of deep longing that is related to the pain of aloneness and separateness in one's childhood. Unable to face the futility of being able to gratify their early dependency needs in their adult life, parents often turn to their children to fill the emotional void. When acted on, emotional hunger is both exploitive and damaging. This type of attention and affection drains the emotional resources of children rather than nourishing them.

Many parents believe that they are being loving and caring when, in fact, what they are actually expressing is emotional hunger. They mistakenly identify their primal longing as love and nurturing affection. They are unaware of the difference between the emotional hunger that comes from deprivation in their own childhood and the feelings of love and regard that a mature adult feels for another person in the present day. While this distinction may be apparent to an objective observer, it is often difficult for parents themselves to see. Three factors are valuable in ascertaining emotional hunger: (a) the internal feeling state of the parent, (b) the actual behavior of the parent in relating to the child, and (c) the observable effect of the parent's emotional state and behavior on the child's demeanor and behavior.

Parental behaviors based on feelings of emotional hunger include parents living through their child, children taking care of their parents (i.e., "parentification" or role reversal), parents exhibiting an anxious overconcern in relation to their child, overprotection of the child, psychological control, and the exclusion of one or the other parent. An extensive body of research now exists explicating several manifestations of emotional hunger (R. W. Firestone, 1997a, 1997b; Note 8). Emotional incest (Love, 1990) is also closely related to emotional hunger (R. W. Firestone et al., 2006) and is discussed further in Chapter 10, "Sexuality."

Emotionally hungry parents offer affection and love at the times they feel the need for it themselves. Often, they use the words "love" or "I love you" not when they feel for their children but rather when they feel a need for reassurance from them. When the word "love" is misused in this way, children become suspicious and distrustful of real emotional sharing and sincere caring. Early on, they come to doubt positive verbal expressions and physical affection because their parents' need and desperation were often covertly expressed in their communications.

Parents who have been emotionally deprived while growing up still have unfulfilled needs for love, attention, comfort, and respect. In acting on their intense needs and desire to be taken care of themselves, they tend to make parents out of their children. Many of these adults turn to their children for reassurances that they are loved and respected. In addition, parents often unconsciously believe that they will live on through their children and thereby manage to allay their anxieties about death.

One common manifestation of emotional hunger is "feeding on" or living vicariously through a child's accomplishments. Many immature parents have unresolved trauma from childhood that makes it difficult for them to relate to their children from an adult perspective. They tend to overidentify with their children's emotions, especially pain and sadness. They project the distress from their own formative years onto their children and are thereby unable to accurately perceive their children or be attuned to their unique experience of life. These parents often overcompensate in an attempt to spare their children the frustration and suffering they are imagining them to be experiencing. They tend to have an exaggerated notion of the helplessness of their children. They are unable to appreciate the maturity and capability of their child because of unresolved feelings of vulnerability and trauma from their own childhoods.

> When Gene was growing up, his mother was in and out of rehab treatment programs. His father traveled for business. During periods in which both parents were absent, Gene was farmed out to different friends and family members. Gene was lonely and emotionally neglected, both when he was at home with his parents and when he was living with others.
>
> Gene married a woman who was prone to depression and often emotionally unavailable, thereby perpetuating the loneliness of his childhood. When they had a daughter, Gene devoted himself to his child. He wanted to make sure that she never felt the kind of loneliness that he had. He dedicated himself to caring for her; he delighted in the toddler's every move. He noticed that when he was with his daughter, his loneliness was gone.
>
> But as the girl got older, Gene's exaggerated focus led to his becoming overly protective of her and overly involved in her life. For example, even though she could walk, he tended to carry her. He interjected himself into her interactions with others, both adults and children, often speaking for her and prompting her responses. When Gene was asked how he was doing, rather than speak personally, he would inevitably talk about how his daughter was doing. Gene's emotional hunger was manifested in his intense awareness of and overidentification with his child as an attempt to assuage the persistent feelings of longing from his childhood.

Emotionally hungry parents often have difficulty reconciling a real desire to protect a child from injury with an overawareness of the child's movements. These parents unduly restrict their children, using psychological control (Barber, 2002), not because of concern for their children's safety but because of the parents' intense hunger and their unconscious need to keep their child close. Their overprotectiveness tends to interfere with the child's developing sense of autonomy (Parker, 1983; Parker & Lipscombe, 1981). However, children of parents who support their child's evolving maturity typically develop a strong sense of personal value and are less likely to maintain an unhealthy dependency on their parents.

The Ideal Parent

Parents who are mature and loving typically have a positive self-image and a healthy self-regard. They have sought to resolve their childhood traumas and strive to challenge the means by which they defend themselves in personal relationships. They are autonomous and are able to tolerate their separateness as individuals. They maintain a sense of compassion for their children and themselves yet remain separate and respectful of the boundaries between them. They have a loving attachment with their children yet do not seek to gratify their basic dependency needs through a connection with them.

Genuine love sustains and nurtures a child. Loving parents have both sufficient emotional resources and the ability to express them and are thus able to provide their child with proper emotional sustenance. They are attuned to their child's wants and are able to consistently offer nurturance and care without arousing unnecessary anxiety in their child. They have the capability and the desire to provide for their infant's needs, necessary elements for the infant's physical and psychological development (R. W. Firestone, 1957). This type of parenting enables a child to grow into a healthy social being (see R. W. Firestone & Catlett, 1999, Chapter 5; Note 9).

Parental love may be operationally defined as those behaviors that enhance the well-being of children and assist them in reaching their full potential (R. W. Firestone, 1990b). Outward manifestations of love can be observed in parents who make real emotional contact with a child. This contact extends beyond practical care and is maintained through play and communication. These parents regularly make eye contact; display spontaneous, nonclinging physical affection; and take obvious pleasure in their child's company.

Loving parents act respectfully toward their children, which is reflected in a tone and style of communication that is natural and easy and indicates an understanding of a child's individuality. Their loving attitude is nurturing of the child's unique personality. Children of such parents are lively and display an age-appropriate level of independence. They have a sense of themselves as a valuable person (Maschi et al., 2013).

Attachment researchers have observed that children develop secure attachment patterns when they have a parent or other significant adult who is, for the most part, sensitive and responsive during interactions with the child, attuned and available in ways that make the child feel seen and safe, compassionate and comforting, especially when the child is hurting or distressed (Lyons-Ruth et al., 2013; Note 10). Such an adult is a strong and consistent presence in the child's life, encouraging the child's independence with a caring interest that is supportive, comforting, and fortifying as the child matures and goes forth into the world.

In encouraging their child's individuation, these parents challenge the fantasy bond in the family. They do not adhere to the notion of unconditional love for family members. Rather, they are aware that love is not constant. They accept that, just as they have ambivalent feelings toward themselves, they have ambivalent feelings toward their children. They have both tender, loving impulses and aggressive feelings. The fact that parents want to nurture their children does not invalidate any anger and hostility they may feel toward them. Conversely, the fact that they have destructive feelings toward their children does not negate their love or concern for them (R. W. Firestone, 1990b; Rohner, 1986a, 1986b, 1991; Rohner & Khaleque, 2010; Note 11). These parents understand that it is healthy to accept all feelings, no matter how negative; however, they also have the maturity to decide which feelings are appropriate to express and in what manner to express them. Parents who understand the ambivalent nature of emotions are comfortable knowing that each family member may, at any given time, have positive and/or negative feelings toward one another.

Parents who challenge illusions of connection do not engage in playing the roles of "the perfect parent" or "the perfect family," nor do they demand that their offspring play "the loving child." These parents recognize that they have limitations resulting from their own defenses. They appreciate that their children have their own unique experiences in the family and the larger world. They do not pressure their children to protect the couple's and family's illusions by hiding the truth about their experiences in the family. Engaging in this type of cover-up makes children doubt their feelings and perceptions and leaves them confused. When children are cut off from being able to express their pain and unhappiness, they are denied the possibility of healing. Confronting the fantasy bond in these ways offers family members the chance to maintain an honest relationship with genuine regard for one another.

THE IMPACT OF THE FANTASY BOND ON COMMUNICATION WITHIN THE COUPLE AND FAMILY

Personal communication in the couple is often distorted by the dishonesty and pretense involved in maintaining a fantasy bond. For this reason, communication in the nuclear family can be restrictive and duplicitous. In both couples and families, the dynamics of the fantasy bond interfere with the flow of free speech and lead to verbal communication that is manipulative and controlling. In fact, the members of a couple may develop a style of talking with each other that is dishonest and misleading long before they have children.

Certain types of interactions are more apparent between people engaged in a fantasy bond. These include sarcasm, criticality, advice giving, and even outright verbal abuse. However, there are also more subtle styles of relating that help keep the illusion of connection intact. For example, partners tend to talk for each other and represent themselves as a unit, using "we" and "our" rather than "I" and "my." In general, members of a couple progressively limit the sharing of relevant personal feelings and lose the ability to straight-forwardly articulate their wants in relation to one another. They are especially reluctant to challenge each other's defenses by engaging in exchanges of honest feedback, whether offering it in a nonhurtful manner or accepting it without retaliation.

Communication between individuals in a bond is most often directed toward sustaining the form of the relationship while disguising the fact that the substance is disappearing. In their interactions, partners avoid discussing important issues and expressing genuine emotions while at the same time using language that serves to maintain the illusion that feelings of love and compassion still exist. This style of communication, or lack of communica-tion, serves the purpose of sustaining emotional distance while preserving the fantasy bond.

The *double message* is a style of relating in which a person's nonverbal behavior and spoken words do not coincide. This acts to support the form, while negating the substance, of a relationship. In a fantasy bond, partners give double messages to one another far more often than they realize. Believing the words of one's partner while ignoring their contradictory actions leads to distortion and confusion of one's sense of reality (Gottman & Krokoff, 1989; Note 12).

To the extent that parents are involved in a fantasy bond and are deceptive about themselves or the nature of their relationship, the personal communi-cations between parents and children will be duplicitous and manipulative. Parental dishonesty and the pretense of closeness have a damaging effect on the child's developing sense of reality. Parents often give their children mixed messages to cover up their actual sentiments, especially any "unac-ceptable" negative feelings and attitudes they might have. For example, a parent may tell a child, "It's time to go to bed; you need your rest," when their actual desire is to be free of the child for the evening. The child picks up the rejecting attitude of the underlying message in the parent's tone of voice, body language, and expressive movements but is confused by the seemingly caring words. Children register, on a deep level, when they are receiving conflicting messages. However, they sacrifice their sense of reality because of their dependence on their parents and their need to believe their parent's words. Parental dishonesty and the pretense of closeness have a damaging effect on the child's developing conception of the world.

In the family, the fantasy bond leads to the curtailment of freedom of speech because certain topics are taboo. Conversations that threaten to dis-rupt the bond or interrupt the illusion of enduring love between parents or family members are discouraged or avoided. When personal communication is restricted, a toxic environment that fosters hostility and resentment is created for the developing child. The child must not exhibit signs of pain or unhappiness because this would expose negative family dynamics. Perceptions and emotional responses that disrupt the illusion of love are suppressed. This, in turn, increases the child's tendency to become inward, secretive, and cynical.

CONCLUSION

People's pseudo-independence and self-protective defenses are interrupted when they turn to another person for love. As they develop a closer, more intimate relationship, they break out of their more inward orientation and shift to wanting their needs to be met by their partner and desiring to meet their partner's needs. But this emotional give-and-take often leaves people feeling vulnerable and anxious. To relieve these feelings, they unconsciously turn to familiar defenses and begin to establish a fantasy bond with their partner. Their genuine feelings of love are slowly replaced by the illusion of being merged with and magically connected to each other. They have a fantasy of being one with their partner, just as they did with their parent in infancy and early childhood.

In the family constellation, factors such as parental ambivalence, duplicity, and role-playing lead to fundamental distortions of each member's sense of reality. Emotional hunger and the myth of unconditional parental love have a negative impact on the development of the child. Within a fantasy bond, children are regarded as possessions of the family rather than as belonging to themselves and having the right to an independent existence.

Essentially, individuals face a fundamental dilemma when entering into an intimate relationship: whether to invest fully and remain vulnerable to possible rejection and loss or to attempt to protect themselves by retreating to a more inward, defensive posture and impersonal, self-gratifying modes of relating.

Partners must be willing to face the threats to their defense system evoked by loving another person and being loved for oneself to sustain a loving relationship and avoid forming a fantasy bond. To be able to accept affection, tenderness, and love, they must be willing to challenge their negative voices, give up their well-entrenched defenses, and endure the anxiety that this would cause them.

In relation to the fantasy bond in the family, parents can come to understand that all people suffer a certain amount of trauma during their developing years. They can use this knowledge to develop compassion for themselves and feeling for what happened to them as children. They can realize that, despite their desires to do the best for their offspring, remnants of their own trauma will negatively impact their children today. They can achieve relationships with their children that are respectful and loving by recovering feeling for themselves and their own lives.

People can choose to go against their voice attacks and retain their feelings of love and affection for each other. Couples and family members can learn to share their feelings about the existential realities inherent in the human condition. In recognizing that all human beings face the same existential crisis, they can approach each other with a sense of understanding and empathy. Embracing life fully with minimal defenses enables individuals to remain open and vulnerable to the people they love. People who have the courage and determination to achieve these goals are better able to maintain an equal, respectful relationship with their partner and other family members.

PART **II** DIMENSIONS OF THE FANTASY BOND

3 IDEALIZATION OF PARENTS AND THE FAMILY

Among the adult's true motives we find. . . . Self-defense: i.e., the need to
idealize one's childhood and one's parents by dogmatically applying the
parents' pedagogical principles to one's own children.

—Alice Miller, *For Your Own Good*

A significant dimension of the fantasy bond is the idealization of the family and the protection of a positive view of the parents, particularly the mother or primary caregiver. The idealized image of the parent must be preserved because the child cannot feel safe or secure with a parent whom they perceive to be inadequate or destructive. This idealization is difficult to alter or refute because, to a large extent, it is supported by society's belief in the sanctity of parents and family. In commenting on this belief, James Garbarino (2017) observed,

> We consider ourselves a nation that cares about children and their families. Yet, this notion is something of a romantic, or self-serving idealization: policies and practices at every level in our society reveal subtle biases against children and their families. (p. 272)

https://doi.org/10.1037/0000268-004
Challenging the Fantasy Bond: A Search for Personal Identity and Freedom,
by R. W. Firestone

This cultural bias is an extension of the individual defense of idealizing the parent (Note 1). Typically, the collective glorification of the family is questioned only when there are instances of blatant child abuse or extreme neglect.

Because children imagine their parents to be more ideal and loving than they are, they tend to deny parental abuses or traumatic experiences. The illusion they develop exaggerates the parent's positive qualities and minimizes or even denies the negative. They may actually ascribe admirable traits to parents that contradict reality (Ainsworth, 1985; Reiner & Spangler, 2013; Note 2). If parents are hurtful to their offspring, their children cannot acknowledge that the parent is destructive but instead consider themselves to be at fault (R. W. Firestone, 1985, 1990b; R. W. Firestone & Catlett, 1999; Karson & Sparks, 2013; Oaklander, 1978). These children often believe that the parent is right and justified in their reactions and tend to accept the parent's distorted perception of them.

This preservation of the idealized image of the parent is possible because children have the capacity to block from their consciousness the most unpleasant or toxic qualities of the parent. This removal from awareness is made easier by their tendency to accept at face value their parent's verbal proclamations of love and concern. Children use a process of selective inattention to keep themselves unaware of indications of hostile and rejecting behavior. Paradoxically, the more the young child suffers from neglect, rejection, or mistreatment, the greater the degree of idealization of the parental figure (J. P. Allen et al., 1996; Bloch, 1978; Brennan & Shaver, 1998; Note 3). Children do not necessarily maintain a conscious, idyllic picture of their families; typically, idealization is manifested by the denial or minimization of parental abuses and trauma.

Progress in therapy involves both disrupting the client's idealization of the parent and challenging their negative self-concept. This acts to diminish a person's negative attitudes and hatred toward self; however, these changes create anxiety. As people gradually learn to stop criticizing and belittling themselves, they begin to perceive their family more realistically. They stop blaming themselves for being rejected and realize that their parents, because of their own unresolved childhood pain and unconscious defenses, were unable to provide them with much of what they wanted or needed as children. Clients begin to feel better but also experience a sense of aloneness.

Relinquishing the idealization process leads to a breakdown in the internal system of self-parenting. As people come to perceive themselves as being the same size and overall stature as their parent, they realize that they can no longer lean on the now diminished parental image for support. While they see life more realistically and develop a sense of autonomy, they generally experience varying degrees of separation anxiety. This anxiety stems from two sources: feeling more individuated from their idealized view of their parents while, at the same time, giving up the corresponding negative image of themselves. There is always some degree of resistance to a therapy that challenges these developments (R. W. Firestone, 1988, 1997a, 2018).

CHALLENGING THE IDEALIZED IMAGE OF PARENTS AND FAMILY

Throughout my career as a psychologist, I have been concerned with people's resistance to changing a conception of self that is self-critical, self-accusatory, and self-punishing. While studying for my PhD, I had the opportunity to work with schizophrenic patients in an in-residence program. It became increasingly clear to my colleagues and me that these seriously disturbed people were involved in the process of idealizing their parent, specifically their mother or primary caregiver, at their own expense (Arieti, 1955; Harrop & Trower, 2001; Searles, 2013; Note 4). When we challenged the idealization, we noted that there was marked resistance to changing both the positive image of the parent and the negative image of self, and it became apparent that the two processes were interrelated (Note 5).

To counterbalance the patient's self-parenting process, my colleagues and I attempted to provide an external form of care and nurturance. Our therapy comprised a direct attack on the patient's internal source of gratification through fantasy, along with an effort to make reality more welcoming. In therapy sessions where we exposed and confronted the aggrandizement of the parent, these patients manifested a reduction of bizarre symptoms and thought disturbance. This, along with the emotional support provided, enabled them to progress in moving through the early stages of development at which they had been fixated.

Early in my psychotherapy practice, I treated a young asthmatic girl (Note 6). Again, I observed the startling effect that exposing negative parental qualities had on symptom manifestation.

> When I met Lena, she was 11 years old and dying of intractable asthma. I had been referred by her doctor because he felt she was depressed and was interested in addressing any psychological components of her symptomology. Lena was frail, and her situation seemed hopeless. I was chilled by the depths of her despair during the initial weeks of therapy. In our first meeting, she looked me in the eye and vowed, "You'll follow me to the hospital and then to the grave." She had little desire to live. All she wished for was to be released from her psychological and physical suffering.

As Lena and I investigated her depression, I became aware of her under-lying anger. I observed that her asthma flare-ups seemed to follow times when she felt angry at her mother. Rather than acknowledging her anger, Lena internalized her feelings, which only exacerbated her physical symptoms. I conjectured that if she could begin to accept her anger, her asthma attacks might subside. And indeed, as we worked together and her anger came out, she began to feel better physically and emotionally. However, this was not a smooth and continuous process. There were still periods of regression, anxiety, and depression, as well as occasions when she had serious asthma attacks that required hospitalization and emergency treatment.

One day, her mother called, begging me to come to the hospital; Lena was failing rapidly. When I entered the hospital room, Lena was weak and fright-ened. As I sat with her, I recalled an incident from the previous week in which she had been especially angry at her mother. I had a strong feeling that she needed to reaffirm this anger. Given Lena's physical state, this idea frightened me, and I knew that she was too weak to speak for herself. So, I voiced her anger for her, expressing the feelings toward her mother she had confided to me the week before. Lena remained listless and unresponsive, and she showed little improvement. I was not encouraged.

Later that day, Lena's mother called again. I anticipated bad news; I thought this was the end. When her mother asked, "What did you do to her?!" I became frightened. I thought that she was accusatory and angry, but the opposite was true. The news was good; Lena had made an unexpected recovery, and her mother was calling to thank me for saving her child. The paradox was amazing to me. What had I done with her daughter? I had helped her to face her rage toward her mother and to see her mother realistically so that she might live.

Lena was desperately holding onto a self-critical attitude and could not accept her hostile feelings toward her parents. She was defensive about her family. She was especially reluctant to acknowledge any inadequacies in her mother, in part because her illness made Lena extremely dependent on her mother for medications and shots and other lifesaving medical care. Thus, if Mother is "bad," Lena would surely die. However, in this emergency situa-tion, merely listening to my verbal expression of her anger toward her mother, having her anger externalized, had been enough of an intervention to break into her idealized image of her mother and to bring about a remission of life-threatening symptoms.

For most people, protecting the idealized image of the family takes a much less severe form than the two examples just mentioned (Note 7). However, as explained in Chapter 1, early in life, people tend to establish a dichotomy of superior and inferior qualities in relation to an idealized parental image. Within this system, the parent is clean, whereas the child is dirty; the parent is right and good, whereas the child is wrong and bad; the parent is normal, and the child is abnormal; the parent is proper and refined in their wants and desires, whereas the child is animalistic and needy; the parent is powerful, and the child is weak.

People are resistant to having their unrealistic image of their parents or parental substitutes challenged. This exposure often leads to angry, defensive reactions. They can take the form of rationalizing the idealized person's weaknesses and shortcomings: "My father was basically absent from my childhood . . . but he was busy making a living to support us" or "My mother was a tyrant . . . but she made us tough and pushed us to be successful."

These rationalizations protect both parent and child, and they serve to maintain the positive image of the parent. Even though they may contain some truth, they cannot undo the pain of being hurt or the objective reality of what actually happened in the family. People use these explanations to justify destructive behavior in an attempt to cut off their pain and hurt and deny their anger. It is psychologically harmful for people to protect their parents in this manner, but it is successful in preserving the idealization of the family and, on some level, offers an illusion of safety.

THE PORTRAYAL OF THE FAMILY AS SPECIAL

People often believe their family to be exceptional compared with other families. The sense of security that the fantasy bond offers is supported by an identification with the distinct characteristics of one's family unit; this can be done by maintaining an image of one's family as special—for instance, as especially dysfunctional, especially quirky, or especially superior in relation to other families.

John's family placed an emphasis on status. His father was a doctor, which he flaunted, much to his son's embarrassment. For instance, he would loudly demand immediate seating and special services in restaurants. John's mother cultivated an image of being a descendant of prominent families. The family lived in a nice house and enjoyed a comfortable lifestyle.

Yet, John's childhood was traumatic. His mother was determined that John would become a doctor and drove him toward that goal with extracurricular tutoring in advanced courses and a curtailing of any extraneous social activity. She demanded that he maintain an excellent grade point average. Meanwhile, his father's behavior at home was erratic and explosive; he blew up at the family without provocation. John was continually built up by his mother and demeaned by his father. He felt like a fraud. He was afraid not to excel and existed in a state of pressure and tension.

Nevertheless, John upheld his family's expectations of him and went to medical school. On graduation, he continued to push himself to live up to his family's image of perfection in his medical career. John's relentless ambition and insensitivity to the level of tension it was causing him led to his developing stomach ulcers. His doctor stressed that it was necessary for John to modify his lifestyle to control his symptoms and suggested that he would benefit from psychotherapy.

The challenge for John was not only taking the practical steps to develop a life that was healthier and more balanced but also dealing with the feelings that arose in taking these steps. In therapy, he realized that by altering his drive and his goals, he was losing his connection to his family's image of being special. He had to be a great doctor if he was to be a part of their greatness. Ultimately, the fallacy of his family's attitudes and expectations became apparent to him. As he progressed in therapy, he came to see them more realistically—that is, as no better or worse than anyone else. In the process, John was able to begin to relax and to stop holding himself to such severe standards.

When people begin to develop a clearer view of themselves as an individual and a more realistic view of their family, the change in their perception jeopardizes the image of having an exceptional family. The child, and later the adult, is reluctant to break with this distorted or exaggerated family image. Many people grow up and leave home physically but do not leave emotionally. This kind of idealization is apparent when people are hurt or offended if one of their family members is criticized. Their identification with the family makes them react as though it were a criticism of them and tends to diminish their self-esteem.

For many, a united family is the ideal; therefore, emancipating oneself from it can signify a flaw or weakness in the family structure. People who are breaking away from a family constellation, whether through forming other strong emotional ties, striking out on their own, or surpassing a parent's accomplishments with their own achievements, tend to experience separation anxiety and guilt in relation to the loss of a sense of connection to the idealized family unit (R. W. Firestone et al., 2012).

IDEALIZATION OF SUBSTITUTE PARENTAL FIGURES

Many people go through life trying to get the love that was missing from their childhood in a symbolic form from parental substitutes. They unconsciously transfer the feelings and attitudes they had toward their parents to other significant people in their current lives—a romantic partner, a friend, a colleague, a celebrity, a leader, or someone else they admire. For example, many people continue to idealize leaders, disregard their weaknesses, and accept their rationalizations for failing to pursue their stated objectives. They do not hold leaders responsible when they become ineffectual or use immoral means to further personal power or agenda (R. W. Firestone & Catlett, 2009b; Lipman-Blumen, 2005; Note 8).

People often enter a romantic relationship with the unconscious expectation that all their needs will be met by the other, which places a heavy burden on their partner. Obviously, no one person can fulfill such unrealistic expectations or live up to such an idealized image of power and goodness. Just as people idealized their parents to gain a sense of security, they now idealize the new individual for the same purpose. Concomitantly, they manifest feelings of childishness and unworthiness. They are often deferential to this person, engaging in maneuvers to please and compromising their own point of view to get approval. An effective way to prevent reality from tarnishing the images of substitute parental figures is to exaggerate their real strengths or admirable qualities (Mikulincer & Shaver, 2016; Note 9).

> Sherise met Tyrone when she was in her early 20s. Being 5 years older, Tyrone seemed mature to her. He was also self-assured and outgoing; he was enthusiastic and had a take-charge attitude. Sherise was not overshadowed by Tyrone's strong personality. She had her own goals and an independent spirit. She valued and maintained friendships that had been important to her before she met Tyrone.
>
> Nonetheless, Sherise did gain a degree of security from Tyrone's confidence and assertive nature. She felt like no matter what the challenge, Tyrone would figure out what to do. This was a relief to her because, as a child, she had often felt unsafe with a father whom she experienced as weak and passive.
>
> Sherise had been vaguely aware of Tyrone's obsessive-compulsive disorder (OCD). They had spoken of it, and it had even been the subject of some of their jokes. But during a time that was emotionally stressful for him, Tyrone became overwhelmed with symptoms of his OCD. He was alarmed about coming into contact with germs and felt compelled to warn Sherise of the dangers that were threatening them. He became obsessed with cleaning their home. He was barely functional.
>
> At first, Sherise felt angry at Tyrone and personally let down by him. She was confused and frightened by his behavior. She felt powerless to help him. Her idealization of Tyrone's competence and her imagination that he would always know what to do in any given situation were shattered. She was forced to see Tyrone as a person with human limitations and fears, like her. When she realized that he needed to be able to depend on her for support during this time, she took action to get him the help he needed to deal with his current crisis.

CONCLUSION

The idealization of the parent plays a significant role in the formation of a fantasy bond. This dynamic is extended into adulthood by maintaining the special image of one's family and by distorting substitute parental figures and romantic partners in a similar manner. Both children and adults are resistant to challenging this process because it arouses separation anxiety. Unfortunately, by preserving the fantasy bond, people also preserve the negative self-concept that necessarily accompanies it.

When people are able to accept a more realistic appraisal of their parents and become aware of them as people with weaknesses, mistakes, immaturities, and inadequacies, as well as strengths, the fantasized connection to the idealized parent is challenged. The corresponding negative self-image is also exposed, allowing people to come to know themselves without the usual overlay of their defenses. They no longer need to build up the parent and denigrate themselves.

As the disruption of the idealization process progresses, people become more compassionate toward themselves and more understanding of their parents. Only when they work through their misconceptions and develop a realistic picture of both can individuals free themselves from past programming and achieve a better sense of self-worth, autonomy, and independence.

4 THE NEGATIVE SELF-CONCEPT

Our life is what our thoughts make it.

—Marcus Aurelius, *Meditations*

The negative self-concept originates in early childhood when the infant suffers varying degrees of emotional deprivation from parents who are limited or misattuned to their child and who lack either the desire or the capability to meet the child's emotional and physical needs. Parental indifference, hostility, and rejecting attitudes become part of the child's negative self-concept. People's negative view of themselves is perpetuated by holding onto an identity that reflects their parents' negative definition of them and includes the acceptance of their parents' distorted views about life. As explained in the previous chapter, children are also inclined to idealize and exonerate their parents by denying or rationalizing the negative traits that have caused them emotional harm (R. W. Firestone, 1985).

Maintaining negative thoughts, feelings, and attitudes about oneself is an integral part of the self-parenting process and is inextricably tied to an

https://doi.org/10.1037/0000268-005
Challenging the Fantasy Bond: A Search for Personal Identity and Freedom,
by R. W. Firestone

idealized image of one's parents. The negative self-concept that is an out-growth of the "bad child" image becomes an essential part of a person's overall system of defenses (R. W. Firestone et al., 2012); altering their basic identity by moving away from negative self-evaluations would cause anxiety because it would necessitate a rupture of the family bond, leaving them with a feeling of loneliness and fear, as described in Chapter 3.

It may seem perverse that people have such a strong need to hang onto self-hatred, an inclination toward self-denial and self-criticism, and resistance to changing their negative self-concept. Yet, viewed from the perspective of protecting the fantasy bond, these human tendencies become understandable. Adhering to a negative self-concept indirectly protects against intrusions into the fantasy bond and its illusion of self-sufficiency.

People who are self-deprecating and self-hating tend to predict rejection by others because, on a deep level, they experience themselves as unlovable. Their anticipation of rejection explains their avoidance of close, personal relationships (Bosmans et al., 2010; Cassidy & Shaver, 2016; R. W. Firestone & Catlett, 1999; R. W. Firestone & Firestone, 2004; Note 1). They do not want to take a chance on being hurt again and, therefore, tenaciously hold on to their feelings of worthlessness.

Modifying the negative self-concept temporarily leaves a person without a secure sense of self because it involves a fundamental contradiction of people's earliest conception of reality. Many people define themselves as basically unlovable and, though this negative attitude causes a great deal of suffering, it serves to provide a familiar and stable identity, which helps to maintain a psychological equilibrium. Thus, circumstances that could lead to a positive change in a person's self-concept are often unconsciously avoided because of the anxiety that the perceived loss of identity entails.

ORIGINS OF THE NEGATIVE SELF-CONCEPT

An infant senses a parent's emotional state through touch and facial expression long before they understand the parent's words (Badenoch, 2008; Cozolino, 2014; Schore, 2019; D. J. Siegel, 2001; Note 2). When parents fail to be attuned to the child's needs, the infant comes to feel confusion, shame, and guilt for wanting. Young children blame themselves for their parents' misattunement while, at the same time, they attempt to keep the negative emotions this brings up below the level of awareness. As adults, they experience this same confusion, shame, and guilt when they are made aware of things that they want or that would be fulfilling to them in any aspect of their lives, personal, professional, financial, or romantic (R. W. Firestone, 1990b; Note 3).

Parental characteristics that are most conducive to the formation of a negative self-concept are those that cause the child to feel ashamed and self-hating. For example, parents may find themselves reacting angrily when they experience their child's aliveness and spontaneity as an intrusion into their defense system. They may try to quiet the child or stifle their child's enthusiasm. They may accuse their child of being bad, greedy, demanding, or inconsiderate. These responses mask the fact that the parents are defended emotionally in a manner that cuts them off from being vulnerable to tender feelings for or from their offspring (R. W. Firestone, 1990b).

The child's negative self-concept is internalized and reinforced most powerfully when the parent and/or child is under emotional distress. For example, when parents are excessively angry and punishing toward their offspring, children become frightened, turning against themselves and internalizing the parents' anger in the form of self-hatred. The child's pain, humiliation, and fear are repressed, and feelings of blaming themselves for real or imagined wrongdoing take their place. In addition, children feel threatened by their reactive anger toward the punitive parent because they fear losing the parent. Again, they turn their anger inward.

Many parents attempt to disown their disagreeable characteristics by projecting them onto their offspring. In a sense, these parents use their child as a receptacle for qualities they hate in themselves. They then punish the child for these traits. Children, who naturally see themselves through their parent's eyes, accept this negative projection as an accurate reflection of who they are (Kerr & Bowen, 1988).

Talia's mother was a childish woman who struggled to function as an adult. She was easily overwhelmed in her daily life and had difficulty holding down a job. Talia's mother denied her own ineptitude by treating her daughter with condescension, as though she were stupid and dysfunctional, continually criticizing and correcting her behavior. Talia grew up believing her mother's view that she was limited in her ability to operate as a normal person.

As a young woman, Talia understandably lacked confidence in herself. She was tentative in her job for fear of making a mistake. In her friendships, she doubted her opinions and sought direction from others. She accepted disrespectful and abusive treatment in relationships. A friend noticed that Talia seemed lost and confused about who she was and suggested that she might benefit from therapy.

In therapy, Talia began to investigate her negative self-concept and began to know herself as a woman with a distinct point of view. In her therapeutic development, she had to question her mother's destructive ways of seeing her and examine her own acceptance of them. Talia explored the pain this brought up and the anger she had toward her mother for building herself up by tearing Talia down. As Talia gained a more accurate picture of her mother and changed her view of herself, she became more self-assured. She garnered recognition at work, and eventually, she started a relationship with a man who was kind and respectful.

THE DIVISION OF THE MIND

As stated earlier, children incorporate their parents not as they are most of the time but when they are most hurtful. Children's efforts to remain intact under stressful or frightening conditions produce a division within the self or personality (R. W. Firestone, 1997a; see Figure 4.1).

The *division of the mind* refers to a primary split between forces that represent the self and those that oppose it. As described in Chapter 1, these propensities can be conceptualized as the self system and the anti-self system, respectively. The two systems develop independently; both are dynamic and continue to evolve and change over time. They are susceptible to influence from significant people and events throughout life (R. W. Firestone, 1997b).

The *self system* consists of the unique characteristics of the individual, including biological, temperamental, and genetic traits and the positive attitudes and traits of the parents that the child assimilates harmoniously. Parents' warmth and nurturance, as well as their ability to repair misattunements, support the development of vital functions of the prefrontal cortex in the child's brain: body regulation, attunement, emotional balance, response flexibility, empathy, self-knowing awareness (insight), fear modulation, intuition, and morality (D. J. Siegel, 2007, 2010). The effects of ongoing psychological development, further education, and imitation of other positive role models throughout an individual's life span continue to contribute to the evolution of the self system.

One's personal goals, including the basic needs for safety, water, food, and sex; the desire for social affiliation, achievement, and life-affirming activity; the capacity for compassion, empathy, and generosity; and the pursuit of transcendent goals related to seeking meaning in life are all aspects of the self system. Positive environmental influences allow the evolving individual to formulate a value system and develop the ability and courage to live with integrity—that is, according to personal ethical principles.

The *anti-self system* refers to internalized parental hostility and cynicism that represents an alien aspect of the personality. It is a defensive response to the destructive side of parents' ambivalence toward their children: their rejection, hostility, neglect, and unresponsiveness. In addition, parents' emotional hunger, overprotectiveness, ignorance, and lack of understanding of a

FIGURE 4.1. Division of the Mind

Division of the Mind

Self-System

Parental Nurturance/Genetic Predisposition/Temperament

Attunement, affection, control

Other factors: effect of positive experience and education on the maturing self-system

Greater Degree of Differentiation

Unique makeup of the individual—harmonious identification and incorporation of parent's positive attitudes and traits

Personal Goals/Conscience

Realistic, Positive Attitudes Toward Self	Behaviors
Realistic evaluation of talents, abilities, and so forth, with generally positive/compassionate attitude toward self and others	Ethical behavior toward self and others
Goals Needs, wants, search for meaning in life	**Goal Directed Behavior**

Anti-Self System

Destructive Parental Behavior/Genetic Predisposition/Temperament

Misattunement, lack of affection, rejection, neglect, hostility, permissiveness

Other Factors: Accidents, illnesses, traumatic separation

The Fantasy Bond

The fantasy bond (core defense) furthers a self-parenting process made up of both the helpless, needy child, and the self-punishing, self-nurturing parent. Either may be acted out in a relationship context. The degree of reliance on this defense is proportional to the amount of damage sustained while growing up.

The Self-Parenting Process

Self-Punishing Voices

Voice Process	Behaviors
1. Critical thoughts toward self	Verbal attacks—a generally negative attitude toward self and others predisposing alienation
2. Microsuicidal injunctions	Actions contrary to one's own interest and goals and emotional/physical health
3. Suicidal injunctions—suicidal ideation	Actions that jeopardize one's health and safety; physical attacks on the self, and actual suicide

Self-Soothing Voices

Voice Process	Behaviors
1. Self-soothing attitudes	Self-limiting or self-protective
2. Microsuicidal injunctions (seductive/self-indulgent thoughts)	Addictive patterns
3. Aggrandizing thoughts toward self	Narcissism/vanity
4. Suspicious, paranoid thoughts toward others	Alienation from others and hostile attitudes toward others

Note. From "Separation Theory and Voice Therapy Methodology," by R. W. Firestone and L. Firestone, in P. R. Shaver and M. Mikulincer (Eds.), *Meaning, Mortality, and Choice: The Social Psychology of Existential Concerns* (p. 355), 2012, American Psychological Association (https://doi.org/10.1037/13748-020). Copyright 2012 by the American Psychological Association.

child's nature negatively impact children's development (Note 4). The anti-self system is also affected by other negative events that occur during life: birth trauma, illnesses, traumatic separations, and the actual loss of a parent, sibling, or other significant figure. While influenced primarily by interpersonal pain, the anti-self system is also reinforced and compounded by the suffering inherent in the human condition, such as poverty, economic recession, crime, natural disasters, accidents, physical and mental deterioration, and death anxiety.

This antagonistic part of the personality predominates to varying degrees at different times throughout the life span. When individuals are in their own point of view, they seem to be very different people than when they are not; when they "feel like themselves," they are generally more relaxed and likable, but when the balance shifts and the anti-self-system becomes dominant, people are usually more withdrawn, self-hating, hostile, and toxic to those around them. Often, when a person is under stress, there is a breakdown in the self system, and the anti-self prevails (Note 5).

People are resistant to recognizing this essential division within their personalities because they are subconsciously fearful to discover irrational, hostile attitudes toward themselves and others. Becoming aware of this alien and destructive component within themselves leads to a sense of fragmentation. They attempt to deny this fracture by identifying negative traits predisposed by the anti-self system as their own. In refusing to tolerate the lack of integration, they tend to suppress their essential aliveness, spontaneity, and individuality and move in the direction of the prescriptions of the critical inner voice.

THE CRITICAL INNER VOICE AND THE NEGATIVE SELF-CONCEPT

As outlined in Chapter 1, the *critical inner voice* refers to a self-destructive thought process that exists to varying degrees in every person and actively perpetuates the negative self-concept. The adverse point of view of the critical inner voice represents the anti-self element of the personality by supporting an individual's defensive adaptations—in particular, the fantasy bond and the self-parenting orientation. The voice reflects the introjection of the parent's hostile, rejecting, or hurtful attitudes toward the child, both spoken and unspoken. This internal dialogue serves to protect the defensive process by interpreting reality in such a way as to preserve the image of the good parent and the resultant negative self-concept.

The voice is experienced within a person as though it were coming from an external source, as if another person were speaking to them. Voices do not reflect a personal, compassionate, or objective point of view but rather one that is detached, judgmental, and often irrational. For example, when a person misses a deadline at work, an appropriate reaction would be, "I feel bad that I didn't make the deadline. I should've allowed more time for that. Next time I'll be more careful." The reaction of their critical inner voice would be, "You really messed up! You can't be counted on to do anything right! No one's going to trust you again."

This negative inner dialogue takes a toll on people's efficiency, vitality, and basic regard for themselves. The voice acts to block the feeling part of the personality, leaving individuals in an emotionally deadened, depressed state, which makes them all the more vulnerable to self-attacks. Even in its mildest forms, the voice interferes with a person's ability to cope with everyday living and functioning.

The voice is not experienced as an auditory hallucination or an audible sound; more precisely, it is a set of negative perceptions and attitudes toward the self and others. It may take the form of conscious thought, but often it remains unconscious or partially conscious. It operates as an ongoing dialogue that runs down the self and others and, as such, is often cynical and even paranoid in nature (R. W. Firestone et al., 2002, 2012; Note 6).

People sometimes become conscious of their voice attacks when they are in stressful situations. For example, they may blame themselves for making a mistake: "Why did you do that, you idiot? Can't you ever do anything right?" A person about to address a group may think, "You're going to forget your speech! Look at your hands, they're shaking so much the audience will see that you're nervous." These more common self-attacks are easily recognized and are generally accompanied by agitation, irritability, or a slightly depressed mood.

Destructive voices that often go unnoticed are those that condone and encourage self-denial because they appear to be altruistic: "Don't draw attention to yourself; don't be conceited. It's best to stay quiet and be humble. Always put others before yourself; don't be selfish and self-centered!" This seemingly moral aspect of the voice is not truly humanitarian in nature. On the contrary, it supports people's tendency to give up their wants and needs and, ultimately, to surrender significant parts of their identity. People who are self-denying and self-sacrificing are usually cruel and harsh toward themselves and resentful and condemning of others whom they view as selfish.

The critical inner voice may become particularly active following an achievement, especially one that contradicts a person's negative self-concept. People often have thoughts such as "Who do you think you are? You don't really deserve this." The voice insinuates that actual accomplishments are a quirk of fate, an accident, or somehow the result of others being deceived: "You've got everyone fooled! You're basically a phony and a fraud. You will never be able to repeat that performance." Many high-achieving individuals have reported experiencing this type of self-attack, described by researchers as the *imposter phenomenon* (Clance & Imes, 1978). This derisive aspect of the voice contributes to the empty feeling or the sensation of being let down that many people notice following a significant success.

The critical inner voice is often contradictory, both instigating actions and then condemning them: "It's okay to have another beer tonight; it's the weekend" and afterward, "You're drinking way too much! You're such a lush!" (L. Firestone & Catlett, 2004; R. W. Firestone, 1993; Note 7). In their most pathological form, voice attacks against the self can ultimately lead to suicide, and the hostile voices toward others can foster aggressive or even homicidal behavior (R. W. Firestone, 1997b, 2018).

Seemingly positive self-nurturing voices that appear to be supportive are also an indication that individuals are fragmented or removed from themselves. For example, thoughts that reinforce vanity or an inflated self-image represent a compensation for feelings of inferiority and a negative conception of self, which are also mediated by the voice. When destructive thought processes take precedence over rational thinking, the self can become the object of a false build-up and subsequent self-attack. Self-aggrandizing voices such as "You're smarter than they are. You don't need their help" are often followed by "You're a complete failure. You never do anything right" if things do not work out. Or the voice may attribute the blame to someone else: "It's all their fault. Your idea was perfect."

The voice is not a conscience or a representation of moral attitudes but rather a system of misconceptions about and negative attitudes toward the self and others. It does not function as a positive set of values; instead, it interprets an external system of values with a judgmental attitude and expresses this with vicious attacks and castigation. The voice does not reflect a person's sense of morality; rather, it operates as an overlay on the personality that is an essential element of a negative defensive process. As a result of internalizing negative parental attitudes, most people grow up adopting an external value system (e.g., that of their parents) rather than gradually developing their own internal set of principles. They judge themselves by these external standards and maintain a feeling that they are deficient in relation to them.

Although voices may appear at times to reflect a moral value system, voice attacks are typically vindictive and judgmental in tone, which serves to increase people's self-hatred rather than motivate them to amend behavior as a conscience would: "You should have been more sensitive to her in that exchange. You have no idea how to relate to women" or "You shouldn't have teased him about that. You really know how to make a person feel bad" or "Don't even try to start a conversation. They obviously have zero interest in you."

The voice engenders hopelessness about gaining control over behaviors that a person wants to change. Unlike a true sense of moral conscience, which inspires people to act according to their stated values, the voice, instead, condemns and demoralizes them. For example, a person who struggles with shyness may have a voice: "Don't even bother trying to be more social; you are just a misfit. It's not worth trying!" When people objectively know themselves to be at fault or acknowledge that they have committed an error in judgment, it serves no useful purpose to punish or hate themselves. It is more appropriate and functional to work on changing future behavior.

People can learn to better identify their critical inner voices by using the techniques of voice therapy. In this process, people free associate about their self-attacks, verbalizing them in the second person format: "You are foolish. You are stupid." Once they have formulated their voices in this way, people can identify the content, analyze the sources, recognize the impact on their behavior, and then challenge their self-attacks. Verbalizing the self-attacks in this manner facilitates the process of separating their point of view from the hostile thought patterns that make up their negative point of view toward themselves and others. Voice therapy is explained in detail in Chapter 12 (Note 8).

When the voice is not challenged but is accepted and believed, it predisposes behavior that can cause negative traits to become a major part of a person's approach to life. By habitually acting on their voices' prescriptions, people eventually become what the voice tells them they are. Thus, the voice becomes the agent of an ongoing, self-fulfilling process.

RESISTANCE TO CHANGING THE NEGATIVE SELF-CONCEPT

The negative self-concept persists into adulthood. As described in Chapter 3, most people are reluctant to give it up because, paradoxically, feeling positive about themselves can cause anxiety and pain. In therapy sessions with individuals of all ages, when I have encouraged them to say positive statements about themselves with feeling, they generally experience sadness as they give themselves value and see themselves as likable. Interfering with a person's negative self-concepts arouses deep emotions, but it also leaves them feeling more compassionate toward themselves.

> In one of Talia's sessions, her therapist suggested that she describe herself objectively. Talia was hesitant. She became silent and avoided making eye contact. Eventually, she began speaking cautiously: "I'm good at my job. [pause] I'm smart. [pause] I care about people." Then she suddenly stopped talking and, after a long silence, finally said, "This is too hard." Her therapist encouraged her to keep going. "I am a kind person, and I care about my friends." At this point, Talia broke down crying and put her hands over her face. She said that she felt like she was going to be slapped. When her crying subsided, Talia felt relief.
>
> This seemingly simple exercise accessed deep feelings and fears. In effect, when she objectively described herself, Talia was going against her mother by contradicting her mother's point of view, and she literally felt that she would be punished for doing so. In subsequent sessions, Talia continued to explore and challenge the voice attacks that supported her negative self-concept.

Challenging the distorted and exaggerated negative evaluations of the voice is a necessary prerequisite to effect a positive change in one's concept of self. Yet, the process of identifying and rejecting voice attacks creates an internal conflict; people are losing or giving up an old image of themselves. A consistent self-concept, even though negative, cannot be altered without causing anxiety and emotional upheaval. Confronting the critical inner voice separates the person from the internalized parent and arouses a fear of fracturing the fantasy bond.

CONCLUSION

Regrettably, people tend to see themselves as bad or flawed, not as the basically decent human beings they actually are. Nevertheless, they can learn to give up these long-standing defensive adaptations and cope with the ensuing anxiety. Using voice therapy procedures, people can expose the dynamics of the voice and identify the various aspects of the internal thought process (R. W. Firestone, 1988, 1997a). They can learn to control the self-destructive behaviors that are dictated by the voice and behave in constructive ways that go against the negative thought process.

Challenging the critical inner voice that supports their outdated ways of defending themselves is an integral part of breaking the idealization of the parent and the negative self-concept and is vital to a person's development. As people free themselves from their misperceptions of the past, they are able to express their authentic identity and live life from a more realistic and compassionate point of view.

5 PROJECTION AND INCORPORATION OF PARENTS' NEGATIVE TRAITS

Children have never been very good at listening to their elders, but they have never failed to imitate them.

—James Baldwin, *Nobody Knows My Name*

To preserve an idealized image of their parents, children must find a means to deny or minimize their parents' negative qualities. When they find it intolerable to perceive their parent realistically, they can displace their parent's harmful traits by either projecting them onto other people or incorporating them into themselves. As children block from awareness the parental characteristics that they experience to be especially threatening, they often distort other people to see them as being more like their parents. They identify these people as being more hostile or untrustworthy than they are, and they react according to these misperceptions. Gradually they develop a disordered and sometimes paranoid style of thinking and viewing the world (R. W. Firestone et al., 2012).

Children also protect themselves and the parent's image by imitating their parent's undesirable traits, behaviors, and points of view about life.

https://doi.org/10.1037/0000268-006
Challenging the Fantasy Bond: A Search for Personal Identity and Freedom, by R. W. Firestone

The process of imitation has been shown to be more impactful than direct learning (Bandura et al., 1963; Bandura & Walters, 1977; Garrels, 2011; Note 1). Differentiating from a parent's negative qualities threatens the fantasized connection with that parent. Incorporating a parent's undesirable traits not only helps the child to negate the harmful characteristics that are part of the parent's personality but also acts to deny the hurt that these traits cause. Therefore, children find safety in becoming more like their parents (R. W. Firestone et al., 2012).

PROJECTION OF PARENTS' NEGATIVE TRAITS ONTO OTHERS

To varying degrees, adults perceive the world in terms of the generalized misconceptions they developed early in their lives. As a result, they see the inadequacies and weaknesses of their parents in other people and react to present-day events as they responded to the original family situation. These misperceptions and distortions tend to be impervious to reality testing; they require little information to confirm and are difficult to refute logically. They are appropriate only in the sense that they once applied to the parent's behavior. This process leads to overdramatic and inappropriate responses to present-day circumstances and interferes with a person's ability to adapt and function in life.

People often behave in such a way as to make their critical or cynical views of others come true. They are adept at proving their negative allegations about other people by provoking the treatment they have come to expect. When the hostility they induce in others is directed back toward them, it escalates their own reactive behaviors. The tragedy is that to rationalize and justify their negative perceptions of others, people increasingly damage their ability to develop satisfying relationships.

Projection and the Paranoid Process

Paranoia is a self-confirming system that precludes the awareness of conflicting perceptions. It is analogous to the work of a scientist who rigs the data to fit a prior hypothesis. Paranoid individuals are generally unconscious of this process and genuinely feel threatened from without. They perceive others as hostile or frightening and are unaware that their distorted perception of danger causes them to be the hostile ones.

Paranoid thinking is a disorder of focus and perspective whereby the subjective world of the individual (i.e., their feelings and reactions) is experienced as happening to the person, rather than originating from within them. This distortion leads to an abnormally high sensitivity to aggression in others, a tendency to imagine malice in other people, and an expectation of harm from the outside world.

> Briana and her sister were only 2 years apart, yet there was a marked discrepancy between how the girls were treated by their parents. Briana, the eldest, was seen as a difficult child, whereas, as far as her parents were concerned, her sister could do no wrong. Her parents reacted to Briana's liveliness and enthusiasm by continually reprimanding her and telling her to calm down. She was a bright and naturally inquisitive child, but her parents criticized her for being nosey and demanding. They obviously preferred her sister, who was quiet and subdued.
>
> Briana saw herself as she was seen in her family: as an unruly troublemaker. She considered her parents to be loving and good parents, especially because she saw them as being this way toward her sister. Briana grew up always expecting to get into trouble. In her teens, she began to act out and engage in rebellious and self-destructive behavior. Eventually, she was expelled from high school.
>
> As an adult, Briana continued to anticipate disapproval from others. She performed well at work, but she had difficulty when she was given feedback by her boss. Rather than objectively considering the information, she felt criticized and angry. In her personal relationships, she would react to conflict by feeling attacked and misunderstood.
>
> When her father died, Briana went into therapy to deal with the depression she felt. Initially, she felt that if she were to really open up about her thoughts and feelings to her therapist, she would be met with criticism. Sometimes when her therapist was listening with interest, Briana imagined he had an angry expression. She began to talk about her various reactions and perceptions to her therapist in the moment to gain insight into how she was distorting reality.
>
> As Briana developed trust in her therapist, they began to investigate her perceptions of other people and their motives. She became comfortable discussing specific situations in which she thought people were mistreating her. She spoke about the times she thought her boss was against her. She talked about difficult interactions with her partner. Over time, she learned that being given feedback was not the same as being condemned or personally attacked. She came to realize that disagreement was not the same as disapproval or criticism. She began to recognize how she tended to distort people as being against her. As Briana came to understand that these misperceptions did not fit her current life but instead were accurate reflections of her experience in her family, she was better able to deal with the strong emotions that still tended to come up and choose a more productive way of responding in those situations.

When people are in a paranoid point of view, they have a heightened sense of self-protection, which they feel is necessary to survive in the harsh, dangerous world that they perceive. When their misperceptions and paranoia intensify, they can become aggressive and explosive. In extreme cases, paranoid individuals may act out violence or criminal activity with an absence of guilt because they feel wronged and therefore justified in their behavior.

Role of the Voice in Paranoid Thinking

The critical inner voice is instrumental in fueling the distrust and cynicism toward others that play a prominent role in paranoid thinking. Paranoid individuals have voices that run down other people or distort their motives: "They are selfish and self-centered." "She's really two-faced; don't trust her." "He's out to exploit you and take advantage of you." Their voices encourage feeling victimized or wounded: "Nobody understands you." "You deserve better than this." "You're much too good for them." "They don't treat you right." When people act on these voices and the paranoia they provoke, their voices justify their overreactions: "You had to stand up for yourself; he was disrespecting you." "You had to stop her from trying to humiliate you." "Of course, you got angry; they were lying to you." Voices support a paranoid person's strong need to be right by defending their feelings of being mistreated and justifying their feelings of martyrdom.

The voice can exaggerate other people's irritation and anger: "He's furious! He's about to hit you." "Look at her expression. She hates you!" "They're going to fire you!" They can misinterpret momentary outbursts of frustration as expressions of hostility directed toward them. These types of voices cause people to overreact to variations in other people's moods and take them too personally (Fenigstein & Vanable, 1992; Note 2).

In the mid-1990s, my colleagues and I conjectured that identifying critical inner voices would prove effective in predicting violence. We subsequently developed an instrument, the Firestone Assessment of Violent Thoughts (Adult and Adolescent; R. W. Firestone & Firestone, 2008a, 2008b) for assessing violence potential for both criminal and family violence. In developing the scale, we found a close connection between negative, cynical, or paranoid thought processes and destructive behavior toward others. Specifically, voices that related to being misunderstood or disrespected fostered violent behavior (R. W. Firestone, 2018; Note 3).

When paranoid individuals act on the warnings and advice of their voices, they tend to provoke other people, which intensifies their own hostile response, thereby establishing a cycle in which their paranoid system is strongly reinforced. People who continue to act on their paranoia fail to develop appropriate reality testing, mature coping behavior, or mastery in overcoming problems.

INCORPORATION OF NEGATIVE PARENTAL TRAITS

As has been explained, children emulate their parent's feeling reactions and behaviors as part of the developmental process (Note 4). As we discussed in Chapter 1, this is supported by brain-imaging studies in which neuro-scientists traced the ability of children to imitate specific behaviors that they observe in a role model to the activation of mirror neurons in a specific region of the brain (D. J. Siegel, 2001). In the process of modeling their parent's behaviors and reactions, children take on their parent's traits and attitudes. Attachment researchers have noted that when caregivers are largely misattuned, "the infant registers it (most often unconsciously) as a lack of reliability of the object . . . [and] begins to live with an internalized object that is essentially negative and feared" (K. M. Newman, 2013, pp. 61–62; see also Provenzi et al., 2018; Note 5).

In this way, children incorporate their parents' psychological defenses, undesirable characteristics, toxic behaviors, and dysfunctional ways of coping with life. For example, a child whose parents are suspicious and distrustful will adopt the parents' paranoid orientation to life and adapt by anticipating mistreatment and harm from others. Children whose parents are self-denying and emotionally self-contained will come to view their natural wants and desires as excessive and needy. They will adapt by mimicking their parents' self-denying posture and assimilating the belief that personal wants are selfish and undesirable.

Identification With the Aggressor

When, from the child's perspective, a parent's reaction is felt as threatening, the child disassociates and identifies with the aggressor—in this case, the all-powerful, angry parent. This defense helps to allay severe anxiety reactions, but in the process, the child internalizes the qualities of the parents at their worst. Psychoanalyst Sandor Ferenczi (1933/1955) asserted, "The weak and undeveloped personality reacts to sudden unpleasure by anxiety-ridden iden-tification and by introjection of the menacing person or aggressor" (p. 163).

By identifying with the aggressor and detaching from themselves in this way, children feel as if they have gained some mastery over a stressful situa-tion. In some instances, this internalized parent can seem to "take over" the personality of the child, as R. D. Laing (1960/1969) described:

A most curious phenomenon of the personality, one which has been observed for centuries, but which has not yet received its full explanation, is that in which the individual seems to be the vehicle of a personality that is not his own. Someone else's personality seems to "possess" him and to be finding expression through his words and actions, whereas the individual's own personality is temporarily "lost" or "gone." There seem to be all degrees of the same basic process from the simple, benign observation that so-and-so "takes after his father," or "that's her mother's temper coming out in her," to the extreme distress of the person who finds himself under a compulsion to take on the characteristics of a personality he may hate and/or feel to be entirely alien to his own. (p. 62)

By emulating the very qualities that caused them pain, children absolve their parents and obscure the fact that these undesirable traits are part of the parent's personality. As a consequence, people continue to imitate the destructive parental mannerisms, behaviors, and attitudes that were especially hurtful to them. Unfortunately, this reenactment typically plays out in people's destructive actions and attitudes toward their children.

Incorporated Negative Parental Traits in Adulthood

There is usually a fantasy bond with a specific parent that leads to an incorporation of that particular parent's attitudes and an imitation of their lifestyle. Although these characteristics may not manifest themselves initially, they tend to become progressively more dominant in people's personalities as they move through life. Any significant transitions in life can trigger this process—for example, moving out on their own, starting a job, exploring their sexuality, sharing a home, establishing a committed relationship, getting married, or starting a family. Most people fail to distinguish between the incorporated parental view and their own point of view.

Typically, as people go through life, the parental traits they have incorporated tend to persist and grow more prominent within their personalities. They often begin to strongly resemble the parent in style, temperament, and mannerisms. This recapitulation of their parent's negative characteristics, especially the traits that they dislike the most, leads to a sense of demoralization and increased voice attacks and self-hatred. This dynamic is particularly pronounced following the death of the parent with whom a person most identifies. The loss of this primary figure in the fantasy bond often triggers a regression, characterized by a more extreme manifestation of negative characteristics of the deceased parent, with the internalized parental image taking more and more precedence over other facets of their real identity.

Paul's father had a small business, but he did not run it well. When Paul was growing up, his father filed for bankruptcy twice. Paul worked in his father's company through high school and witnessed his father's poor judgment and rash business decisions. He was critical of his father and vowed that he would be different.

Paul's first serious job was with a real estate firm. While there, he saw an opportunity to renovate houses in an area of town, and he began buying and flipping houses. He and a friend started their own business, which Paul ran intelligently and efficiently, and their company grew steadily.

Three years later, his father passed away. Paul's relationship with his father had been distant and strained, and he did not feel an immediate effect from the loss. However, during the following year, his partner noticed that Paul was making questionable business decisions. He was missing deadlines on projects, and subcontractors were getting disgruntled. For the first time, the business was losing money. His partner confronted Paul with his concern.

This forced Paul to recognize his mismanagement of the company, but he was confused about why it was happening. He felt alarmed that he was behaving in ways that he did not understand and by the serious impact it was having on his business. Paul sought therapy to address this issue.

Paul spoke to his therapist about being mystified about why these problems were occurring. As they investigated this further, he traced the beginning of his troubles to just after his father's death. The connection between the timing of his sudden failures in business and his father's death became obvious to Paul.

He became aware that he had unknowingly started to imitate his father's traits, even though he had been critical of them. By eliminating a major distinction between himself and his father, Paul was attempting to reconnect with his father. In a sense, he was symbolically attempting to keep his father alive. He was avoiding facing the loss of any opportunity to have the loving father–son relationship they had not had but that he had always wanted. As his therapy progressed, Paul was able to feel the emotions that were aroused in him from his father's death and began to understand the effect that they were having on his life.

Challenging Incorporated Negative Traits

When individuals associate closely with a person whom they particularly respect and like, they tend to identify with and unconsciously imitate and internalize that person's characteristics. People naturally assimilate new traits that are in harmony with their own identity. Therefore, to disrupt the imitation of negative parental characteristics and defenses, it is generally advisable for individuals to associate with and use new people whom they admire as role models. It is valuable to imitate positive and likable traits that differ from one's parents'. However, there is often guilt involved in choosing to emulate someone from outside of the family rather than a family member.

The processes of identification and imitation continue throughout life, enabling people to use an admired person's values, goals, and other positive attributes to strengthen their self-system. As part of the process of self-development, it is advisable to choose and associate with people and circumstances that are conducive to one's development and be aware of and avoid destructive influences.

This modeling effect occurs in the therapy process as well. Positive transference implies an identification with the therapist and an imitation of their good qualities. On some level, this dynamic is ongoing during the course of therapy; thus, it is important that the therapist have personal qualities that are admirable and affirmative. A strong and positive identification with the therapist supports a client's movement toward a new sense of identity that is stable and healthy.

CONCLUSION

The interrelated dimensions of the fantasy bond and defensive process consist of the idealization of parents and family, the development of a negative self-concept, the projection of negative parental traits onto other people, and the incorporation of parents' undesirable characteristics, behaviors, and defensive point of view. These are not discrete defenses but overlap and combine to injure a person's ability to function in the real world.

Children tend to internalize and take on as their own their parents' destructive attitudes, perceptions, and points of view about personal relationships. They incorporate their parents' distorted views of other people, as well as their set of beliefs about the world. These internalized attitudes and traits become a basic part of the developing individual's personality (Note 6). Thus, the parents' mistaken perceptions of the external world influence the misconceptions that their children carry with them throughout their lifetimes.

Children also incorporate their parents' undesirable traits and behaviors to maintain the imagined fusion with the idealized parental figure. This incorporation helps to obscure what would be a more realistic perception of parental weaknesses and inadequacies. People often adopt the very behaviors and attitudes that were the most harmful to them. In becoming like their parents in ways that they felt critical of, they gradually come to dislike themselves.

In addition, children try to block from their awareness parental limitations and destructive qualities by projecting them onto the interpersonal environment. The process of redirecting hostile feelings onto people outside of the family acts to preserve the myth of family solidarity and the idealized image of the parents. This projection creates a distortion of one's perception of other people and the world in general that continues into adulthood and is perpetuated and strengthened by destructive voices. Mistaking these misperceptions to be real sets off personal interactions that are character-ized by a general feeling of distrust, a fear of involvement and vulnerability, and a good deal of cynicism and hostility. People come to feel wronged, mis-judged, and mistreated by others. Feeling victimized is a core component of paranoid thinking and behavior and can lead a person to seek isolation.

Most people who seek therapy bring with them false notions, ideas, or beliefs about themselves, other people, and the world that they learned in their family and that need to be questioned and relinquished to expand their personal lives. These incorporated misconceptions protect the fantasy bond in two ways. First, the person remains undifferentiated from the family's views and thus remains connected to the family. Second, by being distrustful and suspicious of others, they are able to maintain the aura of exclusivity and uniqueness of the family, thereby preserving the family's idealized image. Challenging these misapprehensions and gaining an objective view of one-self and the world at large increases a person's ability to find gratification in and cope with the exigencies of life.

PART **III** BEHAVIORAL
MANIFESTATIONS
OF THE FANTASY
BOND

6 INWARDNESS AND THE LOSS OF FEELING

*I consider many adults (including myself) are or have been, more or less in
a hypnotic trance, induced in early infancy: we remain in this state until—
when we dead awaken, as Ibsen makes one of his characters say—we shall
find that we have never lived.*

—R. D. Laing, *The Politics of the Family and Other Essays*

The majority of individuals in our society exist in a somewhat deadened state
of mind, partially removed from feeling and unaware that they are involved
in a defensive process that, to a large extent, diminishes their human qualities. This lack of emotional awareness precludes the realization that they
are living out a life that does not reflect their true selves. As explained previously, when people are damaged in their upbringing, they tend to develop a
negative conception of self and a cynical view of other people and progressively lose feeling for themselves and others. They gradually retreat into an
inward state characterized by varying degrees of withdrawal of interest in
and involvement with others.

https://doi.org/10.1037/0000268-007
Challenging the Fantasy Bond: A Search for Personal Identity and Freedom,
by R. W. Firestone

In my theoretical approach, the term *inwardness* refers to a syndrome characterized by a general retreat from relationships and life, including self-denial and withholding, a preoccupation with fantasy, a tendency to seek isolation, varying degrees of withdrawal of affect, and a reliance on addictive substances and routines (R. W. Firestone, 1997a). It is necessary to distinguish inwardness from self-reflection, introspection, time spent alone for creative work or planning, meditation, and other forms of spiritual or intellectual pursuits. It is also important to distinguish it from introversion (vs. extroversion), which refers to the personality type that is more comfortable in small groups and one-on-one relationships and empowered by spending time alone (Note 1).

By contrast, inwardness implies a defended state of mind in which people narrow their life experience by turning within in a manner that cuts them off from feeling for themselves and other people. This orientation involves a gradual withdrawal from the exchange of emotional products in the interpersonal world, a preference for isolation, and a reliance on addictive habit patterns. Inwardness also encompasses microsuicidal behaviors, which are destructive behaviors that, while not immediately life threatening, are so prevalent in the general population that I have characterized them as the "microsuicides of everyday life" (R. W. Firestone & Seiden, 1987, p. 31, 1990a; Note 2). These include tendencies toward progressive self-denial, isolation, excessive use of addictive substances, feelings of self-hatred and cynicism toward others, lack of direction in life leading to a sense of hopelessness and despair, and a withdrawal from those activities and relationships most prized by the individual.

In a defensive posture, children become increasingly dependent on fantasy gratification and imagine, to some extent, that they are self-sustaining. In less-than-optimal circumstances, many cease to identify with themselves or fail to give themselves value and, instead, build a self-protective facade as a self-protective response to their parent's critical, rejecting, and/or hostile attitudes and feelings toward them. This facade or social image also represents a futile attempt to deny the allegations of destructive voices (R. W. Firestone et al., 2012; Laing, 1960/1969).

An inward person's life is primarily guided by the dictates of the voice, which encourages isolation and distrust. This internal dialogue consumes a great deal of energy and leaves the person with diminished vitality. Growing older, the child and eventually the adult becomes progressively more inward and removed from directly experiencing the world around them.

Most people move between an inward state and a feeling state and manifest almost two completely separate approaches to life as they fluctuate.

Some live suspended in a defended, cut-off condition, with little compassion or love for long periods. This unfeeling approach and its opposite, an open, feeling state, represent end points on a continuum. Between these extremes lies a middle ground in which most people live, neither deeply possessed by a critical point of view toward themselves nor completely removed from their feelings for themselves and others. However, their spirit and sensitivity can be considerably dulled, and they are, at times, capable of unconsciously acting out destructive behavior toward themselves and/or others.

INWARDNESS

The process of turning inward begins as early as the first few months of infancy and is reactivated by critical events during the life span (Liotti, 1999, 2004; Note 3). At these times, there is some extent of depersonalization, which impacts a person's ability to develop or maintain a sense of their own identity and personal value. In this condition, fantasy gratification takes precedence over feeling, precluding genuine involvement with other individuals (Healy, 2014; Somer & Herscu, 2017; Note 4). For children, this inward world is completely under their control; they can escape from a frustrating emotional climate by withdrawing and resorting to fantasy whenever they feel the need. This alternative is more reliable than depending on a parent whose attention or lack of attention is influenced by variables beyond the child's influence.

Both the child and later the adult unconsciously deny the extent of their inwardness, yet they invariably develop a strong sense of guilt about seeking internal gratification while rejecting emotional exchanges in the real world. In pulling away from others, a person necessarily distorts other people's real qualities and becomes critical of them to justify being isolated. In losing compassion for and sensitivity to others, they also turn away from feeling for themselves. By misperceiving others and holding on to a negative view of themselves, they avoid becoming too attached to those closest to them.

To preserve this inward world and resist exposure, individuals must protect the illusion of being undefended. They maintain the belief that they are pursuing realistic goals—love, close friendships, a rewarding career—when, in fact, they are engaged in self-denial and are sabotaging their lives. When this reality becomes apparent to them, they rationalize their failures and frustration and consider themselves to be victimized by other people and/or circumstances.

Manifestations of Inwardness

Indications of an inward state include a tendency toward isolation, progressive denial of priorities, withdrawal from relationships and favored activities, withholding personal feelings, and a preference for fantasy gratification over pursuing satisfactions in the real world. None of these manifestations are separate and discrete; they tend to converge and overlap. For purposes of clarity and elucidation, however, they are discussed here as separate entities and are illustrated by the example of Steven.

Case Example

Steven first came to see me shortly after he had moved from the Midwest and was living by himself, isolated in his apartment. He had been rejected by his girlfriend and had quit his job and moved across the country. As his withdrawal from people became more extreme, he became concerned about himself and sought therapy. When I first met Steven, his posture and mannerisms revealed the imprint of the abuse and neglect he had endured during his childhood. His self-consciousness and low self-esteem were evident in the way he lowered his head and avoided direct eye contact and in his hesitant style of talking.

In our sessions, Steven spoke of the severe limitations his inwardness imposed on his life. Over the time we worked together, he explored his self-critical thoughts and expressed the inner voices that directed him to isolate himself and distance himself from people. As he came to understand the reasons and feelings behind his tendency toward inwardness, he became more outgoing, developing friendships and a gratifying social life. By the time he terminated therapy, Steven's life had stabilized, and he was reasonably happy.

Five years later, Steven reached out to me again because he had been struggling with isolation and inwardness following his older brother's suicide the previous year. Steven's reaction had been to withdraw into himself and to cut off from the pain and confusion he felt. In our sessions, Steven spoke of how, throughout his childhood, he had looked up to his brother, believing that he had been strong enough to escape their neglectful and violent childhood unscathed. His suicide had destroyed Steven's idealized picture of him and had precipitated a strong guilt reaction for surviving when his brother did not. In therapy, Steven was able to access and process the different emotions he had about his brother's death, which allowed him to come out of his self-protective isolation.

Toward the end of therapy, Steven and I discussed what he had learned about himself and about inwardness, specifically. Steven began our conversation by discussing his childhood.

STEVEN: My family was not accepted in the town I grew up in. The neighbor kids couldn't play with us because we weren't the "right kind of people." I always felt on the outside. One of my first memories is of walking down the street and repeating to myself, "I don't care, I don't care." My life was just me. I hardly remember ever talking to anyone, even in my family. My mother left us before I can remember. I basically spent all of my time alone, daydreaming and living in a fantasy world. And my father was unpredictable. We never knew what to expect when he came home. If he was sober, he would cook dinner for us, but if he was drunk, he'd beat everyone in sight. I was the youngest kid, and I'd hide and try to stay out of the way. Our nights were filled with terror. Talking about this now, I can still feel the emotions of watching my father beating my brother. I felt scared and helpless. There was nothing I could do to save him. All I could do was try to save myself by being quiet.

Tendency Toward Isolation

In this part of the conversation, Steven revealed his state of mind when he is inward and isolated. He talked about the self-critical thoughts and voices that encourage him to withdraw from people.

STEVEN: I still have a tendency to spend a lot of time alone, like I did as a kid. Sometimes I'm worried about how inward and isolated from people I can get.

DR. F: What does "inwardness" mean to you when you think about it?

STEVEN: I know that it has caused me the most problems in my life, in relation to everything in my life, in relation to my family and my girlfriend and friends. I withdraw into my own world. It feels like survival to me.

DR. F: How do you lead this inner life? What is it like? What do you do?

STEVEN: I try to make myself okay. That's the thing that's utmost in my mind. I'm always thinking about how to improve myself. It can be the simplest thing. It can be organizing my office or exercising or doing chores.

DR. F: So, time alone is spent fixing yourself. Why do you need to fix yourself?

STEVEN: It's like I feel like I'm the worst person. Everything is wrong with me, my actions, my thinking, my speech, and the best thing I can do is be quiet. The best thing I can do is just stay out of people's way.

DR. F: What is the voice behind that? What you are telling yourself.

STEVEN: Look, just be quiet. Don't cause any trouble. Get everything right. Stand up straight! Talk straight! Don't be so stupid. (*Speaking with more intensity*) You're so stupid. Every word out of your mouth is stupid! You don't know how to talk. You don't know the right words for things. You don't know how to be with people.

DR. F: Keep going.

STEVEN: Just look at you. You're bothering everybody. Don't look at people. You better not look at people because then people will see deep down inside you're just basically bad.

DR. F: These voices must make you feel tense when you are around people.

STEVEN: I do. And I can never feel relaxed. But when I'm alone, I feel more relaxed when I'm by myself doing something.

DR. F: You see it as a way of relaxing. But does it really work that way?

STEVEN: It doesn't make me feel better. I may feel a little relieved, but the truth is that I'm lonely. And the voices are still there attacking me. Telling me I've got to fix myself.

Isolation is a primary aspect of an inward, self-destructive lifestyle. It can be a significant sign of suicidal ideation and a central element in actual suicide. As illustrated in Steven's case, self-critical attitudes and feelings of worthlessness lead to an avoidance of meaningful social relationships. However, people who are inward are rarely aware of the extent of their self-hatred. Instead, rationalizations preclude awareness of the retreat from life: "I need some space. I need more quiet time, time alone to think things over" or simply "I'm too busy" or "I don't have enough money to go places and do things."

Progressive Withdrawal From Priorities

A propensity toward isolation can lead to the abandonment of friendships and significant relationships. Continually changing jobs or frequent moves to a new location are other indications of withdrawal. Losing interest in activities, hobbies, or causes that previously had meaning or brought pleasure to a person is evidence of a progressive descent into an inward state in which one no longer cares or where nothing seems to matter.

Steven's tendency to withdraw escalated into a pattern of running away at crucial points in his life. In this conversation, Steven refers to this method of escape and connects it to extremely self-deprecating voices.

STEVEN: You know, when I was living with my girlfriend, life was going along okay. Then one day, it felt like everything was closing in on me, and I just had to get away. I felt like I would go crazy if I didn't get out of there.

DR. F: Closing in on you.

STEVEN: Yeah, like I was trapped. Like I was going to suffocate.

DR. F: What were the voices that went with those feelings?

STEVEN: Get out of here! You won't be able to breathe. You aren't safe. You're going to die. Get out of here so you can breathe!

DR. F: So, you left.

STEVEN: Yeah. But you know that even today, the slightest thing can set that reaction off in me. Like if anyone is ever critical of me, then I feel like "I've got to go away. I've got to get out of here." It doesn't even have to be that critical, even a slight request—"Would you move over so I can see better?"—or something as innocuous as that. It's not at all like somebody being really critical or angry toward me.

DR. F: It takes practically nothing to set you off.

STEVEN: Right. It's like when I come out of the inward state, and then if there's anything that bothers me or hurts me, I'm just set off, and the voice starts again: "You see, I told you. You should just go off by yourself. Just get out of here."

As the conversation progressed, Steven discussed the connection between his impulse to run away as an adult and the fear that drove him to hide out and search for a safe place as a child.

STEVEN: I feel exactly how I felt as a kid. It's like I'm back in that dangerous situation. In my house, it was very dangerous. My brother was older than me, and he would try to protect me. But he was just a kid, too. It was much safer for me to go off by myself.

Withholding of Personal Feelings

When people are inward, they tend to hold back from having personal exchanges with others. They can even seem extroverted or outgoing while actually investing little real affect in their relationships. They may be refractory when simple kindness is extended to them. They often react against someone who expresses interest in them.

In this part of the conversation, Steven talked about his lack of tolerance for genuine interactions with the people closest to him.

STEVEN: There have been times when I have gotten to a place where I'm not having any meaningful conversations with anyone. It feels like I almost can't stand to have a real interaction with another person.

DR. F: So, you're cheating yourself out of your real life.

STEVEN: That's how it feels. It's kind of extreme, actually. I hardly speak to anybody, really. Even though I have a girlfriend. And I have friends I joke around with and stuff, and they seem to like me and say nice things about me. I have a good career. I have things that are important to me in my life.

DR. F: How does that realization get lost?

STEVEN: They're all lost to me because of the inwardness. It's like it keeps me removed from everything.

DR. F: It's like a shield.

STEVEN: Yeah. It's a struggle for me. Like, with my girlfriend, I imagine being intimate and loving and being tender. But in the actual situation, I freeze up, and I feel like I'm going to jump out of my skin. And then, there are times when I am vulnerable and expressive like what I imagine, but afterward, it's hard to go back to that level of intimacy. It's like, deep down, I'm scared to death to really relate on that level.

Fantasy Gratification

Fantasy is a major defense against emotional pain, a self-soothing mechanism that is immediately rewarding. In defending against disappointment, sadness, anger, and other disturbing emotions, the inward person gradually comes to prefer fantasy over striving for life's rewards (Healy, 2014; Somer & Herscu, 2017; Note 5). Reliance on this type of self-gratification tends to be progressively incapacitating as it interferes with the active pursuit of goals and leads to passivity and distorts everyday experiences. People who are inward often appear indifferent to significant events in life while responding melodramatically to less important ones. This preoccupation with fantasy is extensive and pervasive. The key issue is that fantasy, along with the habit patterns that support and supplement it, acts to deprive the individual of the necessary ingredients for a fulfilling life (R. W. Firestone, 1990c, 1993).

Steven went on to describe how he retreated into an inward world of fantasy to escape the pain and guilt surrounding his brother's suicide.

STEVEN: I felt like I was getting somewhere in my life, and then when my brother died, I somehow went back into that inward world. I just couldn't cope with his death.

DR. F: So, then you became more inward after his death?

STEVEN: Yeah, I couldn't resolve his death. [*Sad*] Why would he kill himself? He was the strong one when we were growing up. He was the one who stood up to my dad.

DR. F: Yes, you were confused because you always looked up to him.

STEVEN: I was. I just withdrew. I didn't feel anything. Nothing! When I came out of it a little bit, I was afraid it was going to be too painful. But I've come to realize that isn't true. It's not as painful as I thought it would be. It feels better to be in real time in real situations and feel the real feelings. But if I withdraw, I get in trouble. I have to put myself back into the real situation. I have to put myself back into the feelings.

DR. F: You have to feel your pain in order to stay alive.

STEVEN: Yeah, because if you withdraw, you only keep withdrawing.

People who live largely in fantasy are usually more concerned with image or appearance than with actual personal satisfactions. They refrain from initiating actions that might lead to real rewards because achieving their goals in reality threatens to disrupt the fantasy process. Passivity and indifference signify surrender to an unfeeling, deadened state in which the person experiences spontaneous activity or productive work as an unwelcome intrusion. A passive lifestyle also fosters a helpless, victimized, paranoid posture in which people perceive forces as acting on them rather than seeing themselves as being able to impact their environment.

A Negative Self-Image
Negative attitudes toward oneself, as well as cynical, hostile attitudes toward others, support defenses and encourage inwardness. This destructive outlook, along with negative anticipations about the world, is based on painful

experiences within the family of origin. When the general atmosphere at home is harsh and the parents are inadequate or untrustworthy, a child's feeling reaction to these conditions will be to defend themselves, which, for Steven, meant withdrawing and isolating himself.

Some characteristics common among inward, self-destructive individuals include low self-esteem and a deep sense of shame. Such individuals tend to hold on to snide, self-depreciating attitudes toward themselves they internalized early on and find it difficult to adjust to a more positive or realistic point of view. With Steven, old feelings of worthlessness and shame from his childhood were aroused by his guilt in relation to his brother's suicide.

DR. F: What voices do you think you had after your brother's death? What did you tell yourself?

STEVEN: Oh, my God. There was so much guilt. There were voices like: How can you be alive? You're the screwed-up one. You're the one who never did anything right, never did anything responsible, never did anything. You did everything wrong, and he did everything right. And he's dead. He's the one who's dead.

DR. F: Keep going.

STEVEN: You should be dead! You're the one who should be dead, not him. He did everything right; he was smart. He had a family! He had a wife! He had everything! You're the one who's supposed to be dead! (*Sobs deeply*) I was never supposed to have a life, much less a life like I have now with my girlfriend and a good job.

THE LOSS OF FEELING

Inwardness leads to a state of diminished feeling and emotional reaction. Individuals who are close to their feelings experience a sense of inner harmony, respond appropriately to positive and negative events in their lives, and are generally more capable of coping with life than people who are less tolerant of their feelings. Being in contact with one's emotions—sadness, anger, fear, disgust, envy, shame, joy, happiness, amusement, exhilaration—is essential to maintaining one's unique sense of identity, leading a life of integrity, and finding meaning in life (Note 6). Indeed, life and the external world have no inherent meaning in and of themselves. There is no hidden significance to life that may be discovered; rather, it is only a person's investment in themselves, their feelings, their interest in life, other people, and activities that gives life its particular meaning for that person.

Emotional processes are inextricably tied to the motivational system—that is, to one's wants, needs, and desires. Therefore, remaining connected to one's feelings is crucial to pursuing one's goals in life (K. L. Davis & Panksepp, 2011; Plutchik, 2001; Plutchik & Kellerman, 2013). According to L. S. Greenberg (2019), emotions are "the basic datum of experience and . . . (provide) information, action tendencies, and motivation" (Abstract). L. S. Greenberg (2012) stressed the central role that feelings play in motivating human behavior and facilitating progress in psychotherapy, highlighting "the importance of both emotion awareness and emotion regulation in therapeutic change" (Abstract).

Feelings can be conceptualized as flowing through the individual freely. When that natural flow is interfered with—for example, when pain and sadness are blocked—individuals tend to become suspended in a cut-off and defended state. They disengage from themselves as a center of emotion, perception, cognition, and behavior. In an effort to disown their "unacceptable" feelings, they unconsciously deny or repress them or project them onto others.

Avoiding undesirable emotions that inevitably arise in the course of living has a number of negative consequences. People not only cause themselves considerable harm but they also cause harm to others. They are more likely to act out behavior that is detrimental to their well-being. Referring to one of the many psychological costs of suppressing feelings, Harré and Parrott (1996) emphasized the part that feelings play in self-control:

> Feelings inform our reflective selves about our current automatic tendencies. Only if we are aware of these tendencies can we exercise self-control over them. Therefore, if we are to have more control over our emotions we must become more aware of their existence. (p. 18)

Similarly, L. S. Greenberg (2002) stressed another value inherent in being aware of one's emotions:

> We order our reality by forming stories that tell who we are. No story is significant without emotion, and no emotion exists without a story to provide its context. We thus integrate head and heart in authoring who we are. (p. 303; Note 7)

The Role of the Voice in Cutting Off Feeling

As described earlier, in the context of the overall defensive process, the voice represents the person's self-destructive and critical thoughts. It promotes feelings of self-hatred and sets the person up to become defended, inward, angry, and depressed (Note 7). My concept of inwardness denotes a combination of specific propensities and microsuicidal behavior patterns regulated by the voice that plays a role in a withdrawal from personal interactions, an overall divestment in life, and, indeed, in most forms of psychological suffering. They are particularly evident in suicidal individuals. Essentially, the primary intent of the voice is directed toward self-denial and ultimately toward the destruction of the individual (R. W. Firestone, 1997a, 1997b).

Some of the voices that encourage inwardness are self-soothing rather than harsh or critical: "Why go out with those people again? Stay home; take some time for yourself. You like being alone. You enjoy your own company." Other voices are assertive and critical of others: "She's so needy. Does she want you to be with her all the time?" "He's going to take away your independence!" As previously explained, critical inner voices can be projected onto others: "They think you are being too loud!" "They are irritated with you." "They are planning to attack you!" "Just shut up!" People's excessive concern over what others are thinking about them is an attempt to externalize self-attacks and is indicative of underlying feelings of self-hatred.

The obsessional quality of self-attacks is antithetical to maintaining an ongoing state of feeling. When emotions such as anger or competitiveness arise, the voice may judge them as inappropriate, wrong, or bad, causing the individual to suppress these feelings: "What are you getting so worked up about?" "You sound like a crazy person!" "Look at you, crying like a baby!" "Pull it together; have some dignity!" Vulnerable feelings, such as loving and wanting, are also judged and censored by the voice to the person's detriment: "You're so overly sensitive." "You're just a sentimental old fool!"

Clinical evidence from individual and group therapy sessions and non-clinical participants in a longitudinal study (see Firestone, 1997b) supporting the relationship between internal voices and self-destructive living has suggested research possibilities that could lead to an accurate gauge of an individual's suicide potential. I hypothesized that the level of suicidal intent could be assessed by identifying where and with what frequency an individual's thoughts lie along the continuum of negative thought patterns (Table 6.1; Note 8). My daughter, Lisa Firestone, PhD, and I went on to create the Firestone Assessment of Self-Destructive Thoughts (2006), a self-report questionnaire that distinguishes between suicidal and nonsuicidal individuals.

The self-attacks of the voice vary along a continuum of intensity from mild self-reproach to stronger self-accusations to self-destructive and suicidal ideation. Actual self-harm in the form of addictive disorders, recklessness, and other risk-taking behavior are more likely to be acted out when people retreat into an inward state, withdraw their interest and emotional investment in themselves and others, and avoid pursuing significant personal goals

TABLE 6.1. Continuum of Negative Thought Patterns

Levels of increasing suicidal intention	Content of voice statements
Thoughts that lead to low self-esteem or inwardness (self-defeating thoughts):	
1. Self-depreciating thoughts of everyday life	You're incompetent, stupid. You're not very attractive. You're going to make a fool of yourself.
2. Thoughts rationalizing self-denial, thoughts discouraging the person from engaging in pleasurable activities	You're too young (old) and inexperienced to apply for this job. You're too shy to make any new friends. Why go on this trip? It'll be such a hassle. You'll save money by staying home.
3. Cynical attitudes toward others, leading to alienation and distancing	Why go out with her [him]? She's cold, unreliable; she'll reject you. She wouldn't go out with you anyway. You can't trust men [women].
4. Thoughts influencing isolation; rationalizations for time alone, but using time to become more negative toward oneself	Just be by yourself. You're miserable company anyway; who'd want to be with you? Just stay in the background, out of view.
5. Self-contempt, vicious self-abusive thoughts and accusations (accompanied by intense angry affect)	You idiot! You bitch! You creep! You stupid shit! You don't deserve anything; you're worthless.
Thoughts that support the cycle of addiction (or addictions):	
6. Thoughts urging the use of substances or food followed by self-criticisms (weakens inhibitions against self-destructive actions while increasing guilt and self-recrimination following acting out)	It's okay to do drugs; you'll be more relaxed. Go ahead and have a drink; you deserve it. [Later] You weak-willed jerk! You're nothing but a drugged-out drunken freak.
Thoughts that lead to suicide (self-annihilating thoughts):	
7. Thoughts contributing to a sense of hopelessness, urging withdrawal or removal of oneself completely from the lives of people closest	See how bad you make your family [or friends] feel. They'd be better off without you. It's the only decent thing to do—just stay away and stop bothering them.
8. Thoughts influencing a person to give up priorities and favored activities (points of identity)	What's the use? Your work doesn't matter anymore. Why bother even trying? Nothing matters anyway.
9. Injunctions to inflict self-harm at an action level, intense rage against self	Why don't you just drive across the center divider? Just shove your hand under that power saw!
10. Thoughts planning details of suicide (calm, rational, often obsessive, indicating complete loss of feeling for the self)	You have to get hold of some pills, then go to a hotel, and so forth.
11. Injunctions to carry out suicide plans, thoughts baiting the person to commit suicide (extreme thought constriction)	You've thought about this long enough. Just get it over with. It's the only way out!

Note. Any combination of the voice attacks can lead to serious suicidal intent. Thoughts leading to isolation, ideation about removing oneself from people's lives, beliefs that one is a bad influence or has a destructive effect on others, voices urging one to give up special activities, vicious self-abusive thoughts accompanied by strong anger, voices urging self-injury, and a suicide attempt are all indications of high suicide potential or risk. From *Suicide and the Inner Voice: Risk Assessment, Treatment, and Case Management* (p. 219), by R. W. Firestone, 1997b, SAGE. Copyright 1988 by The Glendon Association. Reprinted with permission.

(Note 8). A number of theorists have described the continuous nature of self-destructive behavior, isolation, and restrictive lifestyles (Farberow, 1980a, 1980b; Menninger, 1938). For example, Shneidman (1966) highlighted the "multitudinous ways in which an individual can reduce, truncate, demean, narrow, shorten, or destroy his own life" (p. 199). As the voice gains ascendance over rational thoughts, people become increasingly dissociated from themselves and immune to feeling. Dire predictions about the self, others, and the future are accepted by the person as accurate statements, and as a consequence, suicidal ideation increases dramatically. In these circumstances, microsuicidal behavior has lethal potential as one approaches the extreme end of the continuum.

Inward, Impersonal Relating

Any interaction between two people can be analyzed in terms of whether it is personal and conducive to the expression of feelings and encourages closeness or whether it is impersonal and serves to cut off feeling and promote inwardness. Impersonal relating is characterized by a lack of genuinely connecting on a personal level; people are less communicative and more indirect, and there is a discrepancy between their affect and verbal expression. The minimal nature of personal feelings, eye contact, and physical affection gives the impression that the person is not completely present. This quality of dissociation is characteristic of the inward individual's detached style of relating. In some instances, communications are glib, sarcastic, or condescending to ward off establishing an emotional connection. Often, all that remains in this style of relating is the illusion of a friendship.

In couples where partners are inward, their communication often involves an unspoken agreement to not intrude on one another's defenses and self-contained style of living. Each is protective of this pact because they are reluctant to be independent and, at the same time, fear intrusion into their isolation. The result is a relationship characterized by duplicitous communication and defensiveness about the emotional distance the couple maintains in their relationship. Therefore, both partners operate out of guilt, fear, and obligation to be able to sustain their mutual fantasy of intimacy. Some couples increase the amount of time they spend together and develop a false sense of unity to reassure themselves that they are still engaged on a feeling level.

The antithesis of this mutually agreed-on inward state is a style of relating in which the individuals are equal and independent. Neither acts superior or inferior to the other, and each partner acts out of free choice rather than obligation. This interactive relating is generally more personal, dynamic, and feeling and includes genuine companionship. A person who is authentic in a close, intimate relationship experiences their feelings toward the other person and expresses these feelings outwardly.

By contrast, in a more impersonal mode of relating, while people may know intellectually what they feel for another, they do not experience it on an emotional level. When a person withdraws into an inward, defended state, they tend to hold back their feelings, a process that hurts those dearest to them. Often, they will protect their defended position over any real concern for a relationship. In the process, without intention, people cause a great deal of harm to themselves, their loved ones, and their closest relationships. There is no way for a person to be innocently defended or inward; these defenses inevitably cause some amount of damage, particularly to those who are open or vulnerable.

Suppression of Pain and Loss of Feeling

Much of human behavior is directed toward the avoidance of painful primal feelings from childhood, as well as sad and hurt feelings in the present. Existing in an inward state provides a partial escape. This condition may not necessarily be an unhappy one; it can even provide a seemingly com-fortable way of life for some. However, repressed emotions eventually find expression through neurotic acting out, withdrawal into fantasy, addictions, or psychosomatic illnesses.

Many still view psychological pain as abnormal and think that people suffering from this form of distress are mentally ill. This is a common fallacy related to a misconception about feeling. As noted, feelings arise involun-tarily and are felt as sensations in the body; they cannot be forced. Neither can they be successfully suppressed. Typically, in the nuclear family, the child must not show pain or unhappiness because that would be a betrayal; revealing discontent would expose the parents' inadequacies. Instead, chil-dren turn their reactions of anger, sadness, and hatred on themselves and become inward and secretive about how they actually feel. In a sense, they learn to go underground with any feelings or thoughts that threaten to reveal negative aspects of family life, intuitively knowing that to exhibit these feelings might make their parents angry or guilty.

It is the nature of emotional trauma that if it is suppressed instead of experienced, it does not dissipate or disappear but retains a bodily com-ponent. Pain that is not fully experienced at the time continues to exert its damaging effect on the person and finds symbolic expression through patterns of self-limiting, self-destructive, or aggressive acting out behavior. L. S. Greenberg (2002) observed,

> Over-control of emotion often leads to its opposite—the possibility of break-down of rational control. Emotional control fails when stress becomes too great. . . . Left on their own in murky darkness, emotions can become painfully tortured and twisted. This occurs when, for example, unresolved anger turns to thoughts of revenge. (p. 304)

The avoidance of feeling leads to compulsive reliving and repetition. The defended person continually manipulates the interpersonal environment so that the repressed pain from the past will not resurface. Primitive pain and longings that have been suppressed often cause tension and psycho-somatic illnesses, as well as depression and anxiety. According to Bessel van der Kolk (2015),

> Long after a traumatic experience is over, it may be reactivated at the slightest hint of danger and mobilize disturbed brain circuits and secrete massive amounts of stress hormones. This precipitates unpleasant emotions, intense physical sensations, and impulsive and aggressive actions. (p. 2)

Defense mechanisms that repress spontaneous emotions keep people from feeling fully alive. Their reactions become more automatic and cere-bral, and they become less emotional and more detached from their bodies. This unconscious effort to repress their pain and fear keeps them from being able to experience the richness of their inner life. Nevertheless, if a person enters psychotherapy where the atmosphere is conducive to the expression of these suppressed emotions, they can access and experience the original trauma, which results in a reduction of rigidity and bodily tension (Fosha, 2005; L. S. Greenberg, 2002; Note 9). The expression of these repressed feelings is often accompanied by clear memories, compassion for the self, and intellectual insights. When people learn the value of feeling freely and not consciously controlling their emotions, they also discover that actions based on feelings are fully controllable.

CONCLUSION

The inward state is a mode of defense adopted by the child when faced with environmental deprivation and external threat. The child's renunciation of the true self and the subsequent retreat into an emotionally deadened existence is the best adaptation that can be made in the struggle to pre-serve some rudimentary sense of self in the midst of toxic influences. These self-protective measures help an individual to survive a painful or traumatic childhood but at the expense of a richer, fuller life as an adult. They serve to restrict or impede the possibility of intimacy in close relationships and significantly reduce individuals' capacity to relate to their offspring.

On an unconscious level, when people are inward, they gradually give up goal-directed activity and avoid real gratification to cling to the safety of an internal world over which they have control. The process of nurturing themselves in the inward state becomes addictive and habitual because it has immediately rewarding properties that dull psychological pain. Becoming aware of this process is essential for understanding and facilitating a person's movement toward achieving their full potential.

In losing feeling for themselves, inward people also lose the ability to act spontaneously in response to their desires. On a behavioral level, when people exist in an inward state, they drastically reduce emotional transactions and hold back appropriate responses from others in the interpersonal environment. Active strivings are replaced by passive fantasy, which damages people in their efforts to cope with the realities of life.

At any given moment, a person can either retreat into themselves and seek gratification through their imagination or pursue satisfaction through interactions in the real world. These options are mutually exclusive. Understanding these dynamics is all the more important because the damage caused by inward defenses to themselves, their loved ones, and their children is far more extensive than people would like to believe. People will encounter internal and external pressures as they attempt to emerge from a self-protective, inward state and face painful truths about their lives. However, with self-compassion, they can expose the causative factors that predisposed their inward retreat and its resultant misery, develop themselves, and adopt a more positive approach to life.

7

WITHHOLDING

You can hold yourself back from the sufferings of the world
this is something you are free to do and is in accord with your nature,
but perhaps precisely this holding back is the only suffering that
you might be able to avoid.

—Franz Kafka (quoted in R. D. Laing, The Divided Self)

Withholding is a defense mechanism encompassing a wide range of inter-related behaviors that helps to maintain the illusion of self-sufficiency that is fundamental to the fantasy bond. It involves the holding back of pleasure or fulfillment from the self and others, including positive feelings, actions, and competence, each an innate expression of one's identity. This defense is largely unconscious and is therefore enacted with little awareness, not as a deliberate manipulation that is intended to be hurtful (R. W. Firestone & Catlett, 2009b).

When children are in pain and frustrated, they tend to suppress the spon-taneous expression of their natural feelings. They gradually substitute a defensive, self-protective posture toward life, which keeps the emotional

https://doi.org/10.1037/0000268-008
Challenging the Fantasy Bond: A Search for Personal Identity and Freedom,
by R. W. Firestone

impact of personal exchanges manageable. In addition, children tend to react to a parent's physical and emotional neglect, indifference, and other withholding behaviors by turning away from the parent as a source of support and becoming increasingly self-nourishing (Note 1). Later, as adults, they tend to withhold from themselves potential sources of gratification and fulfillment, especially in their more intimate relationships.

MANIFESTATIONS OF WITHHOLDING

Being especially valued or loved can precipitate anxiety and reawaken feelings of sadness along with other painful emotions from the past. *Withholding* is a person's attempt to restore psychological equilibrium by creating and maintaining a safe emotional distance from anything that might arouse those feelings. Therefore, it is particularly directed toward the people and endeavors most meaningful to them.

Examples of the diverse patterns of withholding can be observed in every realm of human experience. Individuals may limit their potential and fulfillment in life; in couple relationships, partners may self-protectively withdraw the love they once felt and expressed (Love & Shulkin, 1997); in families, parents may unintentionally hold back their love and affection from their children, who then retaliate by withholding from their parents; and in the workplace, people may sabotage their careers by acting out passive aggression (R. W. Firestone, 1990b).

Behavioral manifestations of withholding have a destructive impact on the individual. These include withholding as a form of self-denial, a defense used to maintain inwardness, and a manifestation of passive aggression, an indirect way of expressing anger.

Withholding as a Form of Self-Denial

Being close to feelings and existing in a state of genuine wanting lends excitement and vitality to a person's life. It contributes to the development of a strong sense of identity. Conversely, self-denial includes avoiding and/or retreating from happiness and gratifying experiences. This unconscious reaction causes pain and distress for both the self-denying individual and the person being withheld from. If children feel unloved and/or rejected, they learn to stop wanting affection; that is, they become self-denying and withdraw from their natural feelings of love and affection toward their parents. These children learn to arrest the flow of their genuine feelings and substitute a fantasy of affection, love, and closeness.

Self-denying responses—that is, failing to act on one's authentic inclinations—must be distinguished from altruistic behaviors that are generous and self-fulfilling and generally motivated by feelings of empathy and compassion for others. In contrast, despite rationalizations to the contrary, self-denial can be a form of microsuicide. It represents a giving up of investment in and excitement about life and a withdrawal from significant activities and relationships. This tendency is built into an individual's defensive posture and often manifests itself early in life. In effect, self-denial is a destructive form of self-parenting and generally represents the internalization of excessive or even hostile parental prohibitions.

Some people make a virtue of self-denial and are proud of their asceticism, considering it to be moral and beneficial (Banks, 1996; Fromm, 1939; Note 2). Self-righteous attitudes in the service of self-denial are damaging to others, particularly to one's children. Rationalizations supported by the voice enable people to easily give up activities and friendships they especially enjoy. Relinquishing one's special desires and passions often leads to a self-destructive, downward spiral that, in the extreme, could result in actual suicide.

Maintaining a sense of control is an essential component of the process of self-denial. Withholding individuals feel the need to protect and regulate their inner fantasy world so that it remains stable, predictable, and under their command. In contrast, they see spontaneous responses and free-flowing interactions in their interpersonal environment as out of their control and therefore threatening and potentially harmful. Their need to limit their generosity and giving to others stems from a primitive, deep-seated fear of being emotionally depleted or drained.

Human beings have a natural tendency to avoid feelings of fear, anger, and hurt, yet paradoxically, the very act of holding back to fend off these emotions can exacerbate their suffering. Whenever people unconsciously inhibit loving and affectionate responses that have been a part of their behavior, they are, in effect, going against their own nature, which arouses guilt. These withholding responses combine with the substitution of fantasy for security and partial satisfaction, further turning people against themselves. However unintentional, the damage caused to personal relationships adds to an individual's guilt and self-hatred, progressively leading to still more self-denial.

In families with a withholding or self-denying parent, other family members are often manipulated into feeling guilty, fearful, and/or angry in relation to the self-denial or victimized posture that parent may exhibit. The intimidating effect of this dynamic significantly restricts the flow of honest communication. Being raised in this type of situation often limits a person's ability to become independent, autonomous, and self-reliant.

Withholding as an Expression of Passive Aggression

Passive aggression based on suppressed anger is a form of withholding that is manifested in oppositional, negativistic actions and personality traits, as well as in more covertly controlling behaviors. Passive aggression, an indirect way of expressing hostility, may appear innocent, but it is often as harmful as, or more devastating than, expressions of direct aggression toward others (Cavaiola & Lavender, 2000; Note 3). Controlling others through weakness is a particularly treacherous form of passive-aggressive withholding. It operates as a subtle kind of terrorism that induces guilt in others and supports their voices and self-attacks. Entire families may be manipulated by a weak, victimized family member, hurting everyone, including the perpetrator.

In most families, children have limited channels through which to express their frustration, anger, or emotional pain. When their feelings and reactions are not tolerated, passive aggression toward their parents offers them a means of retaliation while keeping direct expressions of rage concealed. In light of the power differential within families, children find it safer and more comfortable to express their anger in nonstraightforward ways by refusing to behave or respond as they know their parents would like or expect. For the child, covert expressions of anger are more effective than directly expressing rage toward a more powerful adult.

The child's early stubbornness, often beginning during the second year of life, arises partly from the natural desire to express independence and separation from the parental figure. However, defiant and rebellious behavior beyond a certain age is symptomatic of more general withholding. When children withhold their abilities and engage their parent in an ongoing battle of wills, they significantly limit their own growth and potential. Children can become so accustomed to withholding that they eventually believe they are unable to perform certain tasks that are, in reality, within their capabilities.

Adults develop more sophisticated equivalents of this childish stubbornness. For example, people who as children refused to function at their level of competency in school often have difficulty reaching their potential in their careers. Those individuals who, as children, were uncommunicative and silent have difficulty relating to their partner. People's adopted style of withholding operates even in areas of their adult lives where they want to excel. In a sense, they have learned to automatically respond with a "no," including to their own wants, desires, and life goals. As such, withholding is a learned, largely unconscious reaction that is difficult to modify once it has become well established.

People tend to repeat withholding patterns learned in childhood with individuals in their adult lives, especially authority figures. For instance, withholding and passive-aggressive behaviors are prevalent between employee and employer (Cramerus, 1989; Note 4). Employees often resort to withholding when they perceive that there is no other outlet available to them for expressing criticism or anger. In business, at school, and in other formal situations where there is little tolerance for overt anger, hostility comes out in passive ways. This type of withholding can be expressed through procrastinating, exhibiting fatigue, using disorganized and nonproductive working styles, complaining, acting overwhelmed, being forgetful, using ineffective modes of communication, and making mistakes that could be easily prevented (R. W. Firestone & Catlett, 2009b).

> Naomi had proven herself to be a skilled and dependable software engineer and was promoted to a position that commanded more responsibility. Soon after her promotion, she realized that her new boss was not qualified for his job. Not only did the man lack leadership skills, he also did not have an understanding of the program they were using. He disregarded Naomi's suggestions and made ill-informed decisions. When this resulted in mistakes, her boss covered himself by blaming them on his staff. Naomi was frustrated and discouraged and felt less invested in her job. She withdrew into herself and interacted less and less with her fellow employees. She took longer lunch hours and started leaving work early. Her performance, which she had taken such pride in before, began to suffer.
>
> Naomi turned to Joe, a friend who had mentored her early in her career. She described the frustration and anger she felt in the situation with her boss. She explained that she had decided not to leave her job because she liked the work and it paid well, but she realized that on an emotional level, she had already quit. As they spoke, Naomi could see that holding back her abilities was an expression of her anger. Joe pointed out that while these actions were aimed at her boss, they were ruining Naomi's professional life.
>
> In their conversation, Naomi was able to express all of the anger she felt toward her boss, and afterward, she felt relieved. For the first time in a while, she was able to think clearly. With Joe's help, Naomi came up with a plan for taking a more effective approach to her problem. She arranged for a meeting with one of the senior partners and spoke of her concerns regarding the issues in her current department and about her desire to develop more skills and move into a different part of the business.

THE EFFECTS OF WITHHOLDING

As has been established, there is a wide range of withholding responses with variations in intensity, persistence, and strength. As a result of this defense, children are damaged unknowingly, adults spend years sabotaging their careers, and relationships are ruined by one or both persons withdrawing the love they once expressed. Once people begin to hold back their responses, they begin to lose a sense of what they feel and who they actually are.

The Effects of Withholding on Parent-Child Relationships

Several environmental influences are integral to the child's developing withholding patterns of behavior. These consist primarily of the primary caregiver's intolerance and rejection of the child's love, response to this withholding, and modeling of these withholding behaviors.

When parents are defended against experiences that might cause them to feel anxiety or other painful emotions, they must avoid or inhibit interactions that would threaten to disturb their emotional homeostasis. This is especially true in relation to their children, whose natural spirit and un-self-conscious expressions of love would intrude on the parents' self-protective, defended state. For this reason, many well-meaning parents unconsciously discourage loving responses from their offspring (R. W. Firestone, 1990b).

Children whose parents find it difficult to accept their expressions of love gradually learn to disengage from themselves and suppress their positive feelings. Many come to believe that there is something wrong with their loving feelings and that their affection or their basic physical nature is somehow unacceptable or offensive. They experience shame about this deep form of rejection and often hold back expressions of love, tenderness, and affection in future relationships. When parents' withholding involves the withdrawal of a loving, attuned response that was previously experienced by the child, it creates intense feelings of longing and desperation. The child is driven to try to recapture that love, and this emotional hunger persists into adult life (R. W. Firestone & Catlett, 2009b).

Children also observe and are compelled to imitate the withholding behaviors they see acted out between their parents. Unconscious guilt and anxiety are aroused if there is a distinct difference between the style of relating learned in the family and the style of relating one develops as an adult. Thus, people often become locked in a defensive posture that limits their lives.

> Tony's father had many of the attributes of a narcissist. He had an entertaining and lively personality, but he could also be self-centered and often lacked empathy for others. He was the "life of the party" and the "fun dad" who everyone liked to be around. However, alone with his family, he was often disengaged and self-absorbed. He would be irritable and demanding toward his wife and disinterested and dismissive toward Tony. Tony wished that his father would be the same warm, outgoing person at home that he was with other people.

As an adult, Tony was glad not to have the attention-seeking qualities that his father did. He was modest and acknowledging of others. While not the "life of the party," he was a caring person whose friendship was valued. But when Tony had a child of his own, he struggled to connect with him. When his son was an infant, Tony thought maybe he just was not drawn to babies. But as his son grew, Tony realized that the issue was more complicated than that. He was often distracted and unacknowledging of his son. He felt awkward and self-conscious when he tried to bridge the gap between them.

Tony's wife was aware of times her husband held back from their son. She saw when he would run over to Tony, and Tony would not notice. She noticed that even when Tony was not busy, he did not seek out spending time with their son. She talked to Tony about this and, at first, he felt criticized and angry. But she reassured him that her interest was in helping to bridge the gap between him and their child. Tony became less defensive and more willing to listen to his wife. With her help, Tony began to become aware of times when he was emotionally removed and also of steps he could take to be more engaged. Tony was determined to develop a close relationship with his son, unlike the one he had had with his father.

The Effects of Withholding on Couple Relationships

Withholding has a delimiting impact on a person's capacity for maintaining feelings of love and closeness in an intimate relationship. Usually, one partner tries, or sometimes both try, to adjust the exchange of love and affection—the amount of pleasure and fulfillment they are willing to accept or give. They may gradually hold back the very qualities that originally attracted their partner: their unique way of expressing themselves, their looks, their friend-liness, their simple acts of consideration and kindness, and their enjoyment of each other's company. Partners who withhold emotional and physical inti-macy become increasingly self-hating and guilty, which in turn leads to more self-denial, inhibition, and avoidance.

When they were introduced, Marie thought Kristy was one of the most inter-esting people she had ever met. Kristy was impressed by Marie's energy and intelligence. When they started living together, their house became the hub of their social circle. Friends were drawn to the lively conversations, good meals, fun get-togethers, and generally warm and inclusive atmosphere that the two women generated.

The couple started to talk about wanting to get married and share a future together. Soon afterward, Kristy began dropping out of some of their shared activities. When friends came by, she often retired to the bedroom, leaving Marie to socialize alone. Kristy was less enthusiastic about having people over. When she and Marie were alone, where before they had always talked and joked around, Kristy was now distracted by watching shows or playing games on her computer.

Without being aware of it, Kristy was pulling away from Marie. When they had first talked about getting married, she had been overwhelmed by the love she felt for Marie and that she knew Marie felt for her. Her behavior since then put an emotional distance between them and made both Kristy and Marie feel detached from the closeness they had felt to the point where they had stopped thinking about getting married.

The partner who is being withheld from frequently ends up feeling empty and emotionally hungry. When positive responses are held back, it provokes longing and desperation, causing the person to focus intensely on the partner who has become remote. The unconscious withholding of personal qualities and actions that are loved and admired fosters confusion and frustration and can provoke resentment, anger, and distancing responses (Betchen, 2005; Love & Shulkin, 1997). Both parties then become more unresponsive and defended against each other as the withholding patterns become more established. Much of the suffering and conflict within relationships is due to one or both partners taking back the love and affection they once felt and expressed (R. W. Firestone & Catlett, 2009b).

The Effects of Withholding on Sexuality

Sexual withholding refers to the inhibiting of natural sexual desire and its expressions: an appealing manner, an open attitude, physical affection, touching, lovemaking, and any other aspects of the personal expression of one's sexuality (Carnes, 1998; R. W. Firestone et al., 2006; Love & Shulkin, 1997; B. McCarthy & McCarthy, 2003; Mitchell, 2002; Note 5). People tend to hold back loving feelings and sexual responses from their partners as part of an overall defense against closeness and intimacy. Thus, the withholding partner is able to maintain a comfortable emotional distance in the relationship. Although this particular form of self-denial and holding back takes place primarily in the privacy of the bedroom, its harmful effects are not confined to that setting. They are prevalent and disturb every aspect of family life. This facet of withholding is discussed in more detail in Chapter 10, "Sexuality."

The Effects of Withholding on Communication

In relationships characterized by a fantasy bond, mixed messages play a significant role in maintaining the form of the relationship while negating the fact that affection, companionship, and sexual responses are being withheld, to varying degrees, by one or both partners (Bateson, 1972; R. W. Firestone & Catlett, 1989; Gibney, 2006; Note 6). Withholding behaviors combined with positive verbal messages create confusion and conflict in intimate relationships. If these partners were to become aware of their withholding patterns and recognize their underlying hostility or grudges, their illusion of closeness and connection would necessarily be disrupted.

As has been noted, when people become withholding and therefore less functional, they feel guilty and self-hating about their withdrawal from the real world. In an unconscious attempt to cover up their inwardness and withholding, most individuals rationalize their behavior and deceive themselves that they are still pursuing satisfying relationships and meaningful goals. However, when people fail to pursue their goals, they cannot speak about themselves honestly. If they deny having specific wants or desires, they are being dishonest because wants and desires are a fundamental part of a person's identity as a human being. However, if they formulate a goal but are not taking constructive actions, they are also being dishonest. As a result, their communications become duplicitous and confusing to their partner, which further complicates their lives.

Mixed messages combined with withholding have been observed in videotaped interactions between partners as part of a research study conducted by Gottman and Krokoff (1989). Their studies showed that when double messages are a customary part of partners' interacting, their negative emotions tend to be communicated nonverbally through their posture, tone of voice, and other bodily cues. A preponderance of negative implicit messages, especially body language indicating contempt, in conjunction with positive verbal messages between partners is often predictive of the eventual dissolution of the relationship.

Bach and Deutsch's (1979) book, *Stop! You're Driving Me Crazy*, examines myriad ways that people in everyday life attempt to disguise their aggression through double messages, resulting in what they term "crazymaking" (Note 7). Citing cases from their clinical research, Bach and Deutsch reported, "From thousands of stress reports during individual and group psychotherapy sessions, a linkage emerged between pathogenic communication patterns and indirect, so-called passive aggression" (p. v). The greater the discrepancy between the manifest content of a communication and its underlying or latent meaning, the greater the potential for disturbance. Furthermore, within the couple, there are usually implied prohibitions against making any commentary about these discrepancies, which worsens the situation and leads to increased feelings of alienation (R. W. Firestone & Catlett, 2009b).

THE ROLE OF THE VOICE IN WITHHOLDING

Both self-denial and withholding from others are mediated by the voice. Behaviors that would naturally be manifested are held back because of a person's self-critical thoughts or distorted views of others. People regularly withhold their natural responses in everyday life in reaction to the dictates of the voice: in relationships, partners may withhold companionship and communication to avoid being vulnerable, employees may become ineffectual and fail to follow directions, children may procrastinate in doing their schoolwork. These recognizable examples of withholding are so commonplace that they tend to be accepted as normal; nevertheless, they have an undermining effect on a person's life.

In listening to the voice and following its injunctions, people restrict the excitement and enjoyment they could experience in their work and personal lives. They lose the natural capacity for joy and enthusiasm they had as children. The resulting posture is one of insulation and self-deprivation whereby an individual, in denying themselves loving responses, pleasure, and happiness, also deprives others of warmth and acts of kindness.

When parents are inconvenienced or threatened by the child's desires, they may tune the child out altogether or see them as being selfish. Children are often criticized for wanting: "You're so demanding," or "You're greedy and self-centered," or "You always have to have things your own way." By taking no notice of a child's desires or distorting and labeling them as negative, the parents, and later, the incorporated voice, effectively stop the child from expressing genuine wants that would otherwise be a natural part of personal interactions. Consequently, children often become self-conscious whenever they feel free and their spirit is unrestrained. The voice warns about exuberance in the same style that the parents cautioned, "Don't get so excited," "Don't make a fool of yourself," "What's the big deal anyway?"

Later, as adults, if they feel generous, they are likely to have voices telling them, "He doesn't want anything from you," "You're just going to be bothering her." If they want to give a gift to someone, they might think, "It's not good enough. They won't like it." Voices encourage people to be self-denying: "Don't text them. Leave them alone; don't bug them"; "Don't ask for that! You're going to look pathetic!" Voices distort others as being powerful and threatening, thereby influencing passive-aggressive withholding: "Your boss doesn't respect you. She doesn't even know you exist!" "That woman's been badmouthing you!" "You could never compete with that guy. He's much better than you."

Other voices warn against getting attached or emotionally close: "You've been spending too much time together. You need to get off by yourself." "Do you think it's such a good idea to share all of your thoughts with her?" "You're all over him. Give him some room to breathe." Some voices create fear about differentiating from one's parent's style of withholding. For example, when a person feels kind and loving toward their children, they might have voices telling them, "You're indulging your kids. They don't need so much attention. You're spoiling them."

In relation to intimacy, a person whose parents were cold and emotionally unavailable to each other might think, "You're placing too much value on this relationship. Get a life!"

Voices influence people to be withholding in their closest relationships (Dallos, 2004; R. W. Firestone & Catlett, 1999; Mikulincer & Shaver, 2016; Note 8). For example, people might have voices saying things such as, "Don't let him know how much he matters to you. That will give him the upper hand" or "She isn't all that amazing. There's so much wrong with her" or "They don't feel the same way toward you; don't get your hopes up." If people deprive themselves or their loved ones by acting out withholding patterns, their voice attacks them from all sides. First, it may castigate them for damaging the relationship: "See, now you're all alone" or "They'll never want you back." Then it attacks them for hurting their partner: "You really made them feel terrible! You're just not sensitive enough to be in a relationship."

Withholding and self-denial often become habitual and involuntary over time. Because withholding is largely an unconscious process and primarily manifested in passive behaviors, it is difficult to confront directly or pinpoint the specific actions that are being withheld. The person who is made aware of acting out this type of passive aggression tends to react defensively and feel wounded and misunderstood.

In therapy, clients can become conscious of their particular methods of withholding. They can learn to correct their withholding habit patterns through identifying and challenging the voices that are prompting them and then altering those behaviors. They need to persevere through the anxiety caused by modifying their withholding patterns. The goal of therapy is to interfere with each person's withholding and gradual self-destruction and help adjust the balance in the direction of live pursuits.

CONCLUSION

Withholding and self-denial are aspects of a defensive, inward process that has a profound effect on people's lives, relationships, careers, and children. The holding back of abilities, loving responses, and positive traits particularly prized by others alleviates anxiety and helps to maintain the fantasy bond. The diverse manifestations of withholding described in this chapter are familiar and commonplace; nevertheless, they are damaging to all parties.

The ultimate impact of chronic patterns of withholding is a shutting down, a paralysis, of that side of the individual that strives for emotional health and growth, the side that contributes to positive feelings of self-worth and self-esteem. Left unchecked, withholding can evolve into a decline in the pursuit of goal-directed activity and a progressive elimination of the self, culminating in the obliteration of a person's most desirable qualities. In the process of destroying oneself as a lovable person, a person also inadvertently disrupts the love and affection of those closest to them.

My conceptualization of the predicament facing most children is that because of their comparative powerlessness, when they are made to be afraid, they resort to the only tactic available—that of not responding, of not directly expressing the anger they feel at a given moment. Children turn their anger inward and withhold strivings toward life in a misguided drive to preserve their sense of self through self-denial and destruction. Their early strategies of holding back from the people who are most significant to them, at a period in life when they are the most vulnerable, eventually evolve into the major character defenses of later life. Because these specific traits are unconsciously determined and closely tied to the fantasy bond, withholding patterns are difficult to change.

Acts of kindness and generosity are the most effective antidotes to withholding and self-denial. People can learn how to be generous to others and how to accept love and friendship. Being altruistic under circumstances in which a person would usually be withholding neutralizes the inward, defensive patterns formed early in childhood. Acting on the desire to ease the suffering of others, contribute to their well-being, and sustain one's transcendental goals brings one pleasure and infuses life with meaning (Dovidio et al., 2006; Note 9). Breaking patterns of withholding and self-denial results in a freer, more vital existence and sense of fulfillment. Changing habitual responses that have functioned to alienate others significantly expands a person's emotional life and social experience.

Learning to give is important, but it is equally important to learn how to receive. Accepting kindness and affection, contrasted with being wholly self-reliant or pseudo-independent, is an offering to others. Being receptive and appreciative brings joy to the giver and is fundamental to a personal interaction that is mutually gratifying. Learning how to accept love, friendship, and kindness contradicts tendencies to be withholding and self-denying and shifts the balance toward the pursuit of a more fulfilling life. People can learn to give themselves value and look for pleasure and joy in their lives without feeling guilty. They can overcome destructive voices that restrict them and recognize that it is ethical, as well as emotionally healthy, to pursue their dreams (R. W. Firestone & Catlett, 2009b).

8 SELF-NOURISHING HABITS AND ADDICTIONS

Most addicts appear reluctant or unable to seek satisfaction in normal
interpersonal relationships and instead remain aloof and independent and
use the drug to induce a blissful, symbiotic, narcissistic state. The drug
replaces interpersonal relationships as a primary source of achieving
satisfaction and pleasure.

—Blatt et al., "Psychodynamic Theories of Opiate Addiction:
New Directions for Research"

Self-nourishing habits serve the function of self-parenting and thereby establish a pattern of pseudo-independence. These practices temporarily satisfy emotional hunger and primitive longings left over from infancy and early childhood and support the illusion that one can take care of oneself without the need for others. As people deny themselves fulfillment and gratification through emotional exchanges with other people, they come to increasingly rely more on self-nurturing, self-soothing behaviors as substitutes. A self-nourishing lifestyle emerges that shuts off personal feelings and is primarily defensive and self-protective.

https://doi.org/10.1037/0000268-009
Challenging the Fantasy Bond: A Search for Personal Identity and Freedom,
by R. W. Firestone

Self-nourishing habits also serve the purpose of blocking out painful experiences and emotions. In psychoanalytic terms, self-soothing, self-nurturing habit patterns are categorized as *ego-syntonic*; that is, they tend to be acceptable to the self and arouse little conflict with normal ego functioning. However, when their use becomes obviously self-destructive or potentially dangerous, they are no longer acceptable to the person's ego (S. Freud, 1916/1963). Well-established, self-nourishing habits usually become self-destructive because they progressively limit the person's capacity to cope with everyday life. When these behavior patterns become associated with a more generalized retreat from the real world, they are no longer compatible with the person and arouse guilt (R. W. Firestone, 1997a, 1997b).

Habits that serve as a psychological means to dull pain generally become addictive. Like drugs, they temporarily reduce anxiety and are followed by a period of feeling better. However, people who rely on painkilling habits become increasingly crippled in their ability to function and find fulfillment in personal relationships. They tend to limit their pursuit of actual goals and become more involved in an inward lifestyle of fantasy, dependency, and addiction. In the case of long-standing addictions to harmful substances, these self-nurturing habits can even lead to ultimate self-destruction, such as death by alcoholism or drug overdose.

The pertinent issue is that addictive patterns often come to be preferred over satisfaction in the interpersonal environment. People fearful of taking the chance of being hurt again develop an inward lifestyle in which emotional risks are limited and achievements curtailed. To varying degrees, human beings exist in conflict between an active pursuit of goals in the real world and a reliance on fantasy gratification, including addictive behaviors and destructive relationships.

In the course of the developmental sequence, psychological equilibrium is achieved when a person arrives at a particular solution to this basic conflict. Equilibrium is often attained at the expense of satisfying relationships and is threatened by positive or constructive events that contradict earlier painful or traumatic experiences. The defensive process within the person eventually becomes addictive in itself. It persists long after the predisposing factors are no longer active.

As in all other aspects of the defensive process, the critical inner voice is influential in supporting addictive tendencies, first by influencing people to engage in the destructive behavior and then by punishing them for it. For example, the voice encourages a person struggling with alcohol abuse: "Take one more drink—what's the harm?" Then it attacks them when they submit: "You have no willpower. You're a hopeless alcoholic!" In response to these attacks, a person attempts to alleviate the ensuing guilt and self-hatred by resorting to more painkillers, which can result in a continuous loop of self-enabling and self-castigation.

When the addiction is given up, the anxiety and other negative emotions that have been allayed by the substance come to the foreground. This can be perceived as a loss of control over the unwanted feelings of pain and sadness that accompany withdrawal and can leave the person in a disoriented state, feeling helpless and at the mercy of seemingly overwhelming emotions. People often feel edgier and dysregulated and are more prone to lashing out until they are able to establish healthy coping strategies.

HABITUAL AND ADDICTIVE SELF-NOURISHING PATTERNS

Self-nourishing habits come into play early on as survival mechanisms that the infant develops in an attempt to adapt to deprivation and parental mis-attunement. Primitive self-nourishing behaviors—such as thumb sucking, hair twirling, or stroking a blanket—become associated with the fantasized image of the mother or primary caregiver, acting to reduce the baby's tension and partially assuage their hunger. Later, in times of emotional stress, children retreat into an inner world of fantasy and use modified versions of these early techniques to soothe and comfort themselves.

Children's patterns of self-parenting persist and may manifest in new behaviors over time as they grow older. These behaviors, which may include nail-biting, playing computer games excessively, overeating, and compulsively masturbating, can be simultaneously self-nourishing and self-punishing. Self-critical thoughts, voice attacks, and guilt reactions often accompany these self-soothing defenses. Self-parenting can be manifested in addictions to alcohol, drugs, food, cigarettes, sex, or other compulsive habits and routines. Theoretically, the self-parenting process can be conceptualized as an addictive psychonutritional system in which the person imagines that there are limited quantities of nourishment available in the interpersonal environment, and they, therefore, must take care of themselves.

A comparative model of mental health versus psychopathology can be conceptualized in terms of the self-parenting process. The degree to which a person depends on self-nurturing mechanisms and internal fantasy processes can be conceived of as a progression ranging from interpersonal gratification to an acute involvement in self-gratification. At one end of the continuum, a person essentially lives a realistic, engaged life with actions that match aspirations and capabilities. At the other end is a person with an extreme tendency toward fantasy, self-nourishment, and isolation (R. W. Firestone, 1993).

There are two general categories of addictive behaviors that can become associated with a self-nourishing lifestyle, both of which function to dull emotions: addiction to physical substances and addiction to routines or other habitual behaviors. Because the illusion of connection provided by the fantasy bond is used to defend against both interpersonal and existential pain, it falls into the category of an addictive pattern as well.

Addiction to Physical Substances

While the determinants of substance addiction (e.g., alcoholism, drug abuse, eating disorders) are varied (Epps & Holt, 2011; Feng, 2008; Lewis, 2018; Note 1), my focus is on the emotional aspect, specifically the drive to deaden pain and suffering, both from past experiences, as well as from current frustration and stress. While the addiction perpetuates the illusion of pseudo-independence, in actuality, addicts become more incapacitated in their ability to work productively and function adequately in social situations. They come to exist in a dazed, cutoff state for long periods, thus damaging their personal relationships. Friends and family experience considerable suffering and become increasingly alienated as this process spirals downward.

> Even as a small child, Danielle was highly sensitive and often highly reactive. Her parents were distracted by a growing animosity between them, and they separated when she was still young. They each withdrew even more from Danielle, becoming preoccupied with their jobs and the other practicalities of their daily lives. Without a consistent parental figure, Danielle lacked a supportive relationship with someone who could help her stabilize her mood swings and contain her emotional reactions. In her early teens, Danielle started drinking and smoking marijuana to ease her anxiety and emotional unrest.
>
> In her late teens, Danielle was diagnosed with diabetes. She was told that she could regulate her disease with diet, exercise, and insulin injections. Nonetheless, she was traumatized to learn of the impact it could have on her health and that it could lead to an early death. To cope with these fears and quell her anxiety, she increased her alcohol use and turned to heavier drugs. Throughout her 20s, Danielle lived a self-destructive lifestyle; in addition to her ongoing addictions, she abused her body with an unhealthy diet, little physical activity, and irresponsible use of insulin.
>
> In her early 30s, Danielle could no longer block out reality: Her harmful behavior was taking a toll on her health. When her legs started tingling, a sign of nerve damage from diabetes, she became alarmed about the dangerous direction in which she was heading. She reached out for help, and family members supported her enrollment in an intensive rehab program. In the program, she began to address the emotional issues underlying her addictions. As time went on, she came to understand and gain compassion for herself. She also developed skills for dealing with her moods and reactions. Achieving

sobriety was difficult for Danielle, with relapses from which she had to recover. But with support from the program and her sponsor, as well as from family members, Danielle was able to gradually create a life for herself that was free from addiction.

Some children come to substitute eating for the emotional nurturance that is missing in the family. When food becomes their major source of comfort and gratification, eating can turn into a compulsion. Later, the cycle of over-eating and chronic dieting that is often repeated throughout the course of a lifetime not only affects people's physical health but can also be equally damaging to their emotional well-being. Both aspects of this destructive cycle are elements of the same self-nurturing, self-punishing process.

Eating disorders, such as anorexia nervosa, bulimia, binge eating, and severe obesity, are conditions that reflect the use of food for purposes other than sustenance (Kaye, 2008; Note 2). Some indicate a self-parenting process in relation to the excessive control a person exerts over their food intake. Because people with eating disorders are often detached from themselves, they have little sense of what they feel, physically or emotionally, and lack a clear awareness of the sensation of hunger or satiety. They typically experience intense feelings of low self-esteem and dissatisfaction with their appearance. As is the case with all self-nourishing habits, the dynamics of eating disorders revolve around the central issue of self-parenting as a means to allay a person's emotional chaos.

Addiction to Routines

Although structure and discipline are necessary to function and succeed in life, almost any behavior can be misused in a repetitive or ritualistic manner to dull a person's sensitivity to painful feelings and thereby become addictive. The predictability of habitual activities, such as eating the same meals every day or performing the same tasks at the same time, can provide an illusion of certainty and control, thereby relieving the anxiety caused by spontaneity. Yet, their negative side effect is to deaden the individual as a feeling person. Many destructive habits and routines are viewed as acceptable—for example, binge-watching shows, excessively surfing the internet, or spending disproportionate amounts of time playing video games. Some are even seen as productive—for example, an exaggerated and intense involvement in one's work or exercise program. Once these patterns are formed, the behavior can become preferable to the anxiety that the person would experience if these routines were to be interrupted or ended (Estévez et al., 2017; R. W. Firestone, 1985, 1990c, 1993; Note 3).

Sexual Addiction

Early in their development, children learn that physical self-soothing behaviors yield pleasure and satisfaction. Later, they discover that touching their genitals leads to pleasant sensations, as well as relief from tension. Masturbation can gradually develop into a habitual method of self-soothing that reinforces an illusion of not needing gratification from outside of oneself. In addition, if the child is reprimanded for masturbating, they may feel ashamed and become secretive about the activity. As they get older, children create sexual fantasies while gratifying themselves and often become embarrassed about their sexual thoughts as well.

After reaching maturity, continuing excessive masturbation and/or extensive use of pornographic materials, internet pornography, or other forms of cybersex when sexual partners are available reflect a pseudo-independent posture. An individual can maintain an illusion of being in control, not being vulnerable to another person, not needing to rely on anyone for satisfaction. They can also avoid taking another person's needs into account. This absence of interpersonal exchange is indicative of an individual's involvement in a fantasy bond (Dryer & Lijtmae, 2007; R. W. Firestone, 1993; Note 4).

> Noah, 29, began therapy because his wife had left him. He had been married for 3 years and was happy in his marriage. In fact, he and his wife had begun talking about starting a family. However, recently, Noah had registered on some online dating sites. He said that he had been bored and thought it would be harmless fun. At first, he was flirting with a number of women, but soon he was focusing on a few, and their interactions became more sexual.
>
> He became infatuated with these women, texting them day and night. He seemed distracted and preoccupied both at home and at work. He was sexual with his wife less often. Noticing a difference in him, his wife accused him of losing interest in her, which he denied. One day, she went on his computer and found a communication between him and one of the women that contained explicit sexual content, as well as photographs. She felt betrayed. She accused him of cheating on her and left him.
>
> Noah went to therapy because he wanted to save his marriage. He realized that his involvement with the women online had not been innocent and harmless. It had become an obsession for him that was not only secretive but also commanding all of his attention. As he spoke of how exciting and compelling it had been to him, he recognized that it was a sexual addiction. He understood why his wife felt that he had been unfaithful to her.
>
> When Noah and his therapist talked about his marriage, he came to see that his addiction began around the time he and his wife had started talking about having a baby. He said he looked forward to becoming a father, but he also felt pressure from the responsibility that came with it. He was afraid that the carefree days of his young adulthood would be gone. In his future sessions, Noah addressed how his sexual addiction had been an attempt to escape from his perceived burden of fatherhood and to recapture the youth that he feared losing.

When sex is used primarily as a mechanism for self-gratification—that is, with the focus on using the other person's body as a means to satisfy the self rather than on having an interpersonal exchange—it can serve the same function as any other addiction that reduces tension and cuts off feeling (Carnes, 1991, 1992). When a focus on self-gratifying sexuality predominates, both individuals are often left with a sense of emotional dissatisfaction, including feelings of loneliness and emptiness. The lack of personal relating between sexual partners is hurtful to the well-being of the individuals involved. In relationships where the partners have formed a fantasy bond, their physical intimacy can gradually devolve into a routine, habitual pattern of lovemaking that progressively diminishes the closeness in the relationship. The impact of the fantasy bond on sexuality is discussed in more detail in Chapter 10, "Sexuality."

Addiction to Working

The person who is a workaholic has developed compulsive and routine patterns of work that ease anxiety in a manner that is often accepted and even admired by society. They are, in effect, using work to block out their personal lives.

Liza, one of four sisters, was identified as "the smart daughter." She excelled in school, which was greatly admired by her parents. She was given preferential treatment in her family. For example, she was exempt from chores around the house so that she could concentrate on her studies. Shy and socially awkward among her peers, Liza compensated for her lack of friends by focusing her attention on her academic achievements.

Once she graduated, Liza dedicated herself to pursuing a career in nursing. During the next 10 years, she advanced to a top position in a hospital. However, the lives of people around her were changing. Her sisters were having families of their own. Contemporaries at work were falling in love and getting married. Liza began to sense that something was missing in her life. Where she had always regarded her tireless work ethic as an admirable quality, she began to wonder whether she was devoted to her career at the expense of her personal life.

Liza entered therapy, where she came to see how her intense focus on working was cutting her off on a feeling level. She was avoiding having to deal with her extreme shyness and her discomfort with emotional exchanges. This defense had allowed her to overlook the deeper psychological issues in her life for years. It had undermined the effect on her ability to establish friendships and have a meaningful life outside of work. She realized that her feelings of self-worth had always been tied up in how devoted she was to her work, first as a child in school and now as an adult in her career.

However, it was hard for Liza to break with her addiction to overworking. She had to discipline herself to not work extra shifts. She had to force herself to take time off. She had to consciously reach out to develop friendships and carve out time for socializing. She had to be suspicious of and ignore the voices that were chastising her for slacking off and accusing her of doing a bad job. As she continued to challenge her work compulsion, Liza came to understand herself more fully and was able to experience the world beyond her career. Her life became more balanced as she allowed herself the pleasure of relaxing and sharing close times with friends and family.

People who work in isolation have the potential to use their job destructively because their working conditions are congruent with an inward lifestyle. With the increase in remote work, many individuals are no longer working in offices with colleagues or within the confines of established work hours. And while, for some, this has allowed for more personal time with their loved ones at home, many others have become, in effect, digital nomads who toil in isolation for unlimited periods.

Addiction to Isolation

As explained in Chapter 6, there are both positive and negative ways to use private time. Individuals can spend time alone creating, planning, relaxing, or introspecting. People who are introverts take pleasure in solitary activity and are energized by spending time alone. However, isolation can also lead to inward ruminations and indulging in self-nourishing habits, both of which leave a person cut off emotionally. Because of this, isolation itself can become an addictive means for avoiding feeling and detaching from the self and others. An increase in time spent alone, unless used in a personally constructive manner, often leads to an increase in depression and self-hatred. Conversely, reducing the amount of time spent in isolated activities can have a positive impact on a person's psychological well-being. There is a correlation between minimizing solitary, inward time and maximizing a sense of vitality, optimism, and enthusiasm.

Addiction to Another Person

When a fantasy bond is extended to include another person, an addictive relationship is created. Forming a fantasy bond with and becoming dependent on another person out of an unconscious desire for security is one of the most prevalent forms of addiction and plays a prominent role in the deterioration of relationships, particularly within the couple and family. This addictive style of relating disengages people from feeling for themselves and the person with whom the addictive dependency has been formed. In the couple, it leads to a decline in intimacy, sexual attraction, and desire. Externalizing the self-parenting process in the form of addictive interpersonal relationships allows people to maintain a pseudo-independent orientation to life.

THE ROLE OF THE CRITICAL INNER VOICE IN SELF-NOURISHING HABITS AND ADDICTIONS

The critical inner voice encourages the acting out of self-destructive tendencies and addictive behaviors. As noted, voices that influence addictive behavior take two contradictory forms, first urging people to indulge the habit and then castigating them for yielding to temptation (R. W. Firestone et al., 2002, 2012).

The voices that encourage people to engage in the addictive behavior tend to have a seductive tone and are often mistaken as caring for or acting in the person's best interests. For example, the voice of a binge eater may say, "Go ahead, have another helping. You deserve it. What's the harm?" Or the voice of a workaholic may say, "If you work late tonight, you'll be ahead of the competition. The boss will be impressed. The kids are expecting you to be home, but they'll get over their disappointment." The individual with an addiction to pornography may have a voice that says, "It's no big deal. This only involves you. It's not like you're hurting anyone else."

Once people act on their voices and engage in their addictive behavior, the critical inner voice switches its tone and becomes harsh and punishing: "You're so weak-willed!" "You stuffed your face, and now you feel sick. You're gross!" or "You promised the kids you'd be home tonight, and you didn't get in until after they were asleep. You are a terrible parent!" or "I can't believe you watched porn and jerked off, again. You are pathetic."

After this repetitive chain of self-attacks, people feel worse and experience a great deal of emotional pain and turmoil. In this state, the critical voice is more likely to influence them to once again engage in the addictive behavior to numb their pain, ease their agitation, or get rid of their uneasy feeling: "What's the use. Why even try to deal with this? You might as well give up."

When people who are challenging an addiction find themselves having been drawn back in, they need to have compassion for themselves. They must have a patient attitude and a realistic understanding of the effort and struggle involved in overcoming an addiction and achieving and maintaining sobriety. It is difficult to break these patterns because the anxiety and intense emotions that have been relieved by the addiction resurface during withdrawal. Believing the punishing attitudes of the critical inner voice only makes people feel disheartened and self-hating. The judgmental statements of the voice do not inspire change in a positive direction. When people know they have acted in a way that they do not approve of, their self-attacks may seem justified. However, the contradictory nature of the voices that enables addiction makes it clear that voice attacks are fundamentally part of a destructive process.

IMPLICATIONS FOR THERAPY AND TREATMENT

The use of self-nourishing patterns, deadening habitual practices, and addictive behaviors are often rationalized in everyday life. People may insist that drugs give them self-confidence and the additional enthusiasm needed to perform well or be more creative. They may claim that the consumption of a few drinks makes them less inhibited and more relaxed in social situations. Workaholics may boast about their superior work ethic. People with eating disorders may insist that healthy eating habits are impossible to sustain when they are traveling, for instance, or under stress. However, these rationalizations are irrelevant considering the self-destructive effect of the excesses.

When people are dulled and cut off from themselves because of these types of excesses, they are easily capable of going against their own interests. They are more likely to behave in ways that deviate from their stated goals and damage their most valued relationships. People need all of their consciousness and sensitivity to cope with the stresses encountered in everyday life. Therefore, it is harmful to try to justify the use of self-destructive substances. Even where the pattern does not lead to actual life-threatening situations, the negative effects of these abuses should not be minimized.

The goal of therapy is to help clients move away from compulsive, addictive behaviors so that they can expand their lives and tolerate more gratification in reality (R. W. Firestone, 1993, 1997a, 1997b; Flores, 2001). For effective therapy to take place, clients need to relinquish their addictions, whether to behaviors or substances. An addiction functions to numb emotions, and a person cannot effectively deal with an addiction if they are not able to experience their feelings.

The Therapist–Client Alliance

When dealing with an individual's resistance to controlling an addiction, a therapist who exhibits strength, concern, and sensitivity can effectively establish a preliminary contract with the client. The therapist points out, in nonevaluative, nonjudgmental terms, the serious consequences of the addiction. The behavior is not considered or dealt with as a moral issue; instead, it is addressed with the purpose of helping the client understand, on a feeling level, the harm they are inflicting on themselves. The therapist's warmth, independence, and maturity are essential in gaining and holding a client's respect and trust, particularly in cases of addiction, where this is especially relevant to the client's continued motivation to give up their addictive behaviors and move toward sobriety.

However, clients often project their own desire to develop and their original wish to break their destructive habit onto the therapist and perceive the therapist as trying to get them to change. These clients then take an oppositional position in relation to the therapist, imagining that if they indulge in the harmful behavior, they are defying the therapist's demands. To counter this resistance, therapists must not engage in a battle of wills but instead be steady and matter-of-fact.

When treating addiction, the therapist must provide clients with an authentic relationship during the transition from relying on addictive substances to seeking and finding satisfaction in genuine affiliations outside of the therapy setting (R. W. Firestone, 1990c). While actively confronting the client's self-nourishing habit patterns, the positive rapport with the therapist makes reality more rewarding.

On the basis of my clinical experience, I have concluded that all clients, indeed most people, suffer from some degree of addiction that interferes with their living fully. The primary goal in therapy is to help people reexperience and gradually come to terms with the painful feelings and frustrations that originally caused them to retreat into fantasy and self-nurturance. These emotions need to be explored as they recur in the context of therapy.

The initial deprivation, which began when the child was dependent on the primary caregiver for survival and environmental support, persists into adulthood, where people continue to believe, on a subconscious level, that they cannot endure reexperiencing the trauma of these primitive wants and the anticipated rejection. As clients become aware of their ongoing needs and desires, they can use the therapeutic partnership to ask for what they want symbolically, learn to tolerate the resulting frustration, and discover that they can survive without having these specific needs met.

This is the crux of positive or lasting therapeutic progress with addicted individuals. In the course of facing their anger in the transference onto the therapist, clients strengthen their autonomy and become emancipated from remnants of the original fantasy bond formed in their family of origin. They come to relate to the therapist on an equal basis. By recognizing that they can never obtain the gratification they so desperately needed as children and that, in fact, these needs are no longer vital for survival or even for happiness, they can progress to a point in their development where they are able to tolerate and even enjoy their separateness and independence.

Voice Therapy as a Treatment for Addiction

Voice therapy can be effective in treating addictions and challenging the affective, cognitive, and behavioral manifestations of the self-parenting process.

Clients verbalize their negative thoughts, along with the associated emotions. Then they identify and come to understand the original source of their negative thinking. And last, they work on strategies for changing the destructive behavior patterns that are based on their inner voices. Maintaining a daily journal can be a valuable adjunct to therapy because it helps clients identify specific events or emotional "triggers" that precipitate a self-attacking thought process (L. Firestone & Catlett, 2004; R. W. Firestone, 2004; Note 5). When clients write down the thoughts that induce them to engage in an addictive behavior, they are better able to resist the temptation to indulge in their drug of choice.

Through this process, the therapist helps the client identify the destructive cycle involved in addiction, from the soothing, seductive voices that enable it to the vicious, self-recriminating voices that follow and back again. Clients then confront these voices, thereby strengthening their point of view about their addiction, which helps them interrupt the cycle. Client and therapist subsequently collaborate in formulating steps to break the addictive behaviors and translate these plans into action. Together, they work through the symptoms of withdrawal, including feelings of disorientation, anxiety, and increased voice attacks. These will gradually diminish as the client continues to refrain from addictive behaviors. The process of consistently identifying their critical inner voices and working on behavioral suggestions over an extended period can eventually free clients from their addictions and self-destructive habit patterns.

CONCLUSION

Most people develop and use numerous habit patterns and routines in an effort to blunt painful feelings from the past, as well as from the present. When addictive behaviors are used to diminish or repress emotions, they generally have a destructive influence on the ability to feel love, closeness, happiness, and excitement. They predispose attitudes and circumstances that are oppositional to a person's human potential for a richer life.

The gratification afforded by addictive patterns can come to be preferred over the satisfaction offered in personal relationships. Self-nourishing defenses are difficult to break because it is not always apparent that they are self-destructive. They can be viewed as positive in that they offer temporary relief from anxiety and other unpleasant emotions. For this reason, they are often rationalized as being in one's interest. The first step toward challenging an addiction or self-nourishing habit pattern lies in fully recognizing that it is not, in fact, in one's self-interest.

Self-compassion is necessary for taking on the challenge of giving up an addictive behavior (Neff, 2011; Phelps et al., 2018; Note 6). It is an awareness that no one is inherently different from anyone else; everyone is defended and has suffered varying degrees of emotional pain. Self-compassion enables people to maintain a kind attitude toward themselves as they contend with their long-standing, self-nourishing habits. It encourages them to be patient with themselves and with the necessary time it takes to conquer addictive behavior and achieve sobriety (Note 7). They will come to realize that, while an addiction cannot be given up overnight or without pain and anxiety, it can eventually lead to recovery and a more fulfilling life.

A congenial attitude toward oneself helps counter the critical inner voice that plays an influential role in addiction. Armed with the knowledge of how the inner voice operates, people can identify the enemy within that is enabling their self-destructive habits and then behave in ways that go against its advice. The reward for this hard work is increased strength and energy for further growth and development.

9 INDIVIDUATION, REGRESSION, AND THE FANTASY BOND

Although many human problems are similar, they are never identical. . . .
Because of these factors of sameness and difference, it is difficult to summarize
the infinite variations of the process of individuation. The fact is that each
person has to do something different, something that is uniquely his own.
—Carl Jung, *Man and His Symbols*

The process of *individuation*, whereby a person increasingly differentiates from the family of origin, occurs as a natural development throughout a person's lifetime. However, psychological growth and independence never proceed smoothly, nor is any person's development consistently directed toward progressive differentiation (R. W. Firestone et al., 2012; Jenkins et al., 2005; Kerr & Bowen, 1988; Skowron & Friedlander, 1998; Note 1). Each successive stage of maturity confronts the child and, later, the adult with a sense of aloneness and separateness. This predicament is compounded by a person's already established psychological defenses, including the fantasy bond, which are responses to the natural fear and anxiety that surround the awareness of death.

https://doi.org/10.1037/0000268-010
Challenging the Fantasy Bond: A Search for Personal Identity and Freedom,
by R. W. Firestone

Feelings of anxiety, frustration, and aloneness are the infant's immediate responses to painful emotional experiences. After the child learns about death, both fears become operant—the fear related to interpersonal trauma and the fear of death—and these affect children as they move from complete dependence and symbiosis to independence and self-support.

When the fear and anxiety that are aroused at different stages of individuation become overwhelming or when the guilt or anger that arises becomes too intense, people revert to self-nourishing behaviors and a variety of other psychological defense mechanisms to allay these emotions. Generally speaking, there is regression to a previous level of development, along with the tendency to form or strengthen fantasy bonds with significant others (R. W. Firestone, 1990c).

DEVELOPMENTAL STAGES OF INDIVIDUATION

Separation is a vital part of human life. It begins at birth with the actual physical separation from the mother and the cutting of the umbilical cord, the first experience in a person's ongoing individuation process (Rank, 1999). The realization about this basic condition of separateness can, in some sense, be considered an emotional shock from which the individual never fully recovers.

The growing child passes through different stages of individuation. For example, at the time of weaning, children experience intense longings and frustration, which lead to an expanding awareness of being separate and independent. When the infant is weaned, the toddler learns to walk, the child starts school, the adolescent graduates (Burston, 2007; Erikson, 1968; Meeus et al., 2005; Note 2), or other significant transitions occur, such as getting a first job, moving away from home, or entering into a committed relationship and/or having children, the individual is forced to recognize that there is movement further and further away from the parent and other family members.

Each milestone creates a new situation that is potentially traumatic because it signifies the loss of parental support (R. W. Firestone, 1990a; Lapsley & Edgerton, 2002; Note 3) and is therefore capable of causing a person to regress to a previous emotional state. Adulthood is fraught with a series of separation experiences, each one triggering its own set of emotional reactions, which are impacted by the reverberations of prior separation experiences. Often, people seek psychological help at times of separation because of the emotional distress caused by having their bonds broken.

Children and adolescents typically have feeling responses to separations, whether symbolic or real, that mark the transition from one developmental stage to the next. Powerful emotions, which may include anxiety, anger, and guilt, accompany each critical step in the process of individuation.

Anxiety

Separation anxiety naturally occurs in the course of a child's growing up. However, when young children receive inadequate or inconsistent care, their anxiety and frustration are intensified. In addition, if blatant or even subtle indications of parents' self-destructiveness, illness, or mental instability are evidenced, they amplify children's fears of abandonment. At some point in a child's development, separation anxiety becomes associated with the knowledge and dread of death. After this time, whenever people progress to a new stage of individuation, their anxiety is intensified as they are struck simultaneously with an awareness of both their aloneness and their eventual death (R. W. Firestone & Catlett, 2009a; R. W. Firestone et al., 2012; Piven, 2004; Note 4). These anxiety reactions do not necessarily diminish in intensity as people mature.

Anger

Anger can be aroused when children are separated from the parent, both by benign periods of separation that occur naturally and malevolent types of separation, such as punishment by isolation, threats of abandonment, and other forms of rejection. This creates a dilemma for the child. On the one hand, children are enraged at being terrified by the parent's absence, while on the other, they dare not express their anger because they fear that this would bring about the actual loss of the parent. They find themselves feeling furious with the parent at one moment, while at the next, desperately seeking reassurance and contact from that same parent (Lyons-Ruth et al., 2005; Note 5). As described in Chapter 5, a child's "unacceptable" anger toward the parent is usually repressed and projected outward onto others or inward toward themselves.

Guilt

Individuation and emancipation from the parent are a natural part of growing up; therefore, many of the events that lead to separation are initiated by the child. However, young people often feel guilty as they take the tentative steps toward breaking the emotional ties of their fantasy bond with their parents. This imaginary connection is a powerful agent of security, often far more important than the realistic security in the actual functioning relationship. Symbolically, breaking a bond is analogous to letting the other person die.

A child's guilt is exacerbated when a parent experiences distress at their growing freedom and independence. If the parent is emotionally hungry, immature, or dependent, these feelings are exaggerated, and children will come to feel that movement toward adulthood and personal power is mean or a betrayal. Parents who engage in self-destructive behaviors, as well as those who habitually deny themselves happiness and enjoyment, are more likely to arouse feelings of guilt in their children.

REGRESSION

Regression is a psychological retreat to a prior stage of development to relieve the emotional distress and anxiety that accompany separation or loss. This denial is accomplished by forming a fantasy bond or a sense of merged identity where feelings of connection, possessiveness, and belonging obscure the knowledge of one's existence as a separate person. The tendency of human beings to revert to a mindset and style of behaving that support this illusion is universal and occurs whenever the fear of aloneness and death becomes overwhelming.

On a behavioral level, regressed individuals tend to give up autonomy and authority over their own lives and actively try to elicit parental responses from others. This is accompanied by a desire to reestablish the dynamics of their original relationship with their parents in their current lives. They tend to imagine or even provoke rejection from people close to them by overreacting to slights, pleading for reassurances of love, withholding personal responses and affection, and acting overly dependent (R. W. Firestone & Catlett, 1999; Hainlen et al., 2016; Mikulincer & Shaver, 2016; Note 6). Regressive trends also manifest themselves in self-destructive and careless actions that cause concern and worry in loved ones.

In regressing, people block out reactions that are appropriate to the present, while at the same time, they manifest childlike, dramatic, or intense emotions. They move toward an inward existence, often returning to a previous state of passivity and confusion.

Experiences that remind people that they possess strength, independence, and personal power or that acknowledge their unique value as a human being will make them acutely conscious of their life and its eventual loss. This increased sense of self and individuation threatens to break the fantasy bond (R. W. Firestone & Catlett, 2009a). In the face of this perceived threat, people give up mature pursuits, adult responses, and genuine relating for a more childlike orientation. They often regress to more dependent, destructive modes of interacting in their personal relationships.

> Andrea had become dissatisfied with her relationship with Jessica. Over the years, Andrea had developed and matured and was not the insecure, dependent girl she had been when they first became a couple. Where she had once turned to Jessica for guidance and deferred to her opinions, she now found her girlfriend's assertiveness to be disrespectful and stifling. Andrea felt that she had outgrown their relationship and longed for her independence. After much self-reflection, she decided to leave Jessica.
>
> At first, Andrea was excited to be on her own, making her own decisions and discovering new facets of who she was. In time, however, she began to feel more unsure of herself. Where she had felt empowered and self-confident, she began to feel overwhelmed and helpless. Even though they were separated, she found herself reaching out to Jessica for help and then being angry at her for not responding. She started seeking advice and reassurance from her other friends as well.
>
> With her therapist, Andrea discussed the unexpected changes in her attitudes and behaviors regarding her independence. She came to see how the excitement she had initially felt from moving forward in her personal development had turned into anxiety. She had reacted by backing away from being a capable, autonomous individual and had returned to functioning in a more dependent and childlike way. Andrea missed the exhilaration she had felt when she first emancipated herself. In therapy, she addressed her anxiety and began to take steps toward regaining her sense of self. She gradually came out of her regressed state and was able to continue to develop and value herself as a discrete and strong individual.

Regressive behavior in adults indicates a certain lack of personality integration and individuation. As a result, individuals react in ways that were appropriate to their past, not to the current interpersonal environment. Under particularly anxiety-provoking circumstances, these immature levels of functioning come to the foreground. This unconscious recapitulation of the emotional state of a person's child-self creates an illusion of being suspended in time and contributes to a false sense of immortality.

The Bipolar Causality of Regression

Regression has long been recognized as being caused by environmental and interpersonal stress and/or events that remind people of trauma from their past. Negative occurrences such as financial loss, academic failure, and personal rejection arouse levels of anxiety and psychological pain that are difficult to tolerate. The inevitable unpleasant and painful aspects of life, such as illness, accidents, and physical pain, as well as reminders of death, can also act to precipitate regressive behavior (R. W. Firestone, 1990a; R. W. Firestone & Catlett, 2009a).

However, positive events are also causative factors of regression and are often overlooked as such. Therefore, regression can be described as having a bipolar causality—that is, it is just as likely to be activated by significant positive events in people's lives as the opposite. For instance, it may occur as an after-reaction to experiencing unusually deep personal feelings. Many times, members of a couple withdraw from each other after sharing a close, emotional interaction because it makes them feel vulnerable. Intimacy, characterized by patterns of closeness, is often followed by behaviors that create emotional distance, such as emotional withholding, disrespectful interactions, or even hostile exchanges.

As indicated, any experience that leaves people with a heightened sense of individuality can make them aware of being separate and alone. For example, behaving in a nonconforming, unconventional manner or expressing a strong point of view in the face of controversy may generate anxiety in a person, which in turn can lead to regression. Being vulnerable can arouse fear and may influence a return to a more isolated, pseudo-independent posture. This can often be the case for people who are taking an emotional risk by developing a deep friendship or beginning a romantic relationship (Note 7).

Serious, long-term regression can occur in reasonably well-adjusted individuals when they experience unusual success or achievement. For instance, it is not uncommon for a person who has received a promotion or unexpected acknowledgment at work to become unexplainably incompetent and ineffective. It is difficult for people to recognize the cause of their retreat from power or responsibility because this type of regression is largely an unconscious reaction. They tend to blame circumstances or other people rather than look for the cause in themselves.

> Sam was an assistant manager in a growing company. For the first 2 years, he succeeded in his job. He took on more and more responsibility and proved to be a capable and competent asset to the organization. Sam had become invaluable to his boss, and he appreciated her confidence in him.
>
> When the company was looking for a new manager, Sam's boss recommended him for the position. To his surprise, he felt unsure of himself. He knew his misgivings did not make sense, but he could not shake them. He worried that he was not qualified, doubting that he had the necessary leadership skills, even though he had already been directing the staff and performing other relevant tasks.

When Sam spoke to his boss about his doubts, she pointed out that the only difference in his new situation would be that he would be the boss; he would have the final say and be ultimately responsible for the outcome. He realized that this is what had shaken him up. Rather than feeling self-assured and independent as he had always had at work, he felt inadequate and self-doubting. With this awareness and his boss's support through the transition to his new job, he was able to assume his new position with optimism and confidence.

Another experience that implies a separation from, or letting go of, the connection to the fantasy bond is that of having a child of one's own. Though in and of itself this event is usually a rewarding experience, becoming a parent symbolizes the ultimate emancipation from childhood. It represents an end to the hope of getting taken care of or ever receiving the ideal parenting that one did not receive as a child (Note 8).

To avoid this reality, many new parents hold on to remnants of their past by engaging in behaviors and attitudes more characteristic of childhood and adolescence than adulthood. This particular type of regression can occur during pregnancy and continue after the birth of the baby. Both parents may react to the reality and responsibilities of parenthood by experiencing a decline in feelings of engagement and enjoyment while caring for their child and, instead, experience some resentment and a feeling of wanting to be taken care of themselves.

Critically, this transition in life denotes the natural progression that moves a person one step closer to the end of life. It tends to confront the individual with the inevitability of their death, a terrifying thought that has been repressed on many levels (R. W. Firestone & Catlett, 2009a; Solomon, 2019; Yaakobi et al., 2014; Note 9).

Regression at Termination of Therapy

The client who is approaching the termination of therapy often reverts to former symptoms and problems because of a fear of not needing the therapist anymore. By regressing, the client is reacting adversely to their psychological growth and coming to know themselves as an individual and, in essence, is trying to create a fantasy bond with the therapist. Paradoxically, the client's satisfaction with change and improvement leads to the inevitable issue of separation, which can be frightening (Note 10).

Otto Rank (1936/1972) contended that "the authentic meaning of the therapeutic process . . . comes to expression only in the end phase" (p. 195)—that is, in the termination of therapy when the client must separate from the therapist. Rank recognized that regression was likely to take place at the time of this crucial separation. Throughout treatment, he made the dynamics of ending therapy a focal point in the hope that his clients would learn to cope with the problem of separation. He theorized that the central issue of separation represented the core conflict in life. He was well aware of the client's desire to remain ill and dependent on the therapist, a wish that expressed itself in the client's efforts to prolong the therapeutic process by reverting to old symptoms and revisiting material that had previously been worked through (R. W. Firestone, 1997a; Note 11).

Regression as a defense in the service of denying death on an unconscious level is another dimension of a client's resistance to progress in psychotherapy. As the therapist becomes acquainted with the events, whether positive or negative, in clients' lives that have symbolic meaning for them in relation to the trauma of separation and eventual death, patterns of resistance are revealed that need to be addressed with insight and compassion. The resultant awareness helps to facilitate clients' independence and understanding of the termination phase and is also a fundamental aspect of the client's overall movement toward autonomy (R. W. Firestone et al., 2012; P. Johnson & Buboltz, 2000; Note 12).

CONCLUSION

Individuation, which involves becoming a differentiated person, is a lifelong project. It necessitates separating from internalized negative elements that interfere with the fulfillment of one's unique potential. It entails emancipating oneself from fantasy bonds and other defenses developed in adapting to painful circumstances in childhood. It means learning to accommodate to the anxiety and guilt aroused by having one's own point of view and living according to one's own ideals and ethical principles. Individuating involves identifying aversive behaviors and faulty programming in the family and society and developing insight into the relationship between these and the negative internal voices that cause personal distress. It requires understanding the source of these emotional problems and modifying one's negative attitudes, personality traits, and behaviors accordingly.

The processes of individuation, self-differentiation, and regression are affected by how a person resolves the fundamental conflict between the drive toward assertion, autonomy, and separateness and the perceived need to remain dependent and fused with another. On the one hand, human beings have powerful strivings toward fulfilling their potential as unique and independent individuals, while, on the other hand, they have self-destructive and self-limiting tendencies and strong unconscious longings to be taken care of. People usually feel the best when they are experiencing a clear sense of self and personal identity, yet these occasions are often fraught with separation anxiety and, consequently, may be of brief duration.

Regression is a defense mechanism that is used to contend with the fracture in the fantasy bond caused by individuation and other indicators of separation. It represents an unconscious return to the imaginary fusion with the parent. This internal connection is expressed externally by acting in a passive or dependent mode in relation to the real world. By regressing, people attempt to elicit parental responses from others to create the illusion of being taken care of. In a sense, regression signifies a desperate effort to recapture the security and sense of oneness originally associated with one's parents.

The longing to merge with the parental figure or its substitutes by forming a fantasy bond is the most basic response to the fear associated with separation, individuation, and later, death. This fear can be aroused by both positive and negative events. Most people live within a narrow range of experiences, bound on one side by defensive emotional responses to negative incidents and failures and on the other by adverse reactions to atypical positive events.

The bipolar causality of regression becomes logical when the universal human propensity to deny death is considered. Positive or fortunate circumstances, unusual successes, or a close, loving relationship tend to shatter people's fantasy bonds and make them especially aware of their existence. This realization is tinged with poignancy when people contemplate their limitation in time.

At various stages of individuation, people experience a profound feeling of aloneness and uncertainty in life. At the same time, this evolution is alive with a potential for personal gratification, self-expression, and unlimited possibilities. Striving to lead an undefended life is well worth the effort. The feeling of freedom inherent in perceiving oneself as a separate person is both rewarding and exhilarating.

10 SEXUALITY

When people become fused—when two become one—connection can no longer happen. There is no one to connect with. Thus, separateness is a precondition for connection: this is the essential paradox of intimacy and sex.

—Esther Perel, Mating in Captivity

Sex is one of the strongest motivating forces in life. The enjoyment of eroticism and passion, along with the offering and accepting of affection, are fundamental aspects of living. For most people, a fulfilling sex life is central to their sense of well-being and a potential source of pleasure, happiness, and satisfaction. The combination of loving sexual contact and genuine friendship that can be shared in a close relationship is conducive to good mental and physical health.

However, sexual relationships may also cause distress and unhappiness. Indeed, a good deal of human misery centers on sexuality and the difficulties that so many individuals encounter in attempting to achieve and sustain a satisfying sex life. Disturbances in sexual relating can have consequences

https://doi.org/10.1037/0000268-011
Challenging the Fantasy Bond: A Search for Personal Identity and Freedom,
by R. W. Firestone

that affect every facet of a person's life, including activities and pursuits far removed from that domain (R. W. Firestone et al., 2006; H. S. Kaplan, 1995, 2013; Kipnis, 2003; Laumann et al., 1994, 1999; Simons & Carey, 2001; Note 1).

Human sexuality is manifested in many ways, most commonly as heterosexuality, homosexuality, monosexuality, bisexuality, solosexuality, and asexuality. This discussion does not pertain to people who identify as solosexual or asexual. Nor does it refer to those who are alone because of their life circumstances. Rather, this chapter concerns people who desire sexual relationships with others and to whom such relationships are available. Moreover, its primary focus is on the sexuality that exists in adult couple relationships.

I view human sexuality as a simple and pleasurable combination of attitudes and actions that involve giving and receiving for both parties. This refers to all aspects of interpersonal relationships and sexuality between consenting adult partners and makes no distinction between sexual preferences. Sexual experiences can be gratifying on both an emotional and physical level, whether within a committed relationship or in a more casual encounter (R. W. Firestone et al., 2006).

Although people enjoy a wide range of sexual experiences, many describe their ideal situation as one that combines tenderness, warmth, friendship, and sexual fulfillment (R. W. Firestone et al., 2006, p. 3). If not corrupted by ignorance, prejudice, childhood trauma, or sexual abuses, people can enjoy this natural function. Often, in growing up, however, a person's sense of their sexuality is restricted or damaged, and the resultant emotional pain can give rise to long-standing psychological defenses (Note 2). These can be self-protective and/or self-nurturing and often preclude personal vulnerability, interfering with an individual's full and uninhibited participation in sexual relating.

The fantasy bond plays a fundamental role in how people relate sexually. The way children cope with pain in their earliest relationships and the defenses they adopt to deal first with separation anxiety and later with the awareness of death are preserved intact within their personalities as adults. In particular, the self-protective process of the fantasy bond is threatened by the wanting and the necessary give-and-take inherent in the sexual experience.

A sexual encounter that is both emotionally and physically fulfilling can serve to enhance a person's awareness of being truly alive, of really existing. This can make a person acutely aware of the fragility of life and the ultimate separation, through death, both from loved ones and from one's self (R. W. Firestone et al., 2006, p. 24). This heightened sense of vulnerability makes a relationship that combines physical and emotional intimacy hard to establish and even more difficult to sustain.

"NORMAL" SEXUALITY

In contemporary discourse about sex, the terms "normal," "natural," and "healthy" have all been used to describe sexual behavior in human beings. Some significant distinctions can be drawn between these terms. "Normal" is a word generally used to indicate the statistical norm—that is, what most people do—whereas the terms "natural" and "healthy" are more likely to be used as value judgments regarding the moral dimensions of a given sexual behavior or practice (Sandfort & Ehrhardt, 2004; Strong et al., 1999; Note 3).

Sex researchers have stressed the vast diversity of sexual behaviors and practices across different cultures (Suggs & Miracle, 1993). Therefore, what is considered normal, natural, or moral in one society may well be considered abnormal, unnatural, or deviant in another (Heinemann et al., 2016; Note 4). Furthermore, what was considered abnormal or immoral in the past may be considered normal and acceptable today (L. Stone, 1985). As historian Lawrence Stone (1985) rightly observed, "What is absolutely certain . . . is that over the long history of Western civilization, there has been no such thing as 'normal sexuality.' Sexuality is a cultural artifact that has undergone constant and sometimes dramatic changes over time" (p. 42).

The concepts of normality or abnormality are embedded in people's beliefs about the morality or immorality of certain sexual practices, and these convictions can vary significantly across cultures, social classes, ethnic groups, and historical eras (Richardson & Monro, 2012). My views regarding moral and natural sexuality are congruent with many of the sentiments expressed by Klein (1992) and Singer (2001). In discussing how to evaluate the morality of a specific sexual practice, Klein (1992) cited three criteria as a basis for making a responsible choice: "Is it consenting (and is the other person really in a position to give consent)? Is it exploitative? Is it self-destructive?" (p. 5).

The frequency of sexual relations is often used as a criterion for healthy sexuality or an indicator of "normality." Indeed, many are curious about how often the average person has sex, a question that has led to myriad sex surveys that report the frequency of sexual relations for single, cohabiting, and married people (Note 5). The types of sexual activities that people engage in are also used as criteria for normality. For instance, many gauge the "success" of their sexual performance in terms of whether the sex act culminates in orgasm for both partners. However, research evaluating the dimensions of healthy sexuality places emphasis on the emotional satisfaction or dissatisfaction attained by individuals during a sexual experience rather than focusing solely on the physical component (D. Davis et al., 2006; Gonzaga et al., 2006).

TWO MODES OF SEXUAL RELATING

In general, there are two modes of sexual relating: (a) an outward form of contact that is a natural extension of affection, tenderness, and companionship between two people and (b) an inward, more impersonal, self-gratifying expression in which sex is used primarily as a form of self-gratification. Sexual encounters can be viewed as existing on a continuum between these two modes of sexual expression (R. W. Firestone et al., 2006; Fortenberry, 2013; Maltz, 1995; Ventriglio & Bhugra, 2019; Note 6).

Outward, Personal Sexuality

An outward, personal mode of sexual relating between two people includes a sense of mutual give-and-take during which a person is fully present emotionally with the other. This type of personal exchange is evident not only during the sex act itself but also more broadly in a person's facial expression, friendly manner, sense of humor, playfulness, spontaneity, and enthusiasm. This outward mode of sexual relating has been referred to as "positive sexuality" and "sex positivity" (Ferreira et al., 2012; Levine, 2002; Schnarch, 1991; Note 7).

Positive sexuality presumes an acceptance of one's animal nature and an affirmative attitude toward one's body, nudity, and sexual urges. Like all feelings, sexual feelings arise naturally and involuntarily and are experienced as sensations in the body. In this regard, people who are close to these feelings are better able to respond favorably to expressions of loving and being loved in an intimate relationship than those who have less access to them.

In an ideal sexual encounter, partners would proceed naturally from one level of arousal to the next, undisturbed by critical inner voices about their bodies, their sexuality, or their performance. Both would be spontaneous in their sexual responses, and neither would try to inhibit or otherwise control the sex act. In this scenario, both individuals would take responsibility for their own sexual desires and needs and indicate their wants, engendering a basic feeling of equality in their interaction that then contributes to their general sense of well-being and individuality. There would be an absence of guilt, self-critical ruminations, or criticality toward one's partner. The encounter may be playful, carefree, sensuous, affectionate, serious, sad, or any combination of these qualities and emotions. Afterward, partners would experience feelings such as happiness, sadness, relaxation, and fulfillment and express their mutual appreciation for the pleasure they received (R. W. Firestone et al., 2006).

In my work, I have focused on the psychological factors that tend to give sexuality its depth and meaning. From this perspective, physical intimacy would ideally occur between two individuals who have mature attitudes toward sex and regard being sexual as an opportunity to offer pleasure to each other. Both partners would have an active desire for sex, a positive body image, and congenial attitudes about themselves and their partner that are relatively free of distortion. If in a relationship, the nature of the personal interaction that is characteristic within the sexual relationship is carried into other aspects of their daily lives.

Inward, Impersonal Sexuality

Inward, impersonal modes of sexual relating represent a movement away from genuine intimacy and emotional exchanges and toward a reliance on the sex act primarily as a vehicle to assuage feelings of emptiness and insecurity. The attempt to find security in an illusion of fusion with another person contributes to a progressive loss of identity for each person. When one or both partners sacrifice their individuality in this way, their basic attraction to one another is jeopardized (R. W. Firestone, 1985). Couples in a fantasy bond often treat each other as though they were an appendage, which causes their feelings of sexual attraction to wane. The increasing dependence on habitual contact with decreasing personal feeling and emotional closeness adds to a continuous deterioration in the quality of sexual relating. These couples often find themselves being sexual out of a sense of obligation and responsibility rather than a genuine desire to be together.

This chapter follows Brittany and Rick as they addressed the sexual problems they were having in their relationship.

> Brittany and Rick came to couples therapy because, since their daughter was born, Rick had not felt sexual toward Brittany. They had always been a particularly compatible couple. They still enjoyed spending time together, especially sharing the tasks of parenthood. Rick delighted in being a father. He and Brittany were respectful and supportive of each other's individual friendships and interests. They laughed easily and rarely argued. Theirs was an especially harmonious relationship, except that they were no longer sexual.
>
> Rick loved Brittany and his life with her, and he knew that she was hurting from his disinterest in being sexual. He was puzzled about this himself, but he thought he was just going through a phase and that it would pass. Even though

he assured her that it had nothing to do with her, she struggled not to take his lack of sexual interest personally as a rejection of her.

Rick was raised in a basically matriarchal family structure, where his mother and grandmother were the dominant parental figures. His father was a shadowy figure whom he barely knew. His father's job had required that he travel, and Rick felt that his father was glad to be away from them. As he grew older, he heard rumors about his father "running around" and having girlfriends. On the occasions in his childhood when his father was present, his mother and grandmother's hostility toward him was apparent.

When Rick was in his mid-20s, he met Brittany and was immediately attracted to her. He actively pursued her, and when she finally responded to his overtures, they entered into a serious relationship. They shared a sense of fun and adventure, and they also enjoyed a lively sexual relationship. Brittany was impressed by the earnestness with which Rick approached his life. He was hardworking, financially responsible, and had concrete plans for his future. He told her that above all else, he would be different from his father; he would be devoted to his family.

In general, in a sexual situation, whenever there is a switch from close, emotional contact to a more inward, impersonal style of relating, the transformation is hurtful to the well-being of both partners. Many people report a sense of discontent or irritability after a sexual experience in which a less personal mode of relating predominated.

The first change in Rick's sexuality occurred shortly after he and Brittany were married. Brittany thought his diminished interest in sex might be from the stress of the wedding and moving into their new home. After a time, they did become more sexual but not as frequently and with as much passion as before. Brittany especially enjoyed the time when they were trying to get pregnant because they were sexual often. However, after she became pregnant, they were less sexual than they had ever been. And after their daughter was born, Rick stopped being sexual altogether.

Sexual Withholding

Sexual withholding can be defined as an inhibition of expressions of sexual desire and interest, including physical affection, touching, desirability, and other attributes of outward, personal sexuality (R. W. Firestone, 1985, 1997a; R. W. Firestone & Catlett, 1999, 2009b). This does not refer to people who simply choose not to be sexual (Note 8), nor to those who withhold consciously as a calculated manipulation that is meant to be hurtful. The focus here is on individuals for whom sexual withholding is largely unconscious yet causes both partners distress.

The avoidance of physical intimacy may be tied to unconscious feelings associated with early needs met unsatisfactorily in childhood, such as inadequate feeding interactions and other reciprocal communications and exchanges with the primary caretaker. In effect, a person may be saying, "I don't need anything from outside; I can feed myself." Moreover, people who grow up feeling uncared for or deficient are often uncomfortable with the emotional and physical interactions inherent in being sexual. They may be self-doubting about being able to respond to or satisfy their partner. They may perceive their partner's sexual wanting as desperation or hunger. On an unconscious level, they may feel resentful of needing someone else for sexual fulfillment and engage in behaviors that support the fantasy that they can take care of themselves.

Adults in an intimate relationship who are sexually withholding often construe spontaneous sexual interactions and physical intimacy as threatening to their defended state. Consequently, they try to regulate, control, or direct various aspects of the sex act, such as dictating the frequency of sex, the time, place, conditions, movements, positions, and manner of expressing affection.

Sexual withholding may involve a holding back from or distancing of oneself from one's partner or a holding back of pleasure from oneself, both of which unintentionally hurts the other person. While distancing oneself from one's partner can have obvious effects, when people deny themselves sexual pleasure, they become increasingly more self-hating and guilty for going against their natural needs and desires. This, in turn, leads to more self-denial, sexual inhibition, and avoidance of sexual situations (Note 9). Those who are being withheld from feel hurt, frustrated, and angry, emotions which they often attempt to suppress. This can lead to unconscious reactions, such as irritability or desperation toward the partner who is being withholding.

The process of denying oneself sexual pleasure and fulfillment can become automatic and involuntary over time, and the causative destructive attitudes can be deeply repressed. Habitual patterns of self-denial have a progressively deadening effect on the feelings of excitement and attraction typically present at the beginning of a relationship. In a long-term relationship, if partners become withholding, they tend to avoid spontaneous sexual interactions, limit giving to and taking from their partner, and control the emotional transactions in the relationship. All of these behaviors contribute to a deterioration in the quality of their sexual relating.

> Brittany and Rick described how their sex life had changed. At night, Rick would go to bed early and be asleep by the time Brittany came to bed. During the day, even though their interactions were fun and friendly, Rick was no longer affectionate or flirtatious. Their communications had become more practical and less personal. Their activities centered on their daughter, to the exclusion of the two of them spending romantic time together. If Brittany reached out to Rick, he turned away. When he was sexual, he did it out of a sense of obligation.

Rick's disinterest in sex was taking a toll on Brittany. She did not feel sexy or attractive. She started to feel like it did not matter whether or not she made an effort to look good. She could not remember the last time she had enjoyed flirting and the excitement of feeling sexually interesting and interested.

Sex as an Addiction

Self-involved modes of sexual relating often reflect the fantasy bond's illusion of self-sufficiency developed in childhood and its persistence through adolescence into adulthood. Early self-nourishing tendencies that evolve into more sophisticated means of self-gratification can be manifested in addictive sexual activity, such as compulsive involvement in pornography, prostitution, or even excessive masturbation.

Impersonal sexuality can function as a painkiller to inhibit feeling reactions. When people use sex for this purpose, they often rely on fantasy to enhance their excitement and lose emotional contact with their partner (Note 10). Their sexual interaction tends to become more mechanical and focused on performance.

The crucial distinction between personal sexual relating and an addictive style of sexuality (Note 11) lies in the awareness of one's partner as a distinct, separate person, as opposed to the use of the other as an instrument to assuage primitive needs and longings—that is, to relieve fears of aloneness, separateness, and death. A person's primary mode of sexual expression can be either based on a fantasy of self-sufficiency or an emotional and physical vulnerability to their partner.

OTHER INFLUENCES ON SEXUALITY

As explained earlier, the same developmental influences that lead to the formation of the defense system and fantasy bond impact an individual's sexuality. The process of defending against the hurt, fear, and frustration in their earliest relationships leaves people suspicious and self-protective and turned away from wanting to have their needs met by another person. Other significant factors that affect a child's emerging sexuality include parental attitudes toward the body and sex, child sexual abuse, and cultural and societal attitudes toward sex.

Parents tend to pass on to their children, both directly and indirectly, the same values and views of sexuality that were passed on to them. Parental attitudes toward nudity, masturbation, and sex play have a powerful influence on a child's sexual development. This process has a destructive effect when these views are restrictive, narrow, or distorted.

Psychologists have stressed the fact that during early childhood, masturbation and sex play between children are normal and typically not harmful (Bonner, 2001; Martinson, 1994; Zoldbrod, 1998). However, many parents have difficulty accepting this view and often respond with disapproval or anger. Similarly, negative views held by parents in relation to nudity and the human body contribute to children developing feelings of shame and guilt about their bodies and their sexual feelings. These attitudes are often retained throughout life, causing problems in personal relationships and sexual relating as the person matures. As Kaplan (2014) noted,

> Parents who think of themselves as liberal may voice enlightened views, but their deeper negative sexual attitudes are transmitted by their subtle, nonverbal, negative responses to a child's expression of sexual interest or pleasure. . . . In our sexually ambivalent society, such negative associations are likely to be repeated on countless occasions, which leaves few of us entirely free of sexual conflict. (p. 51)

Excessive parental intrusiveness or control, as well as an overconcern with cleanliness and orderliness, can damage a child's sense of autonomy and their understanding that their bodies belong to them (R. W. Firestone, 1990b). In his extensive studies of shame, Lewis (1992) called attention to the fact that parents often express disgust or contempt when socializing their children, especially during toilet training. Other studies have shown that severe, harsh, or intrusive toilet training is correlated with later emotional and sexual disturbances (Fisher & Fisher, 1986; Flanagan, 2014). When parents hold rigid, dogmatic beliefs or repressive attitudes that they apply to sex and the human body, these combine with their own sexual tensions and are inevitably conveyed to the child—consciously or unconsciously—and usually with damaging consequences (Davidson & Darling, 1993; Negy et al., 2016; Zoldbrod, 1998; Note 12).

Within many families, there is little or no indication that the parents enjoy an emotionally close, active sexual relationship. Some parents even believe that it is wrong to express any physical affection in front of their children. However, some parents have an exaggerated focus on sexuality and an overly sexualized style of relating that can be just as damaging. Although many parents feel that children should learn healthy attitudes about sex, few discuss sex openly and personally with their offspring (Afifi et al., 2008; R. W. Firestone, 1990b; R. W. Firestone et al., 2006; Robinson et al., 2017; Schiffer, 2004; Shtarkshall et al., 2007; Note 13).

> In examining his family's history, Rick began to see attitudes that he had incorporated from his family. He realized that from the opinions of his mother and grandmother and by the example of his father's behavior, he had grown up

with the point of view that there are two kinds of women: those who are clean and maternal and those who are carnal and sexual. He had regarded Brittany as sexual until she became a wife and a mother. After that, on an unconscious level, those feelings became taboo. In effect, Rick had recreated his parents' platonic relationship.

Childhood Sexual Abuse

Clearly, acts of a sexual nature performed by an adult on a child are especially traumatic and damaging to the child. The effects of child sexual abuse are often manifested in symptoms of disassociation and numerous sexual dysfunctions and disorders of sexual desire in adults (Kinzl et al., 1995; Maltz, 2002; Pulverman et al., 2018) and contribute to other psychiatric disorders, including suicide risk throughout the life span.

Incestuous sexual abuse is especially destructive because the parent, the person responsible for the safety of the child, is the person who has betrayed the child's trust (Courtois, 1999; Dorais, 2002; Freyd, 1996; Herman, 1981, 1992; Sarwer & Durlak, 1996). Incest interferes with the child's ability to form a sense of safety with either parent, the abusing parent, or the "enabling" nonabusing parent, preventing the development of basic trust in other people. Both limitations clearly have negative consequences in the exploited child's adult relationships.

Even in the absence of physical sexual abuse, emotional incest—that is, a parent's seductive behavior or inappropriate, exaggerated focus on a child—can also lead to numerous sexual difficulties later in life. An emotionally incestuous relationship, also known as *covert incest*, is a sexualized relationship "even when there is no clear-cut, explicit sexual activity between the individuals" (Gartner, 1999, p. 26). Manifestations of emotional incest include flirtatiousness, sexualized affection, inappropriate touching and handling of the child's body and clothing, and sexual innuendos, as well as possessiveness, jealousy of other people in the child's life, a strong focus on and preference for the child, and/or sexualized excitement when in close proximity to the child (Çimşir & Akdoğan, 2021).

According to Love (1990), *emotional incest* has two defining features: "The parent is using the child to satisfy needs that should be satisfied by other adults" (p. 9), and "The parent is ignoring many of the child's needs" (p. 10). A child who has been subjected to emotional incest learns to relate primarily in a sexualized manner, often leading to engaging in promiscuous behavior, even when such behavior is unacceptable or unfulfilling to them. In discussing sexual problems that are common among victims of emotional incest, Love (1990) stated that these people often repress their sexuality:

"The man may be impotent or disinterested in sex. The woman may be afraid of sex or have difficulty achieving an orgasm" (p. 54).

The implications and long-lasting effects of incest and child sexual abuse are pervasive and far-reaching and extend beyond the sexual sphere. Individuals who were damaged in this way become injured in their overall capacity for wanting and specifically in their desire to seek satisfaction in a mature sexual relationship. They may unconsciously inhibit their sexual responses in their adult relationships in various ways. In particular, as a sexual relationship becomes emotionally closer and more meaningful to a victim of childhood sexual abuse, they may experience a diminution in sexual desire or an increasing aversion to being sexual.

Specific problems in intimate relationships and outcomes in terms of adult sexual functioning have been delineated by several clinicians and researchers (Doll et al., 2004; Heiman & Heard-Davison, 2004; Purcell et al., 2004; Roberts et al., 2004). These effects include "sexual aversion or avoidance, decreased sexual desire or sexual self-esteem, inhibited sexual arousal or orgasm, vaginismus, dyspareunia, and negative attitudes toward sexuality and intimate relationships in general" (Meston & Heiman, 2000, p. 399). Kirschner and Kirschner (1996) found that "86 percent [of child sexual abuse survivors] had difficulties dealing with close relationships" (p. 408; Note 14).

Cultural and Societal Attitudes Toward Sexuality

In working with clients and in observing individuals and families in their everyday lives, I have become increasingly impressed with the prevalence of sexually related disturbances in our society. These are related to a variety of social and cultural factors that influence children's development as sexual beings (R. W. Firestone et al., 2006). Each person growing up today is impacted by both repressive and exploitative attitudes toward sexuality. Distorted beliefs about sex and prejudicial, sexist views of men and women are widely disseminated through books, magazines, popular music, radio, television, the internet, and other areas of popular culture. Sex as presented in numerous film and television productions is too often sensationalized and trivialized and is, at times, presented in conjunction with scenes of violence. This combination desensitizes viewers and blurs the distinction between appearance and reality.

Rick grew up in a culture where the mothers are the primary caregivers in the family and are praised for their dedication to their children. Mothers and sisters are seen as being innocent and pure and are discouraged from revealing their sexual nature. There tends to be suspicion of women who dress "too sexy" or are "too into getting men's attention." Women who embrace their sexuality are often viewed as "sluts." In these ways, the biases that Rick acquired in his family were supported by the culture in which he grew up.

In today's society, there is still considerable support for the point of view that sex is inherently bad (Francoeur, 2001; Leander et al., 2018). This concept of sexuality continues to influence the cultural definition of "normalcy," despite scientific, social, and medical advances regarding sexuality over the past 60 years (Baumeister et al., 2002; Baumeister & Vohs, 2004; Note 15). As Esther Perel (2006) noted,

> Religion, government, medicine, education, the media, and pop culture all labor tirelessly to define and regulate the parameters of our sexual well-being. . . . Much of what we learn about sex comes from the street, the movies, television, and school. But before any of these reach us, our family gets to us first. (p. 106)

THE CRITICAL INNER VOICE AND SEXUALITY

The voice process regulates inward, impersonal modes of relating and, as such, can interrupt and interfere with the sexual experience. It often encourages sexual withholding and self-denial, promotes self-gratification over interpersonal sexuality, and encourages addictive sexuality, effectively sabotaging the equality inherent in an ideal sexual experience. Self-critical attitudes, as well as thoughts reflecting animosity toward one's partner, can erupt into consciousness at any time during a sexual experience, decreasing sexual desire and increasing performance anxiety and self-consciousness. As a result, individuals often shift their focus to the technical aspects of sex in an effort to circumvent these inhibitions and complete the sexual act. The negative prescriptions of the critical inner voice may inhibit a person's spontaneous, natural responses before, during, and/or following a sexual experience.

Self-attacks and the accompanying anger affect people's basic feelings about themselves, their bodies, their sexual identity, and their ability to both give and receive sexual pleasure and gratification. Voices may increase a person's self-hatred: "Your body is so ugly. Keep it hidden as much as possible." They may discourage sex by attacking one's partner: "They're all sweaty and smelly. How can you be attracted to that?" Even the mildest voice attack can interfere with a sexual experience: "There's so much noise outside. It's too distracting." Voices also reinforce feelings of shame and guilt that, in turn, effectively tone down or squelch sexual desire and arousal: "Listen to how loud you're being! Have some modesty!"

Before a sexual encounter, voices may undermine a person's confidence: "There's something wrong with you. You aren't like normal people." They may encourage people to be self-denying: "You just had sex the other night. Why do it so soon?" They may support sex addictions and self-gratification: "Say you're tired tonight; then you can take care of yourself after they've fallen asleep. It's so much simpler." Or they may justify being withholding: "It's natural to have less desire for sex. You're getting older; this is what happens."

During sex, voices can make people begin to doubt themselves: "You aren't excited enough. This is going to end badly." They may cause individuals to become self-conscious and withholding: "You look really stupid doing that! You're embarrassing yourself." They may trigger people into regressing into either a parental state—"He's so self-conscious and insecure; you're going to have to take charge"—or a childish state: "She's so critical and frustrated with you, you better figure out what to do to satisfy her!"

Afterward, voices often try to undermine people and put distance between them and their partner—"You weren't very good, he must be disappointed"— or "They didn't seem that into you" or "You acted too needy" or "You weren't passionate enough" (Kaplan, 1995; Note 16).

In listening to individuals talk about their sexual encounters, I have learned a great deal about how the critical inner voice interrupts the flow of feelings and sensations during the sexual act. Although the voice is often unconscious, many people are aware of it while being sexual as a running commentary that criticizes and attacks them and ultimately interferes with the experience, transforming it from an affectionate and pleasurable experience into an anxiety-provoking activity (R. W. Firestone, 1990d).

Voice Therapy Applied to Problems in Sexual Relating

When applied to sexual relating, the goal of voice therapy is to help people access and identify the destructive thoughts that interrupt the smooth progression of feelings that would naturally occur during a gratifying sexual experience (R. W. Firestone, 1990d). Voice therapy procedures have been used to identify a wide range of self-attacks in individuals who reported a variety of difficulties in achieving sexually fulfilling relationships. The presence of negative thoughts during sex has an adverse effect on people's physiological responses and, at times, their ability to enjoy the sexual experience fully (R. W. Firestone, 1990e). When people learn to talk openly about their relationships and disclose specific voice attacks that they have regarding sex, there are often significant positive changes in their sexual relating.

In the context of couples therapy, in sessions where both partners are present, each reveals their negative thoughts and attitudes toward themselves and their partner. They are supported in understanding that their voices are the cause of their overreactions, dramatic hostile thoughts, and grudges, even when these critical views have some basis in reality. As they verbalize their attitudes about their partner's traits and behaviors, they often become aware that their voice has taken on a cynical, disrespectful tone and that these attacks are exaggerating their partner's negative characteristics. Disclosing these angry, judgmental views in the form of the voice helps people to separate them from a more realistic, objective view of their partner.

In tracing the source of their self-attacks and hostile attitudes to childhood and early family interactions, people gain perspective into each other's areas of difficulty and feel more compassion for their partner, as well as for themselves. In this sense, they are sharing each other's individual psychotherapy. Recognizing that the purpose of voice attacks is to create distance and alienation within the relationship is effective in improving partners' attitudes toward one another, as well as in enhancing each individual's personal growth. Each partner learns to accommodate to the anxiety associated with challenging the fantasy bond by breaking inward, self-protective defenses and is gradually able to tolerate more love and intimacy in their life (see R. W. Firestone et al., 2006, Chapter 9, "Voice Therapy Applied to Problems in Sexual Relating," pp. 229–262).

Voice Therapy Applied in a Case Example

In therapy, Rick examined the voices that were interfering with his being sexual. He reported that, before being sexual, he would tell himself, "This isn't going to work. You're not going to feel anything. This is going to end in disaster. Just avoid the whole situation!" When he was sexual, he had voices telling him, "You're losing feeling. Just hurry up and get this thing over with." He was surprised to recognize that he had voices in relation to Brittany: "She's so frantic. She wants too much from you. She's oversexed."

With voice therapy, Rick learned to respond to his voice attacks from his own point of view. He acknowledged that he liked sex. He said that being sexual was important for him, Brittany, and their relationship. He did not see Brittany as oversexed but as a woman with a normal enjoyment of sex.

Rick realized that his sexual difficulty had to do with old feelings triggered in him by getting married and having a child. Without realizing it, he had been responding to voices that were distracting him during lovemaking. His negative voices about sex made making love with Brittany feel like a chore to avoid rather than an experience to enjoy.

Rick and Brittany continued to work on their sexual relationship in couples therapy. They gradually resumed their sexual relationship. Even though he continued to struggle with a lack of sexual drive, Rick had tools to help him when he was sexual. When his voices would start to attack him, he was able to discuss them with Brittany in the moment, which dissipated his voices and enabled him to continue feeling intimate and sexual.

In therapy, as clients challenge their defenses against intimacy, their communications improve, and they are less secretive or self-protective in relation to their sexuality. This allows for more empathy and an increased ability to communicate with compassion and respect for the other person's wants, attitudes, and values. In a committed relationship, they are also less embarrassed or ashamed to disclose their fears or doubts about personal matters to their partner; they are able to candidly discuss their differences, as well as their commonalities. As a result, there is an increase in forthright communications, both in sexual encounters and more generally. This has the positive effect of making each person feel acknowledged and seen. By using voice therapy techniques, people can begin to counteract the dictates of the voice, disrupt the fantasy bond, and achieve greater emotional and sexual fulfillment in their lives.

THE EFFECTS OF DEATH ANXIETY ON SEXUAL RELATING

While a sexual experience can cause anxiety due to the implied intrusion into the fantasy bond, fears of sexual intimacy are also generated by existential concerns. Being intimate with another person in a sexual encounter can heighten a person's appreciation of their existence, as well as of its fragility. This enhanced awareness of mortality and the pain and loss associated with it causes many to withdraw from such experiences. In extreme cases, they may avoid sexual gratification altogether.

As described in Chapter 2, the sex act can be conceptualized as a meaningful, physical coming together that is followed by a clear separation. Thus, a satisfying sexual relationship is capable of arousing separation anxiety, causing people to retreat to a more inward, self-protective mode of sexual expression. Understanding the anxiety stimulated by an awareness of separation and death helps explain many puzzling phenomena about human sexual behavior, including people's tendencies to pull away from intimate relating in their adult associations.

Being sexual is also inextricably linked to the body, which is subject to deterioration and, eventually, death. As Becker (1973/1997) put it, "Sex is of the body, and the body is of death" (p. 162; Birnbaum et al., 2011; Goldenberg et al., 1999; Watter, 2018). According to Goldenberg et al. (2006),

> In addition to enjoying pleasurable bodily activities, people appear threatened by the physical aspects of the body; they experience anxiety and inhibitions surrounding sex, eating, bodily appearance and functions. Based on terror management theory, we posit that people are dually motivated to approach the life-affirming properties of the physical body, and to avoid the physical or animalistic aspects of the body because of their association with death. (Abstract; Note 17)

In general, the more a person becomes connected to their body and emotionally invested in a sexual partner, the more they tend to feel anxiety and sadness about the reality of the potential loss of the relationship. They often reexperience feelings of aloneness, separateness, and existential anxiety that have previously been successfully repressed. I have found that, in therapy, when clients are relieved of a sexual symptom or problem, they often have an increased apprehension about death.

> Even though Rick's retreat from being sexual was primarily tied to learned childhood attitudes and defenses and the voices that supported them, death anxiety also played a role. The birth of his daughter and starting a family of his own was the high point in his life. He felt a depth of love and commitment to his wife and their newborn that he had not felt before. In a session, Rick spoke of how the combination of his loving feelings toward their daughter and the intense closeness and intimacy with Brittany had left him feeling vulnerable. He speculated that it made him feel anxious to feel so invested in his life.

To varying degrees, people tend to adapt to death anxiety through a process of depersonalization, self-denial, and withdrawal of vitality from other people and life-affirming activities. Specifically, their denial of death can generalize to an antifeeling, antisexual existence and support addictive attachments over involvement in loving and sexually satisfying relationships.

CONCLUSION

A combination of sexuality, close emotional contact, and personal communication is the ideal formula for a fulfilling couple relationship. However, as people begin to invest meaning in an intimate relationship or become more committed to their partner, the fantasy bond is seriously threatened, and couples tend to revert to a more self-protective or defended style of sexual relating (R. W. Firestone & Catlett, 1999, 2009a; Mikulincer & Shaver, 2007). In addition, lovers frequently feel uniquely vulnerable to the possibility of future loss or rejection when they remain close to each other during sex.

They are deeply touched to be gratified by another yet are painfully aware of how much they stand to lose.

Most people are unaware of reacting negatively to love and sexual fulfillment. A person's withdrawal from these situations is usually unconscious and can become habitual, at times leading to a significant decrease in sexual function, activity, and/or gratification. When a person has reacted in this manner, sexual encounters can change from being largely outward and personal to being more inward and impersonal.

At these times, a person's sexuality is particularly vulnerable to critical inner voices that distract them from being fully present with their partner. These voices serve to reinforce negative attitudes toward their body, nudity, and sexuality; they are directed toward a person's sexual "performance," increasing anxieties regarding their sexual enjoyment and/or satisfying their partner. The voice process supports a person's self-denying tendencies and influences them to give up their natural sexual desires and wants.

However, I have found that when people become more aware of their negative voices and destructive tendencies in relation to their sexuality and work through them in therapy, they are able to expand their boundaries and enjoy more satisfaction in life. In understanding and challenging their retreat from closeness and intimacy, people can gradually change attitudes and behaviors that limit or control expressions of sexuality in their intimate relationships. They can come to value vulnerability, openness, and equality in their sexual relationships and view these aspects of their relationship as a fundamental part of life. At those moments when ecstasy and exhilaration combine with feelings of sorrow and existential pain, lovers never feel more together, yet more alone (R. W. Firestone et al., 2006).

PART **IV** IMPLICATIONS FOR
PSYCHOTHERAPY

11 MY APPROACH TO PSYCHOTHERAPY

The ultimate aim of therapy is to encourage clients to challenge their defenses and inner world of fantasy and risk seeking satisfaction in the real world through goal-directed behavior. In *What Is Psychotherapy? Contemporary Perspectives* (Zeig & Munion, 1990), I wrote,

> The psychotherapeutic alliance is a unique human relationship, wherein a devoted and trained person attempts to render assistance to another person by both suspending and extending him or herself. Nowhere in life is a person listened to, felt, and experienced with such concentrated sharing and emphasis on every aspect of personal communication. As in any other human relationship, this interaction may be fulfilling or damaging to either individual.
>
> To the extent that a new fantasy bond or illusion of connection is formed (doctor–client, therapist–client, parent–child), the relationship can be detrimental; whereas in a situation that is characterized by equality, openness, and true compassion, there will be movement toward individuation in both parties. My therapy helps a person to expose and challenge fantasy bonds and destructive "voices," remnants of negative childhood experiences that seriously impair people's sense of self, spirit, and individuality. (p. 68)

My approach to psychotherapy is multidimensional and has evolved into a synthesis of psychoanalytic techniques, feeling release therapy, and voice

https://doi.org/10.1037/0000268-012
Challenging the Fantasy Bond: A Search for Personal Identity and Freedom, by R. W. Firestone

therapy. These methods have proven to be beneficial in overcoming resistance and promoting therapeutic movement. I have used all these methods and procedures in my work but not as a rigid system applied to all persons seeking help or therapeutic intervention. My work is adapted to the personal needs of each individual (R. W. Firestone, 1990c, 1997a, 2018).

HISTORICAL DEVELOPMENT OF METHODOLOGY

My psychotherapeutic orientation is the outcome of more than 60 years of investigating the problem of resistance. It broadens the concept of resistance in psychotherapy to include an understanding of people's fundamental refusal to accept a "better life." The concepts and methods described here and in previous chapters have been drawn from three populations: individuals suffering from psychoses, clients in psychotherapy, and a "normal" community of comparatively high-functioning individuals.

As I mentioned in Chapter 3, from 1956 to 1957 I worked as a psychotherapist with schizophrenic patients in an internship at a residential treatment center. This unique setting allowed me to study the full range of mental illness manifested by these patients day and night, as contrasted with the narrow scope available in the once or twice weekly, 50-minute office visit. Our therapy involved the direct exposure and analysis of patients' internal sources of gratification through fantasy, combined with an attempt to make reality more inviting for them. My colleagues and I provided an interim form of parenting that endeavored to compensate for the early emotional deprivation these patients had endured. My basic attitude toward persons with schizophrenia was one of respect for their attempt to maintain some form of integrity in the face of severe trauma and support for the fact that their symptoms made logical sense. I believed that these people had come by their mental disorder honestly; that is, I felt that real events harmful to their psyche had occurred, which led to their level of disturbance (R. W. Firestone, 1990c, p. 629)

During this internship, I developed the basic concepts of my theoretical approach to schizophrenia. In my doctoral dissertation, *A Concept of the Schizophrenic Process* (R. W. Firestone, 1957), I described the dimensions of the fantasized, self-mothering process that the person with schizophrenia relies on for gratification at the expense of interpersonal relationships. Schizophrenic patients, in effect, mother themselves. That is, in their imagination, they are joined or connected to the image of the good, powerful parent. In fantasy, they are split between being the all-powerful parent and the weak, helpless child, a conflict that leads to a certain amount of ego fragmentation. Later, I extended and applied these concepts to the neuroses.

After receiving my PhD, I entered private practice and used a psycho-analytically oriented therapy model for many years. Essentially, I used the technique of free association and the interpretation of my clients' material (Note 1). I helped them to deal with their resistance and resolve their trans-ference reactions. My therapeutic approach progressed further as I integrated what I was learning in my practice with the knowledge I had gained from my work with the patients with schizophrenia.

Since the beginning of my working with clients, I have recognized and understood the value of patients' expressing feeling in psychotherapy. Some-time later, I became interested in Arthur Janov's (1970) primal therapy. My goal was to help people access a depth of feeling to match their intellec-tual understanding of the problems they were addressing in therapy. Primal therapy presented a means for subjects to express deeper emotions, so I developed a modification of Janov's methodology, which I called "feeling release therapy." My associates and I applied the method to over 200 clients. We found that as they released intense feelings and relived core incidents from their childhood, they formulated powerful insights. We spent exten-sive periods evaluating our data, recording and transcribing the substantial amounts of material from individual and group sessions, and assessing the advantages and disadvantages of this form of therapeutic intervention. We came to realize that everyone has a considerable amount of deep-seated pain and sadness that they are continually suppressing and, indeed, may be completely unaware of. It seemed that virtually no one was immune to this primal pain, and none had escaped childhood without being scarred to some extent. Feeling release therapy became an integral part of my treatment format, which proved to be quite effective when combined with a psycho-analytic approach.

These studies led to my investigation of voice therapy techniques. Through my understanding of destructive thought processes, I was able to develop methods that allowed clients' voices to be expressed together with the accom-panying affect. This was often followed by a spontaneous understanding of their source. Voice therapy has proved invaluable in helping clients cope with their harmful thoughts and has been a substantial addition to my overall therapeutic methodology.

For the past 40 years, I have also been involved in a longitudinal study of approximately 200 individuals and their families. In this setting, I was pro-vided with an unusual opportunity to match observations of internal dynamics, exposed through participants' honest self-disclosure, with observations of their interactions with their families of origin, their mates, and their children, as well as their relationships with other participants (R. W. Firestone et al., 2003; Note 2).

From this experience, I developed a number of hypotheses that I believed were generally valid as applied to individuals' behavior in the larger society. Most important, I discovered that essentially all people are divided, to varying degrees, between the self and the anti-self. As already described, the latter represents the incorporation of parents' rejecting and hurtful attitudes, as well as the internalization of other emotionally painful trauma. Negative attitudes or voices toward the self and others are primarily responsible for the majority of a person's painful and destructive experiences, especially problems in one's closest relationships.

By working together in a direct and open forum for self-expression, participants in the group discovered that they were able to challenge long-standing negative attitudes and hostile feelings toward themselves and others. In addition, my associates and I discovered a paradox: Most people do not want what they say they want. Instead, they tend to avoid human interactions that are especially meaningful and experiences that are particularly constructive and have difficulty assimilating a new, more affirmative image of themselves. As previously documented, significant positive movement in one's life arouses anxiety, particularly when it represents a marked difference from the habitual behavior and lifestyles of one's parents and family members. This is often accompanied by an increase in both separation anxiety and death anxiety (R. W. Firestone, 1990c, 2018; R. W. Firestone & Catlett, 2009a).

PRINCIPLES OF AN EFFECTIVE PSYCHOTHERAPY

The treatment strategies used in an effective psychotherapy are based on fundamental philosophical assumptions held by the therapist about the nature of human beings and the society in which they live. As Robert Langs (1982) underscored in his classic work *Psychotherapy: A Basic Text*, "The nature of this therapeutic relationship, and of the transactions between the two participants, is structured and shaped by the implicit and explicit attitudes and interventions of the therapist" (p. 3). Langs (2006) described how these attitudes are "expressed [by the therapist] through a basic caring attitude, securing the ground rules of treatment, and making deep unconsciously validated interventions" (p. 13; Note 3).

A basic attitude underlying my approach to psychotherapy reflects my personal view of people as being innocent rather than inherently destructive or self-destructive (R. W. Firestone, 1997a, p. 4). My focus is on the development of a sense of self in opposition to the invalidation of one's identity that is caused by maintaining destructive voices and self-limiting defenses. As a therapist, I have always viewed hostility and aggression as part of the defense system that people form to cope with life's adversities. They are an overlay on the personality that can be dealt with in therapy with compassion and understanding. When an individual has been hurt or suffered personal abuse, there is a reflexive and understandable reaction of anger and outrage that must be acknowledged and worked through in the therapeutic setting.

I believe that an acceptance of one's sexuality is a vital part of the therapy process and essential to developing one's sense of self. I also believe that people need to develop their own personal value system; individuals can chart the course of their lives in a manner that is harmonious and well integrated when they formulate moral and ethical considerations from within themselves rather than from external sources. My approach also emphasizes the pursuit of transcendent goals that go beyond the narrow confines of self and family. By involving themselves in aspirations that have meaning beyond immediate gratification, people increase their capacity for feeling worthwhile and expand their life space (R. W. Firestone et al., 2003).

Last, I believe that the therapist should develop a personalized approach for each individual rather than applying a specific theoretical orientation to all clients (R. W. Firestone, 1997a, p. 164). This does not negate the therapist having a particular theoretical orientation or background of understanding but rather emphasizes a flexibility and openness regarding the unique needs of each client. Moreover, for effective therapy to take place, I believe the therapist must be sensitized to and able to access clients' special points of identity to help them to give value to themselves.

A comprehensive theory of psychopathology and a comparative mental health model combine to help therapists develop a treatment strategy for their clients. Human beings exist in a state of conflict between the active pursuit of their goals in the real world and the urge to live within an inward, self-protective defense system characterized by reliance on fantasy gratification and manifestations of self-nurturance. The greater damage individuals sustain early in life, the less willing they are to undertake the risks necessary for self-actualization. The resolution of this conflict in the direction of a self-nourishing lifestyle has a damaging effect on individuals' overall functioning.

The defended person's life is distorted by a desperate clinging to addictive attachments, a dependence on self-nourishing habit patterns, strong guilt reactions, low self-esteem, and a distrust of others, whereas a relatively undefended or mentally healthy individual is capable of responding to change, moving toward increased autonomy and more satisfying relationships. Both approaches to life have advantages as well as disadvantages. The "adjusted," albeit defended, person may feel less anxious and temporarily more secure; nevertheless, this adaptation has negative consequences in terms of a loss of personal freedom and a more constricted life. It often leads to new symptom formation or a recurrence of old patterns. The comparatively less defended individual generally feels more integrated, has a stronger identity, has a greater potential for intimacy, and is more humane toward others. However, being relatively free of symptoms and the compulsion to repeat familiar destructive patterns leaves a person with a sense of vulnerability and an awareness of and sensitivity to the events in life that impinge on one's well-being. The poignancy aroused can lead to an increase in death anxiety because, in being open, people are aware of investing in a life they must certainly lose.

The dilemma facing both therapist and client brings these two alternatives to the foreground. Endeavoring to live nondefensively is an ethical choice, given the inherent harm caused by defenses that limit one's capacity for living and feeling, which inevitably causes damage to loved ones. Ideally, an effective therapy would enable a person to discover a moral and compassionate approach toward oneself and others. My basic philosophy stresses the primary value of each client's unique personality, personal freedom, and potential for self-realization (see R. W. Firestone, 1988, Chapter 12, "The Dilemma of Psychotherapy," pp. 252–272).

THE THERAPEUTIC PROCESS

For the therapeutic process to lead to basic character change, it must involve making incisive therapeutic inroads into the client's defense system rather than focusing primarily on symptom reduction or minor shifts in defense mechanisms or addictions.

My therapeutic approach is twofold: (a) to challenge addictive attachments and self-nourishing habit patterns and (b) to encourage movement toward gratification and personal power in the external environment. I have found the methods and procedures described next to be valuable, as well as consistent with separation theory. These techniques are not used in any specific order, nor is there a regimented treatment plan implied for all clients.

Psychoanalytic Methodology

In my multidimensional approach to therapy, I generally use the techniques of psychoanalysis; free association, direct interpretation, and analysis of resistance and transference are essential components of my work. Furthermore,

I believe in the importance of long-term therapy, as contrasted with short-term approaches, which I feel do not do justice to the therapeutic process. It takes a sustained period to address deep-seated character defenses effectively, and without this effort there will be a tendency to revert to previous symptoms (R. W. Firestone, 2018; Note 4).

Historically, psychoanalysts were concerned with developing a method whereby they could obtain a free release of thoughts, as well as an emotional catharsis. They turned to free association as the "royal road to the unconscious" and believed that if the impulses and repressed emotions and memories were recovered, they could be integrated into the ego, and the client would ultimately benefit in the process. The use of free association permits clients to let their thoughts flow in a stream of consciousness unhampered by the rules of logic or censorship. Clients not only learn to think creatively but also come to understand on an emotional level that any thought or feeling is acceptable. At the same time, they are taught to examine the consequences of their behavior in regard to their own best interests and an overall moral perspective (Aron, 1996; Kris, 2013).

Feeling Release Therapy

Feeling release therapy uses techniques that elicit deeply repressed feelings and reawaken emotional pain from the past. It makes use of techniques similar in many respects to those of Arthur Janov's (1970) primal therapy, as described in *The Primal Scream* (Note 5). When applied appropriately, feeling release therapy can be a significant advance over free association as a procedure for recovering memories and experiences from one's childhood. It is more direct and allows for a fuller expression of feeling than traditional practices aimed at bringing unconscious material to the client's awareness.

When I began using the techniques of feeling release therapy, I found that many of my conceptions of the neurotic process were validated by the revelations and insights of clients, as they interpreted their own material and integrated it without assistance or interpretation from me. Because of this lack of therapeutic interference in the process, feeling release therapy has valuable research potential, which heretofore has been neglected by practitioners and theorists in the field.

Before the initial feeling release session, clients spend 24 hours in isolation and self-contemplation while writing down their thoughts and feelings. They are asked to avoid cigarettes, alcohol, and other painkilling and self-soothing substances or habits. The combined effect of prohibiting the use of substances and interrupting routines results in creating an immediate state of heightened tension and deprivation. This allows clients' emotions to become more easily accessible.

In the sessions, clients are encouraged to breathe deeply, allow sounds to emerge as they exhale, and verbalize any thoughts that come to mind. As feelings are released, clients are supported in amplifying this emotional expression. Many times during the process, they appear to genuinely relive events and feelings from early childhood. Afterward, clients are typically relaxed and self-reflective. They tend to form their own insights with unusual clarity, relating irrational or primitive emotional responses to negative experiences in their early lives. They then associate these to current-day limitations. Due to the lack of need for outside interpretation, transference reactions tend to be minimal during this phase.

The knowledge of self and personal understanding gained through feeling release sessions are surprisingly direct and pure. It is as though clients are able to step back into their childhoods and gain insight that fundamentally shifts their view of their present-day problems rather than intellectually "figuring them out" or analyzing them.

My experience working with a large number of individuals in feeling release therapy confirmed Janov's (1970) findings and supported his view that defenses are a protection against feeling primal pain. However, in contrast to Janov, who felt that repeated expression and release could empty the reservoir or "pool of primal pain" and lead to a "cure," our investigations showed that this "pool" cannot be emptied as such. If defenses formed early in relation to interpersonal traumas stood alone and were not reinforced by reactions to death anxiety, Janov's assumptions and hopes might have been realized. The dread of vulnerability and the fear of being overwhelmed by the irrational feelings characteristic of early childhood are reactivated later on when children become aware of their personal mortality. Once again, they are vulnerable and at the mercy of forces beyond their control. This is an existential reality that impacts people throughout life (R. W. Firestone, 1997a).

RESISTANCE IN PSYCHOTHERAPY

Resistance occurs in all forms of therapy and is indicative of an underlying fear and aversion to change (Cozolino, 2016; C. F. Newman, 2002; Note 6). It is at the core of the neurosis itself and is expressed in every aspect of the defended person's lifestyle. Resistant behavior ranges from the intense, at times aggressive, reactions and regressions manifested by psychotic patients to the more common forms of resistance exhibited by clients in psychotherapy. Everyone has an unwillingness to reach certain levels of differentiation. Although most people who seek professional help are dissatisfied with their current situation and want to feel better, they are often also heavily invested in a defended lifestyle, which inhibits their pursuit of a better life.

Overt and Covert Resistance

Clients' resistance in psychotherapy can take two different forms: overt or covert. The more overt behaviors include arriving late for appointments, manifesting inappropriate hostility toward the therapist, being delinquent in paying for therapy, or acting out self-nourishing or self-destructive behaviors outside the sessions. Other more covert or unconscious forms of resistance include the client's reluctance to explore painful repressed material, make positive changes in identity and relationships, and alter addictive behaviors.

In psychoanalysis and depth psychotherapy, clients may become antagonistic, refuse to free associate, or remain unwilling to explore and work through transference phenomena. They may be reluctant to reveal family secrets or express feelings with respect to the material they uncover or the insights they achieve. In voice therapy, which is described in Chapter 12, clients may become resistant to using the techniques that help them separate out discordant elements of the personality. They may find it difficult to articulate their self-attacks in the second person as outside attacks, and they may hold back significant feelings.

Resistance as Defined in Separation Theory

In addition to the specific types of resistance to psychotherapy noted earlier, separation theory focuses on the resistance related to maintaining defenses that protect the fantasy bond: the idealization of parents and family; the preservation of a corresponding negative self-image; the displacement of negative parental traits onto others and/or incorporating them into the self; a tendency to retreat from feeling; the development of an inward, self-protective posture; the withholding of positive emotional responses and adaptive behaviors; and a reliance on self-nourishing habits and routines. The therapist who understands these specific components of the fantasy bond can be alert to signs of opposition and negativity as the client's progress encroaches on these defenses (R. W. Firestone, 2018).

Unconscious separation anxiety and death anxiety constitute the ultimate opposition to therapeutic progress and a better life in general. In that sense, resistance and subsequent defensive behaviors act to prevent death fears from surfacing. Certain attitudes, defensive reactions, behaviors, and belief systems that support illusions of connection and safety help "cool down," in a manner of speaking, unconscious existential fears, whereas other events and circumstances exacerbate death anxiety, causing these emotions to "heat up." For example, fantasy bonds, substances, and even political affiliations or religious faith can be used to ease existential angst, whereas both especially fortunate circumstances and especially negative events can disrupt defensive adaptations, making one more aware of death's eventuality (R. W. Firestone, 2015). However, because defensive reactions to death anxiety are primarily put into motion before people become fully conscious that their anxiety has been aroused (Abeyta et al., 2014; Pyszczynski et al., 1999), it is often difficult for clinicians to identify the crucial events that trigger resistance and regression.

Effective psychotherapy helps clients face and work through the resistance aroused by challenging their defenses. Clients first learn to recognize and acknowledge their aversion to change and then come to understand its origin in the context of their lives. Becoming aware of their tendency to retreat to a defensive posture and challenging and overcoming their resistance to positive movement leaves clients more vulnerable, open, and better able to cope with life. In relation to existential issues, depth therapy enables clients to speak freely about and express the wide range of emotions related to their personal mortality. When people work through existential issues, they tend to place greater value on their lives.

THE EFFECTIVE THERAPIST

The personality of the therapist (Note 7) sets the tone, emotional quality, and strength of the therapeutic alliance (Note 8) between therapist and client and therefore cannot be divorced from the interventions described here. Ideally, therapists would exhibit integrity and personal honesty and be uncompromising in their approach to the defenses that limit and debilitate their clients. As a catalyst and facilitator, they would be sensitive to the wide range of addictive patterns manifested by their clients and have the courage to help expose and interrupt them (R. W. Firestone, 1990c, 1997a).

As emphasized earlier, effective therapists do not attempt to fit their clients into a particular theoretical framework or model. Instead, they are willing to experience the painful truths their clients reveal over the course of treatment and respond as clients' individual needs dictate. Because they are cognizant of the inherent destructiveness of personal defenses and their harmful reflection in society, therapists ideally would refrain from placing social conformity above the personal interests of their clients (Note 9).

Some therapeutic failures can be attributed to limitations imposed on the client by the therapist's own defensive adaptation. Resistance to addressing significant topics can be aroused in the client by damaging aspects of the therapist's personality, specifically, negative characteristics and defenses involving relational issues. When therapists are unaware of their own resistance, they may be unable to recognize the serious restrictions inflicted on the self by destructive internal forces and external social pressures (Schore, 2003; Note 10). The fact that the resultant impairment in the functioning of their client may fall within the range of statistical normalcy is not necessarily an indicator of mental health. A large percentage of people in our culture suffer from disturbances in their psychological functioning (McGinty et al., 2016; Note 11). This fact can obscure the recognition of pathological manifestations, causing both client and therapist to overlook dysfunctional behaviors and symptoms. To ameliorate the risk of their clients unknowingly yielding to a process of progressive limitation through conformity, it is imperative that the therapist be able to motivate their clients to identify and value the unique points of identity that make up their individual nature.

Therapists can be conceptualized as "transitional objects" in that they provide an authentic relationship for their clients during their shift from dependence on self-nourishing processes to seeking and finding satisfaction in genuine relationships in their interpersonal world. As such, therapists must remain human—that is, be interested, warm, caring, and empathic as well as direct and responsible—to temporarily support or sustain clients as they move away from sources of self-gratification toward real relationships. Effective therapists anticipate the termination phase by continually encouraging the independent development of healthy ego functioning in their clients. Excessive dependence on the therapist and attempts to seek fusion are discouraged; instead, transference reactions are interpreted and worked through with sensitivity and proper timing (Note 12).

Fundamentally, a therapist must have an understanding of the conditions that hurt children originally and that continue to detract from their humanness as adults. Viewed from this perspective, the therapist's task and the goal of therapy are self-evident. The therapist must maintain an intentional focus on helping their clients reconnect to themselves and their lives. To move toward this goal, the therapist must be attuned to their clients' authentic feelings, unique qualities, and priorities and help their client to distinguish those from the overlay on the personality that would prevent them from reaching their full potential for living (R. W. Firestone, 2018).

CONCLUSION

As indicated, I have used a multidimensional approach to psychotherapy in my work, consisting of psychoanalytic techniques, feeling release therapy, and voice therapy. As a basic part of my therapeutic effort, I have relied on the theory and methods of psychoanalysis. Free association allows clients to experience their emotions without the impediment of rational constraints or judgment and leads to a deep understanding of self-defeating behavior. Clients are then better able to consider the impact their decisions have on themselves and the world around them and realize the power they have to structure their lives accordingly.

I have also found feeling release therapy to be a significant tool in helping people understand themselves and their emotions. The method is an advance over free association as a technique for recovering traumatic experiences from childhood because it reveals memories in a more direct, feeling context. Clients are also able to interpret their own material and develop a clearer understanding of themselves. The insights that are unearthed verify basic dynamics that operated within their families of origin. This therapy offers a heightened awareness of how childhood experiences affect a client's current behavior. Feeling release sessions help a person become far less defensive and also facilitate a reduction in the tension and anxiety associated with repressing feeling (R. W. Firestone, 1990c).

With the help of therapy, people can challenge their basic character defenses. More significant, they can develop a tolerance for the inevitable discomfort and sense of aloneness that come from confronting destructive fantasy bonds. As they learn to accommodate to a more positive image of themselves and recover a realistic picture of their early lives (Note 13), their life will be enriched by coming to know and appreciate themselves as an individual.

12 VOICE THERAPY

No treatment could do any good until I understood the voice and saw that it was running me, that I was an automaton . . . I feel as if I've been reprieved from a lifelong sentence.

—From a patient's journal, James Masterson, *The Real Self*

The therapeutic method I developed is called "voice therapy" because it is a process of giving language to the negative thought process at the core of people's maladaptive or self-destructive behavior (R. W. Firestone, 2018; Note 1). Expressing voices in the second person format enables clients to separate their own point of view from the thoughts and attitudes antithetical to self and hostile toward others that were incorporated during their formative years. It also facilitates the expression of emotions associated with these negative introjects. The rationale underlying voice therapy is that of exposing the client's negative thoughts and the accompanying affect, forming insight into their sources in parental abuses and gradually modifying behavior toward one's stated goals in juxtaposition to the dictates of

https://doi.org/10.1037/0000268-013
Challenging the Fantasy Bond: A Search for Personal Identity and Freedom,
by R. W. Firestone

the voice. These procedures disrupt fantasies of fusion with the internalized parent by exposing voices that both aggrandize and punish the self and distort and deride others. They challenge each dimension of the fantasy bond and other self-limiting defenses. Breaking away from the imagined connection with parental figures allows a person to move toward independence and autonomy (R. W. Firestone, 1998, 1997a).

In a sense, individuals live in two different worlds, experiencing strong ambivalent feelings and entertaining contradictory viewpoints of the events in their lives. When the self is ascendant, people regard themselves, their loved ones, and others in warm, friendly, compassionate terms. When the anti-self is dominant, they are detached, cynical, and critical. While one part of them is generally open and vulnerable, the other sees life as meaningless and insignificant. From my theoretical vantage point, the critical inner voice keeps people locked into their defense system while their healthier side strives for freedom from the constraints of these defenses.

As the language of the anti-self, the voice opposes the expression of feeling, undermines rational thought, and sabotages the pursuit of real satisfaction and goals. It represents an unconscious, ongoing pattern of thought that acts to suppress feeling and motivates behavior that has negative, self-limiting, or self-destructive consequences. Hatred toward oneself is a direct result of this negative thought process. Even when voice attacks involve accurate content, their underlying intent is characterized by a mean, accusatory, and hostile tone. The inherent anger and aggression of the critical inner voice toward the self can be easily discerned when it is spoken aloud in voice therapy sessions.

HISTORICAL DEVELOPMENT OF VOICE THERAPY

As noted previously, in my early work with patients with schizophrenia and later in my private practice, I was pursuing my understanding of self-destructive processes (Note 2), but essential aspects were missing. However, in the early 1970s, when my associates and I began conducting psychotherapy groups, we were faced with material that deepened my comprehension of this issue (R. W. Firestone, 1988).

I became aware of the emotional pain that participants often experienced when they were confronted with certain types of feedback about themselves. They would have strong negative responses to selective aspects of the information and would feel bad or depressed afterward. Initially, I attributed this to the old adage "the truth hurts." But then I realized that the evaluations people overreacted to supported their distorted views of themselves and tended to activate an obsessive negative thought process. From these observations, I hypothesized that most people evaluate themselves in ways that are often negative and self-punishing. Thus, their reactions to external criticism are usually out of proportion to content, severity, or manner of presentation.

I thought it would be beneficial for people to become aware of the areas and issues about which they were especially sensitive and self-critical and be alert to the events that stimulated their self-attacks. Research into this subject matter became a significant part of my initial explorations of the techniques of voice therapy. In 1973, I formed a therapy group made up of a number of psychotherapists who were also interested in further investigating this issue and pooling our information. The ongoing study of the specific thought patterns associated with neurotic, repetitive behaviors and self-destructive actions and lifestyles led to further research on the mechanism of self-attack.

Concurrent with the therapists' group, my colleagues and I began studying the manifestations of the critical inner voice in our clients. From verbalizing their self-critical thoughts, clients learned that it was not the adverse circumstances in their lives that caused them the most discomfort; rather, it was their interpretation of these events. Early on, we were impressed by the ease with which clients not only grasped the idea of an internal self-attacking thought process but also with how they were able to apply this idea to their everyday lives. In sessions, our clients were surprised, even shaken, by the intensity of their self-attacks and by the degree to which this negative thought process undermined them, interfered with their ability to function effectively, and limited their satisfaction in life.

As participants in both groups continued to identify and express their self-attacks, they often launched into angry diatribes against themselves that they recognized as relating to specific experiences within their family of origin. They uncovered core defenses and well-established habit patterns that clearly originated in early traumatic circumstances. Some identified their self-criticisms as statements they had heard one or both parents make to them as children. Others recognized their voice attacks from attitudes that had been reflected in their parents' tone of voice, body language, or other behavioral cues.

My associates and I observed conspicuous changes in people's physical appearance and expression during voice sessions. These were especially apparent when there was a cathartic release of feeling while verbalizing voice attacks. People's bodies assumed postures and mannerisms that were uncharacteristic of their own. In some cases, when we were familiar with two generations of a family, we noted that the tone of voice and body language of a person became similar to their parent's, most commonly to those of the parent of the same sex. Phrasing and speech intonations underwent basic transformations and sometimes even took on the regional accent of the parent. It was as though the parental figure were living inside the person and could be brought out by this method.

As clients explored the attacks of their critical inner voices and expressed some of the repressed rage they had turned inward, they became aware of the extent to which they had accepted their self-destructive thoughts at face value. The affect that was often released with the exposure of the voice process relieved clients of the tension and anxiety caused by suppressing their emotions. Participants in the therapy groups found that there was considerable commonality in the content of the negative thinking that was being expressed.

I was also impressed that people in both groups arrived at their own insights and interpretations of the material revealed in their voice attacks. Their conclusions about the sources of their critical inner voice did not reflect an a priori interpretation by a therapist. People also became cognizant of how much the voice influenced them to maintain certain self-destructive attitudes and behaviors. These undesirable traits validated the negative self-image they had internalized as part of the original fantasy bond.

From these investigations, I reasoned that we were witnessing manifestations of parental warnings, directions, labels, definitions, and feelings. The hostile attitudes toward the self appeared to have been incorporated into a person's thinking process during the formative years. Eliciting the expression of the voice and the intense emotion that often accompanied it became a fundamental part of my methodology; it represented a more direct pathway to deeply repressed material in the unconscious. Moreover, my associates and I felt that the technique had potential as a research tool to study the unconscious cognitive processes involved in neurotic disorders, depression, and self-destructive or suicidal behaviors (R. W. Firestone, 1997b, 2018).

VOICE THERAPY METHODOLOGY

Voice therapy is a cognitive–affective–behavioral methodology that brings internalized destructive thought processes to consciousness with accompanying affect in a dialogue format such that clients can confront the alien components in their personality (Note 3). The basic techniques expose critical attitudes toward self and others, fantasies of fusion, and addictive, self-limiting patterns of behavior that interfere with clients' movement toward autonomy and independence.

The process of conceptualizing and articulating negative thoughts acts to lessen the destructive effect of the voice on the client's behavior. In voice therapy, clients learn to verbalize their ongoing internal dialogue, expose their self-attacks, challenge their negative attitudes toward self and others, and develop a more objective, nonjudgmental view of people and events in their lives. They become capable of distinguishing the cynical defensive attitudes they incorporated early in life from their actual point of view. In countering their internal criticisms and accusations with realistic appraisals of themselves, they improve their reality testing and attain mastery over the voice and its influence.

My approach to eliciting and identifying the contents of the voice is not didactic; that is, I do not directly try to persuade clients to think or behave rationally. Rather, I help them discover the contents of the voice's malicious coaching in various situations and attempt to assist them in moving away from these negative attitudes and prohibitions. The treatment process has five steps (summarized in Exhibit 12.1); however, they are not discrete and often overlap (R. W. Firestone, 2018).

Step 1: Verbalizing Critical Inner Voices

First, therapist and client discuss the client's self-critical thoughts and self-attacks. They may also review the client's hostile thoughts about a significant person in the client's life, often a romantic partner. Together, they identify the negative thought that is predominant or particularly hurtful. For example, a client may think, "I'm so shy. I'm socially awkward. I get nervous in social situations. I never know what to say." The therapist explains how to

---

EXHIBIT 12.1. The Five Steps of Voice Therapy

- Step 1: *Verbalizing critical inner voices.* Clients identify their critical thoughts and attitudes about self and others, express them in the second person format, and release any associated affect.

- Step 2: *Discussing voice attacks.* Clients discuss their thoughts and insights after verbalizing their voice attacks.

- Step 3: *Confronting voice attacks.* There are two aspects of implementing this process: (a) a cathartic approach that involves clients directly confronting voice attacks with strong emotions and (b) an analytic approach that involves clients offering a rational and realistic evaluation of their point of view.

- Step 4: *Understanding the impact of voice attacks.* Clients identify the negative impact the voice attacks are having on their present-day behavior, therapeutic goals, and desire to change.

- Step 5: *Challenging negative traits and behaviors.* Clients collaborate with the therapist in the planning and implementation of corrective behaviors to challenge negative traits and actions dictated by the voice.

verbalize these criticisms as voice attacks by expressing them in the second person, as though someone else were addressing them. For example, the client might say, "You're so shy. You're socially awkward. You get nervous in social situations. You never know what to say."

The therapist urges the client to continue to verbalize any other attacks that come up, with statements such as "Let go and say anything that comes to mind," making sure that any new voice attacks are articulated in the second person. When this format is used, strong affect and emotions usually accompany the self-attacks (Note 4). The therapist encourages the expression of these emotions with statements such as "Say it louder," or "Let yourself really feel that."

When clients are addressing voice attacks about a partner, it is helpful for them to think of their critical inner voice as a mean internal coach who is against both them and their mate. For example, when the thought "She doesn't care about me" is converted to "She doesn't care about you," it becomes an attack on both parties.

Step 2: Discussing Voice Attacks

In this step, clients discuss their reactions to verbalizing their voice with the therapist. The transition from emotionally expressing voice attacks to rationally reflecting on them often occurs naturally. Typically, after saying the voice, clients have their own insights and draw their own conclusions about the material that has been revealed. Becoming aware of this destructive internal process often leads to an overall feeling of clarity. Expressing the critical inner voice often reveals core negative beliefs that clients had previously only been vaguely aware of. They connect specific voices with identifiable parental attitudes and interactions that defined them, either explicitly or implicitly. As clients realize the cruelty of the negative views being directed toward them and trace the sources of these attitudes to experiences in their early lives, they develop compassion for themselves (R. W. Firestone, 1989, 1990b).

Step 3: Confronting Voice Attacks

Once clients have identified, verbalized, and reflected on the negativity of their critical inner voice, it is necessary for them to take their own side by confronting their internal enemy. In this step, they express their responses to the voice in the first person. The therapist encourages them to respond directly and forcefully to the attacks of the voice and assert their point of view. In following these prompts, clients often confront the voice as though addressing an actual person. Because clients tend to identify the voice in relation to parental figures, they often end up talking directly to their parents in a form of psychodrama.

In the cathartic approach, clients are emotional and irrational when expressing their feelings. When they first take a stand against the negative ways in which they have been viewing themselves, clients often experience intense emotions, including indignation, anger, or deep sadness.

In the analytic approach, clients respond with a more realistic, objective self-appraisal. When they use this rational approach, they confront the unreal basis of their voice attacks in a more logical way. It is beneficial for clients to use the rational approach after having experienced the cathartic one. Responding logically helps them make sense of their anger, sadness, or other strong reactions and encourages them to speak with the strength and authority of an adult.

Contradicting the voice by asserting one's point of view represents an assault on introjected parental images and is often emotionally akin to attacking the parents directly. As a result, it can cause a buildup of tension and self-recrimination. Voicing these angry, hostile feelings toward parental introjects tends to disconnect a client from imagined or symbolic sources of security, and regressive trends may follow. Therefore, I recommend discouraging the emotional cathartic method for clients who appear to lack sufficient ego strength to cope with the resultant guilt and anxiety. In these cases, a nondramatic evaluation of voice attacks on a cognitive level is less threatening while still serving the purpose of separating from destructive elements (Note 5).

Step 4: Understanding the Impact of Voice Attacks

Clients attempt to understand the relationship between their voice attacks and their self-limiting and self-destructive behavior patterns. They identify how the voice has influenced the constraints that they impose on themselves in everyday life. Becoming aware of self-imposed restrictions is empowering and reduces paranoid reactions to others and feelings of victimization.

Clients also evaluate the truth or falsity of their self-criticisms; that is, they subject their voices to a process of reality testing. Although people's negative thoughts toward themselves may contain accurate elements of their undesirable behaviors or personality traits, angry affect toward and malicious attacks on the self are always unjustified. Self-evaluations that are realistically negative yet objective and based on the underlying premise that people can change even long-standing character traits are fundamentally different from voices that categorize a person as inherently defective.

During this phase of therapy, clients learn that it is not appropriate to berate themselves for shortcomings or weaknesses; rather, it is more productive to adopt a compassionate attitude toward themselves while working on modifying behaviors they dislike.

Step 5: Challenging Negative Traits and Behaviors

Interventions that affect the client's everyday life are a vital part of a successful therapy. Therapeutic progress is more than a function of freeing repressed material and interpreting it; it must also involve a process of adjusting one's life on an action level. In this final phase of voice therapy, client and therapist attempt to interrupt maladaptive behavior patterns through collaborative planning for changes that are in accord with the client's personal motivation. Corrective procedures involve changes in clients' behavior that lead to a more goal-directed approach to living.

The process of confronting the voice helps shed light on the client's specific point of view and what has meaning for them. This makes clear which new actions and activities clients can engage in that more accurately reflect who they are, free of the influence of their critical inner voice. Therapists can encourage clients to choose one or two goals to concentrate on while supporting realistic objectives that will increase the likelihood of lasting positive change.

Corrective behaviors fall into five general categories, including (a) those that help control self-feeding habits and dependency behavior, (b) those that break into inwardness and involvement in fantasy, (c) those that control noxious or provoking behavior and interfere with withholding patterns, (d) those that explore a new identity and encourage overcoming fears, and (e) those that challenge destructive fantasy bonds (R. W. Firestone, 1997a).

Corrective behaviors, if consistently implemented, bring about changes that lead to a corrective emotional experience (Note 6). Even though this final step of voice therapy appears to be straightforward and practical, it can be challenging. The new set of circumstances, although more positive, is unfamiliar and initially arouses anxiety. Resistance may arise when a particular behavior impacts a well-established defense, even when it was instituted by the client. For this reason, the therapist must pay attention to the proper timing of the initiation of corrective suggestions and carry out a thorough follow-up of the client's reactions.

Clients report that although they often experience strong voice attacks after significant positive behavioral changes, these self-attacks gradually diminish after the new behavior has been maintained over an extended period. It is important for therapists to teach clients to "sweat through" the anxiety initiated by changes in their actions and style of relating. Only by coping with the anxiety generated by positive change can clients maintain the psychological territory they have gained.

Corrective behaviors, undertaken in a timely, carefully monitored, and skillful manner, progressively desensitize clients to the anxiety and pain involved in breaking fantasy bonds, changing their identity, and expanding their lives. Taking action to implement these behaviors teaches people on a deep emotional level that they can apply rational thought and insight to control their defensive responses. By using self-discipline to increase freedom of choice, they are moving away from compulsively repeating past experiences.

TRANSCRIPT FROM A VOICE THERAPY SESSION

In this excerpt from a voice therapy session, a 40-year-old woman explores the voice attacks that are sabotaging her in her career (Note 7).

THERAPIST (LF): So you were saying at work there's been more and more challenges.

CLIENT (KJ): The thing that's interesting is that I've been with this company for 2 years. And it's exciting, and I'm doing work that I feel is really valuable and meaningful to me personally, which is exhilarating. And I'm working with very smart people, and that's great. But because it's a very small staff and we're trying to do a lot of really big things, sometimes it's like, "Oh, my God! What am I going to do?" And we do new things all the time.

Step 1: Verbalizing Critical Inner Voices

THERAPIST: Is there a current challenge that's come up?

CLIENT: Now we're starting to do a weekly column in a local journal, so that's a new weekly thing. I always wanted to be a writer, but now I'm being asked to write all the time. And I'm not writing for other people. I'm getting my own byline, and that makes me feel very anxious. And, like, I don't know what I'm doing. I'm not a journalist. I mean, I know how to write. I can write a good sentence. But nobody cares about what I have to say. That's my attack.

THERAPIST: Try putting that as a voice. Say those same attacks as "you" statements, like someone is saying them to you—like, "You don't know what you're doing."

CLIENT: Okay. Like, who the hell do you think you are? You don't have anything interesting to say. Nobody gives a shit what you have to say. Nobody cares at all what you have to say! You're just nothing. You're just like this chatty little voice. What gives you the right to have an opinion about anything? And what if you're wrong? What if you write something that nobody thinks is interesting? What if you make a mistake? And now your name is on it. That's going to be so humiliating. Who the hell do you think you are? You don't have any right to say anything. You should just go back to crunching numbers. This is ridiculous.

THERAPIST: There's a lot of feeling behind that. If you just let that go and said anything.

CLIENT: Is it okay if I curse?

THERAPIST: Yes. It's very okay. The voice doesn't come out in nice words.

CLIENT: You don't have a degree in journalism. Nobody gives a shit what you have to say. You better find the right source. You better find a good source. You better couch your terms in accurate language. Oh, you're going to be so humiliated. How can you even think that you could do this? Oh, my God! Who does he [her boss] think you are? Why is he asking you to do this? What's he trying to get from you by giving you all this responsibility? He's going to try to take advantage of you in some way. Oh, my God! This is just terrible! You better stop! You're going to fuck up. You better not do this anymore.

It's interesting because then there's an attack also on my boss because he's giving me this. Because he actually is looking to me to give these things, it's like there's something wrong with him or he's going to come after me in some way, or he's trying to get something out of me that I don't have to give.

THERAPIST: It's a real attack on him, too.

CLIENT: It's an attack on him. It's, like, oh, my God, he's such a joke. He thinks you have something to offer. He must be a total joke, or else he's trying to get something out of you. You know, there's got to be something wrong. Who the hell is this person? Who is this guy? What's he trying to get from you? Why's he trying to build you up? What's he looking for? You better be careful!

Which is interesting because that's not the dynamic between us at all. If anything, there's, like, almost a mentor type of relationship. But he's asking me to do things that I don't think I'm able to do but he thinks I'm able to do. It triggers voices about him.

THERAPIST: Very suspicious.

CLIENT: Yeah. Like, you better watch yourself. You better watch yourself because you're going to get out on a limb, and you're either going to have to do something that you're not prepared to do, or, or he's going to leave you high and dry, and you're going to be humiliated. And you're going to fall to the bottom of nothing, and you better watch out because you're going to be so fucking humiliated. You better watch out!

That's like the warning, you know.

Step 2: Discussing Voice Attacks

THERAPIST: Where do you think those attitudes come from towards this guy?

CLIENT: Well, I mean, it's a suspicion of men in general. Especially because I'm being asked to be an equal, which is really different from how my mother saw the world. With her, it was, like, "If you're in a situation with a man who has power, then you better watch out." That's my voice. "If you're in a situation with a man who has power over you and he's asking you to do these things, he's building you up; it's not because he thinks you're smart. It's not because he thinks you have something to offer. It's because he's going to want you to either sleep with him or do something and you're going to be in a situation and it's disgusting! You better watch your back." That's the attack.

This is her [mother's] attitude absolutely; that's what it feels like. I don't feel like this is my attitude, and that's definitely not the dynamic in my current work relationship. It's not that at all. It's very respectful and very supportive. My mother had this worldview about women: that the only way for women to get ahead in this world is you have to be manipulative; you have to look right and look the part, and you have to act like you enjoy everything, you have to cater to the men. Those voices are like, "You have to make men feel good about themselves. You better stroke his ego. You want to get ahead? If you want to make sure you are all right and you want to keep this job, you better stroke his fucking ego. And you've got to manipulate him. And you better be strategic. You better be strategic here. Don't enjoy this too much, don't lose control or you're going to lose everything. You got to stay on top of it. You got to make sure that he knows that you're valuable and you got to position yourself right."

I don't know; it's so crazy. It's so creepy because it's so not who I feel like I am.

Step 3: Confronting Voice Attacks

THERAPIST: So if you were going to answer back to it, what would you say back?

CLIENT: I would say, first of all, I totally reject that perspective. The way that you're seeing the workplace is so wrong, and that's like 1955. That's not this decade, you know. There's none of that in my life. I feel like I'm just a person. It's not like men are one thing and women are another thing. That's not my reality at all. And I would say that it's great to have a good time doing what you're doing. I mean, that's what's wonderful. Why I've been as successful as I've been in this particular job is because I really love what I'm doing, and I bring that into everything. And that's what I've been acknowledged for.

THERAPIST: What's the real truth about why he's giving you all of these things to do?

CLIENT: It's because I can do these things and because I have these skills and I have these talents. And, actually, I am a good writer, and I am a creative person, and I can put things together in a way that makes sense, and, while maybe I didn't realize it, this is part of what I was hired to do. To help shape the message that we're creating. And I have the ability to do that because I understand story, and I understand narrative. So, nothing weird is going on. I can do it. And that's why I'm being asked to do these things—because I can. And I do it well. And I would also say that I've earned my place. It's not like a gift, or it's not like somebody's trying to get something from me because I've earned what I've gotten because I work hard and I do the job, and I am competent at what I'm doing. It's not like I'm manipulating or strategic or anything. I'm just moving forward, you know.

And then in relation to speaking out, I mean, well, first of all, I do have something to say, and I can articulate my position well. And I think I am relatable, so it's not bizarre that people would want to hear what I have to say. All of the reactions I've gotten haven't been what my voice is afraid of. They've been positive, like, "Good work; keep going." I haven't heard anything like "You're an idiot." In fact—it's so hard to say positive things—I would say that I am intelligent, and I do understand how things work. Not only that, but I have a unique perspective that is valuable. And it's not just because of the schooling and the reading that I've done. But it's also because of the way that I've learned to deal with people. And that's something that's valuable. And so those are valuable things. And I am able to write about it in a way that makes sense to other people. So that's a good thing. It's so hard to say the positive things.

THERAPIST: It's important to do that, too.

CLIENT: It made me sad to say that thing about having a unique perspective being a valuable thing.

THERAPIST: You're valued for who you really are instead of something you're trying to do to somebody.

CLIENT: Part of the attack, I think, is that I'm scheming in some way. Or there's a suspicion of me in some way, like, "Who are you? Why did you end up in this situation?" It's like I've gone beyond what I was supposed to do. What I was supposed to do was this little box: "You were supposed to be a secretary. That's a good role for you. You're a good support person." But now, I'm in a leadership role. I'm in a forward-facing role, and I'm not supposed to be here.

THERAPIST: Even though what you would probably say—what you really want is more of that kind of position.

CLIENT: Yeah, exactly. And I've worked hard to try to get into that kind of position. I wasn't satisfied when I was in a support role. Not that there's anything wrong with that. It didn't fit my personal ambition, partly because I love working with other people. I love mentoring people. I love writing. I love writing to a broad audience. I like creating interesting stories. I like sharing information. I like educating, and I'm getting allowed to do that in my job.

Step 4: Understanding the Impact of Voice Attacks

THERAPIST: How are these ways of thinking and these voices affecting you in your life today?

CLIENT: Where the voice hurts me is it makes me less effective and less productive, and it makes it harder to do the work that I'm doing. So, instead of just sitting down and being able to draft a script, I'm too much in my head, and I can't even get the first draft out. It's like pulling teeth. It's like I'm battling against the voice, and it's a painful experience instead of a joyful one. When I am myself, it is a joyful experience because when I forget the attacks, I really love writing. And sometimes, it takes me a long time to forget the attacks. But if I power through, I finally get to something, and then I get in the flow and know that it'll be good. And that's for me how the creative process works. But I feel like if I didn't have the attacks and I could just go right into the creative process, my life would be so much easier.

Step 5: Challenging Negative Traits and Behaviors

THERAPIST: So what are some actions you could take that might help and that would be going against the voices? It sounds like you're powering through it, but you're fighting with the voices.

CLIENT: Yeah. Maybe to start with, I could sit down and spend a few minutes actually writing out my voices and then answer them back. Yeah, yeah. Like if I'm feeling anxious about what I have to say, I could write the attack—like, "You have nothing to say." And then I could confront it, saying, "Yes, I do." That might actually be helpful to spend 5 minutes of cleansing writing; that would be good. And also, I think having this session will help because some of these things I didn't know were there.

THERAPIST: And you know, getting centered in yourself before you start—like, "It's okay to be just me. All I'm supposed to do here is be me."

CLIENT: Probably a mantra I should start: All I have to do is be me.

After reading about voice therapy, Jason Chapman, 35, wrote this heart-felt poem describing the treacherous nature of voice attacks.

Dear voices . . . Goodbye.

You've been with me for all my years,
I never knew who you really were.
Haunting voices without a name,
Are you me? Are you real? Am I insane?
I live in fear, do I exist? Myself I just can't find,
Your loving hate towards me,
An agonizing double bind.
You fill me with your toxic shame,
Your guilt, your fear, and how to take the blame.
You've taught me how to fear success,
And believe I've failed, having done my best.
Sometimes I voice my protest,
At what you say to me,
But you're always there to lead me back
Where you need me to be.
This has to stop, you won't agree,
You can't live on inside of me.
For the ugly truth I'm grateful,
and it's this that sets me free,
We have to go our separate ways,
It's time to live as me.

VOICE THERAPY APPLIED TO COUPLES

Voice therapy can be applied to couples as well as individuals. In conjoint sessions, partners first formulate the problem they perceive is limiting their satisfaction in the relationship and then proceed through the same five steps used in individual voice therapy sessions. Each partner, in turn, verbalizes

(a) voice attacks toward themselves and their partner; (b) negative attitudes they believe their partner has toward them; and (c) criticisms they believe their parents might have about them, their partner, and their life. They also express any feelings that surface while articulating these destructive thoughts and viewpoints. In a real sense, they are sharing in each other's individual psychotherapy (R. W. Firestone, 2018; R. W. Firestone & Catlett, 1999).

Partners can participate in sessions together from the beginning, or the therapist may determine that the couple would benefit first from individual sessions where they might feel less inhibited in expressing their angry, hostile voice attacks. In exposing their self-attacks and releasing the accompanying emotions, partners learn the specific ways they distort each other and are then able to take back their projections. By exploring the connections between their early experiences in the family of origin and their current interactions with one another, they are better able to distinguish between their distortions and the real characteristics and behaviors manifested by their partner. They also learn to assess their own assets and liabilities realistically. This process leads to an acceptance of ambivalent feelings toward themselves and their partner and, therefore, offers a more stable and honest perspective.

Even if a voice attack toward one's partner has some reality, clients are asked to focus on the source of the attack within themselves and relinquish any hostile or blaming attitudes toward the other. Partners discuss the insights they developed and attempt to understand the relationship between their voice attacks and behaviors that create conflict within the couple. They come to understand the sources of the limitations that have been affecting their relationship. By tracing the origin of their destructive attitudes back to early family interactions and witnessing their partner doing the same, clients develop a new perspective on one another's problems and learn to feel empathy for their mates and compassion for themselves (R. W. Firestone, 2018; R. W. Firestone & Catlett, 1999).

VOICE THERAPY APPLIED TO DIFFERENTIATION

When clients want to clarify their point of view about an area in which they are struggling, it is helpful to focus on a parent's point of view in that area. This can include exploring a parent's opinion of specific people or situations, as well as the overarching attitude that parent has toward various aspects of life and the world more broadly. We have found a slight variation in voice therapy techniques to be particularly useful in this endeavor.

This application involves more direction from the therapist; instead of encouraging the client to express their voices and the client then coming to conclusions as to the source, the therapist would, for example, as an adjunct to Step 1, ask the client specifically to express the point of view of one of their parents or a significant family member using the voice therapy format. The client would attempt to reveal that person's point of view in the second person, as though the person were speaking directly to them. The therapist might suggest, "What would your father say about relationships?" The client would respond with something such as "He'd say, 'Relationships are only good at the beginning. If you get married, you're stuck. Be careful. Don't commit to anyone; people always change. You'll both end up getting bitter and resentful after a while.'"

Differentiation from the destructive attitudes of one's parents and other significant figures in one's childhood is essential to pursuing a self-directed and fulfilling life (R. W. Firestone et al., 2012). In the book *The Self Under Siege* (R. W. Firestone et al., 2012), my colleagues and I examined in detail and elaborated on this important subject. As Murray Bowen pointed out, "In a poorly differentiated family, the high intensity of emotionality and together-ness pressure does not permit the child to grow, to think, feel, and act for himself" (Kerr & Bowen, 1988, p. 96; Note 8).

My work has a philosophical basis regarding the ethics of how people might choose to live if they understood how psychological defenses interfere with their ability to formulate and be guided by their values and ideals. Much of what we consider to be our identity or "self" is not truly representative of our own wants, goals, and values. Instead, it often reflects the wants, priorities, and ideals of others. Are we following our own destiny, or are we unconsciously repeating the lives of our parents and automatically living according to these values, ideals, and beliefs? Most people rarely, if ever, consider these questions in relation to how they are conducting their lives. They implicitly trust that their ideas, emotions, beliefs, and ethical principles are their own. They fail to recognize that they have not become emancipated or differentiated from their families of origin and, as a result, are often "channeling" other people's thoughts, feelings, and value judgments.

As noted in Chapter 1, differentiation is an essential part of psychotherapy. There are two aspects of the socialization process that indicate the detrimental impact of a lack of differentiation. The first and most crucial is that the introjection of negative, self-destructive attitudes and related defenses has, in effect, a primary causal relationship in psychopathology. The second aspect relates to the problem of formulating one's own goals, values, and ideals and thereby establishing a separate and unique identity.

The undermining effect of diverse forms of early programming on one's ability to maintain a unique outlook and sense of morality is powerful. It is an ongoing challenge to remain creative, independent, and inner directed as opposed to outer directed. It is necessary to make every effort to differentiate from internalized harmful influences to fulfill one's personal destiny and make full use of one's life and lifetime.

In psychotherapy, the process of differentiation encompasses four tasks. People need to (a) break with internalized thought processes (i.e., critical, hostile voices toward self and others); (b) separate from negative personality traits incorporated from their parents; (c) relinquish patterns of defense formed as an adaptation to painful events in their childhood; and (d) develop their own values, ideals, and beliefs rather than automatically accepting those they have grown up with (R. W. Firestone et al., 2012).

Voice therapy is particularly useful in the process of differentiation. Revealing their parent's critical attitudes toward them in the second person format enables clients to more fully recognize the impact of the incorporated parental point of view on their current behavior. In the process, they not only identify their critical inner voice but also become aware of the specific negative traits of their parents that they have taken on as their own.

Clients are further able to differentiate their own point of view when they respond to these attacks from their own perspective. For example, in the session with KJ, facing her anger toward her mother and confronting her mother's views regarding the dynamics between women and men strengthened her point of view and helped dispel the doubts she had about herself as an intelligent, capable woman. As a result, it became easier for her to assume a leadership position at work. On follow-up, she reported having become increasingly open and trusting in relation to the men in her workplace and personal life, an orientation very different from that of her mother.

The process of becoming a differentiated person is a lifelong project. It involves separating from the internalized negative elements within one's personality that interfere with the fulfillment of one's unique potential. It means learning to accommodate to the anxiety and guilt aroused by having one's own point of view and living according to one's own ideals and ethical principles (R. W. Firestone et al., 2012).

EVALUATION OF VOICE THERAPY

Voice therapy is a psychotherapy technique originally developed to elicit and identify clients' negative thoughts and attitudes toward self, bringing them more into conscious awareness. As a therapeutic methodology, clinical observations, both during and following sessions, have shown it to be effective in gaining access to core negative beliefs and other defenses and facilitating movement away from maladaptive behaviors. The technique has been applied in individual therapy, group therapy, couples therapy, problems in sexual relating (Note 9), and parenting groups (Note 10). It has also been the foundation of creating assessment instruments for evaluating suicide and violence potential (R. W. Firestone, 2018).

The steps of voice therapy satisfy the two key elements that neuroscientists have found to be necessary for change to be brought about in the brain's networks of neurons (Zull, 2004): practice and emotion. Every action either strengthens or weakens connections in the brain. The more often neurons are used, the more frequently they fire and the stronger their connections become. Neurons that are rarely or never used eventually die. Therefore, any action strengthens existing pathways in the brain, and if the activity is new, it builds new pathways.

Voice therapy enables clients to identify the actions that will successfully rewire their brains. By stopping destructive behaviors instigated by the critical inner voice, clients weaken the old neurological connections in the brain. In addition, by identifying and initiating behaviors that reflect their point of view, clients strengthen existing connections and lay down new neural pathways that can lead to long-term change.

Discoveries in interpersonal neurobiology have revealed that the experience of emotion has a double impact: It causes neurons to fire, and it causes the release of adrenaline, serotonin, and dopamine in the brain. These emotional chemicals stimulate change in the brain's circuitry, helping neuronal networks become stronger, larger, and more complex, especially neuronal networks in the right brain (Schore, 2003, 2011, 2018; Welling, 2012; Note 11). In voice therapy, clients experience deep feelings when they verbalize their critical inner voices and again when they answer back to voice attacks from their own point of view.

As is true in most psychotherapies, at the point where clients become aware that present-day limitations are closely related to early experiences in the family, feelings of anger, grief, and outrage are aroused. Some clients tend to turn these emotions against themselves. Regression may occur, and there may be a corresponding breakdown in the therapeutic relationship. However, with voice therapy and a thorough understanding of the theory underlying it, therapists can help clients get through these critical, regressive phases in their therapy (R. W. Firestone, 1990a, 2018).

Therapists can help clients investigate and comprehend their attachment history and how it influences the way they relate to the people in their lives today. Voice therapy helps to reveal the dynamics of their early relationship with their parents, thereby providing insight into the attachment strategies they formed in adapting to specific parental deficiencies. The understanding of their childhood that clients gain from voice therapy helps create a coherent narrative of their attachment history. Developing a coherent narrative rewires the brain as it integrates emotional processes in the right brain with rational, cause-and-effect thinking in the left brain.

Voice therapy can be a valuable tool for developing more secure attachments or "earned security" (Note 12). In building a trusting therapeutic alliance (i.e., a secure base) with the therapist, clients gradually change how they feel about themselves, modify defensive attachment strategies, and gradually develop more satisfying relationships. Psychotherapeutic progress does not eliminate conflict or pain in life; however, it does reduce much unnecessary self-inflicted suffering. The therapeutic process confronts self-limiting defenses and offers human beings the alternative to live with sensitivity, dignity, and self-respect while coping with the pressures of the interpersonal environment and the limitation of mortality.

CONCLUSION

Voice therapy is a broadly based methodology derived from a systematic theory of neurosis. The procedures challenge defenses, break into destructive bonds, and support clients' gradual relinquishing of the authority of the voice as an antifeeling, antilife regulatory mechanism. Voice therapy is not practiced as a rigid system applied to all individuals seeking therapy. Rather, the method is adapted to the specific requirements of each client. Although best used as a long-term treatment plan, the specialized techniques of voice therapy have been used effectively as a short-term adjunct in other treatment programs and with therapists whose approaches were based on different theoretical models.

The client's movement toward individuation must be supervised with care and diligence, as well as with a deep understanding of personality dynamics. Moreover, the therapist applying these techniques must come to understand each client's particular areas of resistance. Each step in voice therapy exposes and challenges basic character defenses, internal processes of fantasy gratification, and debilitating fantasy bonds. Therefore, resistance may be encountered at any phase of treatment.

As clients proceed through the steps of voice therapy, they come to understand how their critical inner voice is a limiting factor in their lives. They develop a clearer awareness of their point of view and personal goals. As a result, they develop more compassion for themselves and focus on making choices to defy voice commands and change their habitually destructive habit patterns.

The inimical forces within the personality must be exposed and countered for clients to have the opportunity to develop freely as individuals. It is the therapist's task to help clients realize, on an emotional level, that, as adults, they have substantial control over their lives and that, despite any feelings they uncover, they can no longer be overwhelmed and impacted by them as they once were when they were children.

Ideally, an effective psychotherapy would enable clients to discover an implicit moral approach toward themselves and other human beings. It would allow the client a means through which they could, in effect, become an explorer, uncritically accepting and examining their most irrational thoughts and feelings while at the same time viewing others and the world with real curiosity and concern. They would come to live life as a continuous process of discovery and adventure while respecting the boundaries and freedom of others. Through counteracting the dictates of the voice and disrupting fantasy bonds, the therapeutic venture offers the opportunity for clients to fulfill their human potential, thereby giving life its special meaning (R. W. Firestone, 1990b).

PART **V** **THEORETICAL ISSUES**

13 DEATH ANXIETY

The irony of man's condition is that the deepest need is to be free of the anxiety of death and annihilation; but it is life itself which awakens it, and so, we must shrink from being fully alive.

—Ernest Becker, *The Denial of Death*

The curse of awareness and imagination is that we, as human beings, are self-conscious animals and are therefore able to ponder our beginning and our end. The capacity to conceptualize and imagine is at once a strength and a weakness. It sets us above and apart from other animals with unusual artistic sensitivity and power, yet it leaves us the only creature who is obsessed and tortured by the prospect of our eventual death. As a result, we try to evade the anxiety this awareness causes us through some form of denial (Becker, 1973/1997, 1975; R. W. Firestone, 1994; R. W. Firestone & Catlett, 2009a; R. W. Firestone & Solomon, 2018; Solomon et al., 2015; Note 1).

https://doi.org/10.1037/0000268-014
Challenging the Fantasy Bond: A Search for Personal Identity and Freedom,
by R. W. Firestone

On a conscious level, people are aware of their personal end; they know, intellectually, that they will die someday. Yet, on an emotional level, most people deny this knowledge. Many human endeavors and behaviors are shaped by the desperate attempt to avoid the reality of this limitation in time, yet the fear of death can never be fully quieted or dismissed. In our attempt to avoid the full impact of death's inevitability, we find solutions that bring our imaginations into play (R. W. Firestone, 1985).

Existential dread impels us to form illusory connections, hoping to recapture the infantile sense of safety, security, and omnipotence provided by the original fantasy bond. We are subconsciously looking to a significant person or another external source to guarantee us immortality much as we imagined our parent could. The fantasy bond that was formed originally to cope with separation anxiety becomes the primary defense against death anxiety. In this manner, the fantasy of being merged with another person, group, or cause provides us with the false assurance that we will live forever (R. W. Firestone, 1984, 1985).

There are a number of defenses we enlist to ward off death anxiety (Bassett, 2007; R. W. Firestone, 1985, 1997a, 1997b; R. W. Firestone et al., 2003). We attempt to gain control over death through a process of progressive self-denial; that is, we deprive ourselves of experiences that would enhance our lives and give them value. We strive for immortality through our creative powers, attempting to live on through our children or sacrificing ourselves to a cause. We seek to please a higher power with the hope of attaining some form of life after death. We give up on the most meaningful aspects of our lives to have less to lose.

An analogy can be made to the convict on death row who commits suicide in his cell before he can be executed. In taking his own life, he is regaining some sense of mastery over his death. In the same manner, people slowly give up their lives by withdrawing feeling or affect from personal pursuits and goal-directed activity to maintain a false sense of control and omnipotence (R. W. Firestone, 1997b, 2000; R. W. Firestone & Catlett, 2009a; R. W. Firestone & Seiden, 1987). For this reason, many people unconsciously adhere to self-destructive habit patterns and an unfulfilling, inward lifestyle (Note 2).

Individuals shift the problem of death to the periphery of their consciousness, as does society as a whole, by isolating the phenomenon. Often, when death does come, they have unknowingly retreated from many aspects of living that are personally relevant—that is, from the relationships, work, or play that once gave them pleasure. It takes courage to live fully in the face of death, and without conscious effort, there is always the risk of ceding to a self-protective lifestyle.

DEVELOPMENT OF DEFENSES AGAINST DEATH ANXIETY

The formation of the fantasy bond and the child's increasing dependence on it may well be the most significant developmental process of early childhood. This core defense protects the infant and young child from being overwhelmed by the intensity of their reactions to disturbing events in early life. As noted earlier, in the first weeks and months of life, the helpless, dependent infant is faced with feelings of separation anxiety, frustration, and emotional pain that can reach intolerable proportions (Cozolino, 2006/2014; Winnicott, 1952; Note 3). According to D. J. Siegel (1999/2020),

> In the case of traumatic separation or loss of a loved one, especially an attachment figure, the mind is forced to alter the structure of its internal working models to adjust to the painful reality that the self can no longer seek proximity and gain comfort from the caregiver. . . . The effects of unresolved loss or trauma in relation to specific overwhelming events can be powerfully disorganizing and often hidden from conscious awareness. (pp. 405–406)

The essence of the fantasy bond lies in the child's deeply held belief in their inner world of fantasy in which time has no meaning, there are no separations, and everything is permanent and secure, including one's life and the lives of one's loved ones. The sequence of events in an infant's life is such that this illusion of power is actually reinforced by reality. Because their needs and wants are met frequently enough, young babies are conditioned to associate their desires with their caretaker's act in satisfying those desires. This association of needs and their subsequent satisfaction—even though sometimes delayed—sets up the conditions necessary to further affirm these fantasies of invincibility and self-containment. It verifies their illusion that they are capable of controlling their physical environment; in particular, it reassures them that they can control their caretaker.

By the time children come to the realization that their parents are vulnerable to death, they already have at their disposal this well-developed system of defenses. To avoid the new threat to their security, they generally regress to the stage when they were still unaware of this fracture or separation. They use their illusion of pseudo-independence to reassure themselves that even in the event of their parents' death, they could take care of themselves. Soon, however, they discover that they, too, must die, that they cannot sustain their own lives; that is, they become aware of their ultimate helplessness in relation to life itself. At this critical point of futility, their sense of omnipotence is deeply wounded. People rarely completely recover from this blow. When children are faced with the reality of death, the permanence that they once felt is forever altered (Slaughter & Griffiths, 2007; Note 4).

This new knowledge leads to a strengthening of a person's defenses by returning to the fantasy of connectedness with the primary caretaker, an illusion that alleviates their sense of helplessness. In believing that they can somehow cheat death, they hold on to their infantile feelings of omnipotence. Remnants of this infantile fantasy exist within each adult, and indeed, most people are reluctant to give up the unconscious notion that they can achieve immortality through a connection with significant people or events in their lives. The trauma of the realization of death remains in a person's unconscious, and the repression of this anxiety has a broad-reaching effect throughout their life span (Solomon et al., 2015).

TRIGGERS OF DEATH ANXIETY

Reminders of death, both direct and indirect, threaten to unlock the trauma that was suppressed in childhood (R. W. Firestone, 2015). As described in Chapter 9, both negative and positive events can trigger the awareness of death and thus arouse death anxiety. In everyday life, commonplace occurrences provide constant reminders of mortality. The news media report tragedies, acquaintances are diagnosed with serious diseases, and young children ask questions about what happens when you die. The most obvious way that death awareness is brought to consciousness is through direct reminders and actual events. These can be blatant, such as driving past a fatal car accident, or subtler, such as overhearing someone comment, "My mother is going for another scan, and I'm so worried her cancer has come back."

Positive events can also arouse death anxiety; a unique achievement or personal success causes people to give more value to themselves and their lives (R. W. Firestone, 1994). In particular, death anxiety is often triggered when experiencing special closeness and intimacy in a loving relationship. As elucidated in Chapter 10, love and physical satisfaction remind individuals of the fragility of the physical body and life itself (R. W. Firestone et al., 2006; Note 5).

DEFENSES AGAINST DEATH ANXIETY

The fear of death includes many different aspects of emotion and thought. Death may be conceived of as an annihilation of the self, a discontinuing of consciousness for eternity. There is a natural trepidation when contemplating physical and mental deterioration or the pain of losing loved ones or the dread of being alone. There is the all-too-human reaction of despair and rage in relation to situations and conditions over which one has no control. Consequently, death anxiety is a powerful force in shaping the human experience.

Although death anxiety includes a broad spectrum of painful emotions, my definition involves both the conscious and unconscious reactions to the fact that life is terminal and that individuals face total separation from their loved ones (Klackl et al., 2013; Pyszczynski et al., 2006; Shaver & Mikulincer, 2012; Note 6). My hypotheses about the impact of death anxiety have been validated by empirical data accumulated over the past 35 years by researchers in terror management theory. For example, studies by Sheldon Solomon et al. (2015) in which death salience was experimentally manipulated demonstrated people's increased reliance on defense mechanisms as a direct response to those circumstances and the effect that these defenses have on human behavior personally, socially, and politically. According to Robert Langs (2006), "Given both the pervasiveness and scope of the death-related threats with which humans must deal . . . we can appreciate why virtually every human walking this earth experiences a measure of emotional dysfunction. . . . Such is human nature—and life itself" (p. 112).

The various methods people use to defend against death anxiety affect their lives on many levels. On an individual level, they tend to withdraw from those things most meaningful to them, which negatively impacts their relationships, particularly with those closest to them. On a societal level, there is a propensity toward conformity and subordination to a group or cause, with an associated attitude of superiority toward those who are different. Although these defenses do help to avert anxiety states, they are costly in that they tend to cause damage to the person, the couple, the family, and ultimately, to society.

Individual Defenses Against Death Anxiety

It is essentially impossible for children to face mortality directly without protecting themselves to a certain extent; therefore, some defenses against the realization of death and dying are necessary. Some reactions to death awareness have beneficial effects; among these are the desire to make an enduring contribution in art, literature, or science. Likewise, finding lasting meaning in devotion to family, friends, and community and attempting to leave a positive imprint are also noble goals. A sense of purpose and the pursuit of transcendent goals have considerable value, apart from their limited ability to assuage death anxiety (Frankl, 1959; Ryan & Deci, 2004; Wong, 2008; Note 7).

Even though some people may respond positively to an awareness of death by embracing life more fully, many retreat to a more defended posture; when death anxiety is aroused, most tend to pull away from life-affirming activities in an effort to protect themselves. They instead engage in a variety of behaviors that serve to repress the awareness of death. This defensive posture tends to limit their capacity to relate to others, restricts their ability to make choices, and narrows their life experience.

Progressive Self-Denial

The inclination to give up interest in and excitement about life is built into a person's defensive posture and may manifest itself early in life (R. W. Firestone, 1997b, 2000; Piven, 2008; Rheingold, 1967). Examples of how people constrict their lives and put limits on their experiences can be observed in every area of human activity: a premature giving up of participation in sports and physical activities, a diminished interest in sex, a loss of contact with old friends, and a decline in social life. At the same time, some people may increase sedentary or self-nurturing activities, while others may become plagued with a sense of boredom and stagnation.

Slowly and almost imperceptibly, many people begin losing their spirit and exuberance for life. Over time, they become more rigid and controlling, narrowing their range of self-expression and experiences to such a degree that it could be said they are no longer invested in living. This progressive giving up of interests that once excited them can leave them cynical and self-hating.

Creation of a Legacy

In attempting to satisfy their deepest, most urgent need to survive their own personal ending, human beings often strive for perfection and uniqueness in their life's work. To be able to leave a legacy that will endure after their death, evidence that their existence has made a difference, that they have left their mark on the world, eases people's anxiety about dying. The use of creative works and humanitarian efforts as a defense against death anxiety does not exclude the fact that the desire to make such a contribution can be an integral part of giving value to one's life.

Because human beings are capable of deep feeling, logic, and symbolism, they are motivated to seek authentic personal meaning through their relationships, children, work, and creativity. Myriad endeavors can imbue a person's life with meaning and promise. Health practitioners, mental health professionals, clergy, and volunteers find gratification in serving people; artists through self-expression; and still others by promoting policies or participating in humanitarian causes that will help advance the well-being of future generations. The benefit to the world of these personal offerings is incalculable, even if their impact on a person's death anxiety is limited.

A number of theorists conceptualize creativity as a mode of symbolic immortality. Lifton (1979) emphasized the "continuity of artistic creation through time," in which

> each scientific investigator becomes part of an enterprise larger than himself, limitless in its past and future continuity. Whatever his additional motivations— the need to know and the quest for personal glory and reward—he operates within a framework of larger connectedness. (p. 21)

It does not diminish the significance of these efforts to examine the part played by people's undeniable desire to transcend death through their timeless innovations (Note 8).

Vanity

Vanity is an exaggerated positive image of the self that a person uses to compensate for feelings of inadequacy and inferiority (Miller, 1997). The sense of unlimited power, omnipotence, and immunity to death that comes with having an inflated self-image can be traced to early childhood primary narcissism, which originally offered an illusion of self-sufficiency and invulnerability, serving to protect the child from a sense of helplessness and fears of annihilation.

Vanity represents the remnants of this primitive imagined indestructibility that live on in the psyche. It serves as a survival mechanism in times of stress or when people become too conscious of the fallibility of their physical nature and the impermanence of life. It expresses itself on a deeper, unconscious level in a universal sentiment that death happens to other people, never to oneself. This sense of specialness makes a person feel immune to the fate that awaits the masses. In this magical thinking, "death will spare me because I am special" (Note 9).

Vanity helps people deny their mortality through the construction of various fictions that negate the fact of death. It allows people to have illusions of being extraordinary, superior, and capable of performing at unreasonably high levels (Baumeister et al., 2003; Egan & McCorkindale, 2007; Jordan et al., 2003; Young & Flanagan, 1998). However, when their accomplishments fall short of perfection or are criticized by others, severe self-castigation and demoralization result. Thus, there is pressure to maintain the illusions of grandeur. In addition, the arrogance, defensiveness, and even aggressive responses often manifested by the vain individual can be provoking to others. Nonetheless, people are willing to accept the tension associated with vanity in an attempt to avoid feeling ordinary and therefore subject to death as regular people are.

Accumulation of Power and Wealth

The drive to accumulate power is often motivated by a misguided belief that equates accomplishments and wealth with invincibility. Although conscious fears of death may be temporarily alleviated through the enhanced influence that wealth or accomplishments may confer, fears still exist on an unconscious level and often increase in intensity as an individual amasses greater power. Yalom (1980) rightly observed,

> Absolute power, as we have always known, corrupts absolutely; it corrupts because it does not do the trick for the individual. Reality always creeps in— the reality of our helplessness and our mortality; the reality that, despite our reach for the stars, a creaturely fate awaits us. (p. 127)

Power-seeking individuals are addicted to the illusion of control. They compulsively strive to increase their wealth or other power base in an attempt to offset feelings of vulnerability, irrelevance, or inferiority. When their authority is threatened, it brings up intolerable feelings of anxiety and dread, which they try to suppress through seeking greater and greater dominance. These people have an exaggerated suspicion of potential threats from perceived enemies or competitors, which becomes more extreme the more clout they have to wield. Ironically, the more power and wealth people accrue to this end, the stronger their feelings of insecurity and their fears about the future tend to be.

Couple Bonds

As has been explained, closeness and intimacy make people more aware of their separateness, which can arouse conscious death awareness. For instance, when sexual partners feel particularly loving toward one another, they are often distressed by the thought of losing their loved one or themselves. Members of a couple typically quell this anxiety by unconsciously distancing themselves from each other and forming a fantasy bond. Giving up their independence and separate points of view and relinquishing their individuality serves to create and sustain an illusion of safety, security, and ultimately, immortality (J. Hart & Goldenberg, 2008; Hayes et al., 2010; Note 10).

When death anxiety is aroused, there is an unconscious draw to believe that death can be eluded by merging with another person. For example, couples in a fantasy bond often engage in acting out parent–child and dominant–submissive modes of coupling in an effort to seek a false sense of security by establishing one as the savior and the other as the saved, even though these roles often alternate, making it an illogical proposition (Note 11).

Gene Survival

The birth of a child affects parents in conflicting ways. On the one hand, the parents' existential awareness is heightened by the child's vulnerability and complete dependency on them for survival. Also, becoming a first-time parent is another milestone in adulthood that brings a person closer to old age and death. On the other hand, people can use their offspring to establish a feeling of connection to the future. In one sense, children represent a symbolic victory over death by perpetuating the parents' DNA forward in time. Both parents and children imagine that this biological fact somehow imbues them with immortality. The family symbolizes a link to an unending succession of persons passing on unique traits from one generation to the next. To the extent that children resemble their parents in appearance, characteristics, and behavior, they are the parents' legacy to be left in the world as evidence of their existence.

This defense against death anxiety has disadvantages for both the parent and the child. Children are only able to relieve or buffer parents' death anxiety if they adopt the same points of view and lifestyle as their parents. This most often leads to destructive attempts to imprint the child with the parent's attitudes, beliefs, and methods of coping with life (Note 12). The sense of continuity and comfort this would afford is unavailable if children are significantly different from their parents—for instance, if a child has political, sexual, or religious preferences that are dissimilar to the parents'. The desire to have one's children fit into a familial pattern results in misattuned interactions and various levels of alienation. If parents are trying to repress existential anxiety in this way, they cannot truly come to know their child; their distinct perspective and personality, the unique things that light them up—all of this and more is lost when trying to preserve what is familiar and seemingly safe.

In addition, the more children are differentiated from a parent, the more guilt they feel about breaking the chain symbolically linking the generations. By disrupting this continuity, children become acutely aware of their vulnerability to death and of the fact that their movement toward autonomy and independence challenges their parents' sense of immortality. To avoid these reactions, children are inclined to maintain the fantasy bond by asserting a sameness with their parents and rejecting traits that would cause them to stand apart from family patterns and traditions.

Parents' unconscious desire for their children to be the vehicle through which they may prevail, in some sense, over death is the driving force behind the proprietary interest often directed toward offspring. Tampering with these ties is taboo in society because of the threat it poses in relation to the potential arousal of death anxiety. Society goes to great lengths to preserve the sanctity of the family to avoid facing this existential dilemma (R. W. Firestone & Catlett, 2009a).

Societal Defenses Against Death Anxiety

The acute awareness of death and the accompanying anxiety generate strong needs in individuals to become securely embedded in a collective social order (McCoy et al., 2000). The sense of being alone, on one's own, and standing out from the crowd evokes existential fears. Empirical studies by terror management theorists Solomon et al. (2015) have supported Ernest Becker's (1973/1997) assertion that an awareness of death impels people to first construct and then immerse themselves in cultural worldviews and institutions that deny existential realities—that is, the temporal nature of their lives and their basic insignificance in the universe.

Society actively supports people's tendencies to withdraw from life through its assigned rules for role-designated behavior. The general level of pretense, duplicity, and deception in the world also contributes to people's disillusionment, cynicism, and resignation. The pooling of the individual defenses and fantasies of society's members makes it possible for each person to practice self-delusion under the guise of normalcy (R. W. Firestone & Catlett, 1989). Thus, chronic self-denial becomes a socially acceptable defense against death anxiety and a social construct in its own right.

Many defenses against death anxiety are considered to be normal behaviors and are thereby advocated by society. For example, some people numb themselves to existential realities by turning to alcohol or drugs. Others adopt compulsive work habits or routines to distract themselves from the passage of time. Still others preoccupy themselves with trivial matters and obsess over pseudo-problems to divert themselves from realistic concerns about life and death. Some embrace a religion to maintain the hope or promise of an afterlife. Other people overintellectualize about death, taking a more philosophical position to keep themselves one step removed from experiencing feeling about their mortality.

Autocratic Systems of Government

The propensity to subordinate the self in relation to an idea or principle is at the core of nationalism, patriotism, and other isms (R. W. Firestone, 1996,

1997a, 1997b; R. W. Firestone & Catlett, 2009b). The illusion of connection to the group or movement is exhilarating and addictive because it offers a false sense of power and relief from death anxiety. For this reason, a total-itarian form of government is sometimes preferred to a truly democratic system. In a forum where people can speak out or voice their opinions, the inherent freedom makes them aware of their individual existence and iden-tity. This feeling of being alive and separate can cause anxiety rather than relieve it.

By yielding their views to those propagated by dogmatic leaders and con-forming to a group consensus, individuals are able to imagine their identi-ties as merged with that of the majority. This illusory fusion imbues them with a feeling of immortality and invulnerability. They come to feel that, although they may not survive as separate individual entities, they will live on as part of something larger that will continue to exist after they are gone.

In their work, Becker (1973/1997, 1975), Fromm (1941), Kasket (2006), and Videgård (1984b) described people's tendency to seek an ultimate rescuer or idolized hero, whether within a personal relationship, in the entertainment or sports world, or in the business, spiritual, or political sphere. They are likely to transfer the primitive dependency that was once embodied in their bond with their parents onto new figures and ideologies in an attempt to obtain relief from existential fears. Thus, people are espe-cially susceptible to the influence of appealing, authoritarian leaders who promise them certainty and safety (R. W. Firestone & Catlett, 2009a, 2009b; Lipman-Blumen, 2005; Note 13).

Religious Dogma

Many people use religious ideology for the purposes of coping with and allaying death anxiety (R. W. Firestone & Catlett, 2009a, 2009b; J. C. Jackson et al., 2018). These beliefs can offer a good deal of comfort, secu-rity, and meaning (Note 14) but fail to completely reassure a person about the subject of their death. In addition, there is a marked tendency for many people to sacrifice vital elements of their present-day lives for a hypothe-sized afterlife. It is difficult to conceptualize the form an eternal life would take; the concept of an infinite life can, in itself, be disquieting. Nor does the postulation of one's continuing after death, whether through reincarnation or other iterations of this possibility, offer relief from the certainty of a ces-sation of one's current experience.

People are generally apprehensive when faced with any significant change in the structure of their daily lives. This is especially true if the disruption is caused by something that is entirely out of their control. Obviously, death fits this criterion, representing a transition of major proportions. No matter a person's conception of the soul, god, or the nature of consciousness or the spirit, the idea of losing all of one's present-day existence, including the people one holds most dear, is an idea that is fraught with agony.

Most traditional religious ideologies offer protection against death anxiety through a connection with an all-powerful figure and emphasize the submission of the believer's will to God. People who chose to believe in a punitive yet forgiving deity often use this to feel unworthy and powerless in their own right. At the same time, they are able to feel connected and virtuous in believing they are merged with an all-powerful creator. This union is directly analogous to the good parent–bad child dichotomy of the fantasy bond with the primary caregiver. Both provide relief from one's existential fears by offering a sense of immortality.

Religious ideologies that support human beings' tendency to be self-denying and self-sacrificing also contribute to a self-destructive collective defense. Doctrines based on self-abrogation support a person's destructive voices. Acting as external validation, they intensify self-criticism and self-attacks, support the denial of one's physical nature, and contribute to a passive orientation to life (Pagels, 1988, 2003; Vergote & Wood, 1988). This leads to a diminution in feeling, resulting in a restriction of human potential for love and experience.

People are refractory to an unvarnished awareness of their personal death, and most turn away from and try to repress this conceptualization. Even so, unconscious fears of the unknown and the essential ambiguity of life are universal human experiences.

MY APPROACH TO DEATH ANXIETY

Any indication that heightens the awareness that we are leading a separate existence, that we are free agents, or any event that reminds us that we possess strength and power, that we alone are responsible for our decisions, can cause us to be acutely conscious of our life and its eventual loss. I have found that people tend to be more aware of death when they are truly alive to their existence and less aware of it and less caring about it when they are more constrained.

Some existential thinkers have hypothesized that the fear of death is greater in people who do not live up to their potential and achieve fulfillment than in those who succeed in life (Searles, 1961; Sezer & Gülleroğlu, 2017; Yalom, 1980; Note 15). They proposed that death anxiety is a manifestation of unfulfilled strivings and is "inversely proportional to life satisfaction" (Yalom, 1980, p. 207). This thesis leads to the assumption that if people are able to free themselves from their psychological limitations and are therefore better able to actualize themselves, their fears about dying will be reduced. However, in my experience, I have often observed that as clients progress in psychotherapy—that is, as they relinquish well-established defenses, experience their lives more fully, and move toward increased personal freedom and satisfaction—unconscious thoughts of death tend to come to the surface, accompanied by heightened feelings of death anxiety (R. W. Firestone & Catlett, 2009a; Langs, 2004). I have found that when people feel particularly fulfilled and/or valued, they develop a keen sense of what is precious to them and what they have to lose and, as a result, often retreat from or give up these prized experiences in life rather than be deprived of them by external forces in the end. This self-protective process underscores the question, Why invest fully in a life that we know is finite? This dilemma is difficult to cope with.

How can a person find meaning in their lives when faced with such a glaring certainty? I believe the answer lies in accepting our vulnerability without shame—that is, avoiding illusions that promise immortality. Life and death are both mysterious, and to imagine we can know anything about their ultimate nature is vanity. It is possible to live without sacrificing the truth of our experience without choosing to manipulate others or numb ourselves. Even with an inescapable end before us, we can live lives of consequence with genuine regard for ourselves and others. To accomplish this, we must be willing to acknowledge our impermanence (Note 16), feel the pain of the fact of our inevitable death and the inevitable death of our loved ones, and consciously allow the elements of existential despair that arise naturally their full recognition (Emanuel et al., 2021; Stolorow, 2015; Note 16).

We know that something cannot come from nothing, yet I believe we exist. This conundrum unsettles me but is also humbling in its implication (R. W. Firestone & Catlett, 2009a). Many people, both religious and nonreligious, have reported experiencing feelings of reverence and a deep appreciation regarding the wonders of the world and the miracle and mystery of life (Schneider, 2004, 2007). Such events are considered by Tomer et al. (2008) as "peak experiences" that are associated with "feelings of wonder, surprise, awe" (p. 9; Note 17). We all possess the potential to have experiences that transcend the satisfaction of tangible needs and sense mysteries that elude human understanding (R. Beck, 2004; Frankl, 1959; Schneider & Krug, 2010; Spinelli, 1997; Yalom, 1980). I reflected on this in *Beyond Death Anxiety*:

> It is when the search for meaning takes people to the edge of human understanding, where they accept the ultimate mystery of life and the limitations of science and rationality, that they know at the most profound level what it means to be fully human. (R. W. Firestone & Catlett, 2009a, p. 316)

CONCLUSION

It appears that we are caught in an unresolvable dilemma. On the one hand, if free of our customary defenses, we contend with the full emotional awareness of death, with its attendant feelings of fear, despair, and dread; the impact of this awareness threatens to overwhelm us. On the other hand, we will bear the pain of existential guilt if we deny death's reality by employing defensive maneuvers that cut into our real experience while protecting our illusion of immortality.

The point in the developmental sequence when children first discover death is a critical juncture where their defense system crystallizes and helps to shape their future. From this moment in time, most individuals accommodate to the fear of death, to varying degrees, by withdrawing energy and emotional investment in life-affirming activity and close, personal relationships. To whatever extent people renounce real satisfaction, they rely increasingly on internal gratification, fantasies of fusion, and numbing habits and behaviors.

The most effective denial of death lies in the fantasy bond that children develop originally as a compensation for deficiencies in their emotional environment. Death anxiety perpetuates the formation of fantasy bonds throughout a person's life. The image of being merged offers an illusion of immortality, a hope that one can somehow escape death. For the most part, people fail to realize that the use of a fantasy of connection to obtain security—that is, to procure a lie about life and death from another person or institution—is tantamount to invalidating the true nature of the relationship or endeavor.

Human beings are always conscious, on some level, of the fact that they are trapped in bodies that will eventually die. We are faced with an unresolvable dilemma. We fear death and naturally strive to remove the source of this fear from our awareness. To accomplish this, many individuals withhold feeling for the situations and people in their lives that remind them of their mortality. They turn away from that which makes them feel most alive in a futile attempt to avoid the awareness of their death. Anxiety about death, per se, is not unhealthy; however, attempts to deny the fact that one must die can cause psychological disturbance. The capacity to fully embrace life can only be realized if a person is open to experiencing the essential pain and sadness inherent in living (R. W. Firestone & Catlett, 2009a).

14 SOCIETY AND CONFORMITY

Throughout history, human beings have survived because they live in complex and interdependent societies in which people band together in groups for mutual aid and protection. Because the group enhances the members' chances of survival, group survival means personal survival. This adaptation begins with the infant's reliance on its parents and then extends to the family, tribe, and larger society. The benefits of this arrangement are apparent: The individual supports the group, and the group supports the individual.

However, group identification can also have a destructive effect on the individual. In many instances, the social mores propagated in a given culture are, in fact, a manifestation of the pooling of the combined defenses of its members. The fantasy bond and the illusion of connection that it offers individuals are extended to the group and culture in an effort to deny the reality of human separateness and autonomy. Conventionality and conformity tend to support the individual's defense system. When this is the case, both act in concert to oppose the natural strivings of a person. Through social pressure, implicit and explicit value systems act to constrain people in their unique pursuit of life (R. W. Firestone, 1985, 1996).

https://doi.org/10.1037/0000268-015
Challenging the Fantasy Bond: A Search for Personal Identity and Freedom,
by R. W. Firestone

To be defended in these ways—that is, against avenues to one's self-determination—a person must engage in some form of self-deception. Manifestations of the same deceit, duplicity, and double messages evidenced by defended individuals are reflected in the contradiction between the stated values of society and objective reality. Indications of this dishonesty are apparent in society's value systems and its social institutions. Generally speaking, people remain unaware of this duplicity in themselves and others. They repress their perceptions and fail to comment on the discrepancies that they do perceive. Becoming accustomed to mixed messages and regarding them as a normal part of social interaction limits individuals as thinking and feeling members of society. As Timothy Snyder (2017) affirmed,

> You submit to tyranny when you renounce the difference between what you want to hear and what is actually the case. This renunciation of reality can feel natural and pleasant, but the result is your demise as an individual—and thus the collapse of any political system that depends upon individualism. (p. 66)

In this sense, many social mores and conventions act to protect a habitually defensive lifestyle, including the fantasy bond and the attendant fantasies of connection that give a person a false sense of security and an illusion of immortality.

THE INDIVIDUAL AND SOCIETY

Children are initially exposed to parents' defenses and are shaped by the child-rearing practices in their family of origin. As they expand their boundaries to include the neighborhood, school, and larger society, they encounter new imprinting and socialization processes (Bronfenbrenner & Morris, 2006; Note 1). Throughout history, people in all cultures have created increasingly complex conventions and belief systems in an attempt to adapt to interpersonal pain and death anxiety. Ernest Becker (1975) articulated the costs of cultural worldviews that help people deny their personal mortality:

> Cultures are fundamentally and basically styles of heroic death denial. . . . These costs can be tallied roughly in two ways: in terms of the tyranny practiced within the society, and in terms of the victimage practiced against aliens or "enemies" outside it. (p. 125)

Each generation has been raised by people whose ancestors were themselves reared by parents who experienced personal suffering, feared death as a reality, and to a certain extent, defensively retreated from investing in their lives. Each succeeding generation has added its own building blocks to the system of denial and accommodation, contributing to the increased rigidity and universality of the defensive process.

Most adult members of society remain prisoners of their own internal programming while supporting the socialization processes that perpetuate the damage done to them in their families of origin. Negative social pressures exerted by other defended individuals, wielded by the power structure and maintained through contemporary mores and practices generally have a delimiting effect on each person's sense of freedom, sexuality, integrity, and the natural drive for affiliation with others.

CONFORMITY AND SOCIAL PRESSURE

The struggle to become a person in the face of negative elements existing in the family and society begins in infancy and continues throughout the life span (R. W. Firestone et al., 2012). Children are exposed to a distinctive indoctrination into the microculture of their family of origin. Erich Fromm (1944) described this socialization in "Individual and Social Origins of Neurosis":

> The child does not meet society directly at first; it meets it through the medium of his parents, who in their character structure and methods of education represent the social structure, who are the psychological agents of society, as it were. What, then, happens to the child in relationship to his parents? It meets through them the kind of authority which is prevailing in the particular society in which it lives, and this kind of authority tends to break his will, his spontaneity, his independence.
>
> But man is not born to be broken, so the child fights against the authority represented by his parents; he fights for his freedom not only from pressure but also for the freedom to be himself, a full-fledged human being, not an automaton. (pp. 381–382)

The socialization process in the family, be it nuclear, foster, or blended, lends itself to categorizing, standardizing, and putting the stamp of conformity on most children. It often "imposes a destructive structure, a self-regulating system that cuts deeply into [children's] feelings and conditions their thoughts and behaviors to meet certain accepted standards" (R. W. Firestone, 1990b, p. 318). As R. D. Laing (1967) observed,

> The family is, in the first place, the usual instrument for what is called socialization, that is, getting each new recruit to the human race to behave and experience in substantially the same way as those who have already got here. (p. 68)

In many families, the satisfaction of the children's needs for survival, security, affection, and love is contingent on their loyalty to their parents. They are thus successfully socialized to accommodate to the wishes, demands, and opinions of others to their detriment. Thereafter, children continue to impose the same structure and programming on themselves (R. W. Firestone, 1990b). This destructive process leads them to be easily influenced and manipulated by others throughout their lives.

To varying degrees, most people fail to emancipate themselves from the damaging effects of the socialization process of their childhood. They engage in the defensive behaviors that their families condone at the price of their integrity and uniqueness, a process that limits them as thinking and feeling people. On a broader scale, the majority of social structures tend to be restrictive of individuality and personal expression (Cook, 2014; Foucault, 1975, 1980, 1990; Marcuse, 1991, 1992; Renaud, 2013; Note 2). Conformity and adjustment to society are seen as moral and healthy by many, whereas nonconformity to societal expectations is perceived as aberrant and threatening. Therefore, individuals must subordinate themselves to preserve the couple's, the family's, and/or society's norms; otherwise, they are considered peculiar, immature, or abnormal.

Fear of Being Ostracized

The challenge of maintaining one's integrity and personal sense of values is made even more difficult by the individual's inherent need to belong to and be accepted by the group for survival. This dependence on society for care and protection can override one's investment in one's own principles (Baumeister, 2005). According to Baumeister, the "more prevalent and powerful source of anxiety [is] social isolation. It consists of fears of ending up alone" (p. 257). Because people fear exclusion to such an extent, they "conform, comply, obey, ingratiate, improve their appearance and manage their impressions to others in order to be included and feel like they belong" (Williams et al., 2000, p. 749). Significant prejudices, repercussions, and retaliations are often directed against people who espouse views that differ from those of the majority. Nonconformists are often threatened with rejection, aggression, or expulsion because their opinions and beliefs challenge the group's defensive adaptations and arouse its members' existential terror. The anxiety caused by being rejected, which is akin to the fear of death, has its roots in humankind's evolutionary history.

Guilt About Individuating

Guilt reactions are often aroused in people whose behaviors and lifestyles depart from accepted societal norms. When people go against cultural standards to fully embrace their lives, they must deal with the fear aroused by affirming their individuality and personal power. Breaking with tradition and the status quo triggers guilt because it increases a person's sense of being distinct and separate from one's family or society.

Each successive stage in the individuation process is potentially marked by guilt about symbolically leaving one's family behind. This reaction often reflects an unconscious desire to hold on to the fantasy bond with one's parents. A person's guilt can also be activated by self-denying and self-hating people, particularly if they are family members (R. W. Firestone, 1987, 1997a, 1997b). People cannot place restrictions on themselves without also constraining those in close contact with them. They cannot avoid the honest pursuit of goals without exerting pressure on others to follow suit. The guilt about moving in a direction that is different from or more fulfilling than experiences in one's family can lead to regression that limits each person's destiny.

> Ali was the only son in a Middle Eastern family. He was especially close to his father. His family was active in the mosque and well respected in their community. It was assumed that Ali would marry and ultimately join the family business. When he was a teenager, Ali dated girls, but he also had many male friends. In his early 20s, he went to Europe and lived on his own for the first time in his life. And also for the first time in his life, he became aware that he was attracted to men. Without the constraints of his family and culture, he chose to explore these feelings, and he realized that he was gay.
>
> Ali was torn. His father was the most important person in his life, yet Ali knew that his father would disown him if he knew that his son was gay. He also knew that homosexuality was condemned in his culture. When he considered telling the truth about his sexuality, he was frightened of being ostracized by his father and family, and he felt guilty at the thought of rejecting them. So, Ali lived a double life. He resided in Europe, where he lived as a gay man. And when he visited his family, he presented himself as heterosexual. Ali lived with the awareness that if he were truly himself, he would either have to separate himself from the family and the community he loved or be rejected by them.

Forces within the family and the larger culture generate social pressure that discourages individuation, supports conventionality and self-limitation, and inhibits movement toward a creative, fulfilling life. In general, society tends to idealize parents and support the myth of unconditional love; its institutions often reinforce destructive couple and family bonds. These attitudes and standards operate as aversive forces in the larger society and have an enduring negative effect on its members (Note 3).

Eventually, some conventions, however shortsighted and inhumane, become formalized into written laws. However, even when they remain unwritten and implicit, they become the accepted standards by which people evaluate their behavior and attitudes. Many social standards that are viewed as normal and routine are damaging to people psychologically; individuals living by conventional principles are often unknowingly limiting their choices and personal freedom, impairing their emotional health. Social mores and distorted, institutionalized attitudes are likely to have serious consequences because they create obstacles that make it difficult for people who are striving to develop their individuality in ways that defy traditional norms.

Stereotypic Attitudes

In addition to the obvious racism and discrimination that is apparent in today's society, there are more subtle factors that also have a destructive impact on how people regard themselves and others. For example, stereotypic views of age and gender disseminated through the media, educational institutions, and other sources of public discourse restrict people's thinking and adversely affect their behavior. Stereotypes are confusing because they assign individuals to rigid, artificial categories. Grau and Zotos (2016), who reviewed research into stereotyping in the media since 2010, observed, "Stereotypes are beliefs about a social category. . . . They become problematic when they lead to expectations about one social category over another or restrict opportunities for one social category over another" (p. 761; Note 4).

Although in the last decades there have been numerous changes in mainstream gender roles, there are still many residual beliefs that portray people in ways that are harmful psychologically and costly to society. According to Koenig (2018),

> Gender stereotypes have descriptive components, or beliefs about how males and females typically act, as well as prescriptive components, or beliefs about how males and females should act. For example, women are supposed to be nurturing and avoid dominance, and men are supposed to be agentic and avoid weakness. (Abstract)

In the Annual Review of Gender Stereotypes, Ellemers (2018) pointed out that gender stereotyping is discriminatory also because it disregards alternative gender identities:

> Gender continues to be seen as a binary categorization, in which we tend to compare men to women and women to men, anchoring any differences in terms of a contrast between them. Thus, gender categorizations are immediately detected, are chronically salient, seem relatively fixed, and are easily polarized. (p. 177)

With respect to these adverse effects, Ellemers (2018) asserted,

> Gender stereotypes prevent women and men from equally sharing the care of children and family members and from equally benefiting from the interpersonal connections made through these activities. . . . This is not only costly

for the individuals involved but also for society, as it impacts psychological and physical well-being of individuals, the resilience of families, and the long-term availability and contribution of workers in the labor market. (p. 192)

Within most societies, beliefs about male superiority still exist despite advances that have been made toward equality due, in part, to the feminist movement and recent research that contradicts popular stereotypes (Hyde, 2016; Note 5). In describing the harm inherent in the hierarchal structures of patriarchal societies, in which gender stereotyping is still prevalent, C. Gilligan and Snider (2018) stressed this point:

> Our relational desires and capacities—our wish to connect with others and our ability to register our feelings and to communicate them—have to be compromised or reined in, sacrificed or constrained to maintain an order of living contingent on dividing people into the superior and the inferior, the touchables and the untouchables, whether on the basis of race, gender, class, caste, religion, sexuality, you name it. (p. 12; Note 6)

In today's society, conventional attitudes generally define age-appropriate roles and behaviors, be they in relation to children, teenagers, adults, or senior citizens. These often reflect misconceptions and inaccurate assumptions about people at different stages of life that disregard and disrespect their actual experience of life. This is especially apparent in the attitudes that society coveys about aging. For example, despite the current focus on remaining youthful, popular concepts of "maturity" support the gradual retreat from energetic activities as one grows older (R. W. Firestone, 1997b, 2000).

Terror management theorists Martens et al. (2004) attributed ageism, in part, to people's fear of death:

> If . . . we want very much to live in the most secure and death-free way possible, then elderly people are always a potential threat to our equanimity. Elderly people have an uncanny way of exposing the existential dilemma we all can understand on some level, and yet want very much to be free of. They are a living symbol of time running out, of faculties fading, of potentially frightening biological facts. (p. 1534)

These theorists proposed an antidote to the tendency to isolate and stigmatize older people:

> A possibility for reducing ageism might be broadening our values and what makes our lives meaningful. If people value in themselves qualities that are strengths of the elders, such as wisdom, a sense of humor about the dark side of life, or achieving close and rich relationships, perhaps people will have less to fear in elderly people. Perhaps people and culture can still imbue elders with more value than appears to be currently the case. (Martens et al., 2004, p. 1533)

(See R. W. Firestone et al., 2012, pp. 157–158; Note 7.)

Misconceptions About Committed Relationships

An individual's tendency to form a fantasy bond is fortified by conventional attitudes and assumptions about committed relationships, marriage, and family life. For example, in modern society, most people expect far more security from a committed relationship or marriage than it could ever reasonably offer. As Esther Perel (2006) observed, "Love, beyond providing emotional sustenance, compassion, and companionship, is now expected to act as a panacea for existential aloneness as well" (p. 8; Note 8). These anticipations put an unfair burden on relationships; clearly, no one person can fulfill all of another person's needs. When people put such unrealistic expectations on their partner or relationship, the original equality, genuine companionship, and spontaneous affection they once shared are considerably diminished.

> Jason and Beth were introduced by friends on one of the rare occasions that they were both in the same city. Jason worked as a freelance photographer, and Beth's work as a programmer allowed her to travel the world. They hit it off right away, partly because they shared the same independent spirit and love of adventure. They began to plan their schedules to overlap so they could spend more time together. They visited each other, traveled some together, and continued to take trips independently. Neither one of them had ever wanted to be tied down in a conventional committed relationship.
>
> However, as they came to love and care about each other, they decided to get married but were determined to define the parameters of their marriage in their own terms. They would continue to live as they had been, dividing their time between their independent interests and shared experiences. Eventually, though, they began to feel pressured. Beth's parents commented, "What kind of husband takes off like that? If he loved you, he would be with you." Jason's friends asked, "Aren't you afraid of her meeting someone else when she's off traveling around?" Their friends prodded them, "When are you two going to grow up and settle down?" "You're not really planning on living like this forever, are you?" When Beth's friends began having babies, they asked her, "When are you going to have a baby?"
>
> The reactions of their friends and family began to have an effect on Jason and Beth. They grew dissatisfied with each other. He became suspicious and possessive, and she became childish and demanding. They were no longer the fun-loving, free-spirited individuals who had fallen in love with each other. Instead, they were two unhappy people who felt that they and their partner were somehow falling short and not living up to expectations.

Most people profess strong support for close, enduring relationships, but the reality of the number of breakups and divorces leads to cynicism and a feeling of futility about the future of intimate relationships. In addition, stereotypic attitudes learned in the family and other social institutions further strengthen these cynical attitudes. Thus, young people are taught two divergent views, both of which are inaccurate. On the one hand, they are encouraged to regard committed relationships as an idealized promise of everlasting happiness, while on the other, they are taught that they generally end in alienation and heartbreak.

Myths About the Family

The precept of unconditional parental love is a fundamental part of society's idealistic conception of family life. However, the reality is that parents have both positive and negative feelings toward their children (R. W. Firestone, 1990b; Rohner, 1991; Rohner & Veneziano, 2001). These ambivalent attitudes coexist within everyone. Many mothers and fathers honestly believe that they love their children even when their child-rearing practices are indifferent, neglectful, or even abusive. They mistake their loving intent for the presence of love.

The impossibility of living up to the myth of unconditional love often leads to feelings of shame and guilt in parents. These emotions are compounded in families where the parents have difficulty feeling for their children. The unrealistic expectations foster a sense of failure and humiliation, driving parents to cover up the truth of their feelings rather than supporting them taking a compassionate interest in their limitation.

It serves no constructive purpose for parents to attempt to minimize or deny their shortcomings or inadequacies in the eyes of their children. Because many adults find it difficult to realize when they are insensitive, rejecting, or otherwise misattuned toward their offspring, they inadvertently disallow their children the opportunity to recognize and cope with the pain this may cause, thereby hampering their child's ability to develop themselves. The tension and confusion introduced by trying to play down or overlook parents' shortcomings further injure the child. Indeed, an honest acknowledgment of parental deficiencies would enable both parties to deal with and repair any ruptures in their relationship effectively. With a diminution of this pressure and the subsequent relaxation for both parent and child, they can come to experience genuine regard and loving feelings for one another.

Society also supports the belief that children belong to their parents. This assumption of parents' proprietary rights over their children has its source in the fantasy bond and the illusion of connection between parent and child. Within this context, parents are assumed to always have the best interests of their children at heart and the necessary maturity and capability to nurture and raise their children. Many have the attitude that, because they gave life to their offspring and have invested time, energy, and money in their upbringing, their children belong to them, much as any other possession. They establish an exclusive emotional tie with their child that is different from a natural attachment characterized by love and affection. This enveloping, constraining interest reflects the parents' feeling that the child is theirs and is, in fact, an extension of themselves. For these individuals, there is a general blurring of the boundaries between them and their child (R. W. Firestone, 1990b; R. W. Firestone & Catlett, 2009a).

SOCIETY'S IMPACT ON HUMAN RIGHTS

In examining the functions served by a particular social system, it is necessary to consider the extent to which it provides for the welfare of its constituents. The ideal state would be concerned with economic security for all its members, as well as the protection of their personal freedom and basic human rights. Its government would be based on philosophical principles that place value on the life of each person over the survival of a system of rules and regulations (R. W. Firestone & Catlett, 2009b).

In contrast, when protection of the state or political system takes precedence over that of the individual, the needs of most of its citizens are not served. Instead, most members tend to suffer on a personal, economic, and political level. Governments that operate on this philosophy tend to give human rights issues a low priority, which can set the stage for oppression and tyranny. Totalitarian or authoritarian states that demand conformity and submission impose a wide range of rules and restrictions on their citizens. However, a truly just government would allow its citizens personal freedom and mobility and would provide opportunities for the improvement of their economic status. While all social systems involve a certain amount of compromise in relation to the rights of the individual, it is always a matter of degree. According to Moghaddam (2013), "even democracies contain an ever-shifting relationship between democratic and dictatorial tendencies, with elements that can pull democracies back to dictatorship" (Abstract; Note 9).

In general, much of the social control and categorization, as well as the conventional attitudes and stereotypic views propagated by modern society, function to restrict people's thinking and increase their hostility toward one another. Instead of challenging or attempting to modify destructive family practices, modern societies tend to collude with and support the formation of fantasy bonds within the couple and family. It is unethical, as well as illogical, to place primary value on a social institution or system, whether it be the couple, the family, or another bureaucracy, without considering the well-being of the individual people involved—adults and children. Any system is merely an abstraction, whereas the people concerned are real, living entities (R. W. Firestone & Catlett, 1999, 2009b).

With respect to the care of children and child welfare, society's idealization of the family often enables its members to avoid crucial issues that are vital to mental health. For example, the rights of each child are largely dictated by the legal system (Note 10). The court, as a social institution, presumably safeguards the well-being of children by establishing definitions of neglect and abuse and mandating the reporting of incidents of child maltreatment by mental health professionals and educators (Note 11). Child welfare agencies have often overlooked the well-being of children in support of the primacy of the biological family (Baldwin et al., 2019; Note 12).

Ideally, parents would expand their child's world to include other individuals who could be of value by providing a nurturing and supportive environment for the child that would thereby counteract some of the damage that inadvertently occurs within the limitations of the nuclear family. An extended family may be defined as one or more adults, in addition to the child's natural parents, who maintain a relationship with the child over a significant period; an older sibling, a grandparent, favorite relative, godparent, neighbor, teacher, counselor, or mentor often serves this function.

The advantages of an extended family in terms of enhancing children's self-esteem and overall well-being have been documented in research investigating the long-term effects of child abuse. Studies have shown that "resilient" children, those who grew up in traumatic circumstances yet were able to survive emotionally, did so because they had a secure relationship with another adult, generally someone outside the nuclear family (Haskett et al., 2006). Even when the contact between child and adult was of brief duration, it still had an ameliorative effect on the child's sense of self. By offering an alternative point of view and a more congenial, accepting attitude, devoid of negative projections, this type of relationship may help avert a pathological outcome (Note 13).

CONCLUSION

To varying degrees, most social systems and institutions ignore significant issues of human rights by supporting conformity within the group over the individual. Similarly, many families intrude on and violate the innate right of their members to develop as unique individuals. Many parents fail to provide conditions where the child's distinctive personality and special qualities can naturally emerge. This abuse of personal freedom can eventually evolve into an issue of human rights within each individual; children who are mistreated go on to mistreat themselves in much the same manner as they were hurt. The damage is then perpetuated in new relationships and, perhaps most painfully, with regard to their own children, thereby completing a destructive cycle. Therefore, a discussion of human rights issues, values, and ethics is essential if we are to adequately explore the impact of the fantasy bond on the dynamics of family relationships and social structures.

Society can be viewed as a reflection of the self-parenting process in each individual, promoting self-nourishing fantasies and habits over real experience and relationships. The culture presents its members with images in place of experiences, data in place of wisdom, spectatorship in place of participation. In this collusion between negative social pressure and individuals' defenses, people are progressively forfeiting much of their humanness, losing contact with feeling, embracing self-deception, and accepting substitute gratifications that effectively limit their real selves.

A person faces a critical struggle against enormous odds to retain a sense of self as a unique individual. People are not only impacted by psychological and existential challenges but also exist in a cultural structure that imposes restrictions on some of their most human qualities: the capacity for sustaining personal feeling, the desire for meaning and creative expression, and the ability to live in harmony with others. Society exerts its influence through both explicit and implicit demands for sameness and uniformity that tend to reinforce the defensive process in each member. These conventional attitudes and social mores support the formation of fantasy bonds in couples and families and encourage the socialization of children according to "proper" norms, many of which are limiting or harmful to their emotional well-being.

Therefore, overcoming negative social pressures requires that we, as individuals, challenge our personal defenses against leading a feelingful life. As we become aware of the personal demons we carry from the past and how our destructive voices are shaping our lives, we can take measures to progressively free ourselves from these negative influences. We can challenge our fantasy bonds, develop our capacity to feel, cope with anger, move away from addictive lifestyles, form genuine friendships, encourage generosity, control our self-destructive tendencies, and confront our defenses against death anxiety.

As individual members of society, we must reconsider our priorities in relation to family and social values. On a broader societal level, we can challenge harmful institutional practices and work toward building a more inclusive global community based on mutual concern and true interdependence. When individual rights are valued, it allows for more constructive associations between people and enhances each person's development and pursuit of a better life. By becoming aware of the serious and painful issues described in this chapter, we can begin to change these patterns on a personal, familial, and societal level.

15 POLARIZATION, PREJUDICE, AND ETHNIC WARFARE

It seems clear that comfortable illusion is now a danger to human survival.
—Ernest Becker, *Escape From Evil*

Separation theory offers an understanding of the core dynamics underlying human aggression. It explains how people's defensive nature and dependency on the fantasy bond polarize them against others with different customs and beliefs. In a similar vein, Schneider's (2013) concept of "psychological polarization" describes the elevation of one absolutist point of view to the exclusion, even demonization, of all others (Note 1). Such polarization is a reflection of the age-old attempt to quell existential anxiety and panic evoked by the painful realization of the inevitability of one's personal mortality.

As noted, human destructiveness is largely a response to the personal abuses suffered in childhood, which is later intensified by the specter of impending death. The psychological defenses that individuals form early in life in an effort to minimize or shut out psychological pain offer some

https://doi.org/10.1037/0000268-016
Challenging the Fantasy Bond: A Search for Personal Identity and Freedom,
by R. W. Firestone

comfort but also predispose a degree of distortion of and alienation from self and others.

The combined projection of individual defense mechanisms onto a social framework makes up a significant aspect of culture. For example, feelings of vanity and specialness that are part of the defense system that shields individuals from their mortality are extended to a cultural pattern of superiority that has led to virulent racism and genocide throughout history. Entire societies are capable of becoming progressively more hostile, paranoid, or psychologically disturbed in much the same manner that the defended person can become mentally ill. The broadly held destructive and pejorative attitudes of the culture often become administered policies that restrict and debase those considered to be divergent. As these standards become the norm, the inevitable impact on the personality development of the individual constituent creates a cycle that is difficult to interrupt.

ORIGINS OF POLARIZATION

As previously indicated, group identification provides individuals with an illusion of safety and security through an imagined connection or fantasy bond with the membership. Kaiser (Fierman, 1965) proposed that people's compelling need to surrender their will to another person or group through an "illusion of fusion" (p. 208) represents the universal neurosis. Because the fantasy bond is effective as a denial of death anxiety, if this core defense were to break down, individuals would once again be faced with the pain associated with mortality. Therefore, any external intrusion or threat to the fantasy bond is inevitably met with strong and often unconscious resistance. As the language of the defensive process, the critical inner voice fosters distrust and hostility toward others in an attempt to protect the fantasy bond from outside interference. Stereotypes, prejudicial attitudes, and racial biases are extensions of these fundamentally hostile and distorted views. They provide a pseudorational basis for aggressive acts against those people who are perceived as different.

Group Identification

Members of a given social group or society have a stake in their shared perception of reality, and their emotional security is fractured when individuals or other groups express alternative perceptions. Identification with a particular ethnic or religious group is a potent defense against death anxiety and typically includes an ideology—that is, a system of thoughts, beliefs, and prejudicial attitudes that can provide the justification and pave the way for hatred and bloodshed (L. M. Jackson, 2019; Note 2). When people merge their identity with that of a group or nation, they tend to feel hostile toward outsiders whom they experience as a potential threat to their vision of being able to live on as part of something larger and more permanent.

A number of theorists have asserted that group identification is a major causative factor in religious, racial, and international conflict. S. Freud's (1921/1955) work on the subject, which stressed the "mindlessness of the group mind," supports my thesis that group membership offers a false sense of superiority, specialness, and omnipotence to individuals who feel alone, helpless, and powerless in an uncertain world (R. W. Firestone & Catlett, 2009a; see Herrera & Sani, 2013; Hohman & Hogg, 2011; Note 3). Freud (1921/1955) quoted Le Bon's (1895/1920) *"Psychologie des foules"*: "the individual forming part of a group . . . is no longer himself, but has become an automaton who has ceased to be guided by his will" (p. 76). Falk (2004) also described the group dynamics operating within many nationalistic and/or totalitarian societies as "a collective illusion, a fusion of each person's narcissistic image of self with the image of greatness embedded in the national group. . . . Nationalism can be viewed as defensive group narcissism" (p. 99).

In his classic work, *Escape From Freedom*, Erich Fromm (1941) described how existential fears of aloneness and "a feeling of insignificance and powerlessness" associated with "the process of growing freedom" (p. 197) compel people to take actions as a group that would be unthinkable to them as individuals. In *Psychoanalysis and Religion*, Fromm (1950) observed,

> There is nothing inhuman, evil, or irrational which does not give some comfort provided it is shared by a group. . . . Once a doctrine, however irrational, has gained power in a society, millions of people will believe in it rather than feel ostracized and isolated. (p. 33)

Most individuals, though defended, are not emotionally unstable to the extent that the existence of people with different views causes them to strike out with aggressive or violent acts. However, the majority can be induced into a state of hatred or rage by a leader who has pathological needs and who manipulates their fear and insecurity to achieve power (Fromm, 1941; Shirer, 1960).

Nationalism and Totalitarianism

Nationalism and totalitarianism are just two of the myriad causes, malignant and benign, that people may pledge a deep allegiance to and become reliant on for a sense of safety, stability, and relief from existential anxiety (R. W. Firestone & Catlett, 2009b; Fromm, 1964). J. Gilligan (2007) defined nationalism as

> A form of prejudice that privileges members of one's own nation and discredits those who belong to others. Once religion—the divine right of kings—lost its credibility as the source of legitimacy, another basis had to be found. With belief in nationalism came the belief that governments or states derived their legitimacy from the nation they represented and defended. The concept of nationhood and the nation-state thus replaced the now-defunct concepts of God, religion, and the divine right of kings. (p. 39)

Loyalty to and identification with the ingroup and simultaneous devaluation of others feed narcissistic, omnipotent feelings and can instill in a person a false sense of invulnerability. Totalitarian governments epitomize the destructive effect of collective defenses and exaggerated group identification (Arendt, 1968/1994, 1973; Baehr, 2002; Giroux, 2015; Klar & Bilewicz, 2017; Surmelian, 1990 [as cited in Marlinova, 1990]; Young-Bruehl, 2002; Note 4). Although they may offer a sense of unity, there is always a substantial loss of personal freedom and independence and an increase in human rights violations in a homeland that propagates prejudice and hostile attitudes toward other countries.

People who are primarily submissive or conforming in their orientation transfer the desperation and dependency needs that originally characterized their relationship with their parents onto new figures, groups, and ideologies. This makes them particularly vulnerable to manipulation by authoritarian leaders who promise them safety and continuity. The unpredictable nature of the world is frightening, and amidst this chaos, leaders reach out, offering a connection and calming the fear. They can do this by including followers in life-affirming causes and activities or engaging them in a divisive quest for superiority. Either way, the allure of these types of leaders is that they are able to imbue lives that may feel insignificant with significance (Lipman-Blumen, 2005; Note 5).

Within a functional democracy, citizens are ultimately accountable for the goals that their leaders pursue, their government's policies, the actions taken on their behalf, and most important, the means their leaders use to achieve these ends. In such a forum, where people can speak out and voice their opinions, the implicit freedom makes them aware of their individual existence, power, and identity. This feeling of being alive, unique, and separate exposes one's mortal nature. To avoid the anxiety inherent in such a reminder, there will always be those who are driven to pursue persuasive, domineering leaders who assuage this fear by offering illusions of ultimate power and group identification.

Society reinforces the defensive lifestyle, conformity, and conventionality of its members, an unconscious conspiracy that effectively destroys the democratic process. In her description of the "hierarchy enhancing myths" that are touted by many autocratic leaders, L. M. Jackson (2019) suggested that such myths "perpetuate inequality by providing seemingly acceptable explanations for the existing hierarchal social order" (p. 83). Democracy depends on an intelligent, informed, free-thinking, independent populace. Fused identity and blind submission to a group or nation and hero-worship of leaders, together with susceptibility to psychologically based manipulations that offer respite from fear, combine to make true democracy a near impossibility (R. W. Firestone & Catlett, 2009b).

Organized Religion

Many religious teachings presuppose that without the moral rules of a sacred text to guide them, human beings would naturally revert to living unethical, immoral lives that lack spirituality. I strongly disagree with this point of view and concur with the many philosophers who argue that morality and spirituality can exist separate from religion. Among these is E. O. Wilson (1998), who asserted his belief that "moral values come from human beings alone, whether or not God exists" (para. 4). Furthermore, the capacity for empathy, which is the emotional basis for moral behavior, has been identified by evolutionary psychologists and biologists as an innate characteristic of human beings. According to Olson (2007), "a body of empirical evidence reveals that the roots of prosocial behavior, including moral sentiments such as empathy, precede the evolution of culture and religion" (para. 3).

Various moralistic rules and regulations that many religious practices impose serve to increase their members' sense of guilt and shame, particularly in relation to peoples' sexual nature, nudity, and the naturalness of the human body. These judgmental attitudes have been proven to be detrimental to mental health (Pagels, 1988; Prescott, 1996; Vergote & Wood, 1988). For example, Maltby (2005) found that "extrinsic-personal religiosity was . . . related to trait and state guilt" (Abstract). Similarly, Grubbs et al. (2015) reported findings showing that religiosity may increase "the propensity of individuals to see their own behaviors as pathological" (p. 125).

Religious dogma that is rigid, restrictive, and inflexible can also function to instill hatred and malice in believers toward nonbelievers. Throughout history, countless actions that have been taken in the name of morality have, in fact, led to immorality in the form of religious persecution and wars against outsiders or nonbelievers. Many feel that they are connected to God or doing God's work and are therefore in the moral position, or even under a moral obligation, to bring judgment on others. Becker (1975) wrote,

> No wonder the divine kings repeatedly staged their compulsive campaigns and inscribed the mountainous toll of their butchery for all time. . . . Their pride was holy; they had offered the gods an immense sacrifice and a direct challenge, and the gods had confirmed that their destiny was indeed divinely favored, since the victories went to them. (p. 106; Note 6)

THE PSYCHODYNAMICS OF AGGRESSION, PREJUDICE, AND ETHNIC STRIFE

In contrast to theories of aggression set forth by S. Freud (1925/1959) and Klein (1948/1964), who asserted that infants possess innate aggression or a death instinct, I suggest that human beings are not innately self-destructive or aggressive toward others. It is true that they have the capacity for violence, but this is different from having an instinct for violence. People become destructive, violent, or harmful to self and others only in response to emotional pain, fear, rejection, and deprivation. Understanding aggression as a response to frustration and other environmental factors rather than as an inborn instinct allows space for personal power and positive change.

Attitudes held in families often encourage prejudice toward other families, groups, and cultures that approach life differently. These distinctions support core beliefs that individuals who do not look "like we do" and who do not act "like we do" are inferior, worthless, immoral, or even dangerous (Note 7). As described in Chapter 5, children often imitate their parents' defenses by taking on as their own the negative parental attitudes, biases, and prohibitions of their parents through the processes of identification and incorporation (Note 8). In addition, the rigidity of a person's intolerance of and discrimination toward others is influenced by the degree of damage sustained in early family interactions. Individuals who have come to rely heavily on the fantasy bond for security tend to react with amplified hostility and alarm toward those with different cultural and ethnic backgrounds. These influences and their extension into society have a negative effect on individuals and their relationships and set groups of people against one another.

The defense of projecting onto others those characteristics one despises most in oneself is another source of racism and intolerance. This destructive bid to maintain self-esteem as compensation for one's negative self-image is evident at the societal level when members of one group see those of another to be fundamentally subhuman (i.e., immoral, depraved, and unclean). In *The Psychology of Prejudice*, L. M. Jackson (2019) described how "common beliefs often reflect and respond to aspects of the social structure," and "beliefs linked to prejudice perpetuate inequality because they provide a sense of legitimacy to the social system" (pp. 81–82). This thinking becomes a seemingly sound rationale for bettering the world by eradicating all aspects and agents of the perceived evil.

Becker (1973/1997) and Solomon et al. (2000) proposed that group identification functions as a buffer against death anxiety:

> Mortality concerns contribute to prejudice because people who are different challenge the absolute validity of one's cultural worldview. Psychological equanimity is restored by bolstering self-worth and faith in the cultural worldview, typically by engaging in culturally valued behaviors and by venerating people who are similar to oneself, and berating, converting, or annihilating those who are different. (Solomon et al., 2000, p. 203)

The drive to obscure from consciousness the true nature of the human condition stimulates people to oppose those whose solution to this dilemma is different from their own. This mentality is apparent in society when there is strict allegiance to a particular form of patriotism, nationalism, and other alliances of this kind. As Solomon et al. (2000) noted, "Isms make schisms" (p. 201). The choice becomes narrow: Either rehabilitate or eliminate those seen as different and, therefore, the enemy. This explains the ubiquitous nature of ethnic conflict across the globe. Without insight into the profound nature of this urge, people carry on the brutality of age-old battles, despising and attempting to subdue one another in perpetuity. The human species may ultimately be in peril if there is not a concentrated effort on the part of each individual and society as a whole to recognize and address the motivations underlying destructive beliefs and behaviors (R. W. Firestone & Solomon, 2018; Lifton, 2012; Note 9).

EMPIRICAL RESEARCH

Terror management researchers, in their vigorous study of the effect of death salience on human attitudes and behavior, have empirically verified aspects of Ernest Becker's (1973/1997) theoretical formulations and, by extension, the existential insights composing separation theory. Solomon et al. (2004, 2015) conducted more than 350 studies in which the experimental design involved the comparison of two groups: one that was exposed to words that were designed to subtly arouse death awareness and one that was not. The researchers then observed how each group responded to various tasks. Their findings indicate that subjects who were subliminally presented with the word *death* more strongly endorsed the worldview of their own ethnic group or nation; at the same time, they denigrated members of other groups whose worldviews differed from their own (Das et al., 2009; J. Greenberg et al., 2016; Note 10).

Other studies showed that people tend to be more moralistic toward those whose behavior conflicts with society's social or moral codes. For example, judges whose death awareness was raised set higher bails on prostitutes than judges in the control group (Rosenblatt et al., 1989). These reactions were also evident at the behavioral level: In an experimental setting, individuals whose awareness of death was heightened administered larger amounts of an aversive substance to people of a religious denomination and ethnic background different from their own (Lieberman et al., 1999).

These reactions to unconscious stimuli may also affect political choices. For example, two post-9/11 studies found that subjects in the high death awareness group favored a candidate who insisted on an aggressive agenda toward those they believed were the enemy over one who urged a more diplomatic path (Cohen et al., 2004, 2005).

CONCLUSION

The whole of humanity is enriched by the array of color, movement, ingenuity, song, and worship that swirls throughout this world. These same virtues and values that inspire curiosity, awe, gratitude, and a sense of kinship across cultural lines are also capable of generating fear, confusion, discord, and alienation. A major problem facing us today is the hostile divide between peoples of different countries and ethnicities, perpetuating intolerance, long-standing animosities, and continued bloodshed and destruction. There are many threats to civilization at this point in history: climate change, pandemics, the poisoning of our air and water. If we cannot come together as a species with a desire to establish rapport and affiliation, the continued polarization puts us at ultimate risk.

The feeling of helplessness in contemplating the cessation of existence as one knows it provides the impetus that drives members of a group or citizens of a nation to build up grandiose images of power at the expense of other groups or nations, to act on their projections and distortions, and even to attempt to eliminate "impure" and despised enemies. Understanding the root cause of aggression provides a clear perspective and points toward a hope for the future, whereas a deterministic conception of humankind's essential savagery may become a self-fulfilling prophecy. Indeed, negative forecasting precludes constructive action, assuring the uninterrupted continuation of these destructive cycles.

I do not suggest that there is an easy solution for the struggle for peace, and I do not propose that the undertaking is simple. I do, however, hope that with an insight into the source of human aggression, people would be able to understand and have compassion for themselves and begin to alter the harmful child-rearing practices and social systems that foster destructive attitudes and behaviors. Developing self-compassion naturally extends to empathy toward others, which is needed to heal the distrust and hatred that so often permeate relations between different cultures and ethnicities.

The key to our continued survival is the development of an inclusive worldview (Note 11). We must recognize the existential nature of our impulse to shun that which is unfamiliar and transcend these fears to realize the commonality between all people. We must avoid relying on illusion and comfortable beliefs and be willing to become conscious of our pain and the pain of others. This is the common ground, the common humanity, we must acknowledge to achieve a meaningful peace (R. W. Firestone & Catlett, 2009b).

I believe in humankind's capacity to change negative personality characteristics and unethical practices. Just as people can create a more positive identity and new destiny for themselves, a similar result can be achieved in society and culture. In spite of the present state of affairs and the complexity of the battleground—the demonstrable prejudice, polarization and hatred, and the powerful force of resistance to challenging the underlying causes—one must not fail to maintain hope. Without cautious optimism, without giving significant value to life and experience, all that is precious about civilization will be lost.

Notes

CHAPTER 1

1. Ed Tronick (2007) reported findings showing that instances of imperfection are commonplace. In one study, researchers (J. F. Cohn et al., 1985) found that mothers and their infants were in misattuned interactions more than 70% of the time. In other words, most parents are engaged in attuned communications with their infants only 30% of the time.

2. The term *illusion of fusion* was used originally by Hellmuth Kaiser (in Fierman, 1965) to describe a phenomenon he observed in patients' transference reactions. Kaiser suggested that this phenomenon applied to other relationships: "The universal psychopathology is defined as the attempt to create in real life by behavior and communication the illusion of fusion" (Fierman, 1965, p. 209).

3. Cozolino (2020) noted,

   Early relationships with caretakers shape the circuits between the amygdala and OMPFC (orbital medial prefrontal cortex) which stores the memories of how well others are able to regulate our anxiety. The implicit memories stored in this network manifest as what are called secure and insecure patterns of attachment. (p. 26)

   Similarly, Schore (2019) observed, "The child uses the output of the mother's emotion-regulating right cortex as a template for imprinting— the hard wiring of circuits in his own right cortex that will come to mediate his expanding affective capacities" (p. 9).

4. Certain events or situations, which can seem innocuous from a parent's perspective, may appear life-threatening to the baby. For example, an

infant whose mother leaves the room for a few minutes to heat a bottle may feel completely abandoned and suffer a form of anxiety, referred to by Winnicott (1958) as *annihilation anxiety*: "An excess of this reacting produces not frustration but a threat of annihilation. This . . . is a very real primitive anxiety" (p. 303).

5. See Silverman et al. (1982), who demonstrated that the message "MOMMY AND I ARE ONE," presented subliminally, partially relieved symptoms in schizophrenic patients and some groups of nonpsychotic individuals. More recently, Weinberger and Smith (2011) reported the following:

> Two programs of empirical research have endeavored to explicate some of the unconscious processes involved in adult phenomena of merger, symbiosis, or oneness. . . . These lines of research have established links between unconscious processes of oneness and a range of clinical and nonclinical outcomes. (Abstract)

Also see Sohlberg et al. (1998).

6. Developmental psychologists, including Peter Fonagy et al. (2002), have explained how repeated disruptions in parents' attuned interactions, without repair, lead to the formation of an "alien self" within the child. They asserted that

> the alien self is present in all of us, because transient neglect is part of ordinary caregiving; it is pernicious when later experiences of trauma in the family or the peer group force the child to dissociate from pain by using the alien self to identify with the aggressor. (p. 198)

Estela Welldon (2011) referred to the intergenerational transmission of negative parental introjects in asserting that "good-enough mothering," as described by Winnicott (1952), "is more easily said than done, since mothers are also the children of their own mothers, with their own range of early ordeals and traumas" (p. 65). Also see K. M. Newman's (2013) description of the outcome of parenting that fails to be "good enough."

7. My conceptualization of the personality as divided into the self and anti-self systems is closely aligned with the constructs of the libidinal and antilibidinal ego developed by Fairbairn (1952) and Guntrip (1960) and in some areas with Harry Stack Sullivan's concept of a three-way division between the "good-me," "bad-me," and "not-me." According to Sullivan (1953) and Arieti (1955), the "bad-me" develops as a result of perceiving one's parents as good and oneself as bad. Karen Horney's (1950) descriptions of childhood trauma and the defensive adaptations

children make in trying to meet their needs are similar to my formulations. In terms of the division within the personality, however, Horney conceptualized the neurotic person's self as split between an idealized self and a real self. The concept of an anti-self can also be distinguished from R. D. Laing's (1960/1969) and D. W. Winnicott's (1952) conceptualizations of a "false self" or "persona" that, according to Laing and Winnicott, develops in the infant due to a lack of "mirroring" on the part of the mother or primary caregiver (see Chapters 4 and 5, this volume).

8. Investigations into the concept of the voice led to the development of the Firestone Assessment of Self-Destructive Thoughts (R. W. Firestone & Firestone, 2006) and the Firestone Assessment of Violent Thoughts (R. W. Firestone & Firestone, 2008a, 2008b), self-report questionnaires to determine an individual's risk of self-destructive and/or violent behavior.

9. See Lyons-Ruth (2003), who wrote, "Attachment theory is a two-person theory of conflict and defense. . . . Attachment research has uniquely and reliably illuminated the ontogeny of defensive adaptations to caregivers' refusal or failures to provide needed soothing responses to infant fear or distress" (p. 106). Also see Laczkovics et al. (2018).

10. A fundamental aspect of internal working models has to do with the "infant's encoding of interactions in terms of what they implied about the expected availability (and reliability) of the attachment figure" (Cassidy & Shaver, 2016, p. 783).

11. For further reading, see D. J. Siegel (2012), who explained, "We are continually shaping our cortical architecture. . . . Family experience influences our cortical development and may play a part in how attachment relationships shape many aspects of our functioning, including emotion regulation or affect regulation and our narrative self-understanding" (p. 95).

12. According to Tronick and Beeghly (2011),

> infants of abusing or neglectful parents face a dilemma. To avoid the toxic caregiver, infants can either withdraw and self-regulate (a choice that will eventually lead to diminishing complexity and compromised growth) . . . or maintain their presence in the dysfunctional relationship and gain whatever complexity from it is possible, at whatever cost in the long run. (p. 119)

For example, in observational studies, Beebe and Steele (2013) and Tronick (1989) identified both avoidant and "clinging" behaviors (insecure attachment strategies) in 4-month-olds and 12-month-olds.

CHAPTER 2

1. See Person (2006), who commented, "We now know that memory exists in two forms: autobiographical memory and procedural memory. Fonagy et al. (2002) described these two systems as based on two relatively independent, neurologically and psychologically homogeneous systems" (p. 658). Also see Birnbaum et al. (2008), who described the compensatory uses of fantasy in anxiously attached individuals.

2. Kipnis (2003) delineated more than 100 implicit rules and restrictions of "coupledom" that regulate each partner's behaviors in relation to the other:

   > From bathroom to bedroom, car to kitchen, no aspect of coupled life is not subject to scrutiny, negotiation, and rule formation . . . and love means voluntary adherence to them. . . . [Here] is a brief sample of answers to the simple question: "What can't you do because you're in a couple?". . . . You can't leave the house without saying where you're going. You can't not say what time you'll return. . . . You can't go to parties alone. . . . You can't sleep apart, you can't go to bed at different times, you can't fall asleep on the couch without getting woken up to go to bed. . . . You can't get out of bed right away after sex, etc. . . . Thus is love obtained. . . . What matters is the form. (Kipnis, 2003, pp. 84–92)

3. Willi (1975/1982) described the inequality and polarity he observed in many couples: "In the disturbed partner relationship we often observe that one partner has a need for over-compensatory progression while the other seeks satisfaction in regression. They reinforce this one-sided behavior in each other because they need each other as complements" (p. 24). "This progressive and regressive behavior is a major reason for the mutual attraction and the resulting bond" (p. 56).

4. Perel (2006) declared,

   > My belief, reinforced by twenty years of practice, is that in the course of establishing security, many couples confuse love with merging. This mix-up is a bad omen for sex. . . . Eroticism requires separateness. . . . In order to commune with the one we love, we must be able to tolerate this void and its pall of uncertainties. (p. ix)

   Similarly, David Schnarch (1991) stressed the importance of considering existential anxieties and fears of aloneness to help explain why partners with low levels of self-differentiation have boring, routine sex: "[These] people have boring, monotonous sex because intense sex and intimacy (and change itself) are more threatening than many people realize" (p. 143).

5. In describing mating preferences, attachment researchers Mikulincer and Shaver (2016) reported,

> Insecure people tend to possess problematic mate preferences, which further jeopardize their chances of establishing a satisfying relationship. . . . Specifically, anxious individuals were more attracted to anxiously attached partners, and avoidant people were more attracted to avoidant partners. However, Pieetromonaco and Carnelley (1994) and C. Straus et al. (2012) found complementary patterns of mate preferences, by which avoidant people preferred an anxious partner. (p. 299)

6. The critical inner voice strongly influences how individuals relate to each other in an intimate attachment in much the same manner as do internal working models. For example, Rholes et al. (2007) suggested,

> Highly anxious individuals might maintain their negative model of self in relationships by selectively attending to information about their negative behaviors/characteristics. . . . The partners of highly anxious and highly avoidant persons may remain dissatisfied with their relationships in part because they selectively attend to the negative qualities of their insecure partners. (p. 437)

Also see Mikulincer and Shaver (2007), who noted,

> Another common dynamic can be found in couples where the desires of insecure/preoccupied individuals for close proximity to and fusion with relationships partners [encourage them] . . . to project their negative self-views onto relationship partners, thereby creating an illusory sense of similarity and union. (p. 171)

Regarding parent–child relating, Bakermans-Kranenburg and Van IJzendoorn (1993) proposed that "internal working models or current 'state of mind' with respect to attachment relationships determine parents' sensitivity to their infants' attachment behavior, and, in turn, shape the infants' own internal working models of attachment" (p. 870).

7. According to Bowen (1978),

> The two-person relationship is unstable in that it has a low tolerance for anxiety. . . . When anxiety increases, the emotional flow in a twosome intensifies and the relationship becomes uncomfortable. When the intensity reaches a certain level the twosome predictably and automatically involves a vulnerable third person in the emotional issue. (p. 400)

Most often, that third person is the couple's child.

8. Findings from numerous studies investigating manifestations of emotional hunger tend to validate my clinical observations and hypotheses regarding this important family dynamic, described in previous works (R. W. Firestone, 1987, 1990b, 1997a). For example, according to Ungar (2009), "Barber (1996) provides an exhaustive review of the construct of psychological control as a form of overprotection . . . [that] inhibits or intrudes upon psychological development through manipulation and exploitation of the parent–child bond" (p. 3). Also see Lynch et al. (2002), a study conducted by Brussoni and Olsen (2013) regarding fathers' concerns about the effects of overprotection of their children's self-confidence, and research findings reported by P. C. Alexander (2003), Hazen et al. (2005), Kerig (2005), Macfie et al. (2015), and Mayseless et al. (2004), as well as Clarke et al. (2013), who developed the Parental Overprotection Scale.

9. Regarding the "ideal" parent, see Ryan et al. (2006), who pointed out, "Countless studies have established the importance of maternal supportiveness to early child cognitive development. . . . These studies have also shown that, as with mothers, sensitivity, responsiveness, and stimulation among fathers predict better cognitive outcomes for infants and young children" (p. 212).

10. Lyons-Ruth et al. (2013) narrowed the broad term *maternal insensitivity* to a more precise phenomenon, *maternal withdrawal*, a profoundly damaging behavior, specifically when the infant is distressed and/or other exhibiting cues indicate their need for soothing. Also see Beebe et al. (2012), who hypothesized, "Future disorganized infants represent states of not being seen and known by their mothers, particularly in moments of distress; they represent confusion about both their own and their mothers' basic emotional organization" (p. 352).

11. Through extensive long-term research conducted in 35 cultures, Rohner (1986a, 1986b, 1991) and colleagues (Rohner & Khaleque, 2010) examined parents' accepting and rejecting attitudes toward their child. They found that these feelings and attitudes exist on a continuum ranging from parental warmth and acceptance to indifference, rejection, and hostility. Both positive and negative attitudes could be measured intergenerationally (in both parent and child). Also see Rohner (2008), who noted, "Results of most studies reported here conclude that perceived partner acceptance and remembered parental (both maternal and paternal) acceptance in childhood correlate significantly with men's and women's psychological adjustment" (Abstract).

12. Gottman and Krokoff (1989) observed double messages in videotaped interactions between partners where there was a preponderance of negative nonverbal behavioral cues, which each person tried to cover up with positive verbal messages. This dynamic often predicted the eventual dissolution of the relationship. Also see Bach and Deutsch (1979), who applied the Bateson (1972) concept of the double-bind to explore communication between intimate partners, and a more recent analysis by Tramonti (2019), who "addresses the relevance of the work of Gregory Bateson for psychotherapy today" (Abstract).

CHAPTER 3

1. Miller (1980/1984) described the negative consequences of idealizing one's abuser and repressing memories of painful childhood experiences:

    > But the nature of the subsequent enactment reveals that the whole history of early persecution was stored up somewhere; the drama now unfolds in front of the spectators with an amazing resemblance to the original situation but under another guise: in the reenactment, the child who was once persecuted now becomes the persecutor. (p. 145)

    Also see Jessica Benjamin (1988), who contended, "The fantasy of the omnipotent mother is the result of psychic splitting, replicated at many levels of cultural and social experience" (p. 214).

2. Attachment researchers have described the idealization process in children designated as "insecure/avoidant." According to Ainsworth (1985), "[These children] tend to offer an idealized picture of parent or parents, but in response to probes may recall episodes that quite contradict this picture" (p. 796). Other research, using the Adult Attachment Interviews, showed that "Insecure-dismissing individuals . . . usually have trouble remembering childhood experiences and often strongly idealize one or both parents" (Reiner & Spangler, 2013, p. 216). Also see Lanktree and Briere (2015), who found, "In addition to delayed symptom onset [due to trauma], some children, especially those experiencing reduced caretaker support . . . may actively deny abuse effects that they are actually experiencing due to shame or fear of retribution" (p. 65).

3. See J. P. Allen et al. (1996), whose research found a correlation between the severity of childhood trauma of adolescent patients and their idealization of parents, despite their own reports of frightening experiences they had suffered as children. Measures used in this study included the

Adult Attachment Interview. An individual's idealization of parents also can be assessed by using The Mother-Father-Peer Scale, which "consists of dimensions measuring participants' perceived quality of treatment by mother, father, and peers while growing up . . . [including] defensive idealization" of a mother or father who "had not a single fault that I can think of" (Brennan & Shaver, 1998, p. 844). According to Dorothy Bloch (1978), idealizing one's parents at one's own expense acts as a survival mechanism for the helpless, dependent child. Bloch proposed, "That a distorted parental image may be essential to the psyche's defensive system has emerged with great clarity from both my work with children and my psychoanalytic treatment of adults" (p. 162).

4. According to Harrop (2002) and Harrop and Trower (2001), schizophrenia is a form of "blocked development." Harrop and Trower noted, "Some people with a psychosis are not very autonomous, and still have a simplistic and idealized view of their parents" (p. 246). In another study (Trower & Harrop, 1999), the psychotic clients endorsed "questionnaire items reflecting this difficulty (conflict), such as 'People who argue with Mum are awful,' 'I never say things my Mum may not want to hear'" (p. 245).

5. Yalom (1980), Searles (1961), and Karon and VandenBos (1977) have described schizophrenic patients' strong resistance to challenging the idealization of the mother due partly to their inability to cope with existential anxiety. Yalom observed,

> First, the anxiety of facing death is infinitely greater in those who do not have the strengthening knowledge of personal wholeness and of whole participation in living. (Another) source of intense death anxiety emanates from the nature of the schizophrenic *patient's early relationship to mother—a symbiotic union from which the patient has never emerged* [emphasis added] but in which he or she continues to oscillate between a position of psychological merger and a state of total unrelatedness. Furthermore, the schizophrenic patient perceives that the symbiotic relationship is absolutely necessary to survival. (pp. 151–152)

6. Portions of this example include direct quotes and paraphrased sections of a case study originally published in *The Fantasy Bond* (R. W. Firestone, 1985, pp. 87–89). Adapted from *Overcoming the Destructive Inner Voice: True Tales of Therapy and Transformation* ("the work") by Robert W. Firestone. Copyright 2016. Used by permission of Rowman & Littlefield Publishing Group. All rights reserved.

7. There are other emotional disorders and psychopathologies linked to the dynamics of idealizing parents. For example, Cartwright (2002) identified

a number of violent individuals who have a defensive organization characterized by "a rigid split in the psyche between a constellation of idealized object relations and internalized world of bad objects" (p. 113). Also see Ward et al. (2001), who found that in women with anorexia nervosa, "Low levels of reflective functioning and high idealization scores are found . . . [that] may be learned (or transmitted) from mother to daughter . . . [and] act as a risk factor for the development of anorexia nervosa" (Abstract).

8. See Mayseless and Popper (2007), who explained, "Leaders in an attachment capacity, especially in times of turmoil and danger need to be idealized in order to be perceived as stronger and wiser; hence there is a need for some distance to allow for this idealization" (p. 81). Similarly, Shamir (1995) demonstrated that "distant leaders with whom respondents never had close contact (e.g., political leaders) were perceived in a much more stereotyped manner as figures 'larger than life' compared with close leaders whom respondents met face to face" (p. 23). Also see Mayseless and Popper's (2007) *compensation hypothesis*, proposing that "a person with an ambivalent (preoccupied) attachment style . . . [shows] the strongest propensity to form attachment relationships with a leader" (p. 84). "[Their] yearning may lead to the uncritical adoption of certain dogmas and leaders that offer such security, a quite frequent occurrence in adolescence" (p. 82).

9. According to Mikulincer and Shaver (2016), the defensive idealization of others (parents and partners), "like other reality-distorting defenses, creates additional problems for avoidant people because it conflicts with their desire for distance" (p. 147). Regarding mate selection in terms of the idealization process, see Felmlee (2001), who argued that people tend to idealize their partners and also perceive virtues in their partner's faults or weaknesses.

CHAPTER 4

1. Anticipations of rejection are closely related to beliefs and expectations regarding the availability and reliability of attachment figures, originally described as *internal working models* by Bowlby (1972, 1973, 1980): "Bowlby posited internal working models as a mechanism through which interactions with caregivers are internalized. These 'working models' forecast the caregiver's availability and responsiveness" (Cassidy & Shaver,

2016, p. 65). As noted in Chapter 1, there are distinct similarities between the concept of the voice and negative beliefs about the self and others in the context of an attachment relationship (internal working models) held by insecurely attached individuals (Bretherton, 1996; Bretherton et al., 1990; Fonagy et al., 2002; Main, Kaplan, & Cassidy, 1985). For studies investigating *cognitive schema* or thought processes that make up internal working models, see Bosmans et al. (2010), whose findings "confirm the hypothesis that *maladaptive cognitions* related to insecure attachment explain the association between attachment and symptoms of psychopathology" (p. 16) and "internal working models can be better conceptualized as cognitive schemas" (pp. 16–17). Also see Mikulincer and Shaver's (2007) investigations into adult attachment and their descriptions of how internal working models influence how each partner relates to the other.

2. In explaining how infants are able to "read" the intentions of the caregiver, D. J. Siegel (2001) proposed, "Within the child's brain is created a multisensory image of the emerging caregiver's nonverbal signals. These nonverbal signals reveal the primary emotional states of the individual's [caregiver's] mind" (p. 84). As Badenoch (2008) noted, "With the discovery and exploration of *mirror neurons* in the last decade, we are becoming aware of how we constantly embed within ourselves the intentional and feeling states of those with whom we are engaged" (p. 37).

3. Cozolino (2002) observed that our

> most common distortions based on the input of early memory are in the direction of shame, a primary socialization affect starting at about 12 months. . . . Individuals who are "shame based" (Bradshaw, 1990) can find criticism, rejection, and abandonment in nearly every interaction, resulting in a life of chronic anxiety, a struggle for perfection, exhaustion, and depression. (p. 99)

4. See Zeanah and Zeanah (1989) and Belsky et al. (2009).

5. Regarding the anti-self system, other theorists have described the formation of an alien part of the self, similar in some respects to my formulations. For example, Fonagy et al. (2002) referred to this alien part of the self as one outcome of disorganized attachment in childhood:

> In the case of chronically insensitive or mis-attuned caregiving, a fault is created in the construction of the self, whereby the infant is forced to internalize the representation of the object's [caregiver's] state of mind as a core part of himself. But in such cases the internalized other remains alien and unconnected to the structures of the constitutional self. (p. 11)

Also see K. M. Newman's (2013) interpretation of Winnicott's (1965) formulations regarding the "false self":

> In the face of a consistent failure of the environmental objects . . . the infant begins to live with an internalized object that is essentially negative and feared. . . . [The infant] form(s) a compromise bond with the object (e.g., the mother) . . . [constructing the "false self-bond" that] helps create the illusion of a responsive mother. (pp. 61–62)

6. A number of theorists and therapists have described aspects of an internal negative thought process or internal voice, including J. S. Beck (1995), Ellis et al. (1975), and Kaufman (2004), among others. In his work with emotion-focused therapy, L. S. Greenberg (2004, 2015) emphasized the importance of identifying thoughts or cognitions that contribute to clients' avoiding experiencing emotions. According to L. S. Greenberg (2004), "To overcome emotion avoidance clients must first be helped to approach emotion by attending to their emotional experience. This often involves changing the cognitions governing their avoidance" (p. 9). Regarding the dynamics and functions of the voice observed in individuals with more severe emotional disorders, see Osatuke and Stiles (2006) and Fonagy (1997).

7. See R. W. Firestone (1993) and L. Firestone and Catlett (2004). Also see Tierney and Fox (2010):

> Researchers found that in spite of their voice's harsh and forceful character, participants felt an affiliation towards it. . . . Therapists must persist in their endeavors to penetrate this tie, whilst acknowledging the hold this entity has over those with anorexia. (p. 243)

8. Descriptions of voice therapy theory and methodology can be found in Zeig and Munion (1990) and Kannan and Levitt (2013). Voice therapy methodology can be distinguished from "voice dialogue" (Stone & Stone, 1989). For example, in Corstens et al. (2008; an adaptation of Stone & Stone's, 1989, voice dialogue), "The facilitator tries to help the Voice Hearer (VH) recognize and acknowledge the original positive purpose of the voice and change their attitude to it in order to create a more fruitful relationship" (p. 330). An approach more congenial to voice therapy, both theoretically and methodologically, can be found in L. S. Greenberg's (2004) steps in emotional coaching:

> When the person's accessed primary emotions are unhealthy, the person has to be helped to identify the negative voice associated with these emotions . . . [and] people need to be coached to challenge the destructive thoughts, in their unhealthy emotions, [answering back] from a new inner voice based on their healthy primary emotions and needs, and to learn to regulate when necessary. (p. 7)

CHAPTER 5

1. According to Garrels (2011),

   > Imitation may very well be the basis for not only how we learn, but also how we understand each other's intentions and desires, establish relational bonds, fall in love, become jealous, compete with one another, and violently destroy each other, all the while operating largely outside of our conscious awareness. (p. 1)

   In the same volume, Meltzoff and Moore (1998) emphasized, "The imitation of customs, habits, rituals, practices, preferences, social norms, and values is essential to maintaining human culture itself" (p. 57).

   Also see K. E. Hart et al.'s (2006) critical analysis of Bandura et al.'s (1963) original study. According to a recent analysis by Green and Piel (2009), Bandura et al. (1963) expanded on his original social learning theory of imitation to include cognitive factors, which is termed *social cognitive learning theory*, "a learning theory which has come out on the ideas that people learn by watching what others do, and that human thought processes are central to understanding personality" (p. 11).

2. In "Paranoia and Self-Consciousness," Fenigstein and Vanable (1992) cite R. D. Laing's (1960/1969) argument that

   > the self-conscious awareness of oneself as an object of the awareness of others leads to a heightened sense of being seen; as a result, self-conscious persons are susceptible to the paranoid feeling that they are the object of other people's interest more than, in actuality, is the case. (p. 129)

   Regarding the destructive voices that influence paranoia, they noted that

   > activation of the self-schema (voices about the self) not only influences the dimensions along which others are judged . . . but also actively biases the perception of others to make it appear as if their behavior, real or imagined, is somehow related to the self [e.g., that others are watching, thinking about, or perhaps even trying to influence the self]. (Fenigstein & Vanable, 1992, p. 137)

3. See J. Gilligan (2001), who observed,

   > In the course of my psychotherapeutic work with violent criminals, I was surprised to discover that I kept getting the same answer when I asked one man after another why he had assaulted or even killed someone: "Because he disrespected me." In fact, they used that phrase so often that they abbreviated it to, "He dissed me." . . . In my previous book, I spoke of shame as the pathogen that causes violence. (pp. 26, 27)

The reader can find excerpts of interviews with J. Gilligan (2001) in the video documentary *Voices of Violence: Part I. the Roots of Violence* (Parr, 2008), distributed at https://www.psychotherapy.net. Also see the Firestone Assessment of Violent Thoughts (FAVT; R. W. Firestone & Firestone, 2008a, 2008b). Reliability and validity studies conducted on the FAVT found five levels or factors to be significantly correlated with violent behavior: (a) social mistrust, (b) being disregarded, (c) negative critical thoughts, (d) overt aggression, and (e) self-aggrandizing thoughts. An alternative developmental pathway is that, in some cases, as noted earlier, rage reactions to parental dismissal or disrespect are internalized, which later can lead to self-destructive and/or suicidal behavior (R. W. Firestone, 2018).

4. See Kokkinaki and Vitalaki (2013) and Marco Iacoboni et al. (1999), who described the neural mechanisms responsible for imitation. In addition, Ray and Heyes (2011) argued,

> Imitation requires the imitator to . . . translate visual information from modelled action into matching motor output. It has been widely accepted for some 30 years that (this) correspondence problem is solved by a specialized, innate cognitive mechanism. This is the conclusion [that] assumes that human neonates can imitate a range of body movements. . . . [However], the experience necessary for this kind of learning is provided by the socio-cultural environment during human development. (Abstract)

5. Regarding a parent's misreading and thus not mirroring the infant's internal states, see the comprehensive investigation into the complex processes of social cognition, imitation, and mirroring provided by Provenzi et al. (2018), who noted,

> [In conclusion], while there are some constructs that have been analyzed in detail (i.e., contingency, coordination, matching, synchrony), there are still some areas that have not been fully and thoroughly explored and deserve further attention (i.e., reparation and mirroring). It should be noted that these two processes are key dyadic mechanisms respectively involved in achieving better synchrony (i.e., reparation) and in increasing the chances of understanding the other partner's interactive intentions (i.e., mirroring). (p. 19)

Provenzi et al. (2018) also noted,

> Tronick (Dowd & Tronick, 1986) has greatly described how the ability to repair interactive ruptures is one of the central dyadic processes (Fonagy, 2015; Harrison & Tronick, 2011) that associates with adequate and protective caregiving as well as effective psychotherapeutic work. (p. 16)

6. See Sutfin et al. (2008), whose findings are

> consistent with a variety of related results that point to the importance of attitudes, behaviors, and relationships in the family of origin, rather than to structural features of the family such as parental sexual orientation, as the crucial factors that influence children's development. (pp. 509–510)

For example, in studies of children's imitation of parents in same-sex couples, Goldberg et al. (2012) noted, "The perceived play behaviors of boys and girls in same-gender parent families were more similar (i.e., less gender stereotyped) than the perceived play behavior of boys and girls in heterosexual-parent families (which were more divergent; that is, gender-stereotyped)" (Abstract). Refer to Golombok et al. (2014, 2018) regarding children's overall adjustment within adoptive and surrogate same-gender parent families compared with heterosexual parent families.

CHAPTER 6

1. See Janowsky (2001). Also see De Fruyt et al. (2006), who found correlations between depression and introversion "in 599 patients treated for major depression (over a 6-month period) . . . patients described themselves as slightly more extraverted, open to experience, agreeable and conscientious, and substantially more emotional stable after treatment" (Abstract).

2. *Microsuicide* refers to those behaviors, communications, attitudes, or lifestyles that are self-induced and threatening to an individual's physical health, emotional well-being, or personal goals. See R. W. Firestone and Seiden (1987, 1990b). Soubrier (1993) provided a psychoanalytic definition of suicide as "a final act of despair of which the result is not known, occurring after a battle between an unconscious death wish and a desire to live better, to love and be loved" (p. 37). I conceptualize suicide as a triumph of the anti-self—the self-destructive aspect of the personality.

3. Regarding insecure (preoccupied and disorganized) attachments and emotional dysregulation in infants, Liotti (2006) contended, "In stressful circumstances, the segregated negative internal working model may surface to regulate emotions and cognitions in a way that is alien to the person's usual sense of self" (p. 56). For research into emotional dysregulation in borderline personality disorders, see Mosquera et al. (2014), Conklin et al. (2006), and Ebner-Priemer et al. (2007).

4. See R. W. Firestone (1993). Person (1995) provided descriptions and literary examples of the creative and compensatory uses of fantasy. Person emphasized that fantasy processes encompass much of conscious and unconscious mental activity. Compensatory functions of fantasy also have been investigated by Somer and Herscu (2017) and Healy (2014), who noted, "More recently Swygnedow (2010) and Davidson (2012) have used fantasy to analyze the politics (denial) of global warming" (p. 2).

5. See Izard and Buechler (1980), who noted, "All of the discrete emotions have some motivational impact on the individual. . . . The emergence of anger, for example, makes salient the attributes of frustrating restraints and motivates efforts to deal with barriers" (pp. 170, 172). The ability to experience and regulate one's emotions is linked to a secure attachment. For example, Fosha (2005) cited studies highlighting "the moment-to-moment processes by which infants and caregivers mutually regulate affective states and achieve safety and resonance despite vicissitudes of attachment, self-states, and relatedness" (pp. 516–517).

   Schore (2019) reported, "In face-to-face (as well as body-to-body) transactions, the mother is implicitly shaping her infant's unconscious mind" (p. 9). According to D. J. Siegel and Hartzell (2003), "When children experience an attuned connection from a responsive empathetic adult, they feel good about themselves because their emotions have been given resonance and reflection" (p. 66). Also see Brumariu (2015), who noted, "Securely attached children internalize effective emotion regulation strategies within the attachment relationship and are able to successfully employ adaptive emotion regulation strategies outside the attachment relationship, when the attachment figure is not present" (Abstract).

6. L. S. Greenberg (2002) found that

   > Telling oneself it is not rational to be so anxious or depressed is not very effective. In therapy people cannot easily be cured by reason alone. Connections from the emotional centers of the brain to the rational ones are much stronger than those in the reverse direction (Le Doux, 1996). Thus, people are moved far more by their emotions than they are able to move their emotions by rational control. This is a fact of cerebral architecture. (p. 303)

7. For example, L. S. Greenberg (2002) encourages many of his patients to identify the critical voices associated with their maladaptive emotions. See "Exercise 8. The Whole Process of Emotional Coaching . . . 6. Identify the destructive voice and destructive thoughts: 8. Put the hostile, negative thoughts against the self into 'you' language. Say them to yourself: 'You are worthless'" (p. 219).

8. In clinical studies, we were able to identify three levels of the voice in terms of intensity and content: (a) self-critical thoughts and attitudes; (b) self-accusations accompanied by angry affect; and (c) injunctions, often accompanied by murderous rage, to injure or kill oneself. When verbalized out loud, these voices, composed of vicious, degrading self-accusations and injunctions to injure oneself, are powerful and dramatic. It is important to emphasize that, in almost every case, emotional catharsis appeared to decrease the need for destructive action (R. W. Firestone & Seiden, 1990a). See Table 6.1.

9. See Fosha (2005), who described several therapeutic approaches focused on emotional processes that facilitate transformational change and healing in clients and somatic-focused and emotion-focused experiential traditions. They documented how "the psyche is transformed through the simple shifting of focus away from in-the-head cognition and toward moment-to-moment in-the-body sensing and feeling ('lose your head and come to your senses')" (p. 517).

CHAPTER 7

1. Dallos (2004) described this "turning away" in terms of the behaviors or strategies that an avoidantly attached child might develop in response to an emotionally unavailable parent: "If the child's experience is that painful rebuffs may occur when she tries to gain closeness, she may try to evolve ways of distracting herself from her need for attachments" (p. 44), often by engaging in self-soothing and self-nourishing behaviors. In other cases, intrusive and/or unreliable parents can interfere with their children's ability to develop a "core self" or personal identity, including an awareness of their basic wants and needs (Stern, 1985). Also see Bretherton (1995), who suggested, "Misleading, inappropriate, or absent feedback from a parent or other attachment figure . . . may also under-mine an infant's ability to construct adequate, well-organized internal working models of self and the attachment figure" (p. 317).

2. Fromm (1939) described the social and historical sources of modern (early 20th century) views of selflessness and self-denial. Referring to the work of Max Weber (1930), Fromm (1939/1959) noted,

> The tremendous economic achievements of modern society would not have been possible if this kind of asceticism had not absorbed all energy to the purpose of thrift and relentless work . . . [but] man became the slave of a master inside himself instead of one outside. (pp. 5–6)

In some cases, cultural or societal perceptions of asceticism confound research findings and interpretations of such findings, as pointed out by Cole (2008), who argued that "the perpetuation of an image of asceticism may play a role in inhibiting the positive role that vegan diets and lifestyles have to play in reducing serious contemporary social harms" (p. 707). Also see Banks (1996).

3. Cavaiola and Lavender (2000) portrayed this type of hostile withholding as characteristic of individuals who may be diagnosed with passive-aggressive personality disorder (PAPD). However, there was considerable debate over whether to include this diagnostic category in *DSM-IV* (American Psychiatric Association, 1994). For example, see Rotenstein et al. (2007) and Hopwood et al. (2009); the latter argued that "PAPD appears systematically related to borderline and narcissistic personality disorders, sets of personality traits, and childhood experiences consistent with several theoretical formulations, dysfunction, substance abuse disorders, and history of hospitalizations. Overall, results support the construct validity of PAPD" (Abstract).

4. Regarding withholding in the workplace, see Cramerus (1989), who noted, "The self-derogator's continual focus on his or her weaknesses and shameful inadequacies is debilitating in task performance, hinders skill acquisition, and fosters social isolation" (p. 66). In terms of how withholding behavior patterns in employees are influenced by leadership styles, N. J. Johnson and Klee (2007) reported, "In this phenomenological study, 13 experts were asked about passive-aggressive (PA) behaviors in the workplace, specifically, whether leadership styles (autocratic, transactional, and transformational) can predict them . . . most participants viewed the autocratic leadership style as a predictor of PA behaviors" (Abstract).

5. See Stephen Mitchell (2002), who explained why many individuals need to hold back or control sexual passion in a long-term relationship:

> Erotic passion destabilizes one's sense of self. When we find someone intensely arousing who makes possible unfamiliar experiences of ourselves and an otherness we find captivating, we are drawn into the disorienting loopiness of self/other. We tend to want to control these experiences and the others who inspire them. Thus, emotional connection tends to degrade into strategies for false security that suffocate desire. (p. 92)

Also see B. W. McCarthy (1997) and B. McCarthy and McCarthy (2003) regarding interventions for couples in "low or no-sex" marriages.

6. The term *mixed message* refers to double bind theory, developed by Bateson (1972) initially to help clarify environmental factors involved in the etiology of schizophrenia. In reviewing Bateson's double bind theory and extending it to the neuroses, Gibney (2006) stated,

> The essential hypothesis of the double bind theory is that the "victim"—the person who becomes psychotically unwell—finds him or herself in a communicational matrix, in which messages contradict each other. . . . A secondary injunction that conflicts with the first at a more abstract level, and like the rest, is enforced by punishment or signals that threaten survival, is often communicated by posture and tone and may include such "meta-messages" as: "Do not notice the contradiction between my claim to be a loving parent and my willingness to withdraw my love from you." . . . [and] a tertiary negative injunction that prohibits the victim from escaping the field. (p. 50)

7. According to Bach and Deutsch (1979),

> "Crazymaking" derives from the obscure portion of a double message. (p. 20) . . . The open half of the message is always clear and understandable. . . . It is invariably a message of goodwill, acceptance, agreement, love, concern, loyalty. But the second half of the double message is always foggy. It is indirect. And it is always especially hard for us to hear and understand, because it is something we don't want to hear. (p. 2)

Gottman and Krokoff (1989) demonstrated that in these "double-bind" interactions, it was the negative affect communicated nonverbally, especially postural and facial expressions indicating contempt, that predicted the dissolution of the relationship. According to Bateson (1972), in parent–child relations, double messages can be even more devastating.

8. "Don't let him know how much he means to you" and other negative advice by the voice, such as "Don't get too attached. Who needs romance, anyway?" and other voices that influence withholding and self-denying behavior reflect dysfunctional beliefs or internal working models associated with insecure attachment styles. According to Dallos (2004),

> In brief, the working model consists of two interdependent parts: 1. A view of the world in terms of . . . whether the world is a dangerous place in which no one will be willing to help, and the need to deal with feelings on one's own. 2. A view of the self as worthy or unworthy of love and affection. (p. 47)

Mikulincer and Shaver (2016) found that "avoidant people learn . . . not to seek support from attachment figures" (p. 147), and "avoidant people tend to project onto a relationship partner their own undesirable traits, which gives them an added reason to dismiss or disparage others and maintain distance from them" (p. 497).

9. Regarding generosity, see Sober and Wilson's (1999) discussion of altruism. Here, the authors refuted many earlier explanations of the evolutional basis of altruism, notably the concepts of reciprocal altruism and the "selfish gene." Also see Rosas (2010), whose

> approach implies a new concept of altruism: a cooperative behavior is altruistic whenever it requires positive assortment between altruists to evolve. . . . The role of assortment, and its being controlled by individual traits that co-evolve with altruistic ones, is the fundamental new insight promoted by the neighbor modulated fitness approach. (Abstract)

Dovidio et al. (2006) also reported that facing death often makes one more willing to help others. As an example, these researchers tracked the rates of volunteering before and after September 11, 2001, and reported "a two to threefold increase in volunteering following 9/11" (R. W. Firestone & Catlett, 2009b, p. 196, n. 11).

CHAPTER 8

1. See MacKillop and Ray (2018), who concluded, "Across theoretical accounts, there is convergence that addiction is a disorder of 'vicious cycles,' or patterns of maladaptive overconsumption that over time become increasingly difficult to change" (p. 44). Also see Esch and Stefano's (2004) comprehensive analysis in "The Neurobiology of Pleasure: Reward Processes, Addiction, and their Health Implications." Karim and Chaudhri (2012) also noted that "the legitimacy of nonsubstance addictions has received increased attention from clinicians, researchers and the general population as more and more individuals report symptoms consistent with impairment of impulse control" (Abstract). For example, see Peele (2001), who argued, "Gambling provides a vivid and comprehensible example of an experiential model of addiction" (Abstract).

2. Kaye (2008) reported,

> Twin studies of anorexia (AN) and bulimia (BN) suggest there is approximately a 50 to 80% genetic contribution to liability accounted for by additive genetic factors [p. 122] . . . the majority of people with AN and BN exhibit childhood perfectionism, obsessive-compulsive personality patterns, and anxiety that predate the onset of AN and BN. (p. 124)

However, in a more recent study exploring childhood antecedents of eating disorders, K. L. Allen et al. (2014) found that "maternal concern about child weight, children's level of family satisfaction, family exposure to stress, and maternal education are unique predictors of child eating disorder symptoms" (Abstract).

3. According to Estévez et al. (2017), recent research findings have challenged the view that certain nonsubstance behavioral addictions are, in fact, "normal" activities: "For instance, playing video games is an activity that when taken to excess and starts to become problematic has been viewed by many scholars as a type of behavioral addiction with dysfunctional psychological symptoms" (p. 534). In addition, Monacis et al. (2017) called attention to compensatory functions served by excessive online activity: "Positive associations were found between need for approval (referred to as an anxious style) and . . . online addictions. . . . Moreover, individuals with . . . an avoidant attachment, are led by their attachment attitudes . . . to satisfy their need of social belonging by using the online format" (pp. 863–864).

4. See Dryer and Lijtmae (2007) and Coleman-Kennedy and Pendley (2002), who found, "As many as 20 million people in the United States are affected by sexual addiction" (p. 143). de Alarcón et al. (2019) found that "hypersexual disorder fits this model (of behavioral addictions) and may be composed of several sexual behaviors, like problematic use of online pornography" (Abstract). Similarly, Wéry and Billieux (2017) reported, "It is now acknowledged that excessive involvement in cybersex can become dysfunctional and associated with addiction symptoms (e.g., loss of control, mood regulation)" (p. 2). Regarding genetic factors involved in sex addiction, see Blum et al. (2012).

5. See L. Firestone and Catlett (2004) for a specific format for journaling that has been "adapted for use by clients trying to break an addictive pattern of behavior" (p. 52). Also see White et al. (2020).

6. Kristin Neff (2011), who conducted extensive research to identify the dimensions of self-compassion, asserted,

> Self-compassion entails treating oneself with kindness, recognizing one's shared humanity, and being mindful when considering negative aspects of oneself. . . . Research . . . shows that self-compassion provides greater emotional resilience and stability than self-esteem, but involves less self-evaluation . . . it is a kind, connected, and clear-sighted way of relating to ourselves even in instances of failure, perceived inadequacy, and imperfection. (Abstract)

Also see Phelps et al. (2018), who found that "low risk for substance use disorder was associated with higher level of SC (self-compassion)" (p. 78).

7. See Flores's (2001) group therapy model of total abstinence and relapse prevention, in which

> the third step involves learning to gradually build a new life in which relationships now become as rewarding or as gratifying as the addiction once was. . . . [In this respect,] attachment-oriented group therapy can be defined as a way of eliciting, exploring, integrating, and modifying attachment styles represented within a person's internal working model. (p. 75)

CHAPTER 9

1. According to Skowron and Friedlander (1998), individuation and differentiation of self, while having some similarities, still refer to different processes:

> Individuation, from an object-relations perspective . . . involves the achievement of independence and a unique sense of identity. Differentiation of self is the capacity to maintain autonomous thinking and achieve a clear, coherent sense of self in the context of emotional relationships with important others. (p. 237)

As Bowen (in Kerr & Bowen, 1988) explained, "The more differentiated a self, the more a person can be an individual while in emotional contact with the group" (p. 93). Moreover, research conducted by Jenkins et al. (2005) "indicated that differentiation level is significantly predictive of psychosocial development" (Abstract).

2. Eric Erikson (1968) recommended that adolescents search for their own political and/or religious ideology and value system: "A youthful ideology affords young people with an instrument of individuation and self-definition" (Burston, 2007, p. 152). Also see Meeus et al. (2005), who proposed,

> Adolescence is the period in which the parent–child relationship changes in character, and identity is formed. The frequency and duration of contacts between parent and adolescent decrease, the parent–adolescent relationship becomes less authoritarian and more egalitarian, and identity becomes less diffuse and more clear and articulated . . . separation from the parents is not a precondition for individuation, but rather separation and individuation are two parallel processes of development during adolescence. (Abstract)

3. Lapsley and Edgerton (2002) asserted,

> The developmental task for the young adult is to flexibly manage the ongoing dialectic between separation and connectedness, while avoiding the undesirable outcomes of fusion and enmeshment, on the one hand,

and complete detachment and isolation, on the other. One factor that may influence how well this task is managed is the attachment style of the young adult. (p. 484)

Lapsley and Edgerton also found that "college adjustment was counter-indicated by fearful and preoccupied attachments" (Abstract).

4. My investigations (R. W. Firestone, 1994) have supported the proposition that conscious death anxiety is often exacerbated by the degree of individuation and self-actualization. See Piven (2004), who asserted,

> The clinical literature is replete with instances where individuation in adulthood continues to threaten death and annihilation. Experiencing one's own feelings and ideas, acting upon one's own desires against anonymous conformity, even sexual pleasure itself can threaten one with guilt, punishment, loss of love, even psychotic fragmentation, death, and extinguishment of the ego. (p. 174)

Tillich (1952) also noted that "the anxiety of death increases with the increase of individualization" (p. 50). Similarly, Maslow (1971) described the fear of death as closely related to the fear of standing alone, as an individual, apart from the crowd:

> We fear our highest possibilities (as well as our lowest ones). . . . We enjoy and even thrill to the godlike possibilities we see in ourselves in such peak moments. And yet we simultaneously shiver with weakness, awe, and fear before these very same possibilities. (p. 34)

5. For example, Liotti (2011) contended,

> Being exposed to frequent interaction with a FR (frightening/frightened) caregiver, infants are caught in a relational trap: their dense system motivates them to flee from the caregiver, while at the same time their attachment system motivates them, under the commanding influence of separation fear, to strive for achieving comforting proximity to her or him. (p. 235)

Also see Dutra and Lyons-Ruth (2005) and Lyons-Ruth (2008).

6. Mikulincer and Shaver (2016) reported,

> We have repeatedly discovered associations between individual differences in attachment-system functioning and people's perceptions of others (e.g., what one thinks [imagines] about the availability, supportiveness, personal traits, and intentions of a relationships partner) and oneself (e.g., What one thinks [imagines] about one's own value to relationship partners, one's lovability). (p. 147)

Also see Hainlen et al. (2016), who found "a link between higher levels of insecure attachment experiences . . . and fusing with others, as well as a link between attachment anxiety and difficulty maintaining an I-position in relationships" (p. 181).

7. Several measures, including the Experiences in Close Relationships Inventory–Revised (Fraley et al., 2000), and the Differentiation of Self Inventory (Skowron & Schmitt, 2003), have been developed to assess people's internal working models and levels of differentiation of self in the context of an intimate relationship. For example, in "Assessing Interpersonal Fusion: Reliability and Validity of a New DSI [Differentiation of Self Inventory] Fusion With Others Subscale," Skowron and Schmitt (2003) noted, "On an interpersonal level, more differentiated individuals are comfortable with intimacy in close relationships and, therefore, the need to regulate feelings of anxiety with fusion or emotional cut off in relationships is decreased" (p. 210).

8. Becoming a parent, as well as moving toward independence and autonomy, disrupts a major component of the fantasy bond—the idealization of parents. According to Kerr and Bowen (1988),

> The more differentiation between parents and a child, the less likely it is that the child will idealize or denigrate either parent. . . . A reasonable amount of objectivity about self and others, coupled with the ability to act on the basis of that objectivity when it is important to do so, is the essence of differentiation of self. (p. 203)

9. See Solomon (2019):

> From an existential perspective, becoming a parent is a potentially dynamic transition that confers numerous social and psychological benefits, as well as presenting some daunting challenges. [This chapter] present[s] an empirically corroborated account of how parenthood assuages and arouses existential anxieties. (Abstract)

In this regard, Yaakobi et al. (2014) found that avoidantly attached individuals did not find parenthood to be a buffer against death anxiety. Instead, worries related to becoming a parent made death-related thoughts more accessible: "Although one could argue that thinking about parenthood might boost a person's self-esteem, this may not be true for avoidant people who are likely to perceive parenthood as incompatible with their strivings for autonomy and self-reliance" (p. 773).

10. According to J. B. McCarthy (1980),

> If the goal of the psychoanalytic work is the patient's freedom and autonomy, and the [patient] retains the unconscious fears that autonomy equals death or the loss of the self, then the positive outcome of the analysis may be as anxiety-provoking as the original inner conflicts. (p. 193)

Also see Bollas (1987), who focused attention on helping restore the patient's authentic self, which at termination involves separation from introjected "parental views" (aspects of the anti-self) and a strengthening of the patient's point of view. According to Bollas, during the termination phase, "the analyst restores to the patient what I believe we can term genuine or true subjectivity" (p. 63).

11. See Skynner (1991), who described how Bowen (1978) used role modeling in family therapy sessions:

> Bowen promotes the formation of the boundaries of key individuals by clearly defining his own, through indicating what he will do and not do by avoiding manipulative attempts to seduce him or coerce him into taking responsibility for patient or family pathology. By not functioning for the patient, he sets an example from which family members may ultimately learn to function for themselves and to contain their own assets and liabilities. (p. 184)

12. See the Therapeutic Reactance Scale (TRS) by Dowd et al. (1991), as well as P. Johnson and Buboltz (2000), who suggested, "Therapists may find it useful to assess the developmental etiology of the resistance and reactance and to address their clients' reactivity by increasing their levels of differentiation" (p. 99). Also see Przybyła's (2016) comprehensive paper, "Neurobiological Foundations of Psychotherapy," which asserted that "behavioral or cognitive change made through training or reformulation of cognitive schemas, is insufficient. This is because the change in the internal organization of the human mind is possible mainly through affective assimilation of undigested experience" (p. 40). Similarly, in applying voice therapy to the process of differentiation, my associates and I observed that "by expressing the emotions associated with their destructive thought patterns, clients were able to relinquish deeply held misconceptions of self, allowing them to experience increased feelings of compassion for themselves" (R. W. Firestone et al., 2012, p. 44).

CHAPTER 10

1. Portions of this chapter are adapted from *Sex and Love in Intimate Relationships* by R. W. Firestone et al. (2006).

2. Their style of relating is often linked to insecure (avoidant or anxious) attachment strategies they developed early in life. According to adult attachment researchers Mikulincer and Shaver (2016),

> Avoidant people's discomfort with closeness may interfere with psychological intimacy in sexual situations . . . [their] avoidance may be associated with measurable erotophobia (i.e., fearing or backing away from sex) or preference for impersonal, uncommitted sex. . . . Attachment anxiety is

likely to be associated with a complex ambivalent approach to sexuality. . . . Perhaps the most dangerous kinds of sexual difficulties for anxious people can be traced to their interpersonal desires and fears. Their intense desire for closeness can result in intrusive sexual behavior and cause them to engage in unsafe sex. . . . In addition their fear of rejection can create problems in communication about sex, difficulties with sexual assertiveness, and an increased vulnerability to sexual coercion. (p. 372)

3. Sex therapist Wendy Maltz and Beverly Holman defined healthy sexuality: "Healthy sexuality requires that these five basic conditions be met: Consent, Equality, Respect, Trust, and Safety" ("The CERTS Model for Healthy Sex," n.d., para. 1). Also see Sandfort and Ehrhardt (2004), who observed,

> There is a "healthy" suspicion against promoting the use of a health perspective in relation to sexuality. "Health" has been the pretext for suppressing or regulating sexual practices in the past. . . . The pathologizing of masturbation and the battles against STDs and prostitution have a long history in public health and medicine. (p. 184)

Giner-Sorolla et al. (2012) stated, "Recent work suggests that negative moral judgements of sexual activities are informed by disgust and anger. . . . Across scenarios, judgements of abnormality predicted disgust independent of anger, and judgements of harm/rights violation predicted anger independent of disgust" (Abstract). For other definitions of "normal" sexuality, see Magon et al. (2012).

4. As noted, different cultures can hold widely differing views regarding "normal" sexual practices and behavior. See Richardson and Monro (2012) and Heinemann et al. (2016) for reviews of the relevant literature. The latter researchers noted, "In describing some cases where culture has affected sexuality, specific cultural beliefs should not be used to create stereotypes regarding specific cultures, rather, to gain an appreciation for the affect culture can have on sexuality" (Heinemann et al., 2016, p. 144).

5. For example, Stritof (2004) reported highlights of one survey (the 2003 Durex Survey) that found that the average American couple has sex about once a week. The survey also showed that unmarried couples living together have sex 146 times a year, while married couples make love 98 times a year on average.

6. See Wendy Maltz (1995). Also see Ventriglio and Bhugra (2019), who asserted,

> Sexual behaviours and orientations vary and may be related to mental health. . . . Frequently, sexual variations are considered to be pathological

and need to be medically treated. However, it should be accepted that sexuality includes a continuum of behaviours, thoughts, fantasies, acts, and attractions that are beyond procreation. Modern sexology introduced the concept of gender identity and sexual fluidity to describe how gender and sexual orientation vary and are flexible over time. (Abstract)

Otto Kernberg (1980, 1995) also hypothesized a continuum of sexual love based largely on "the capacity—or rather, the incapacity—to fall and remain in love" (Kernberg, 1980, p. 278). Also refer to a panel discussion including Otto Kernberg and Nancy Chodorow in Grossman (2001).

7. Schnarch (1991) portrayed personal sexual relating in terms of an individual's capacity for intimacy and ability to attach "profound emotional meaning to the sexual experience" (p. 143). Schnarch observed that partners with low levels of self-differentiation cling to a conventional form of "other-validated" intimacy, based on the need for fusion, rather than "self-validated" intimacy based on the ability to tolerate separateness and existential aloneness. Knee et al. (2008) conducted research into a phenomenon similar to other-validated intimacy, "relationship-contingent self-esteem" (RCSE): "Although RCSE reflects more commitment to one's partner and the relationship, the relational process is not one that promotes satisfaction or a genuine sense of closeness" (p. 624). Also see Levine (2002) and Ferreira et al. (2012).

8. Brotto and Yule (2017) concluded,

> There is not sufficient evidence to support the classification of asexuality as a psychiatric disorder of as a sexual dysfunction . . . there is modest support for asexuality's placement as a unique sexual orientation. There is, however, likely as much variation among asexual individuals' lack of sexual attraction (and whether it also extends to lack of romantic attraction) as there is among sexual individuals' presence of sexual attraction. (p. 625)

Also see Bogaert (2015), who proposed, "Although more research is needed, there is some evidence that self-identified asexual people are not significantly distressed by their lack of sexual interest/attraction per se" (p. 12); therefore, they do not meet the criteria for being diagnosed with a psychiatric disorder or sexual dysfunction.

9. Schnarch (1991) proposed a new "paradigm" or treatment model— the sexual crucible approach—for overcoming sexual desire disorders that focuses on resolving the need for personal differentiation or self-validation. He suggested that "high desire" and "low desire" are systemic positions in every sexual relationship and that these positions are reflective of other emotional and interpersonal issues.

10. See Katehakis (2017), who asserted,

> Sexual desire is always present in humans, sometimes all the more so when they attempt to suppress it. This paradox leads individuals to engage in some types of sexual fantasies to overcome the kind of guilt about sexual feelings. . . . In sum, the function even of edgy fantasizing is a natural and psychologically neutral, mental power. (p. 258)

However, also see studies by Maniglio (2010): "Results suggest that deviant sexual fantasies can promote sexual homicide when combined with early traumatic experiences and social and/or sexual dysfunction" (Abstract). In my opinion, it is valuable to examine clients' sexual fantasies because they symbolically express their attitudes toward the giving and taking of love in relation to other persons (R. W. Firestone, 1985).

11. For example, in relation to pornography, see Park et al. (2016), who presented

> evidence that Internet pornography's unique properties (limitless novelty, potential for easy escalation to more extreme material, video format, etc.) may be potent enough to condition sexual arousal to aspects of Internet pornography use that do not readily transition to real-life partners, such that sex with desired partners may not register as meeting expectations and arousal declines. Clinical reports suggest that terminating Internet pornography use is sometimes sufficient to reverse negative effects. (Abstract)

12. See Negy et al. (2016), who noted,

> On average, and across the four national groups, the messages young adults received from their parents about broad domains of sexual behaviors (masturbation, non-intercourse types of heterosexual sexual activity, premarital sex, same-sex activity, and cohabiting) were unequivocally restrictive. By contrast, across the four groups, young adults on average held rather permissive sexual values and their values differed significantly from those of their parents. (Abstract)

13. Regarding parents' changing attitudes toward sex education, see Kantor and Levitz (2017), as well as Huber and Firmin (2014) and Lamb (2010).

14. Pulverman et al. (2018) reported the rates of sexual dysfunction among women with CSA histories in random probability studies ranged from 25% to 59% (pp. 2–4). For more detailed studies, see Kinzl et al. (1995), Mullen and Fleming (1998), and Spiegel (2013).

15. For a discussion of changes in societal views of sexuality resulting from the "sexual revolution," see Baumeister and Vohs (2004), who interpreted these changes in terms of social exchange theory, as well as

Baumeister et al. (2002). For a different trend in attitudes, see Leander et al. (2018). Their studies

> revealed an important cultural shift in the attitude toward children's nudity and sexual games, the so-called doctor games. Although these were quite accepted at Danish childcare institutions until the beginning of this century, the study showed that new, pervasive regulations had been established to control the child's body and its sexuality. A new discourse revealed that fear of child sexual abuse, in particular, had influenced views of children's sexual games and nudity and that, at times, the child itself was viewed as a potential threat to other children. (Abstract)

16. Kaplan (1995) described similar negative cognitions or voices that occur before, during, and after a sexual encounter. She called attention to the important part played by "selectively negative cognitive and perceptual processes . . . in the pathogenesis of HSD [hypoactive sexual desire disorders]" (p. 117). Kaplan (1979) also reported specific negative thoughts her patients had reported: "The unconscious injunction—'you are not entitled,' 'something will happen if things get too good,' 'who do you think you are?' 'You can't have everything'—may be the underlying cause of sexual difficulties in such cases" (p. 171).

17. Becker (1973/1997) went on to write, "The sexual conflict is thus a universal one because the body is a universal problem to a creature who must die" (p. 164). Terror management researchers Goldenberg et al. (1999) have hypothesized that "high-neuroticism individuals are conflicted by sex and that the conflict is rooted in mortality concerns" (p. 1184). In an experiment, Goldenberg et al. (2002) found that anxious individuals "who are especially likely to find sex threatening, rated the physical aspects of sex [on a scale] as less appealing when reminded of their mortality" (p. 310). See Birnbaum et al. (2011), who noted,

> Mortality salience (MS) increased the desire for romantic sex, regardless of gender, and the desire for casual sex among more avoidant men. . . . These findings suggest that the variety of meanings sexual behavior has for different people may explain why, in some cases, sexual behavior may function as a defense against mortality concerns, whereas in other cases, it may exacerbate threat. (Abstract)

Also see Watter (2018).

CHAPTER 11

1. See S. Freud (1961), who declared that "a dream is as a rule merely a thought like any other" (p. 112). Carl Jung (1974) proclaimed, "Every dream is an organ of information and control . . . dreams are our most

effective aid in building up the personality" (p. 101). Regarding free association, see Lewis Aron (1996) and Kris (2013).

2. See R. W. Firestone et al. (2003). The book "describes a unique experiment in applied psychology whereby a group of individuals overcame a wide range of defensive behaviors and transformed their lives" (Abstract).

3. See Langs (2006, 2018/1993). In the latter book, Langs (2018/1993) explained why ground rules and "secured frames" are necessary for effective psychotherapy:

> Death is, of course, the existential frame of life; as a result, secured frames, however enhancing they may be, always arouse personal death anxiety and the need to cope with its ramifications. On the other hand, modifying frames allows for grandiose illusions of being able to defy the inevitability of death—though they do so at considerable (usually denied) cost because deviant frames also are persecutory and disruptive in nature. (p. 34)

4. Regarding long-term therapy, see R. W. Firestone (1997a):

> Brief or short-term psychotherapy based on Voice Therapy techniques can be accomplished by a skillful therapist. Nonetheless, the person's potential for future development should not be compromised by treatment processes that focus only on the amelioration of symptoms and relief of anxiety. (p. 166)

Findings from investigations in the neurosciences have led researchers to depict psychoanalysis, depth psychotherapy, and other long-term "talk therapies" as "brain-changing" processes. For example, in *Why Therapy Works*, Cozolino (2015) described, in depth, the neuronal correlates involved in clients' making fundamental changes during psychotherapy. As neuroscientist Joseph LeDoux (1998) suggested,

> Therapy is just another way of creating synaptic potentiation in brain pathways that control the amygdala . . . psychoanalysis, with emphasis on conscious insight and conscious appraisals, may involve the control of the amygdala by explicit knowledge through the temporal lobe memory system and other cortical areas involved in conscious awareness. (p. 265)

5. Regarding primal therapy, see Videgård (1984a). Also see Witty and Khamsi (1995).

6. In terms of the neuronal basis of people's fundamental resistance and fear of change, Louis Cozolino (2015) suggested,

> While most therapists label a client's persistence in maintaining old behaviors, thoughts, and feelings as resistance, I believe that there is a better way to think about it. Our brains weave our experience of reality from millions of unconscious assumptions based on past learning. Interwoven with useful assumptions are those that can make our lives difficult or

impossible. The problem is, our minds usually can't tell the difference . . . so what we usually call resistance may simply be primitive brain circuitry engaging in anxiety reduction by holding onto the beliefs that make us feel safe. (p. 58)

7. Regarding the therapeutic alliance, see Koole and Tschacher (2016), who proposed,

> The core idea of the In-Sync model is that the alliance emerges from the coupling of the neural activity of the brains of the patient and therapist. The more tightly patient and therapist's brains are coupled, the better the alliance. . . . Their coupling can . . . be achieved only indirectly, through the mutual coordination of the patient and therapist's behavior and experiences. . . . Synchrony thus helps to establish the alliance, which in turn promotes adaptive emotion regulation in the patient, and thereby good therapeutic outcomes. (p. 7)

8. See Heinonen et al. (2012), whose research showed that "active, engaging, and extroverted therapists produced a faster symptom reduction in short-term therapy than in long-term therapy. More cautious, non-intrusive therapists generated greater benefits in long-term therapy" (Abstract) and "characteristics inducing patient's hope, initiative and improvement may not, however, be related to therapeutic professional qualities only. . . . Similar outcomes seemed to share certain commonalities (e.g., an invested, non-reclusive manner in personal life)" (p. 310). Also see Jennings and Skovholt (1999), Lafferty et al. (1989), and Delgadillo et al. (2020).

9. See Leong and Lee (2006) regarding differences between "conformity" in individualistic and collectivistic cultures:

> Recent research findings have highlighted that the Asian American worldview emphasizes obligation to family, familial relations, and interpersonal harmony. Furthermore, values such as conformity, obedience, and subordination to authority, role hierarchy versus egalitarianism, and self-restraint versus self-disclosure are also salient for this population. . . . Considerations must be also made for patients' level of acculturation and ethnic identity before developing an adaptive therapeutic approach. (p. 416)

10. Schore (2003) acknowledged what the therapist is up against in striving to maintain the therapeutic stance in relation to unrecognized elements of the anti-self system, which exist in both therapist and patient: "The patient does not project an internal critic [critical inner voice] into the therapist, but rather the therapist's internal critic, stimulated by the patient's negative affective communications, resonates with the patient's and is thereby amplified" (pp. 90–91).

11. McGinty et al. (2016) reported,

> Over the course of a life-time, nearly half of all Americans will meet the criteria for a mental health disorder. Mental illness is now the leading cause of disability in the United States, but only about 40 percent of those affected receive treatment. (p. 1121)

12. Regarding manifestations of the fantasy bond observed in transference reactions, particularly during the termination phase of therapy, see Fierman's (1965) description of Kaiser's concept of the universal psychopathology:

> Whenever the patient comes close to having it driven home to him that it is he himself who is going to make a decision; or that the conviction in his mind is really his, originated by his own thinking; or that it is he, and he alone, who is wanting something, a piece of delusional ideology rolls like a fog over the mental scenery. (pp. 133–134)

Also see Murray Bowen (1978), who proposed,

> [In society], it is possible to identify some of the manifestations of regression. Togetherness forces begin to over-ride individuality, there is an increase in decisions designed to allay the anxiety of the moment, an increase in cause-and-effect thinking, a focus of "rights" to the exclusion of "responsibility," and a decrease in the overall level of responsibility . . . there is another paradox in the focus on togetherness. The more man anxiously strives for togetherness, the more he loses what he strives for. Man needs human closeness, but he is allergic to too much of it. (pp. 279–280)

13. The disciplines of attachment theory and interpersonal neurobiology have an in-depth understanding of psychological trauma and favor psychotherapeutic interventions that involve accessing patients' emotions associated with trauma and other painful experiences from the past. See Schore (2015), who asserted that "the application of attachment principles to psychotherapy models also has been elucidated by focusing the treatment upon the affective dynamics of right brain internal working models encoding coping strategies of affect regulation that are activated within the therapeutic alliance" (p. 30).

CHAPTER 12

1. Portions of this chapter are adapted from *The Enemy Within: Separation Theory and Voice Therapy* (R. W. Firestone, 2018), used with permission from Zeig, Tucker, and Theisen.

2. Regarding patients with schizophrenia, see R. W. Firestone (1997a):

> The hallucinated voices in schizophrenic patients have a parental quality that is similar to the judgmental character of the neurotic patient's self-critical thoughts and negative self-appraisals. Both self-attacking thoughts and auditory hallucinations are indications of a self-parenting process that undermines the personality. (p. 145)

Other studies have investigated the parallels between internal self-statements and auditory hallucinations—see Berry et al. (2017), Smailes et al. (2015), Alderson-Day et al. (2018), and McCarthy-Jones (2012), who observed, "In cognitive behavioural therapy, some voice hearers come to recognize their voices as actually being their own thoughts" (p. 237).

3. In R. W. Firestone et al. (2003), I stated,

> Voice Therapy is cognitive because it helps to elicit and identify, on a conscious level, a person's negative thoughts and attitudes toward self. It is affective in that it brings these thoughts into consciousness, along with the accompanying feelings such as anger and sadness associated with these thoughts. It is behavioral because there is focus on changing the behaviors that are self-limiting or self-destructive. (pp. 77–78)

Voice therapy is similar in some respects to Aaron Beck's "automatic thoughts" (A. T. Beck et al., 1979) in cognitive therapy and Albert Ellis's "irrational beliefs" (Ellis, 1973; Ellis et al., 1975) in rational-emotive therapy; however, there are a number of differences (see R. W. Firestone, 1997a).

4. See J. S. Beck's (1995) emphasis on accessing clients' emotions in cognitive behavior therapy. L. S. Greenberg (2002) described how clients

> can identify the destructive voices associated with . . . [feelings of shame] and recognize the self-contempt that produces the shame probably is a result of a past experience of maltreatment or was learned. . . . Then they are often able to focus on their healthier core feelings of sadness or anger in response to the original situation. (p. 97)

5. Regarding reactions to answering the voice, see R. W. Firestone et al. (2012), Chapter 4. After expressing their parents' distorted attitudes toward them, clients often become aware of a strong urge to angrily contradict these negative views. Therapists need to closely monitor clients' reactions to answering the voice in this way. Individuals who challenge the prescriptions of the voice before they have the emotional maturity to separate from parental introjects may regress and become more resistant to the therapy process.

6. My use of the term *corrective suggestion* is meant to describe techniques that are usually focused on challenging rather than supporting specific defenses of the client. These corrective suggestions often lead directly to a "corrective emotional experience," as described by F. Alexander and French (1946; see Chapter 4, "The Principle of Corrective Emotional Experience," pp. 66–70). Also see "Demon on My Shoulder," in *Overcoming the Destructive Inner Voice: True Stories of Therapy and Transformation* (R. W. Firestone, 2016, Chapter 2, pp. 35–50).

7. This voice therapy session was filmed as part of an e-course about voice therapy produced by PsychAlive.org

8. Murray Bowen (1978) described "differentiation of self," as a concept that "defines people according to the degree of fusion, or differentiation, between emotional and intellectual functioning" (p. 362). According to Skowron and Friedlander (1998), "Differentiation of self is the capacity to maintain autonomous thinking and achieve a clear, coherent sense of self in the context of emotional relationships with important others" (p. 237). See Drake et al. (2015), as well as J. P. Siegel and Forero (2012), who identified specific situations in family life that lead to splitting and low levels of self-differentiation.

9. Schnarch (1991) proposed that low levels of self-differentiation in each partner contribute to disturbances in a couple's sex life. Schnarch observed that partners involved in committed relationships have sexual difficulties because they are operating at relatively low levels of self-differentiation. See Ferreira et al. (2016), whose "results suggest that partners' similarity regarding differentiation of self predicted individual sexual desire. Other findings suggest that couple satisfaction was positively associated with both sexual desire and differentiation of self" (Abstract).

10. See R. W. Firestone (1989). As participants in the group came to a deeper understanding that the sources of their limitations as parents lay in their own painful childhood experiences, they began to adopt a more compassionate, less blaming attitude toward themselves and their children. This preventive model is similar in certain respects to emotion-focused family therapy interventions described by Lafrance et al. (2020).

11. Welling (2012) proposed that the process of accessing implicit memory systems by accessing negative emotional processes may be responsible for basic therapeutic changes observed in emotion-focused therapy and other similar therapeutic models:

> Research on memory reconsolidation has recently shown that a consolidated (long-term) memory trace is not immutable, as neuroscientists

> believed for nearly a century, but can be revised and reconsolidated. Reconsolidation of memory is an adaptive update mechanism by which new information [and more positive emotions are] incorporated into old memories. (p. 127)

12. See Odgers (2018) and Cozolino (2014), who noted that some

> individuals are considered to have accomplished what is called "earned autonomy" . . . meaning that they are capable of interrupting the transmission of negative attachment patterns from one generation to the next (Siegel, 2010) it is what we hope will happen through the process of psychotherapy. (p. 410)

Also see Dansby Olufowote et al. (2020), who "describe a process model of change hinging on three interrelated categories: meta-conditions of positive attachment change, making intrapsychic changes, and making interpersonal changes . . . [and on] clinicians being surrogate attachment figures for clients" (Abstract). Also see Brubacher (2017), who uses "attachment theory [to] set the stage from which to consider individual therapy as a process of love (developing secure connections) between therapist and client, between client and past and present relationships, and within the client's internal processes" (Abstract). Similarly, the techniques of voice therapy help clients uncover and gradually modify negative internal working models or critical inner voices that mediate insecure (avoidant, anxious, and disorganized) attachment patterns, thereby facilitating their movement toward "earned security."

CHAPTER 13

1. Regarding the existential dilemma that all human beings face, Solomon et al. (2015) observed, "This awareness of death is the downside of human intellect. . . . To manage this terror of death, we must defend ourselves" (pp. 6–7). Also see Becker (1973/1997), Binswanger (1958), Bugental (1976), Frankl (1946/1959), Kierkegaard (1954), Laing (1960/1969), Maslow (1971), May (1983), Schneider (2004), Wong (1998), and Yalom (1980). Historically, many concepts in existential psychotherapy are an outgrowth of a philosophical system that has become generally known as *existential phenomenology* (H. W. Cohn, 1997; Cooper, 2003; Spinelli, 2006; Valle & King, 1978; van Deurzen & Arnold-Baker, 2005).

2. Engaging in a wide range of self-destructive or microsuicidal behaviors enables people to gradually adapt to the fear of death by seriously restricting their lives. See Farberow (1980b) and Orbach (2008).

3. See Cozolino (2006/2014), who described the impact on the developing brain when

> withdrawal from those on whom the baby depends for biological stimu- lation and growth causes distress, pain and anxiety. . . . When immature brains depend completely on caretakers for emotional and physical sur- vival, even a brief separation results in measurable hypothalamic-pituitary- adrenal (HPA) responses. (p. 117)

D. J. Siegel (1999/2020) emphasized, "The experience of separation and the distress of disconnection likely create in us a 'sense of self' in which we are isolated and alone. . . . Perhaps (leading to) an 'us versus them mentality'" (p. 487). Also see Bowlby (1973) and Mikulincer et al. (2009).

4. Shaver and Mikulincer (2012) found that

> Unfortunately, unresponsive, unsupportive attachment figures and the attachment insecurities they arouse can leave a person vulnerable to anx- ieties about mortality, meaninglessness, isolation, and lack of freedom, causing him or her to adopt less constructive ways of coping with these existential concerns. (p. 294)

Regarding the stage at which children evolve a more complete under- standing of death, see Slaughter and Griffiths (2007), Hoffman and Strauss (1985), Speece and Brent (1984), and Kastenbaum (2000), who reported a case in which this more complete understanding seemed to occur at the age of 16 months.

5. Terror management researchers Goldenberg et al. (1999) suggested that "sex poses a problem for humans because it reminds them of their animalistic nature and consequently of their finitude" (p. 2). Birnbaum et al.'s (2011) results showed that an increase in death awareness (death salience) "increased the desire for casual sex, but only among more avoidant men" (p. 16).

6. See Pyszczynski et al. (1999)—studies show that

> Distinct defensive processes are activated by conscious and nonconscious but accessible thoughts of death. Proximal defenses, which entail sup- pressing death-related thoughts or pushing the problem of death into the distant future by denying one's vulnerability, are rational, threat-focused, and activated when thoughts of death are in current focal attention. Distal terror management defenses, which entail maintaining self-esteem and faith in one's cultural worldview, function to control the potential for anxiety that results from knowing that death is inevitable. (Abstract)

Also see Klackl et al. (2013), whose "study aimed at demonstrating neuro- physiological correlates of proximal defenses" (Abstract).

7. See Deci and Ryan (2004), who made a distinction between defenses against death anxiety and the search for personal meaning in life, commenting that

> people's search for meaning and significance cannot be wholly reduced to defensive processes because it also reflects intrinsic developmental processes. [They] suggest that self-esteem resulting from defenses against anxiety (whether about death or exclusion) is akin to contingent self-esteem (vanity), whereas true self-esteem is based in ongoing satisfaction of needs for competence, autonomy, and relatedness. (Abstract)

Also see Ryan et al. (2012).

8. Lifton (1979) emphasized the continuity of artistic creation through time. He cited Jacques Choron's (1964) assertion that artistic creation is the means by which "not the individual, but man, human continuity, reveals itself. More than any other activity, art escapes death. . . . Similarly, each scientific investigator becomes part of an enterprise larger than himself, limitless in its past and future continuity" (p. 21). More recently, Perach and Wisman (2019) described "the first empirical report of the death anxiety buffering functions of creative achievement among people for whom creativity constitutes a central part of their cultural worldview" (Abstract). In related studies, Cui et al. (2020) found that "while the benevolent creative task could buffer anxiety in the mortality salience condition, the malevolent creative task did not have the same effect . . . benevolent creativity was more intense for participants with a higher level of search for meaning" (Abstract).

9. "Vanity expresses itself in the secret fantasy that death happens to someone else, never to oneself" (R. W. Firestone et al., 2003, p. 192). See Shaw (2005), who

> noted the importance of this dynamic when soldiers go into combat. These soldiers cherish the conviction that they are mysteriously impervious to spattering bullets and exploding shells; the little spot on which they stand is rendered secure by their standing on it. (p. 5)

10. In relation to couples who have formed a fantasy bond as a buffer against death anxiety, J. Hart and Goldenberg (2008) observed,

> As Becker (1973/1997) suggested, the modern era seems to have ushered in a spirituality of romantic love, an explicitly human-attachment-related solution to merge with others. . . . Modern psychodynamic research shows that people use romantic relations to protect themselves from the fear of death. (as cited in J. Hart and Goldenberg, 2008, pp. 107–108)

This is especially true for individuals with an insecure attachment style.

See Hayes et al. (2010), who reported,

> People who possess a secure attachment style appear more likely to manage existential concerns by seeking romantic attachment partners. Those who possess an anxious-ambivalent attachment style seem to favor parental attachments and cultural worldview defense. Finally, people with an avoidant attachment style seem to engage only in worldview defense, preferring to avoid relationships altogether (Cox et al., 2008; Mikulincer & Florian, 2000). (p. 703)

11. Rank (1941) observed,

> As a rule, we find in modern relationships, one person is made the god-like judge over good and bad in the other person. In the long run, such symbiotic relationship becomes demoralizing to both parties, for it is just as unbearable to be a God as it is to remain an utter slave. (p. 196)

Similarly, Becker (1973/1997) noted,

> If you find the ideal love and try to make it the sole judge of good and bad in yourself, the measure of your strivings, you become simply the reflex of another person. You lose yourself in the other, just as obedient children lose themselves in the family. . . . When you confuse personal love and cosmic heroism you are bound to fail in both spheres. . . . How can a human being be a god-like "everything" to another? (p. 166)

12. Regarding "gene survival," living on through one's children as a defense against death anxiety, see Bassett (2007), who proposed two experimentally testable predictions of terror management theory related to this topic. Also see Solomon (2019), Yaakobi et al. (2014), and Zhou et al. (2008). Levin-Keini and Shlomo (2019) have also drawn on

> Irvin Yalom's . . . theoretical existential model to examine how the transition to parenthood confronts first-time mothers and fathers with ultimate concerns: death, freedom, isolation, and meaninglessness. . . . The chapter demonstrates the way in which the challenges associated with the transition to parenthood arouse these concerns. (Abstract)

13. See Lipman-Blumen (2005), and Piven et al. (2004), who wrote,

> Psychological dependence on a projected fantasy of a deity is an immensely gratifying position. One feels protected, nurtured, loved by the parental surrogate, attains approval in carrying out his commands, feels absolved and adored for pleasing the God with sacrifices and acts of gratitude. . . . And one can find a sense of nurturance in the religious group itself; a nearly maternal gratification in losing one's separateness in that group and participating in a communal merger. (pp. 65–66)

14. Park and Edmondson (2012) noted,

> Religion is central to many people's life purpose. Such purpose can include connecting to the sacred, achieving enlightenment, finding salvation, knowing God, and experiencing the transcendent (Emmons, 1999). . . . It must be noted, of course, that people often embrace troubling goals, such as supremacy and destruction, in the name of religion as well. (p. 151)

15. Research findings are mixed in relation to the proposed inversely proportional relationship between "life satisfaction" and death anxiety in terms of intervening variables, such as age, genetic predisposition, physical health, and previous trauma. See Mroczek and Spiro (2005), Sezer and Gülleroğlu (2017), and Tomaszek and Muchacka-Cymerman (2020).

16. Many of my views regarding death anxiety, existential issues of being and nonbeing, separateness, and the search for meaning, with which less defended individuals contend, are akin to those discussed by Yalom (1980) and other existential and humanistic theorists. See Bugental (1976), Maslow (1971), May (1958), Schneider (2004), Yalom (1980), and Wong (1998). Also see Vahrmeyer and Cassar (2017), who suggested, "an open stance towards death based on faith, and in the mystery of life, offer relief without denying the finitude of physical death" (Abstract).

17. See R. Beck (2004, p. 213). R. Beck (2004) qualified his research as follows: "There is one assumption that is made in this review of literature that should be made explicit. Namely, if Freud, Kierkegaard, James, and Becker are correct, the majority of the religious persons are characterized by the defensive orientation" (p. 217, n. 1). Regarding "the miracle and mystery of life," see Schneider (2004) and Passmore and Howell (2014).

CHAPTER 14

1. Regarding the feedback loop of influence among individuals, family systems, and society, see the bioecological model developed by Bronfenbrenner and Morris (2006, p. 793). Bronfenbrenner's and Morris's conceptualization includes what they refer to as the *microsystem* (e.g., heritability or one-to-one interactions), *mesosystem* (e.g., parents' marital relationship), and *exosystem* (e.g., the neighborhood or parent's work situation). The relationship between the individual, family, and society is a system with continual reciprocal movement among these systems.

2. Nevertheless, a number of distinctions can be made between individualistic and collectivistic societies in terms of values and self-identity. For example, Wang et al. (2021) found

> When the group and individual interests conflict, people from collectivistic cultures more often give priority to the group interests than people in individualistic cultures do . . . and the personal values and identity may be more influential in an individualistic culture than a collectivistic culture. (p. 3)

According to Foucault (1975), social institutions also extend their restrictions to limiting the communication of "truth" as well as producing new "truths." For example, Foucault (1975) asserted, "Each society has its regime of truth, its 'general politics' of truth: that is, the types of discourse which it accepts and makes function as true" (p. 131). Also see Cook (2014), Marcuse (1991), and Renaud's (2013) essay on Foucault's (1975) and Marcuse's (1991) work. Regarding genetic factors that may contribute to social conformity, see Chen et al. (2018). For differences observed in individualistic and collectivistic cultures with respect to social conformity, see Pan et al. (2013) and Panagopoulos and van der Linden (2016).

3. See Perry (2009), who observed,

> Childhood is a dangerous time. . . . It is in the family setting that the child is fed, clothed, sheltered, nurtured and educated, directly and indirectly, in the language, beliefs, and value systems of the culture. It is in the family setting in which the non-genetic "DNA" of the culture is transmitted from generation to generation, allowing the amazing process of sociocultural evolution. (Abstract)

4. Grau and Zotos (2016) also noted that "peoples' perception of social reality is shaped by the media. They incorporate stereotypes presented by the media into their own system of values, ideas, and beliefs about the quality of life" (p. 763). According to Knoll et al. (2011), "the social role of women and men has changed in many Western societies over the past years. At the same time, advertisers still depict women and men in tradition-bound roles to promote their products" (p. 2).

5. See Hyde (2016), who noted, "Meta-analyses of gender differences across a wide array of psychological qualities support the Gender Similarities Hypothesis, which states that males and females are quite similar on most—but not all—psychological variables" (Abstract).

6. C. Gilligan and Snider (2018) also proposed,

> From an evolutionary standpoint, patriarchy posed a threat. To put it starkly, in the words of the evolutionary anthropologist Sarah Blaffer Hrdy (2011), "Patriarchal ideologies that focused on both the chastity of women and the perpetuation and augmentation of male lineages undercut the long-standing priority of putting children's well-being first." (as cited in C. Gilligan & Snider, 2018, p. 9)

Also see Andersen et al. (2013). An analogy can be made between racism and gender discrimination in relation to stereotypic thinking about LGBTQ individuals. See Brown and Groscup (2009), and Snyder (2018), who reported that in Russia in 2012, a confidant of Putin, Vladimir Yakunin, published an influential essay in which he declared, "The spread of gay rights was a deliberate policy intended to turn Russia into a 'herd' easily manipulatable by the global masters of capitalism" (p. 51).

7. More positive views of the elderly that counter ageism, based on recent findings from interpersonal neurobiology, can be found in Cozolino (2016), who emphasized,

> As we age, research has shown that we tend to remember more positive and neutral images than negative ones . . . another study showed that when we look at faces with different emotions, we have greater activation in brain areas that reflect positive emotions as we age. (p. 147)

8. Perel (2006) also pointed out the double messages or "diametrically opposed attitudes" toward marriage operating within our culture:

> The legacy of Puritanism, which locates the family at the center of society, expects marriage to be reasonable, sober, and productive. . . . But alongside this very American notion . . . we believe in personal fulfillment: in life, liberty and the pursuit of happiness. We relish the freedom to spontaneously satisfy our desires. . . . An entire industry of hedonism hovers on the outskirts of marriage, a constant reminder of all we've sacrificed in exchange for the muted sexuality of marital love. (p. 90)

9. See Malti et al. (2014), who stated,

> Morality in individualistic cultures is said to be rights-based and structured by concerns with furthering and protecting the independence and personal choice of the individual. Collectivistic cultures are thought to have an interdependent and duty-based morality structures around the expectations, rules and duties stemming from a person's role in the social system. . . . [However,] a meta-analysis . . . confirmed that differences between "individualistic" and "collectivistic" societies are neither larger nor systematic and that societies and individuals cannot be accurately characteristic in terms of a single orientation. (p. 260)

Triandis (2018) also noted that "both extreme individualism and collectivism are likely to result in poor intergroup relations" (p. 28). Also see Moghaddam (2016). In relation to human rights issues, see González-Suárez (2009): "The synergy formed by the joint work among the academy, grassroots organizations and the government lead to public policies based on solidarity and the distribution of wealth for human rights, mental health and a sustainable environment" (Abstract). The Costa Rican government appears to be based largely on John Rawls's (1999, 2001) principle of distributive justice in which, ideally, the most resources would go to the least advantaged citizens.

10. See van der Kolk (2015), who called attention to the exclusion of "traumatic developmental disorder" as a diagnostic category from the *DSM-5* (American Psychiatric Association, 2013), despite empirical findings demonstrating a positive correlation between adverse childhood experiences and physical and mental dysfunctions in adulthood (Felitti et al., 1998). Specifically, in relation to neglect, Rachel Kelly (2007) cited research showing that "child protective agencies and professional child protection workers tend to look for immediate physical harm. . . . By recognizing neglect only when there is 'imminent harm,' the law fails to recognize or intervene in the majority of neglectful situations" (p. 157). Also see Tyler et al. (2006), who reported,

    > Neglect remains the most cited reason for the placement of children in an out-of-home care situation in the United States. . . . One of the problems with current US child neglect policy is the variance that exists across states regarding mandatory child neglect reporting laws. (p. 12)

11. See Worley and Melton (2013):

    > Legal mandates to report suspected abuse are undermined by ambiguities in definition and inconsistencies across jurisdictions, mired in errors of both under and over-reporting, and lead to a loss of community and professional responsibility in the duty of child protection. (Abstract)

    Also see Gershoff (2002), who noted, "A growing number of countries have adopted policies or laws that prohibit parents from using corporal punishment as a means of discipline (Austria, Croatia, Cyprus, Denmark, Finland, Germany, Israel, Italy, Latvia, Norway, and Sweden)" (p. 539). Also refer to Kolhatkar and Berkowitz (2014) regarding cultural considerations in relation to child maltreatment. With respect to children's rights, Reardon and Noblet (2009) noted, "There are only two nations in the world who have not signed" the United Nations Convention on the Rights of Children—Somalia and the United States—"a government that does not recognize children as rights-bearing citizens" (p. xvii).

12. Regarding "support of the privacy of the biological family," see Biehal (2007), Sheldon (1997), and Baldwin (2002).

13. See the comprehensive report by Haskett et al. (2006) showing, "Relationships with individuals outside the immediate family are important in resilience among children at risk of maladaptation. In particular, high-quality peer friendships and supportive relationships with non-parental adults are linked with success for children at risk" (p. 804). The evolutionary advantage of extended family arrangements was cited by neuropsychiatrist Bruce Perry (2006), who suggested,

> The human brain is designed for a different world. . . . Of the 250,000 years or so that our species has been on the planet, we spent 245,000 years living in small transgenerational hunter-gatherer bands of 40–50 individuals. . . . For each child under the age of 6, there were four developmentally more mature persons who could protect, educate, enrich, and nurture the developing child—a ratio of 4:1. (pp. 44–45)

Also see *Mothers and Others: The Evolutionary Origins of Mutual Understanding*, by Sarah Hrdy (2009), who highlighted the selective advantage evolutionarily of extended family arrangement on an infant's early brain development:

> [This] set the stage for a new kind of ape equipped with differently sensitized neural systems, alert from a very early age to the intentions of others. This novel nervous system would in turn have been exposed to selection pressures that favored the survival of any child with slightly better aptitudes for enlisting, maintaining, and manipulating alloparental manifestations. In this way, natural selection would lead to the evolution of cognitive tendencies that further encouraged infants to monitor and influence the emotions, mental states, and intentions of others. (p. 121)

CHAPTER 15

1. Schneider (2013) cited Arie Kruglanski, "one of the leading investigators of global terrorism," who suggested that "terrorism in particular and polarization in general are rooted in a very profound problem of the human situation." That problem is "what I and others call 'existential anxiety'" (p. 8). . . . "Virtually everyone who is polarized, I contend, has been a victim of existential panic, and virtually all of us, in varying degrees, have experienced this polarization" (p. 9).

2. L. M. Jackson (2019) called attention to subtle forms of control that

> operate at the intergroup level through the use of social ideologies that provide moral and intellectual justification for inequality. These ideologies, often known as "legitimizing myths," involve systems of beliefs about society, why things are the way they are, what types of behavior are more or less desirable, how society should allocate resources and so on. (p. 83)

3. S. Freud (1921/1955) and Fromm (1941, 1964) contended that identification with the group is a significant contributing factor in religious, racial, and ethnic conflict. S. Freud (1921/1955) noted that "a group is extraordinarily credulous and open to influence, it has no critical faculty, and the improbable does not exist for it. . . . A group knows neither doubt nor uncertainty" (p. 78). Also see Herrera and Sani (2013) and Hohman and Hogg (2011), whose findings indicated that "mortality salience strengthened identification *only* among those who were uncertain about the afterlife" (Abstract). Fromm (1964) also stressed the importance of examining "the role of narcissism for the understanding of nationalism, national hatred, and the psychological motivations for destructiveness and war" (p. 62):

> Good examples of this phenomenon in recent years are the racial narcissism which existed in Hitler's Germany, and which is found in the American South today . . . [each member of such a group] feels: "Even though I am poor and uncultured, I am somebody important because I belong to the most admirable group in the world—I am white"; or, "I am an Aryan." (pp. 78–79)

4. See Hannah Arendt's (1973) classic work, *The Origins of Totalitarianism*, where she sets forth her views regarding the historical origins of and the fundamental basis for the totalitarian state. Similarly, Klar and Bilewicz (2017) analyzed the factors that contribute to people's adherence to the principles of authoritarian and totalitarian governments. See Giroux (2015), who cited Ariel Dorfman's (2014) depiction of one effective means of controlling the populace: "Surveillance, in any land where it is ubiquitous and inescapable, generates distrust and divisions among its citizens, curbs their readiness to speak freely to each other, and diminishes their willingness to even dare to think freely" (pp. 103–104). Also see Surmelian (1990; as cited in Marlinova, 1990).

5. Lipman-Blumen (2005) observed that many destructive leaders remain in power because they fulfill one of the most basic needs of their followers:

> The real tragedy of the human condition is not that we must die, but that we choose to live by illusions. Illusions are the umbilical cord linking leaders and followers. Leaders understand their followers' need for

illusions. In a terrifyingly uncertain world, the illusions that leaders spin offer us a lifeline . . . permitting even us small, short-lived creatures to become significant figures in the grand universe. (pp. 50–51)

Similarly, Wilkerson (2020) explained why certain types of leaders appeal to individual group members:

The right kind of leader can inspire *a symbiotic connection* [emphasis added] that supplants logic. The susceptible group sees itself in the narcissistic leader, *becomes one with the leader* [emphasis added], sees his fortunes and his fate as their own. "The greater the leader," Fromm (1964) wrote, the greater the follower. . . . The narcissism of the leader who is convinced of his greatness, and who has no doubts, is precisely what attracts the narcissism of those who submit to him. (p. 271)

6. The Middle Eastern and Balkan conflicts of the early 1990s were based largely on religious motives. According to political analysts, the "ethnic cleansing" that took place in Croatia (Yugoslavia) represented yet another stage in a 600-year-old conflict that began with a religious war during the 14th century (Owen, 1993; Schmemann, 1992). Also see Wirth (2007), who suggested, "Slobodan Milosevic's idiosyncratic disorder—his borderline personality disorder, his sadomasochism, the depression he denied, his latent suicidalism, and his inability to confront the suffering in his life—fit the Serbs' ethnic disorder as a key fits a lock" (p. 125).

7. According to Wilkerson (2020), physical appearance, including observable inherited traits, such as skin color, height, and hair texture, are the criteria used to determine the caste to which each person belongs. For example, "'No one was white before he/she came to America,' James Baldwin once said" (p. 50). Wilkerson contended,

It was in the making of the New World that Europeans became white, Africans black, and everyone else yellow, red, or brown. It was in the making of the New World that humans were set apart on the basis of what they looked like, identified solely in contrast to one another, and ranked to form a caste system based on a *new concept called race* [emphasis added]. It was in the process of ranking that we were all cast into assigned roles to meet the needs of the larger production. None of us are ourselves. (pp. 52–53)

8. L. M. Jackson (2019) reported results of a meta-analysis by Degner and Dalege (2013) of 131 studies representing 45,000 sets of parents and their children. The meta-analysis

showed that, on the whole, parents and children resemble one another in their attitudes from early childhood through young adulthood. The parallels in attitudes have been identified in studies of sexism, racism, attitudes toward specific groups, including ethnic, religious, and sexual minority groups: immigrants, overweight people, and people with disabilities and disease. (p. 131)

In relation to biased attitudes toward sexual minorities, Barringer et al. (2013) found that "men who self-identify as spiritual, but not religious, are more likely to report that homosexuality is not morally wrong than their more religious counterparts" (Abstract). Also see Pettijohn and Walzer (2008).

9. Also relevant is Lifton (2005).

10. See J. Greenberg et al. (2016): "We summarize the theory's core insights into the causes and consequences of prejudice and review substantial lines of research supporting these insights" (Abstract). According to the article "How Terrorism News Reports Increase Prejudice Against Outgroups: A Terror Management Account" (Das et al., 2009), "Consistent with TMT [terror management theory], terrorism news and [Theo] Van Gogh's murder increased death-related thoughts. Death-related thoughts, in turn, increased prejudiced attitudes toward out-group members, especially when participants had low self-esteem, and when terrorism was psychologically close" (Abstract). Also see Pyszczynski et al. (2003) and Hayes et al. (2010).

11. Regarding an inclusive world view, Buddhist leader Daisaku Ikeda (as cited in Toynbee, 1976) declared,

The feeling that the earth is one's homeland and a love of all mankind must take the place of the narrow patriotism of the past. When world-embracing patriotism gains precedence, national patriotism will sink to the level of loyalty to a locality. (p. 198)

References

Abeyta, A. A., Juhl, J., & Routledge, C. (2014). Exploring the effects of self-esteem and mortality salience on proximal and distally measured death anxiety: A further test of the dual process model of terror management. *Motivation and Emotion, 38*(4), 523–528. https://doi.org/10.1007/s11031-014-9400-y

Afifi, T. D., Joseph, A., & Aldeis, D. (2008). Why can't we just talk about it? An observational study of parents' and adolescents' conversations about sex. *Journal of Adolescent Research, 23*(6), 689–721. https://doi.org/10.1177/0743558408323841

Ainsworth, M. D. (1985). Attachments across the life span. *Bulletin of the New York Academy of Medicine, 61*(9), 792–812. https://www.ncbi.nlm.nih.gov/pmc/articles/PMC1911889/

Ainsworth, M. D., Blehar, M., Waters, E., & Wall, S. (1978). *Patterns of attachment: A psychological study of the strange situation*. Psychology Press.

Alderson-Day, B., Mitrenga, K., Wilkinson, S., McCarthy-Jones, S., & Fernyhough, C. (2018). The varieties of inner speech questionnaire–Revised (VISQ-R): Replicating and refining links between inner speech and psychopathology. *Consciousness and Cognition, 65*, 48–58. https://doi.org/10.1016/j.concog.2018.07.001

Alexander, F., & French, T. M. (1946). *Psychoanalytic therapy: Principles and application*. Ronald Press.

Alexander, P. C. (2003). Parent-child role reversal: Development of a measure and test of an attachment theory model. *Journal of Systemic Therapies, 22*(2), 31–44. https://doi.org/10.1521/jsyt.22.2.31.23349

Allen, J. P., Hauser, S. T., & Borman-Spurrell, E. (1996). Attachment theory as a framework for understanding sequelae of severe adolescent psychopathology: An 11-year follow-up study. *Journal of Consulting and Clinical Psychology, 64*(2), 254–263. https://doi.org/10.1037/0022-006X.64.2.254

Allen, K. L., Gibson, L. Y., McLean, N. J., Davis, E. A., & Byrne, S. M. (2014). Maternal and family factors and child eating pathology: Risk and protective relationships. *Journal of Eating Disorders, 2*(1), 11. https://doi.org/10.1186/2050-2974-2-11

American Psychiatric Association. (1994). *Diagnostic and statistical manual of mental disorders* (4th ed.).

American Psychiatric Association. (2013). *Diagnostic and statistical manual of mental disorders* (5th ed.).

Andersen, S., Ertac, S., Gneezy, U., List, J. A., & Maximiano, S. (2013). Gender, competitiveness, and socialization at a young age: Evidence from a matrilineal and a patriarchal society. *The Review of Economics and Statistics, 95*(4), 1438–1443. https://doi.org/10.1162/REST_a_00312

Anthony, S. (1973). *The discovery of death in childhood and after.* Penguin Education. (Original work published 1971)

Arendt, H. (1973). *The origins of totalitarianism* (Vol. 244). Houghton Mifflin Harcourt.

Arendt, H. (1994). *Imperialism: Part two of the origins of totalitarianism* (Vol. 2). Houghton Mifflin Harcourt. (Original work published 1968)

Arieti, S. (1955). *Interpretation of schizophrenia.* Robert Bruner.

Aron, L. (1996). From hypnotic suggestion to free association: Freud as a psychotherapist, circa 1892–1893. *Contemporary Psychoanalysis, 32*(1), 99–114. https://doi.org/10.1080/00107530.1996.10746942

Bach, G. R., & Deutsch, R. M. (1979). *Stop! You're driving me crazy.* Berkley Books.

Badenoch, B. (2008). *Being a brain-wise therapist: A practical guide to interpersonal neurobiology.* Norton.

Baehr, P. (2002). Identifying the unprecedented: Hannah Arendt, totalitarianism, and the critique of sociology. *American Sociological Review, 67*(6), 804–831. https://doi.org/10.2307/3088971

Bakermans-Kranenburg, M. J., & Van IJzendoorn, M. H. (1993). A psychometric study of the Adult Attachment Interview: Reliability and discriminant validity. *Developmental Psychology, 29*(5), 870–879. https://doi.org/10.1037/0012-1649.29.5.870

Baldwin, H. (2002). *Termination of parental rights: Statistical study and proposed solutions.* https://heinonline.org/HOL/LandingPage?handle=hein.journals/jleg28&div=13&id=&page=

Baldwin, H., Biehal, N., Cusworth, L., Wade, J., Allgar, V., & Vostanis, P. (2019). Disentangling the effect of out-of-home care on child mental health. *Child Abuse & Neglect, 88*, 189–200. https://doi.org/10.1016/j.chiabu.2018.11.011

Bandura, A., Ross, D., & Ross, S. A. (1963). Imitation of film-mediated aggressive models. In R. J. Huber, C. Edwards, & D. H. Bownton (Eds.), *Cornerstones of psychology: Readings in the history of psychology* (pp. 215–227). Thomson Learning.

Bandura, A., & Walters, R. H. (1977). *Social learning theory.* General Learning Corporation. http://www.asecib.ase.ro/mps/Bandura_SocialLearningTheory.pdf

Banks, C. G. (1996). "There is no fat in heaven": Religious asceticism and the meaning of anorexia nervosa. *Ethos, 24*(1), 107–135. https://doi.org/10.1525/eth.1996.24.1.02a00040

Barber, B. K. (Ed.). (2002). *Intrusive parenting: How psychological control affects children adolescents*. American Psychological Association. https://doi.org/10.1037/10422-000

Barringer, M. N., Gay, D. A., & Lynxwiler, J. P. (2013). Gender, religiosity, spirituality, and attitudes toward homosexuality. *Sociological Spectrum, 33*(3), 240–257. https://doi.org/10.1080/02732173.2013.732903

Bassett, J. F. (2007). Psychological defenses against death anxiety: Integrating terror management theory and Firestone's separation theory. *Death Studies, 31*(8), 727–750. https://doi.org/10.1080/07481180701490628

Bateson, G. (1972). *Steps to an ecology of mind*. University of Chicago Press.

Baumeister, R. F. (2005). *The cultural animal: Human nature, meaning, and social life*. Oxford University Press.

Baumeister, R. F., Campbell, J. D., Krueger, J. I., & Vohs, K. D. (2003). Does high self-esteem cause better performance, interpersonal success, happiness, or healthier lifestyles? *Psychological Science in the Public Interest, 4*(1), 1–44. https://doi.org/10.1111/1529-1006.01431

Baumeister, R. F., Twenge, J. M., & Nuss, C. K. (2002). Effects of social exclusion on cognitive processes: Anticipated aloneness reduces intelligent thought. *Journal of Personality and Social Psychology, 83*(4), 817–827. https://doi.org/10.1037/0022-3514.83.4.817

Baumeister, R. F., & Vohs, K. D. (2004). Sexual economics: Sex as female resource for social exchange in heterosexual interactions. *Personality and Social Psychology Review, 8*(4), 339–363. https://doi.org/10.1207/s15327957pspr0804_2

Beck, A. T., Rush, A. J., Shaw, B. F., & Emery, G. (1979). *Cognitive therapy of depression*. Guilford Press.

Beck, J. S. (1995). *Cognitive therapy: Basics and beyond*. Guilford Press.

Beck, R. (2004). The function of religious belief: Defensive versus existential religion. *Journal of Psychology and Christianity, 23*(3), 208–218. http://citeseerx.ist.psu.edu/viewdoc/download?doi=10.1.1.548.1204&rep=rep1&type=pdf

Becker, E. (1975). *Escape from evil*. Free Press.

Becker, E. (1997). *The denial of death*. Free Press. (Original work published 1973)

Beebe, B., Lachmann, F., Markese, S., & Bahrick, L. (2012). On the origins of disorganized attachment and internal working models: Paper I. A dyadic systems approach. *Psychoanalytic Dialogues, 22*(2), 253–272. https://doi.org/10.1080/10481885.2012.666147

Beebe, B., & Steele, M. (2013). How does microanalysis of mother–infant communication inform maternal sensitivity and infant attachment? *Attachment & Human Development, 15*(5–6), 583–602. https://doi.org/10.1080/14616734.2013.841050

Belsky, J., Conger, R., & Capaldi, D. M. (2009). The intergenerational transmission of parenting: Introduction to the special section. *Developmental Psychology, 45*(5), 1201–1204. https://doi.org/10.1037/a0016245

Benjamin, J. (1988). *The bonds of love: Psychoanalysis, feminism, and the problem of domination*. Pantheon Books.

Berry, K., Varese, F., & Bucci, S. (2017). Cognitive attachment model of voices: Evidence base and future implications. *Frontiers in Psychiatry, 8*, 111. https://doi.org/10.3389/fpsyt.2017.00111

Betchen, S. J. (2005). *Intrusive partners, elusive mates: The pursuer-distancer dynamic in couples*. Routledge.

Biehal, N. (2007). Reuniting children with their families: Reconsidering the evidence on timing, contact and outcomes. *British Journal of Social Work, 37*(5), 807–823. https://doi.org/10.1093/bjsw/bcl051

Binswanger, L. (1958). Existential analysis and psychotherapy. *Psychoanalysis and the Psychoanalytic Review, 45*(4), 79–83.

Birnbaum, G., Hirschberger, G., & Goldenberg, J. (2011). Desire in the face of death: Terror management, attachment, and sexual motivation. *Personal Relationships, 18*(1), 1–19. https://doi.org/10.1111/j.1475-6811.2010.01298.x

Birnbaum, G. E., Svitelman, N., Bar-Shalom, A., & Porat, O. (2008). The thin line between reality and imagination: Attachment orientations and the effects of relationship threats on sexual fantasies. *Personality and Social Psychology Bulletin, 34*(9), 1185–1199. https://doi.org/10.1177/0146167208319692

Bloch, D. (1978). *"So the witch won't eat me": Fantasy and the child's fear of infanticide*. Grove.

Blum, K., Werner, T., Carnes, S., Carnes, P., Bowirrat, A., Giordano, J., Oscar-Berman, M., & Gold, M. (2012). Sex, drugs, and rock 'n' roll: Hypothesizing common mesolimbic activation as a function of reward gene polymorphisms. *Journal of Psychoactive Drugs, 44*(1), 38–55. https://doi.org/10.1080/02791072.2012.662112

Bogaert, A. F. (2015). Asexuality: What it is and why it matters. *Journal of Sex Research, 52*(4), 362–379. https://doi.org/10.1080/00224499.2015.1015713

Bollas, C. (1987). *The shadow of the object: Psychoanalysis of the unthought known*. Columbia University Press.

Bonner, B. L. (2001). Normal and abnormal sexual behavior in children. *Psychotherapy Bulletin, 36*(4), 16–19.

Bosmans, G., Braet, C., & Van Vlierberghe, L. (2010). Attachment and symptoms of psychopathology: Early maladaptive schemas as a cognitive link? *Clinical Psychology & Psychotherapy, 17*(5), 374–385. https://doi.org/10.1002/cpp.667

Bowen, M. (1978). *Family therapy in clinical practice*. Jason Aronson.

Bowlby, J. (1972). *Attachment: Vol. 1*. Penguin Books.

Bowlby, J. (1973). *Attachment and loss: Vol. II. Separation anxiety and anger*. Basic Books.

Bowlby, J. (1980). *Attachment and loss: Vol. 3. Loss, sadness and depression*. Basic Books.

Bradshaw, J. (1990). *Healing the shame that binds you*. Health Communications.

Brennan, K. A., & Shaver, P. R. (1998). Attachment styles and personality disorders: Their connections to each other and to parental divorce, parental death, and perceptions of parental caregiving. *Journal of Personality, 66*(5), 835–878. https://doi.org/10.1111/1467-6494.00034

Bretherton, I. (1995). A communication perspective on attachment relationships and internal working models. *Monographs of the Society for Research in Child Development, 60*(2–3), 310–329. https://doi.org/10.1111/j.1540-5834.1995.tb00220.x

Bretherton, I. (1996). Internal working models of attachment relationships as related to resilient coping. In G. G. Noam & K. W. Fischer (Eds.), *Development and vulnerability in close relationships* (pp. 3–27). Erlbaum.

Bretherton, I., & Munholland, K. A. (2016). The internal working model construct in light of contemporary neuroimaging research. In J. Cassidy & P. R. Shave (Eds.), *Handbook of attachment: Theory, research, and clinical applications* (pp. 63–90). Guilford Press.

Bretherton, I., Ridgeway, D., & Cassidy, J. (1990). Assessing internal working models of the attachment relationship. In M. T. Greenberg, D. Cichetti, & E. M. Cummings (Eds.), *Attachment in the preschool years: Theory, Research, and Intervention* (pp. 273–308). University of Chicago Press.

Bronfenbrenner, U., & Morris, P. (2006). The bioecological model of human development. In R. Learner (Ed.), *Handbook of child psychology: Vol. I. Theoretical models of human development* (pp. 793–828). Wiley. https://doi.org/10.1002/9780470147658.chpsy0114

Brotto, L. A., & Yule, M. (2017). Asexuality: Sexual orientation, paraphilia, sexual dysfunction, or none of the above? *Archives of Sexual Behavior, 46*(3), 619–627. https://doi.org/10.1007/s10508-016-0802-7

Brown, M. J., & Groscup, J. L. (2009). Homophobia and acceptance of stereotypes about gays and lesbians. *Individual Differences Research, 7*(3), 159–167.

Brubacher, L. (2017). Emotionally focused individual therapy: An attachment-based experiential/systemic perspective. *Person-Centered and Experiential Psychotherapies, 16*(1), 50–67. https://doi.org/10.1080/14779757.2017.1297250

Brumariu, L. E. (2015). Parent–child attachment and emotion regulation. *New Directions for Child and Adolescent Development, 2015*(148), 31–45. https://doi.org/10.1002/cad.20098

Brussoni, M., & Olsen, L. L. (2013). The perils of overprotective parenting: Fathers' perspectives explored. *Child: Care, Health and Development, 39*(2), 237–245. https://doi.org/10.1111/j.1365-2214.2011.01361.x

Bugental, J. F. T. (1976). *The search for existential identity*. Jossey-Bass.

Burston, D. (2007). *Erik Erikson and the American psyche: Ego, ethics, and evolution*. Jason Aronson.

Carnes, P. (1991). *Don't call it love: Recovery from sexual addiction*. Bantam Books.

Carnes, P. (1992). *Out of the shadows: Understanding sexual addiction* (2nd ed.). Hazelden.

Carnes, P. J. (1998). The case for sexual anorexia: An interim report on 144 patients with sexual disorders. *Sexual Addiction & Compulsivity, 5*(4), 293–309. https://doi.org/10.1080/10720169808402338

Cartwright, D. (2002). *Psychoanalysis, violence and rage-type murder*. Brunner-Routledge.

Cassidy, J. A., & Shaver, P. R. (2016). *Handbook of attachment: Theory, research, and clinical applications* (3rd ed.). Guilford Press.

Cavaiola, A. A., & Lavender, N. J. (2000). *Toxic coworkers: How to deal with dysfunctional people on the job*. New Harbinger.

The CERTS Model for Healthy Sex. (n.d.). In *HealthySex.com*. https://healthysex.com/healthy-sexuality/part-one-understanding/the-certs-model-for-healthy-sex/

Chen, B., Zhu, Z., Wang, Y., Ding, X., Guo, X., He, M., Fang, W., Zhou, Q., Zhou, S., Lei, H., Huang, A., Chen, T., Ni, D., Gu, Y., Liu, J., & Rao, Y. (2018). Nature vs. nurture in human sociality: Multi-level genomic analyses of social conformity. *Journal of Human Genetics*, *63*(5), 605–619. https://doi.org/10.1038/s10038-018-0418-y

Choron, J. (1964). *Death and modern man*. Collier Books.

Çimşir, E., & Akdoğan, R. (2021). Childhood Emotional Incest Scale (CEIS): Development, validation, cross-validation, and reliability. *Journal of Counseling Psychology*, *68*(1), 98–111. https://doi.org/10.1037/cou0000439

Clance, P. R., & Imes, S. A. (1978). The imposter phenomenon in high achieving women: Dynamics and therapeutic intervention. *Psychotherapy: Theory, Research, & Practice*, *15*(3), 241–247. https://doi.org/10.1037/h0086006

Clarke, K., Cooper, P., & Creswell, C. (2013). The parental overprotection scale: Associations with child and parental anxiety. *Journal of Affective Disorders*, *151*(2), 618–624. https://doi.org/10.1016/j.jad.2013.07.007

Cohen, F., Ogilvie, D. M., Solomon, S., Greenberg, J., & Pyszczynski, T. (2005). American roulette: The effect of reminders of death on support for George W. Bush in the 2004 presidential election. *Analyses of Social Issues and Public Policy*, *5*(1), 177–187. https://doi.org/10.1111/j.1530-2415.2005.00063.x

Cohen, F., Solomon, S., Maxfield, M., Pyszczynski, T., & Greenberg, J. (2004). Fatal attraction: The effects of mortality salience on evaluations of charismatic, task-oriented, and relationship-oriented leaders. *Psychological Science*, *15*(12), 846–851. https://doi.org/10.1111/j.0956-7976.2004.00765.x

Cohn, H. W. (1997). *Existential thought and therapeutic practice: An introduction to existential psychotherapy*. SAGE. https://doi.org/10.4135/9781446279878

Cohn, J. F., Krafchuk, E., Ricks, M., Winn, S., & Tronick, E. Z. (1985). Continuity and change from three to nine months-of-age in the sequencing of mother-infant dyadic states during face-to-face interaction. *Developmental Psychology*, *22*, 167–180.

Cole, M. (2008). Asceticism and hedonism in research discourses of veganism. *British Food Journal*, *5*(4), 293–309. https://doi.org/10.1108/00070700810887176

Coleman-Kennedy, C., & Pendley, A. (2002). Assessment and diagnosis of sexual addiction. *Journal of the American Psychiatric Nurses Association*, *8*(5), 143–151. https://doi.org/10.1067/mpn.2002.128827

Conklin, C. Z., Bradley, R., & Westen, D. (2006). Affect regulation in border-line personality disorder. *The Journal of Nervous and Mental Disease, 194*(2), 69–77. https://doi.org/10.1097/01.nmd.0000198138.41709.4f

Cook, D. (2014). Foucault, Freud, and the repressive hypothesis. *Journal of the British Society for Phenomenology, 45*(2), 148–161. https://doi.org/10.1080/00071773.2014.919122

Cooper, M. (2003). Between freedom and despair: Existential challenges and contributions to person-centered and experiential therapy. *Person-Centered and Experiential Psychotherapies, 2*(1), 43–56. https://doi.org/10.1080/14779757.2003.9688292

Corstens, D., Escher, S., & Romme, M. (2008). Accepting and working with voices: The Maastricht approach. In A. Moskowitz, I. Schäfer, M. J. Dorahy (Eds.), *Psychosis, trauma and dissociation: Emerging perspectives on severe psychopathology* (pp. 319–332). Wiley-Blackwell. https://doi.org/10.1002/9780470699652.ch23

Courtois, C. A. (1999). *Recollections of sexual abuse: Treatment principles and guidelines*. Norton.

Cox, C. R., Arndt, J., Pyszczynski, T., Greenberg, J., Abdollahi, A., & Solomon, S. (2008). Terror management and adults' attachment to their parents: The safe haven remains. *Journal of Personality and Social Psychology, 94*(4), 696–717. https://doi.org/10.1037/0022-3514.94.4.696

Cozolino, L. (2002). *The neuroscience of psychotherapy: Building and rebuilding the human brain*. Norton.

Cozolino, L. (2006). The social brain. *Psychotherapy in Australia, 12*(2), 12–17.

Cozolino, L. (2014). *The neuroscience of human relationships: Attachment and the developing social brain*. Norton.

Cozolino, L. (2015). *Why therapy works: Using our minds to change our brains*. Norton.

Cozolino, L. (2016). Why therapy works. *The Neuropsychotherapist, 4*(1), 6–19. https://static1.squarespace.com/static/5e1916c3f39c41335c14c63a/t/5e31ec71c048515932962b31/1580330101272/TNPTVol4Issue1pp6-17.pdf

Cozolino, L. (2020). *The pocket guide to neuroscience for clinicians*. Norton.

Cramerus, M. (1989). Self-derogation: Inner conflict and anxious vigilance. *Journal of Contemporary Psychotherapy, 19*(1), 55–69. https://doi.org/10.1007/BF00946061

Cui, Y. X., Zhou, X., Zu, C., Zhai, H. K., Bai, B. R., Xu, Y. M., & Li, D. (2020). Benevolent creativity buffers anxiety aroused by mortality salience: Terror management in COVID-19 pandemic. *Frontiers in Psychology*. https://doi.org/10.3389/fpsyg.2020.601027

Dallos, R. (2004). Attachment narrative therapy: Integrating ideas from narrative and attachment theory in systemic family therapy with eating disorders. *Journal of Family Therapy, 26*(1), 40–65. https://doi.org/10.1111/j.1467-6427.2004.00266.x

Dansby Olufowote, R. A., Fife, S. T., Schleiden, C., & Whiting, J. B. (2020). How can I become more secure? A grounded theory of earning secure attachment. *Journal of Marital and Family Therapy, 46*(3), 489–506. https://doi.org/10.1111/jmft.12409

Das, E., Bushman, B. J., Bezemer, M. D., Kerkhof, P., & Vermeulen, I. E. (2009). How terrorism news reports increase prejudice against outgroups: A terror management account. *Journal of Experimental Social Psychology, 45*(3), 453–459. https://doi.org/10.1016/j.jesp.2008.12.001

Davidson, J. K., Sr., & Darling, C. A. (1993). Masturbatory guilt and sexual responsiveness among post-college-age women: Sexual satisfaction revisited. *Journal of Sex & Marital Therapy, 19*(4), 289–300. https://doi.org/10.1080/00926239308404372

Davis, D., Shaver, P. R., Widaman, K. F., Vernon, M. L., Follette, W. C., & Beitz, K. (2006). "I can't get no satisfaction": Insecure attachment, inhibited sexual communication, and sexual dissatisfaction. *Personal Relationships, 13*(4), 465–483. https://doi.org/10.1111/j.1475-6811.2006.00130.x

Davis, K. L., & Panksepp, J. (2011). The brain's emotional foundations of human personality and the Affective Neuroscience Personality Scales. *Neuroscience and Biobehavioral Reviews, 35*(9), 1946–1958. https://doi.org/10.1016/j.neubiorev.2011.04.004

de Alarcón, R., de la Iglesia, J. I., Casado, N. M., & Montejo, A. L. (2019). Online porn addiction: What we know and what we don't—A systematic review. *Journal of Clinical Medicine, 8*(1), 91. https://doi.org/10.3390/jcm8010091

De Fruyt, F., Van Leeuwen, K., Bagby, R. M., Rolland, J. P., & Rouillon, F. (2006). Assessing and interpreting personality change and continuity in patients treated for major depression. *Psychological Assessment, 18*(1), 71–80. https://doi.org/10.1037/1040-3590.18.1.71

Deci, E. L., & Ryan, R. M. (Eds.). (2004). *Handbook of self-determination research.* University Rochester Press.

Degner, J., & Dalege, J. (2013). The apple does not fall far from the tree, or does it? A meta-analysis of parent–child similarity in intergroup attitudes. *Psychological Bulletin, 139*(6), 1270–1304. https://doi.org/10.1037/a0031436

Delgadillo, J., Branson, A., Kellett, S., Myles-Hooton, P., Hardy, G. E., & Shafran, R. (2020). Therapist personality traits as predictors of psychological treatment outcomes. *Psychotherapy Research, 30*(7), 857–870. https://doi.org/10.1080/10503307.2020.1731927

Doll, L. S., Koenig, L. J., & Purcell, D. W. (2004). Child sexual abuse and adult sexual risk: Where are we now. In L. J. Koenig, L. S. Doll, A. O'Leary, & W. Pequegnat (Eds.), *From child sexual abuse to adult sexual risk: Trauma, revictimization, and intervention* (pp. 3–10). American Psychological Association.

Dorais, M. (2002). *Don't tell: The sexual abuse of boys* (I. D. Meyer, Trans.). McGill-Queen's University Press.

Dorfman, A. (2014, February 3). Repression by any other name. *Guernica.* https://www.guernicamag.com/repression-by-any-other-name/

Doucette-Gates, A., Firestone, R. W., & Firestone, L. A. (1999). Assessing violent thoughts: The relationship between thought processes and violent behavior. *Psychologica Belgica, 39*(2–3), 113–134. https://doi.org/10.5334/pb.947

Dovidio, J. F., Gaertner, S. L., Hodson, G., Riek, B. M., Johnson, K. M., & Houlette, M. (2006). Recategorization and crossed categorization: The implications of group salience and representations for reducing bias. In R. J. Crisp & M. Hewstone (Eds.), *Multiple social categorization: Processes, models and applications* (pp. 65–89). Psychology Press.

Dowd, E. T., Milne, C. R., & Wise, S. L. (1991). The Therapeutic Reactance Scale: A measure of psychological reactance. *Journal of Counseling and Development, 69*(6), 541–545. https://doi.org/10.1002/j.1556-6676.1991.tb02638.x

Drake, J. R., Murdock, N. L., Marszalek, J. M., & Barber, C. E. (2015). Differentiation of self-inventory—Short form: Development and preliminary validation. *Contemporary Family Therapy, 37*(2), 101–112. https://doi.org/10.1007/s10591-015-9329-7

Dryer, J. A., & Lijtmae, R. M. (2007). Cyber-sex as twilight zone between virtual reality and virtual fantasy: Creative play space or destructive addiction? *Psychoanalytic Review, 94*(1), 39–61. https://doi.org/10.1521/prev.2007.94.1.39

Dutra, L., & Lyons-Ruth, K. (2005, April 7–10). Maltreatment, maternal and child psychopathology, and quality of early care as predictors of adolescent dissociation. In J. Borelli (Chair), *Interrelations of attachment and trauma symptoms: A developmental perspective* [Symposium]. Society for Research in Child Development biennial meeting, Atlanta, GA, United States.

Ebner-Priemer, U. W., Welch, S. S., Grossman, P., Reisch, T., Linehan, M. M., & Bohus, M. (2007). Psychophysiological ambulatory assessment of affective dysregulation in borderline personality disorder. *Psychiatry Research, 150*(3), 265–275. https://doi.org/10.1016/j.psychres.2006.04.014

Egan, V., & McCorkindale, C. (2007). Narcissism, vanity, personality and mating effort. *Personality and Individual Differences, 43*(8), 2105–2115. https://doi.org/10.1016/j.paid.2007.06.034

Ellemers, N. (2018). Gender stereotypes. *Annual Review of Psychology, 69*(1), 275–298. https://doi.org/10.1146/annurev-psych-122216-011719

Ellis, A. (1973). *Humanistic psychotherapy: The rational-emotive approach.* Three Rivers Press.

Ellis, A., Harper, R. A., & Powers, M. (1975). *A guide to rational living.* Chatsworth.

Emanuel, L., Solomon, S., Fitchett, G., Chochinov, H., Handzo, G., Schoppee, T., & Wilkie, D. (2021). Fostering existential maturity to manage terror in a pandemic. *Journal of Palliative Medicine, 24*(2), 211–217. https://doi.org/10.1089/jpm.2020.0263

Epps, C., & Holt, L. (2011). The genetic basis of addiction and relevant cellular mechanisms. *International Anesthesiology Clinics, 49*(1), 3–14. https://doi.org/10.1097/AIA.0b013e3181f2bb66

Erikson, E. H. (1968). *Identity: Youth and crisis* (No. 7). Norton.

Esch, T., & Stefano, G. B. (2004). The neurobiology of pleasure, reward processes, addiction and their health implications. *Neuroendocrinology Letters*, *25*(4), 235–251. http://www.wisebrain.org/media/Papers/Neurobioofpleasure_Stefano2004.pdf

Estévez, A., Jáuregui, P., Sánchez-Marcos, I., López-González, H., & Griffiths, M. D. (2017). Attachment and emotion regulation in substance addictions and behavioral addictions. *Journal of Behavioral Addictions*, *6*(4), 534–544. https://doi.org/10.1556/2006.6.2017.086

Fairbairn, W. R. D. (1952). A revised psychopathology of the psychoses and psycho-neuroses. In W. R. D. Fairbairn (Ed.), *Psychoanalytic studies of the personality* (pp. 28–58). Routledge & Kegan Paul.

Falk, A. (2004). *Fratricide in the Holy Land: A psychoanalytic view of the Arab–Israeli conflict*. University of Wisconsin Press.

Farberow, N. L. (1980a). Indirect self-destructive behavior: Classification and characteristics. In N. L. Farberow (Ed.), *The many faces of suicide: Indirect self-destructive behavior* (pp. 15–27). McGraw-Hill.

Farberow, N. L. (1980b). Introduction. In N. L. Farberow (Ed.), *The many faces of suicide: Indirect self-destructive behavior* (pp. 1–12). McGraw-Hill.

Felitti, V. J., Anda, R. F., Nordenberg, D., Williamson, D. F., Spitz, A. M., Edwards, V., Koss, M. P., & Marks, J. S. (1998). Relationship of childhood abuse and household dysfunction to many of the leading causes of death in adults. The Adverse Childhood Experiences (ACE) Study. *American Journal of Preventive Medicine*, *14*(4), 245–258. https://doi.org/10.1016/S0749-3797(98)00017-8

Felmlee, D. H. (2001). From appealing to appalling: Disenchantment with a romantic partner. *Sociological Perspectives*, *44*(3), 263–280. https://doi.org/10.2307/1389707

Feng, Y. (2008). Convergence and divergence in the etiology of myelin impairment in psychiatric disorders and drug addiction. *Neurochemical Research*, *33*(10), 1940–1949. https://doi.org/10.1007/s11064-008-9693-x

Fenigstein, A., & Vanable, P. A. (1992). Paranoia and self-consciousness. *Journal of Personality and Social Psychology*, *62*(1), 129–138. https://doi.org/10.1037/0022-3514.62.1.129

Ferenczi, S. (1955). *Confusion of tongues between adults and the child*. In M. Balint (Ed.), *Final contributions to the problems and methods of psycho-analysis* (pp. 156–167). Basic Books. (Original work published 1933)

Ferreira, L. C., Narciso, I., & Novo, R. F. (2012). Intimacy, sexual desire and differentiation in couplehood: A theoretical and methodological review. *Journal of Sex & Marital Therapy*, *38*(3), 263–280. https://doi.org/10.1080/0092623X.2011.606885

Ferreira, L. C., Narciso, I., Novo, R. F., & Pereira, C. R. (2016). Partners' similarity in differentiation of self is associated with higher sexual desire: A quantitative dyadic study. *Journal of Sex & Marital Therapy*, *42*(7), 635–647. https://doi.org/10.1080/0092623X.2015.1113584

Fierman, L. B. (Ed.). (1965). *Effective psychotherapy: The contribution of Helmuth Kaiser*. Free Press.

Firestone, L. (2004). Voice therapy: A treatment for depression and suicide. In R. Yufit & D. Lester (Eds.), *Assessment, treatment, and prevention of suicidal behavior* (pp. 235–278). Wiley.

Firestone, L., & Catlett, J. (2004). Voice therapy interventions for addicted clients. *Counselor, 5*(5), 49–69.

Firestone, R. W. (1957). *A concept of the schizophrenic process* [Unpublished doctoral dissertation]. University of Denver.

Firestone, R. W. (1984). A concept of the primary fantasy bond: A developmental perspective. *Psychotherapy: Theory, Research, & Practice, 21*(2), 218–225. https://doi.org/10.1037/h0085976

Firestone, R. W. (1985). *The fantasy bond: Structure of psychological defenses*. Glendon Association.

Firestone, R. W. (1986). The "inner voice" and suicide. *Psychotherapy: Theory, Research, & Practice, 23*(3), 439–447. https://doi.org/10.1037/h0085636

Firestone, R. W. (1987). The "voice": The dual nature of guilt reactions. *American Journal of Psychoanalysis, 47*(3), 210–229. https://doi.org/10.1007/BF01250340

Firestone, R. W. (1988). *Voice therapy: A psychotherapeutic approach to self-destructive behavior*. Glendon Association.

Firestone, R. W. (1989). Parenting groups based on voice therapy. *Psychotherapy: Theory, Research, & Practice, 26*(4), 524–529. https://doi.org/10.1037/h0085473

Firestone, R. W. (1990a). The bipolar causality of regression. *American Journal of Psychoanalysis, 50*(2), 121–135. https://doi.org/10.1007/BF01250909

Firestone, R. W. (1990b). *Compassionate child-rearing: An in-depth approach to optimal parenting*. Glendon Association.

Firestone, R. W. (1990c). Prescription for psychotherapy. *Psychotherapy: Theory, Research, & Practice, 27*(4), 627–635. https://doi.org/10.1037/0033-3204.27.4.627

Firestone, R. W. (1990d). Voices during sex: Application of voice therapy to sexuality. *Journal of Sex & Marital Therapy, 16*(4), 258–274. https://doi.org/10.1080/00926239008405462

Firestone, R. W. (1990e). Voice therapy. In J. K. Zeig & W. Munion (Eds.), *What is psychotherapy? Contemporary perspectives* (pp. 68–74). Jossey-Bass.

Firestone, R. W. (1992). *Voices in suicide: The relationship between the Firestone Voice Scale for Self-Destructive Behavior and self-destructive life-styles*. Glendon Associates.

Firestone, R. W. (1993). The psychodynamics of fantasy, addiction, and addictive attachments. *American Journal of Psychoanalysis, 53*(4), 335–352. https://doi.org/10.1007/BF01248800

Firestone, R. W. (1994). Psychological defenses against death anxiety. In R. A. Neimeyer (Ed.), *Death anxiety handbook: Research, instrumentation, and application* (pp. 217–241). Taylor & Francis.

Firestone, R. W. (1996). The origins of ethnic strife. *Human Mind and Interaction, 7,* 217–241.

Firestone, R. W. (1997a). *Combating destructive thought processes: Voice therapy and separation theory.* SAGE.

Firestone, R. W. (1997b). *Suicide and the inner voice: Risk assessment, treatment, and case management.* SAGE.

Firestone, R. W. (1998). Voice therapy. In H. G. Rosenthal (Ed.), *Favorite counseling and therapy techniques: 51 therapists share their most creative strategies* (pp. 82–85). Accelerated Development.

Firestone, R. W. (2000). Microsuicide and the elderly: A basic defense against death anxiety. In A. Tomer (Ed.), *Death attitudes and the older adult: Theories, concepts, and applications* (pp. 65–84). Brunner-Routledge.

Firestone, R. W. (2015). The ultimate resistance. *Journal of Humanistic Psychology, 55*(1), 77–101. https://doi.org/10.1177/0022167814527166

Firestone, R. W. (2016). *Overcoming the destructive inner voice: True stories of therapy and transformation.* Prometheus Books.

Firestone, R. W. (2018). *The enemy within: Separation theory and voice therapy.* Zeig, Tucker, & Theisen.

Firestone, R. W. (2019, November). Basic tenets of separation theory. *Journal of Humanistic Psychology.* https://doi.org/10.1177/0022167819889218

Firestone, R. W. (2021). The enemy within. *Journal of Humanistic Psychology.* Advance online publication. https://doi.org/10.1177/00221678211025354

Firestone, R. W., & Catlett, J. (1989). *Psychological defenses in everyday life.* Glendon Association.

Firestone, R. W., & Catlett, J. (1999). *Fear of intimacy.* American Psychological Association.

Firestone, R. W., & Catlett, J. (2009a). *Beyond death anxiety: Achieving life-affirming death awareness.* Springer.

Firestone, R. W., & Catlett, J. (2009b). *The ethics of interpersonal relationships.* Karnac Books.

Firestone, R. W., & Firestone, L. (2002). Suicide reduction and prevention. In C. Feltham (Ed.), *What's the good of counselling & psychotherapy? The benefits explained* (pp. 48–80). SAGE.

Firestone, R. W., & Firestone, L. (2004). Methods for overcoming the fear of intimacy. In D. J. Mashek & A. Aron (Eds.), *Handbook of closeness and intimacy* (pp. 375–395). Psychology Press.

Firestone, R. W., & Firestone, L. (2006). *Firestone Assessment of Self-Destructive Thoughts (FAST) manual.* Psychological Assessment Resources.

Firestone, R. W., & Firestone, L. (2008a). *Firestone Assessment of Violent Thoughts (FAVT) manual.* Psychological Assessment Resources.

Firestone, R. W., & Firestone, L. (2008b). *Firestone Assessment of Violent Thoughts—Adolescent (FAVT-A) manual.* Psychological Assessment Resources.

Firestone, R. W., & Firestone, L. (2012). Separation theory and voice therapy methodology. In P. R. Shaver & M. E. Mikulincer (Eds.), *Meaning, mortality, and choice: The social psychology of existential concerns* (pp. 353–377). American Psychological Association. https://doi.org/10.1037/13748-020

Firestone, R. W., Firestone, L., & Catlett, J. (2002). *Conquer your critical inner voice: A revolutionary program to counter negative thoughts and life free from imagined limitations*. New Harbinger.

Firestone, R. W., Firestone, L. A., & Catlett, J. (2003). *Creating a life of meaning and compassion: The wisdom of psychotherapy*. American Psychological Association. https://doi.org/10.1037/10611-000

Firestone, R. W., Firestone, L. A., & Catlett, J. (2006). *Sex and love in intimate relationships*. American Psychological Association. https://doi.org/10.1037/11260-000

Firestone, R. W., Firestone, L. A., & Catlett, J. (2012). *The self under siege: A therapeutic model for differentiation*. Routledge. https://doi.org/10.4324/9780203122426

Firestone, R. W., & Seiden, R. H. (1987). Microsuicide and suicidal threats of everyday life. *Psychotherapy: Theory, Research, & Practice, 24*(1), 31–39. https://doi.org/10.1037/h0085688

Firestone, R. W., & Seiden, R. H. (1990a). Psychodynamics in adolescent suicide. *Journal of College Student Psychotherapy, 4*(3–4), 101–124. https://doi.org/10.1300/J035v04n03_07

Firestone, R. W., & Seiden, R. H. (1990b). Suicide and the continuum of self-destructive behavior. *Journal of American College Health, 38*(5), 207–213. https://doi.org/10.1080/07448481.1990.9936189

Firestone, R. W., & Solomon, S. (2018, September). Separation theory: Sheldon Solomon interview with Robert Firestone. *Journal of Humanistic Psychology*. https://doi.org/10.1177/0022167818796881

Fisher, S., & Fisher, R. L. (1986). *What we really know about child-rearing: Science in support of effective parenting*. Jason Aronson.

Flanagan, P. (2014). Unpacking ideas of sexuality in childhood: What do primary teachers and parents say? *Open Review of Educational Research, 1*(1), 160–170. https://doi.org/10.1080/23265507.2014.972436

Flores, P. J. (2001). Addiction as an attachment disorder: Implications for group therapy. *International Journal of Group Psychotherapy, 51*(1), 63–81. https://doi.org/10.1521/ijgp.51.1.63.49730

Fonagy, P. (1997). Multiple voices vs. meta-cognition: An attachment theory perspective. *Journal of Psychotherapy Integration, 7*(3), 181–194. https://doi.org/10.1037/h0101122

Fonagy, P., Gergely, G., Jurist, E., & Target, M. (2002). *Mentalization, affective regulation and the development of the self*. Basic Books.

Fortenberry, J. D. (2013). Puberty and adolescent sexuality. *Hormones and Behavior, 64*(2), 280–287. https://doi.org/10.1016/j.yhbeh.2013.03.007

Fosha, D. (2005). Emotion, true self, true other, core state: Toward a clinical theory of affective change process. *Psychoanalytic Review, 92*(4), 513–551. https://doi.org/10.1521/prev.2005.92.4.513

Foucault, M. (1975). *Discipline and punishment: The birth of the prison.* Allen Lane.

Foucault, M. (1980). *Power and knowledge.* Harvester.

Foucault, M. (1990). *The history of sexuality: Vol. I. An introduction* (R. Hurley, Trans.). Vintage Books.

Fraley, C., Waller, N., & Brennan, K. (2000). *The Experiences in Close Relationships-Revised (ECR-R) Questionnaire.* https://fetzer.org/sites/default/files/images/stories/pdf/selfmeasures/Attachment-ExperienceinCloseRelationshipsRevised.pdf

Francoeur, R. T. (2001). Challenging collective religious/social beliefs about sex, marriage, and family. *Journal of Sex Education and Therapy, 26*(4), 281–290. https://doi.org/10.1080/01614576.2001.11074434

Frankl, V. E. (1959). *Man's search for meaning* (Rev. ed.). Washington Square Press. (Original work published 1946)

Frankl, V. E. (1963). *Man's search for meaning: An introduction to logotherapy* (I. Lasch, Trans.). Pocket.

Freud, A. (1966). *The ego and the mechanisms of defense* (Rev. ed.). International Universities Press.

Freud, S. (1953). *A general introduction to psychoanalysis* (J. Riviere, Trans.). Permabooks. (Original work published 1924)

Freud, S. (1955). Group psychology and the analysis of the ego. In J. Strachey (Ed.), *The standard edition of the complete psychological works of Sigmund Freud* (Vol. 18; J. Strachey, Trans.; pp. 63–143). Hogarth. (Original work published 1921)

Freud, S. (1959). An autobiographical study. In J. Strachey (Ed.), *The standard edition of the complete psychological works of Sigmund Freud* (Vol. 20; J. Strachey, Trans.; pp. 7–75). Hogarth. (Original work published 1925)

Freud, S. (1961). Remarks on the theory and practice of dream-interpretation. In J. Strachey (Ed.), *The standard edition of the complete psychological works of Sigmund Freud, Volume XIX (1923–1925): The ego and the id and other works* (pp. 107–122). Hogarth.

Freud, S. (1963). Some thoughts on development and regression—Etiology, Lecture XXII, introductory lectures on psycho-analysis. In J. Strachey (Ed.), *The standard edition of the complete psychological works of Sigmund Freud* (Vol. 16; J. Strachey, Trans.; pp. 339–357). Hogarth. (Original work published 1916)

Freyd, J. J. (1996). *Betrayal trauma: The logic of forgetting childhood abuse.* Harvard University Press.

Fromm, E. (1939). *Selfishness and self-love.* William Alanson White Psychiatric Foundation.

Fromm, E. (1941). *Escape from freedom.* Avon Books.

Fromm, E. (1944). Individual and social origins of neurosis. *American Sociological Review, 9*(4), 380–384. https://doi.org/10.2307/2085981

Fromm, E. (1950). *Psychoanalysis and religion.* Yale University Press.

Fromm, E. (1964). *The heart of man: Its genius for good and evil.* Harper & Row.

Garbarino, J. (2017). *Children and families in the social environment.* Transaction. https://doi.org/10.4324/9781315081397

Garrels, S. R. (Ed.). (2011). *Mimesis and science: Empirical research on imitation and the mimetic theory of culture and religion.* MSU Press.

Gartner, R. B. (1999). *Betrayed as boys: Psychodynamic treatment of sexually abused men.* Guilford Press.

Gershoff, E. T. (2002). Corporal punishment by parents and associated child behaviors and experiences: A meta-analytic and theoretical review. *Psychological Bulletin, 128*(4), 539–579. https://doi.org/10.1037/0033-2909. 128.4.539

Gibney, P. (2006). The double bind theory: Still crazy-making after all these years. *Psychotherapy in Australia, 12*(3), 48–55.

Gilligan, C., & Snider, N. (2018). *Why does patriarchy persist?* Wiley.

Gilligan, J. (2001). *Preventing violence.* Thames & Hudson.

Gilligan, J. (2007). Terrorism, fundamentalism, and nihilism: Analyzing the dilemmas of modernity. In A. Mahfouz, S. Twemlow, & D. E. Scharff (Eds.), *The future of prejudice: Psychoanalysis and the prevention of prejudice* (pp. 37–59). Jason Aronson.

Giner-Sorolla, R., Bosson, J. K., Caswell, T. A., & Hettinger, V. E. (2012). Emotions in sexual morality: Testing the separate elicitors of anger and disgust. *Cognition and Emotion, 26*(7), 1208–1222. https://doi.org/10.1080/02699931. 2011.645278

Giroux, H. A. (2015). Totalitarian paranoia in the post-Orwellian surveillance state. *Cultural Studies, 29*(2), 108–140. https://doi.org/10.1080/09502386. 2014.917118

Goldberg, A. E., Kashy, D. A., & Smith, J. Z. (2012). Gender-typed play behavior in early childhood: Adopted children with lesbian, gay, and heterosexual parents. *Sex Roles, 67*(9–10), 503–515. https://doi.org/10.1007/s11199-012-0198-3

Goldenberg, J. L., Cox, C. R., Pyszczynski, T., Greenberg, J., & Solomon, S. (2002). Understanding human ambivalence about sex: The effects of stripping sex of meaning. *Journal of Sex Research, 39*(4), 310–320. https://doi.org/10.1080/00224490209552155

Goldenberg, J. L., Kosloff, S., & Greenberg, J. (2006). Existential underpinnings of approach and avoidance of the physical body. *Motivation and Emotion, 30*(2), 127–134. https://doi.org/10.1007/s11031-006-9023-z

Goldenberg, J. L., Pyszczynski, T., McCoy, S. K., Greenberg, J., & Solomon, S. (1999). Death, sex, love, and neuroticism: Why is sex such a problem? *Journal of Personality and Social Psychology, 77*(6), 1173–1187. https://doi.org/ 10.1037/0022-3514.77.6.1173

Golombok, S., Blake, L., Slutsky, J., Raffanello, E., Roman, G. D., & Ehrhardt, A. (2018). Parenting and the adjustment of children born to gay fathers through surrogacy. *Child Development, 89*(4), 1223–1233. https://doi.org/10.1111/cdev.12728

Golombok, S., Mellish, L., Jennings, S., Casey, P., Tasker, F., & Lamb, M. E. (2014). Adoptive gay father families: Parent–child relationships and children's psychological adjustment. *Child Development, 85*(2), 456–468. https://doi.org/10.1111/cdev.12155

Gonzaga, G. C., Turner, R. A., Keltner, D., Campos, B., & Altemus, M. (2006). Romantic love and sexual desire in close relationships. *Emotion, 6*(2), 163–179. https://doi.org/10.1037/1528-3542.6.2.163

González-Suárez, M. (2009). Political psychology for democracy, human rights and academic development: Sharing Costa Rica's experience. *Revista Psicologia Política, 9*(18), 237–257.

Gottman, J. M., & Krokoff, L. J. (1989). Marital interaction and satisfaction: A longitudinal view. *Journal of Consulting and Clinical Psychology, 57*(1), 47–52. https://doi.org/10.1037/0022-006X.57.1.47

Grau, S. L., & Zotos, Y. C. (2016). Gender stereotypes in advertising: A review of current research. *International Journal of Advertising, 35*(5), 761–770. https://doi.org/10.1080/02650487.2016.1203556

Green, M., & Piel, J. A. (2009). *Theories of human development: A comparative approach*. Prentice-Hall.

Greenberg, J., Landau, M. J., Kosloff, S., Soenke, M., & Solomon, S. (2016). How our means for feeling transcendent of death foster prejudice, stereotyping, and intergroup conflict: Terror management theory. In T. D. Nelson (Ed.), *Handbook of prejudice, stereotyping, and discrimination* (pp. 107–148). Psychology Press.

Greenberg, L. S. (2002). *Emotion-focused therapy: Coaching clients to work through their feelings* (2nd ed.). American Psychological Association. https://doi.org/10.1037/10447-000

Greenberg, L. S. (2004). Emotion-focused therapy. *Clinical Psychology & Psychotherapy, 11*(1), 3–16. https://doi.org/10.1002/cpp.388

Greenberg, L. S. (2012). Emotions, the great captains of our lives: Their role in the process of change in psychotherapy. *American Psychologist, 67*(8), 697–707. https://doi.org/10.1037/a0029858

Greenberg, L. S. (2015). *Emotion-focused therapy: Coaching clients to work through their feelings*. American Psychological Association.

Greenberg, L. S. (2019). Theory of functioning in emotion-focused therapy. In L. S. Greenberg & R. N. Goldman (Eds.), *Clinical handbook of emotion-focused therapy* (pp. 37–59). American Psychological Association. https://doi.org/10.1037/0000112-002

Grossman, G. (2001). Contemporary views of bisexuality in clinical work. *Journal of the American Psychoanalytic Association, 49*(4), 1361–1377. https://doi.org/10.1177/00030651010490041401

Grubbs, J. B., Exline, J. J., Pargament, K. I., Hook, J. N., & Carlisle, R. D. (2015). Transgression as addiction: Religiosity and moral disapproval as predictors of perceived addiction to pornography. *Archives of Sexual Behavior, 44*(1), 125–136. https://doi.org/10.1007/s10508-013-0257-z

Guntrip, H. (1960). Ego-weakness and the hard core of the problem of psychotherapy. *The British Journal of Medical Psychology, 33*(3), 163–184. https://doi.org/10.1111/j.2044-8341.1960.tb01238.x

Guntrip, H. (1969). *Schizoid phenomena object-relations and the self.* International Universities Press.

Hainlen, R. L., Jankowski, P. J., Paine, D. R., & Sandage, S. J. (2016). Adult attachment and well-being: Dimensions of differentiation of self as mediators. *Contemporary Family Therapy, 38*(2), 172–183. https://doi.org/10.1007/s10591-015-9359-1

Harré, R., & Parrott, W. G. (Eds.). (1996). *The emotions: Social, cultural and biological dimensions.* SAGE.

Harrop, C. E. (2002). The development of schizophrenia in late adolescence. *Current Psychiatry Reports, 4*(4), 293–298. https://doi.org/10.1007/s11920-996-0049-4

Harrop, C., & Trower, P. (2001). Why does schizophrenia develop at late adolescence? *Clinical Psychology Review, 21*(2), 241–265. https://doi.org/10.1016/S0272-7358(99)00047-1

Hart, J., & Goldenberg, J. L. (2008). A terror management perspective on spirituality and the problem of the body. In A. Tomer, G. T. Eliason, & P. T. P. Wong (Eds.), *Existential and spiritual issues in death attitudes* (pp. 91–113). Erlbaum.

Hart, K. E., Scholar, F., Kritsonis, W. A., & Alumnus, D. (2006). Critical analysis of an original writing on social learning theory: Imitation of film-mediated aggressive models by Albert Bandura, Dorothea Ross and Sheila A. Ross. *National Forum of Applied Educational Research Journal, 19*(3), 1–7.

Haskett, M. E., Nears, K., Ward, C. S., & McPherson, A. V. (2006). Diversity in adjustment of maltreated children: Factors associated with resilient functioning. *Clinical Psychology Review, 26*(6), 796–812. https://doi.org/10.1016/j.cpr.2006.03.005

Hayes, J., Schimel, J., Arndt, J., & Faucher, E. H. (2010). A theoretical and empirical review of the death-thought accessibility concept in terror management research. *Psychological Bulletin, 136*(5), 699–739. https://doi.org/10.1037/a0020524

Hazen, N., Jacobvitz, D., & McFarland, L. (2005). Antecedents of boundary disturbances in families with young children: Intergenerational transmission and parent-infant caregiving patterns. *Journal of Emotional Abuse, 5*(2–3), 85–110. https://doi.org/10.1300/J135v05n02_05

Healy, S. (2014). Psychoanalysis and the geography of the Anthropocene: Fantasy, oil addiction and the politics of global warming. In P. Kingsbury & S. Pile (Eds.), *Psychoanalytic Geographies* (pp. 181–196). Routledge.

Heiman, J. R., & Heard-Davison, A. R. (2004). Child sexual abuse and adult sexual relationships: Review and perspective. In L. J. Koenig, L. S. Doll, A. O. Leary, & W. Pequegnat (Eds.), *From child sexual abuse to adult sexual risk: Trauma, revictimization, and intervention* (pp. 13–47). American Psychological Association. https://doi.org/10.1037/10785-002

Heinemann, J., Atallah, S., & Rosenbaum, T. (2016). The impact of culture and ethnicity on sexuality and sexual function. *Current Sexual Health Reports, 8*(3), 144–150. https://doi.org/10.1007/s11930-016-0088-8

Heinonen, E., Lindfors, O., Laaksonen, M. A., & Knekt, P. (2012). Therapists' professional and personal characteristics as predictors of outcome in short- and long-term psychotherapy. *Journal of Affective Disorders, 138*(3), 301–312. https://doi.org/10.1016/j.jad.2012.01.023

Herman, J. (with Hirschman, L.). (1981). *Father–daughter incest.* Harvard University Press.

Herman, J. (1992). *Trauma and recovery.* Basic Books.

Herrera, M., & Sani, F. (2013). Why does ingroup identification shield people from death anxiety? The role of perceived collective continuity and group entitativity. *Social Psychology, 44*(5), 320–328. https://doi.org/10.1027/1864-9335/a000128

Hoffer, E. (2006). *The true believer: Thoughts on the nature of mass movements.* Harper Perennial Classics. (Original work published 1955)

Hoffman, S. I., & Strauss, S. (1985). The development of children's concepts of death. *Death Studies, 9*(5–6), 469–482. https://doi.org/10.1080/07481188508252538

Hohman, Z. P., & Hogg, M. A. (2011). Fear and uncertainty in the face of death: The role of life after death in group identification. *European Journal of Social Psychology, 41*(6), 751–760. https://doi.org/10.1002/ejsp.818

Hopwood, C. J., Morey, L. C., Markowitz, J. C., Pinto, A., Skodol, A. E., Gunderson, J. G., Zanarini, M. C., Shea, M. T., Yen, S., McGlashan, T. H., Ansell, E. B., Grilo, C. M., & Sanislow, C. A. (2009). The construct validity of passive-aggressive personality disorder. *Psychiatry, 72*(3), 256–267. https://doi.org/10.1521/psyc.2009.72.3.256

Horney, K. (1950). *Neurosis and human growth.* Norton.

Hrdy, S. B. (2009). *Mothers and others: The evolutionary origins of mutual understanding.* Harvard University Press.

Hrdy, S. (2011). *Mothers and others.* Belknap Press of Harvard University Press.

Huber, V. J., & Firmin, M. W. (2014). A history of sex education in the United States since 1900. *International Journal of Educational Reform, 23*(1), 25–51. https://doi.org/10.1177/105678791402300102

Hyde, J. S. (2016). Sex and cognition: Gender and cognitive functions. *Current Opinion in Neurobiology, 38,* 53–56. https://doi.org/10.1016/j.conb.2016.02.007

Iacoboni, M. (2009). Imitation, empathy, and mirror neurons. *Annual Review of Psychology, 60*(1), 653–670. https://doi.org/10.1146/annurev.psych.60.110707.163604

Iacoboni, M., Woods, R. P., Brass, M., Bekkering, H., Mazziotta, J. C., & Rizzolatti, G. (1999). Cortical mechanisms of human imitation. *Science, 286*(5449), 2526–2528. https://doi.org/10.1126/science.286.5449.2526

Izard, C. E., & Buechler, S. (1980). Aspects of consciousness and personality in terms of differential emotions theory. In R. Plutchik & H. Kellerman (Eds.), *Theories of emotion* (pp. 165–187). Academic Press. https://doi.org/10.1016/B978-0-12-558701-3.50013-2

Jackson, J. C., Jong, J., Bluemke, M., Poulter, P., Morgenroth, L., & Halberstadt, J. (2018). Testing the causal relationship between religious belief and death anxiety. *Religion, Brain & Behavior, 8*(1), 57–68. https://doi.org/10.1080/2153599X.2016.1238842

Jackson, L. M. (2019). *The psychology of prejudice: From attitudes to social action* (2nd ed.). American Psychological Association.

Janov, A. (1970). *The primal scream: Primal therapy, the cure for neurosis*. Putnam.

Janowsky, D. S. (2001). Introversion and extroversion: Implications for depression and suicidality. *Current Psychiatry Reports, 3*(6), 444–450. https://doi.org/10.1007/s11920-001-0037-7

Jenkins, S. M., Buboltz, W. C., Jr., Schwartz, J. P., & Johnson, P. (2005). Differentiation of self and psychosocial development. *Contemporary Family Therapy, 27*(2), 251–261. https://doi.org/10.1007/s10591-005-4042-6

Jennings, L., & Skovholt, T. M. (1999). The cognitive, emotional, and relational characteristics of master therapists. *Journal of Counseling Psychology, 46*(1), 3–11. https://doi.org/10.1037/0022-0167.46.1.3

Johnson, N. J., & Klee, T. (2007). Passive aggressive behavior and leadership styles in organizations. *Journal of Leadership & Organizational Studies, 14*(2), 130–142. https://doi.org/10.1177/1071791907308044

Johnson, P., & Buboltz, W. C. (2000). Differentiation of self and psychological reactance. *Contemporary Family Therapy, 22*(1), 91–102. https://doi.org/10.1023/A:1007774600764

Jordan, C. H., Spencer, S. J., Zanna, M. P., Hoshino-Browne, E., & Correll, J. (2003). Secure and defensive high self-esteem. *Journal of Personality and Social Psychology, 85*(5), 969–978. https://doi.org/10.1037/0022-3514.85.5.969

Jung, C. G. (1974). *The collected works of CG Jung: Symbols of transformation* (Vol. 20). Princeton University Press.

Kannan, D., & Levitt, H. M. (2013). A review of client self-criticism in psychotherapy. *Journal of Psychotherapy Integration, 23*(2), 166–178. https://doi.org/10.1037/a0032355

Kantor, L., & Levitz, N. (2017). Parents' views on sex education in schools: How much do Democrats and Republicans agree? *PLOS ONE*, Article e0180250. https://doi.org/10.1371/journal.pone.0180250

Kaplan, H. S. (1979). *Disorders of sexual desire and other new concepts and techniques in sex therapy*. Brunner/Mazel.

Kaplan, H. S. (1995). *The sexual desire disorders: Dysfunctional regulation of sexual motivation*. Brunner/Mazel.

Kaplan, H. S. (2013). *New sex therapy: Active treatment of sexual dysfunctions*. Routledge. https://doi.org/10.4324/9780203727317

Kaplan, H. S. (2014). *Sexual aversion, sexual phobias and panic disorder*. Routledge. https://doi.org/10.4324/9781315803845

Karim, R., & Chaudhri, P. (2012). Behavioral addictions: An overview. *Journal of Psychoactive Drugs, 44*(1), 5–17. https://doi.org/10.1080/02791072.2012.662859

Karon, B. P., & VandenBos, G. R. (1977). *Psychotherapy of schizophrenia: The treatment of choice*. Jason Aronson.

Karson, M., & Sparks, E. (2013). *Patterns of child abuse: How dysfunctional transactions are replicated in individuals, families, and the child welfare system*. Routledge. https://doi.org/10.4324/9780203862728

Kasket, E. (2006). Death and the doctor. *Existential Analysis, 17*(1), 137–150.

Kastenbaum, R. (2000). *The psychology of death* (3rd ed.). Springer.

Katehakis, A. (2017). Sexual fantasy and adult attunement: Differentiating preying from playing. *American Journal of Play, 9*(2), 252–270.

Kaufman, G. (2004). *The psychology of shame: Theory and treatment of shame-based syndromes*. Springer.

Kaye, W. (2008). Neurobiology of anorexia and bulimia nervosa. *Physiology & Behavior, 94*(1), 121–135. https://doi.org/10.1016/j.physbeh.2007.11.037

Kelly, R. (2007). Childhood neglect and its effects on neurodevelopment: Suggestions for future law and policy. *Houston Journal of Health Law & Policy, 8*, 133.

Kerig, P. K. (2005). Revisiting the construct of boundary dissolution: A multidimensional perspective. *Journal of Emotional Abuse, 5*(2–3), 5–42. https://doi.org/10.1300/J135v05n02_02

Kernberg, O. F. (1980). *Internal world and external reality: Object relations theory applied*. Jason Aronson.

Kernberg, O. F. (1995). *Object relations theory and clinical psychoanalysis*. Jason Aronson.

Kerr, M. E., & Bowen, M. (1988). *Family evaluation: An approach based on Bowen theory*. Norton.

Kierkegaard, S. (1954). *The sickness unto death* (W. Lowrie, Trans.). Anchor. (Original work published 1849)

Kinzl, J. F., Traweger, C., & Biebl, W. (1995). Sexual dysfunctions: Relationship to childhood sexual abuse and early family experiences in a nonclinical sample. *Child Abuse & Neglect, 19*(7), 785–792. https://doi.org/10.1016/0145-2134(95)00048-D

Kipnis, L. (2003). *Against love: A polemic*. Pantheon Books.

Kirschner, S., & Kirschner, D. A. (1996). Relational components of the incest survivor syndrome. In F. W. Kaslow (Ed.), *Handbook of relational diagnosis and dysfunctional family patterns* (pp. 407–419). Wiley.

Klackl, J., Jonas, E., & Kronbichler, M. (2013). Existential neuroscience: Neurophysiological correlates of proximal defenses against death-related thoughts.

Social Cognitive and Affective Neuroscience, 8(3), 333–340. https://doi.org/10.1093/scan/nss003

Klar, Y., & Bilewicz, M. (2017). From socially motivated lay historians to lay censors: Epistemic conformity and defensive group identification. *Memory Studies, 10*(3), 334–346. https://doi.org/10.1177/1750698017701616

Klein, M. (1964). *Contributions to psycho-analysis 1921–1945*. McGraw-Hill. (Original work published 1948)

Klein, M. (1992). *Ask me anything: A sex therapist answers the most important questions for the 90s*. Simon & Schuster.

Knee, C. R., Canevello, A., Bush, A. L., & Cook, A. (2008). Relationship-contingent self-esteem and the ups and downs of romantic relationships. *Journal of Personality and Social Psychology, 95*(3), 608–627. https://doi.org/10.1037/0022-3514.95.3.608

Knoll, S., Eisend, M., & Steinhagen, J. (2011). Gender roles in advertising: Measuring and comparing gender stereotyping on public and private TV channels in Germany. *International Journal of Advertising, 30*(5), 867–888. https://doi.org/10.2501/IJA-30-5-867-888

Koenig, A. M. (2018). Comparing prescriptive and descriptive gender stereotypes about children, adults, and the elderly. *Frontiers in Psychology, 9*, 1086. https://doi.org/10.3389/fpsyg.2018.01086

Kokkinaki, T., & Vitalaki, E. (2013). Exploring spontaneous imitation in infancy: A three generation inter-familial study. *Europe's Journal of Psychology, 9*(2), 259–275. https://doi.org/10.5964/ejop.v9i2.506

Kolhatkar, G., & Berkowitz, C. (2014). Cultural considerations and child maltreatment: In search of universal principles. *Pediatric Clinics, 61*(5), 1007–1022. https://doi.org/10.1016/j.pcl.2014.06.005

Koole, S. L., & Tschacher, W. (2016). Synchrony in psychotherapy: A review and an integrative framework for the therapeutic alliance. *Frontiers in Psychology, 7*, 862. https://doi.org/10.3389/fpsyg.2016.00862

Kris, A. O. (2013). *Free association: Methods and process*. Routledge. https://doi.org/10.4324/9780203766439

Laczkovics, C., Fonzo, G., Bendixsen, B., Shpigel, E., Lee, I., Skala, K., Prunas, A., Gross, J., Steiner, H., & Huemer, J. (2018). Defense mechanism is predicted by attachment and mediates the maladaptive influence of insecure attachment on adolescent mental health. *Current Psychology, 39*, 1–9. https://doi.org/10.1007/s12144-018-9839-1

Lafferty, P., Beutler, L. E., & Crago, M. (1989). Differences between more and less effective psychotherapists: A study of select therapist variables. *Journal of Consulting and Clinical Psychology, 57*(1), 76–80. https://doi.org/10.1037/0022-006X.57.1.76

Lafrance, A., Henderson, K. A., & Mayman, S. (2020). *Emotion-focused family therapy: A transdiagnostic model for caregiver-focused interventions*. American Psychological Association. https://doi.org/10.1037/0000166-000

Laing, R. D. (1967). *The politics of experience*. Pantheon.

Laing, R. D. (1969). *The divided self*. Penguin Books. (Original work published 1960)

Lamb, S. (2010). Toward a sexual ethics curriculum: Bringing philosophy and society to bear on individual development. *Harvard Educational Review, 80*(1), 81–106. https://doi.org/10.17763/haer.80.1.c104834k00552457

Langs, R. (1982). *Psychotherapy: A basic text*. Jason Aronson.

Langs, R. (2004). *Fundamentals of adaptive psychotherapy and counseling*. Palgrave Macmillan. https://doi.org/10.1007/978-0-230-62953-0

Langs, R. (2006). *Love and death in psychotherapy*. Palgrave Macmillan.

Langs, R. (2018). *Empowered psychotherapy: Teaching self-processing*. Routledge. (Original work published 1993)

Lanktree, C. B., & Briere, J. N. (2015). *Treating complex trauma in children and their families: An integrative approach*. SAGE.

Lapsley, D. K., & Edgerton, J. (2002). Separation-individuation, adult attachment style, and college adjustment. *Journal of Counseling and Development, 80*(4), 484–492. https://doi.org/10.1002/j.1556-6678.2002.tb00215.x

Laumann, E. O., Gagnon, J. H., Michael, R. T., & Michaels, S. (1994). *The social organization of sexuality: Sexual practices in the United States*. University of Chicago Press.

Laumann, E. O., Paik, A., & Rosen, R. C. (1999). Sexual dysfunction in the United States: Prevalence and predictors. *Journal of the American Medical Association, 281*(6), 537–544. https://doi.org/10.1001/jama.281.6.537

Leander, E. B., Larsen, P. L., & Munk, K. P. (2018). Children's doctor games and nudity at Danish childcare institutions. *Archives of Sexual Behavior, 47*(4), 863–875. https://doi.org/10.1007/s10508-017-1144-9

LeDoux, J. (1998). *The emotional brain: The mysterious underpinnings of emotional life*. Simon & Schuster.

Leong, F. T., & Lee, S. H. (2006). A cultural accommodation model for cross-cultural psychotherapy: Illustrated with the case of Asian Americans. *Psychotherapy: Theory, Research, Practice, Training, 43*(4), 410–423. https://doi.org/10.1037/0033-3204.43.4.410

Lester, D. (2004). The inner voice and the plural self. *Psychological reports, 94* (3 Suppl.), 1455–1455. https://doi.org/10.2466/pr0.94.3c.1455-1455

Levin-Keini, N., & Shlomo, S. B. (2019). Confronting existential concerns in the transition to parenthood: A theoretical and therapeutic model. In O. Taubman-Ben-Ari (Ed.), *Pathways and barriers to parenthood* (pp. 235–249). Springer. https://doi.org/10.1007/978-3-030-24864-2_14

Levine, S. B. (2002). Reexploring the concept of sexual desire. *Journal of Sex & Marital Therapy, 28*(1), 39–51. https://doi.org/10.1080/009262302317251007

Lewis, M. (1992). *Shame: The exposed self*. Free Press.

Lewis, M. (2018). Brain change in addiction as learning, not disease. *The New England Journal of Medicine, 379*(16), 1551–1560. https://doi.org/10.1056/NEJMra1602872

Lieberman, M., Doyle, A. B., & Markiewicz, D. (1999). Developmental patterns in security of attachment to mother and father in late childhood and early adolescence: Associations with peer relations. *Child Development, 70*(1), 202–213. https://doi.org/10.1111/1467-8624.00015

Lifton, R. J. (1979). *The broken connection: On death and the continuity of life.* Simon & Schuster.

Lifton, R. J. (2005). Americans as survivors. *The New England Journal of Medicine, 352*(22), 2263–2265. https://doi.org/10.1056/NEJMp058048

Lifton, R. J. (2012). *Death in life: Survivors of Hiroshima.* University of North Carolina Press.

Liotti, G. (1999). Understanding the dissociative processes: The contribution of attachment theory. *Psychoanalytic Inquiry, 19*(5), 757–783. https://doi.org/10.1080/07351699909534275

Liotti, G. (2004). Trauma, dissociation, and disorganized attachment: Three strands of a single braid. *Psychotherapy: Theory, Research, & Practice, 41*(4), 472–486. https://doi.org/10.1037/0033-3204.41.4.472

Liotti, G. (2006). A model of dissociation based on attachment theory and research. *Journal of Trauma & Dissociation, 7*(4), 55–73. https://doi.org/10.1300/J229v07n04_04

Liotti, G. (2011). Attachment disorganization and the controlling strategies: An illustration of the contributions of attachment theory to developmental psychopathology and to psychotherapy integration. *Journal of Psychotherapy Integration, 21*(3), 232–252. https://doi.org/10.1037/a0025422

Lipman-Blumen, J. (2005). The allure of toxic leaders: Why followers rarely escape their clutches. *Ivey Business Journal, 69*(3), 1–40. https://assess.connectiveleadership.com/documents/why_followers_rarely_escape_their_clutches.pdf

Love, P. (with Robinson, J.). (1990). *The emotional incest syndrome: What to do when a parent's love rules your life.* Bantam Books.

Love, P., & Shulkin, S. (1997). *How to ruin a perfectly good relationship.* Zeig, Tucker & Theisen.

Lynch, S., Hurford, D. P., & Cole, A. (2002). Parental enabling attitudes and locus of control of at-risk and honors students. *Adolescence, 37*(147), 527.

Lyons-Ruth, K. (2003). The two-person construction of defenses: Disorganized attachment strategies, unintegrated mental states, and hostile/helpless relational processes. *Journal of Infant, Child, and Adolescent Psychotherapy, 2*(4), 105–114. https://doi.org/10.1080/15289168.2002.10486422

Lyons-Ruth, K. (2008). Contributions of the mother–infant relationship to dissociative, borderline, and conduct symptoms in young adulthood. *Infant Mental Health Journal, 29*(3), 203–218. https://doi.org/10.1002/imhj.20173

Lyons-Ruth, K., Bureau, J. F., Easterbrooks, M. A., Obsuth, I., Hennighausen, K., & Vulliez-Coady, L. (2013). Parsing the construct of maternal insensitivity: Distinct longitudinal pathways associated with early maternal withdrawal.

Attachment & Human Development, 15(5–6), 562–582. https://doi.org/10.1080/14616734.2013.841051

Lyons-Ruth, K., Yellin, C., Melnick, S., & Atwood, G. (2005). Expanding the concept of unresolved mental states: Hostile/helpless states of mind on the Adult Attachment Interview are associated with disrupted mother–infant communication and infant disorganization. *Development and Psychopathology, 17*(1), 1–23. https://doi.org/10.1017/S0954579405050017

Macfie, J., Brumariu, L. E., & Lyons-Ruth, K. (2015). Parent–child role-confusion: A critical review of an emerging concept. *Developmental Review, 36*, 34–57. https://doi.org/10.1016/j.dr.2015.01.002

MacKillop, J., & Ray, L. A. (2018). *The etiology of addiction: A contemporary biopsychosocial approach.* Routledge.

Magon, N., Chauhan, M., Malik, S., & Shah, D. (2012). Sexuality in midlife: Where the passion goes? *Journal of Midlife Health, 3*(2), 61–65. https://doi.org/10.4103/0976-7800.104452

Main, M., Goldwyn, R., & Hesse, E. (1985). *Adult attachment classification and rating system* [Unpublished manuscript]. Department of Psychology, University of California, Berkeley.

Main, M., Kaplan, N., & Cassidy, J. (1985). Security in infancy, childhood, and adulthood: A move to the level of representation. *Monographs of the Society for Research in Child Development, 50*(1–2), 66–104. https://doi.org/10.2307/3333827

Maltby, J. (2005). Protecting the sacred and expressions of rituality: Examining the relationship between extrinsic dimensions of religiosity and unhealthy guilt. *Psychology and Psychotherapy, 78*(1), 77–93. https://doi.org/10.1348/147608305X39644

Malti, T., Ongley, S. F., Killen, M., & Smetana, J. (2014). The development of moral emotions and moral reasoning. In M. Killen & J. G. Smetana (Eds.), *Handbook of moral development* (pp. 163–183). Psychology Press.

Maltz, W. (1995). The Maltz hierarchy of sexual interaction. *Sexual Addiction & Compulsivity, 2*(1), 5–18. https://doi.org/10.1080/10720169508400062

Maltz, W. (2002). Treating the sexual intimacy concerns of sexual abuse survivors. *Sexual and Relationship Therapy, 17*(4), 321–327. https://doi.org/10.1080/1468199021000017173

Maniglio, R. (2010). The role of deviant sexual fantasy in the etiopathogenesis of sexual homicide: A systematic review. *Aggression and Violent Behavior, 15*(4), 294–302. https://doi.org/10.1016/j.avb.2010.02.001

Marcuse, H. (1991). *One-dimensional man: Studies in the ideology of advanced industrial society* (2nd ed.). Beacon Press.

Marcuse, H. (1992). Ecology and the critique of modern society. *Capitalism, Nature, Socialism, 3*(3), 29–38. https://doi.org/10.1080/10455759209358500

Marlinova, O. (1990). *Group psychology in the totalitarian system: A psychoanalytic view.* https://www.fromm-gesellschaft.eu/images/pdf-Dateien/Marlinova_O_1990.pdf

Martens, A., Greenberg, J., Schimel, J., & Landau, M. J. (2004). Ageism and death: Effects of mortality salience and perceived similarity to elders on reactions to elderly people. *Personality and Social Psychology Bulletin, 30*(12), 1524–1536. https://doi.org/10.1177/0146167204271185

Martinson, F. M. (1994). *The sexual life of children*. Bergin & Garvey.

Maschi, T., Schwalbe, C., & Ristow, J. (2013). In pursuit of the ideal parent in juvenile justice: A qualitative investigation of probation officers' experiences with parents of juvenile offenders. *Journal of Offender Rehabilitation, 52*(7), 470–492. https://doi.org/10.1080/10509674.2013.829898

Maslow, A. H. (1971). *The farther reaches of human nature* (Vol. 19711). Viking Press.

May, R. (1958). Contributions of existential psychotherapy. In R. May, E. Angel, & H. F. Ellenberger (Eds.), *Existence: A new dimension in psychiatry and psychology* (pp. 37–91). Basic Books/Hachette. https://doi.org/10.1037/11321-002

May, R. (1983). *The three modes of world. The discovery of being: Writings in existential psychology*. Norton.

Mayseless, O., Bartholomew, K., Henderson, A., & Trinke, S. (2004). "I was more her Mom than she was mine:" Role reversal in a community sample. *Family Relations, 53*(1), 78–86. https://doi.org/10.1111/j.1741-3729.2004.00011.x

Mayseless, O., & Popper, M. (2007). Reliance on leaders and social institutions: An attachment perspective. *Attachment & Human Development, 9*(1), 73–93. https://doi.org/10.1080/14616730601151466

McCarthy, B. W. (1997). Strategies and techniques for revitalizing a nonsexual marriage. *Journal of Sex & Marital Therapy, 23*(3), 231–240. https://doi.org/10.1080/00926239708403928

McCarthy, B., & McCarthy, E. (2003). *Rekindling desire: A step-by-step program to help low-sex and no-sex marriages*. Brunner-Routledge.

McCarthy, J. B. (1980). *Death anxiety: The loss of the self*. Halsted Press.

McCarthy-Jones, S. (2012). *Hearing voices: The histories, causes and meanings of auditory verbal hallucinations*. Cambridge University Press. https://doi.org/10.1017/CBO9781139017534

McCoy, S. K., Pyszczynski, T., Solomon, S., & Greenberg, J. (2000). Transcending the self: A terror management perspective on successful aging. In A. Tomer (Ed.), *Death attitudes and the older adult: Theories, concepts, and applications* (pp. 37–63). Routledge. https://doi.org/10.4324/9781315784489-3

McGinty, E. E., Kennedy-Hendricks, A., Choksy, S., & Barry, C. L. (2016). Trends in news media coverage of mental illness in the United States: 1995–2014. *Health Affairs, 35*(6), 1121–1129. https://doi.org/10.1377/hlthaff.2016.0011

Meeus, W., Iedema, J., Maassen, G., & Engels, R. (2005). Separation–individuation revisited: On the interplay of parent–adolescent relations, identity and emotional adjustment in adolescence. *Journal of Adolescence, 28*(1), 89–106. https://doi.org/10.1016/j.adolescence.2004.07.003

Meltzoff, A. N., & Moore, M. K. (1998). Object representation, identity, and the paradox of early permanence: Steps toward a new framework. *Infant*

Behavior and Development, 21(2), 201–235. https://doi.org/10.1016/S0163-6383(98)90003-0

Menninger, K. (1938). *Man against himself.* Harcourt, Brace & World.

Meston, C. M., & Heiman, J. R. (2000). Sexual abuse and sexual function: An examination of sexually relevant cognitive processes. *Journal of Consulting and Clinical Psychology, 68*(3), 399. https://doi.org/10.1037//0022-006X.68.3.399

Mikulincer, M., & Florian, V. (2000). Exploring individual differences in reactions to mortality salience: Does attachment style regulate terror management mechanisms? *Journal of Personality and Social Psychology, 79*(2), 260–273. https://doi.org/10.1037/0022-3514.79.2.260

Mikulincer, M., & Shaver, P. R. (2007). *Attachment in adulthood: Structure, dynamics, and change.* Guilford Press.

Mikulincer, M., & Shaver, P. R. (2016). *Attachment in adulthood* (2nd ed.). Guilford Press.

Mikulincer, M., Shaver, P. R., Sapir-Lavid, Y., & Avihou-Kanza, N. (2009). What's inside the minds of securely and insecurely attached people? The secure-base script and its associations with attachment-style dimensions. *Journal of Personality and Social Psychology, 97*(4), 615–633. https://doi.org/10.1037/a0015649

Miller, A. (1984). *For your own good: Hidden cruelty in child-rearing and the roots of violence* (2nd ed.; H. Hannum & H. Hannum, Trans.). Farrar, Straus & Giroux. (Original work published 1980)

Miller, A. (1997). *The drama of the gifted child: The search for the true self* (Rev. ed.; R. Ward, Trans.). HarperCollins.

Mitchell, S. A. (2002). *Can love last? The fate of romance over time.* Norton.

Moghaddam, F. M. (2013). *The psychology of dictatorship.* American Psychological Association. https://doi.org/10.1037/14138-000

Moghaddam, F. M. (2016). *The psychology of democracy.* American Psychological Association. https://doi.org/10.1037/14806-000

Monacis, L., de Palo, V., Griffiths, M. D., & Sinatra, M. (2017). Exploring individual differences in online addictions: The role of identity and attachment. *International Journal of Mental Health and Addiction, 15*(4), 853–868. https://doi.org/10.1007/s11469-017-9768-5

Mosquera, D., Gonzalez, A., & Leeds, A. M. (2014). Early experience, structural dissociation, and emotional dysregulation in borderline personality disorder: The role of insecure and disorganized attachment. *Borderline Personality Disorder and Emotion Dysregulation, 1,* Article 15. https://doi.org/10.1186/2051-6673-1-15

Mroczek, D. K., & Spiro, A., III. (2005). Change in life satisfaction during adulthood: Findings from the Veterans Affairs Normative Aging Study. *Journal of Personality and Social Psychology, 88*(1), 189–202. https://doi.org/10.1037/0022-3514.88.1.189

Mullen, P. E., & Fleming, J. (1998). *Long-term effects of child sexual abuse.* National Child Protection Clearinghouse.

Neff, K. D. (2011). Self-compassion, self-esteem, and well-being. *Social and Personality Psychology Compass, 5*(1), 1–12. https://doi.org/10.1111/j.1751-9004.2010.00330.x

Negy, C., Velezmoro, R., Reig-Ferrer, A., Smith-Castro, V., & Livia, J. (2016). Parental influence on their adult children's sexual values: A multi-national comparison between the United States, Spain, Costa Rica, and Peru. *Archives of Sexual Behavior, 45*(2), 477–489. https://doi.org/10.1007/s10508-015-0570-9

Newman, C. F. (2002). A cognitive perspective on resistance in psychotherapy. *Journal of Clinical Psychology, 58*(2), 165–174. https://doi.org/10.1002/jclp.1140

Newman, K. M. (2013). A more usable Winnicott. *Psychoanalytic Inquiry, 33*(1), 59–68. https://doi.org/10.1080/07351690.2013.743805

Oaklander, V. (1978). *Windows to our children: A gestalt therapy approach to children and adolescents.* Gestalt Journal Press.

Odgers, A. (2018). *From broken attachments to earned security: The role of empathy in therapeutic change.* Routledge. https://doi.org/10.4324/9780429475108

Olson, G. (2007, October 24). Neuroscience and moral politics: Chomsky's intellectual progeny. *Dissident Voice.* https://dissidentvoice.org/2007/10/neuroscience-and-moral-politics-chomskys-intellectual-progeny/

Orbach, I. (2008). Existentialism and suicide. In A. Tomer, G. T. Eliason, & P. T. P. Wong (Eds.), *Existential and spiritual issues in death attitudes* (pp. 281–316). Erlbaum.

Osatuke, K., & Stiles, W. B. (2006). Problematic internal voices in clients with borderline features: An elaboration of the assimilation model. *Journal of Constructivist Psychology, 19*(4), 287–319. https://doi.org/10.1080/10720530600691699

Owen, D. (1993). The future of the Balkans: An interview with David Owen. *Foreign Affairs, 72*(2), 1–9. https://doi.org/10.2307/20045518

Pagels, E. (1988). *Adam, Eve, and the serpent.* Random House.

Pagels, E. (2003). *Beyond belief: The secret gospel of Thomas.* Vintage Books.

Pan, Y., Gauvain, M., & Schwartz, S. J. (2013). Do parents' collectivistic tendency and attitudes toward filial piety facilitate autonomous motivation among young Chinese adolescents? *Motivation and Emotion, 37*(4), 701–711. https://doi.org/10.1007/s11031-012-9337-y

Panagopoulos, C., & van der Linden, S. (2016). Conformity to implicit social pressure: The role of political identity. *Social Influence, 11*(3), 177–184. https://doi.org/10.1080/15534510.2016.1216009

Park, B. Y., Wilson, G., Berger, J., Christman, M., Reina, B., Bishop, F., Klam, W. P., & Doan, A. P. (2016). Is internet pornography causing sexual dysfunctions? A review with clinical reports. *Behavioral Sciences, 6*(3), 17. https://doi.org/10.3390/bs6030017

Park, C. L., & Edmondson, D. (2012). Religion as a source of meaning. In P. R. Shaver & M. Mikulincer (Eds.), *Meaning, mortality, and choice: The social psychology of existential concerns* (pp. 145–162). American Psychological Association., https://doi.org/10.1037/13748-008

Parker, G. (1983). *Parental overprotection: A risk factor in psychosocial development.* Grune & Stratton.

Parker, G., & Lipscombe, P. (1981). Influences on maternal overprotection. *The British Journal of Psychiatry, 138*(4), 303–311. https://doi.org/10.1192/bjp.138.4.303

Parr, G. (Producer & Director). (2008). *The roots of violence, Part I: Voices of violence* [Film]. The Glendon Association.

Passmore, H. A., & Howell, A. J. (2014). Eco-existential positive psychology: Experiences in nature, existential anxieties, and well-being. *The Humanistic Psychologist, 42*(4), 370–388. https://doi.org/10.1080/08873267.2014.920335

Peele, S. (2001). Is gambling an addiction like drug and alcohol addiction? Developing realistic and useful conceptions of compulsive gambling. *Journal of Gambling Issues, 3.* https://doi.org/10.4309/jgi.2001.3.2

Perach, R., & Wisman, A. (2019). Can creativity beat death? A review and evidence on the existential anxiety buffering functions of creative achievement. *The Journal of Creative Behavior, 53*(2), 193–210. https://doi.org/10.1002/jocb.171

Perel, E. (2006). *Mating in captivity: Reconciling the erotic the domestic.* HarperCollins.

Perry, B. D. (2006). Applying principles of neurodevelopment to clinical work with maltreated and traumatized children: The neurosequential model of therapeutics. In N. B. Webb (Ed.), *Working with traumatized youth in child welfare* (pp. 27–52). Guilford Press.

Perry, B. D. (2009). Examining child maltreatment through a neurodevelopmental lens: Clinical applications of the neurosequential model of therapeutics. *Journal of Loss and Trauma, 14*(4), 240–255. https://doi.org/10.1080/15325020903004350

Person, E. S. (1995). *By force of fantasy: How we make our lives.* Basic Books.

Person, E. S. (2006). Revising our life stories: The roles of memory and imagination in the psychoanalytic process. *Psychoanalytic Review, 93*(4), 655–674. https://doi.org/10.1521/prev.2006.93.4.655

Person, E. S., & Klar, H. (1994). Establishing trauma: The difficulty distinguishing between memories and fantasies. *Journal of the American Psychoanalytic Association, 42*(4), 1055–1081. https://doi.org/10.1177/000306519404200407

Pettijohn, T. F., & Walzer, A. S. (2008). Reducing racism, sexism, and homophobia in college students by completing a psychology of prejudice course. *College Student Journal, 42*(2), 459–468.

Phelps, C. L., Paniagua, S. M., Willcockson, I. U., & Potter, J. S. (2018). The relationship between self-compassion and the risk for substance use disorder. *Drug and Alcohol Dependence, 183*, 78–81. https://doi.org/10.1016/j.drugalcdep.2017.10.026

Pines, A. M. (1999). *Falling in love: Why we choose the lovers we choose*. Routledge.

Piven, J. S. (2004). *Death and delusion: A Freudian analysis of mortal terror*. Information Age Publishing.

Piven, J. S. (2008). Death, terror, culture, and violence: A psychoanalytic perspective. In M. K. Bartalos (Ed.), *Speaking of death: America's new sense of mortality* (pp. 197–226). Praeger.

Piven, J. S., Boyd, C., & Lawton, H. (Eds.). (2004). *Terrorism, jihad, and sacred vengeance*. Psychosozial-Verlag.

Plutchik, R. (2001). The nature of emotions: Human emotions have deep evolutionary roots, a fact that may explain their complexity and provide tools for clinical practice. *American Scientist, 89*(4), 344–350. https://doi.org/10.1511/2001.4.344

Plutchik, R., & Kellerman, H. (Eds.). (2013). *Theories of emotion* (Vol. 1). Academic Press.

Prescott, J. R. (1996). The origins of human love and violence. *Pre- and Perinatal Psychology Journal, 10*, 143–188.

Provenzi, L., Scotto di Minico, G., Giusti, L., Guida, E., & Müller, M. (2018). Disentangling the dyadic dance: Theoretical, methodological and outcomes systematic review of mother–infant dyadic processes. *Frontiers in Psychology, 9*, 348. https://doi.org/10.3389/fpsyg.2018.00348

Przybyła, J. (2016). Neurobiological foundations of psychotherapy. *Psychoterapia, 2*(177), 29–42.

Pulverman, C. S., Kilimnik, C. D., & Meston, C. M. (2018). The impact of childhood sexual abuse on women's sexual health: A comprehensive review. *Sexual Medicine Reviews, 6*(2), 188–200. https://doi.org/10.1016/j.sxmr.2017.12.002

Purcell, D. W., Malow, R. M., Dolezal, C., & Carballo-Diéguez, A. (2004). Sexual abuse of boys: Short- and long-term associations and implications for HIV prevention. In L. J. Koenig, L. S. Doll, A. O'Leary, & W. Pequegnat (Eds.), *From child sexual abuse to adult sexual risk: Trauma, revictimization, and intervention* (pp. 93–114). American Psychological Association. https://doi.org/10.1037/10785-005

Pyszczynski, T., Greenberg, J., & Solomon, S. (1999). A dual-process model of defense against conscious and unconscious death-related thoughts: An extension of terror management theory. *Psychological Review, 106*(4), 835–845. https://doi.org/10.1037/0033-295X.106.4.835

Pyszczynski, T., Greenberg, J., Solomon, S., & Maxfield, M. (2006). On the unique psychological import of the human awareness of mortality: Theme and variations. *Psychological Inquiry, 17*(4), 328–356. https://doi.org/10.1080/10478400701369542

Pyszczynski, T., Solomon, S., & Greenberg, J. (2003). *In the wake of 9/11: The psychology of terror*. American Psychological Association. https://doi.org/10.1037/10478-000

Rank, O. (1941). *Beyond psychology*. Dover.

Rank, O. (1972). *Will therapy and Truth and reality* (J. Taft, Trans.). Knopf. (Original work published 1936)

Rank, O. (1999). *The trauma of birth* (Vol. 23). Psychology Press.

Rawls, J. (1999). *A theory of justice* (Rev. ed.). Harvard University Press.

Rawls, J. (2001). *Justice as fairness: A restatement.* Harvard University Press.

Ray, E., & Heyes, C. (2011). Imitation in infancy: The wealth of the stimulus. *Developmental Science, 14*(1), 92–105. https://doi.org/10.1111/j.1467-7687.2010.00961.x

Reardon, K. K., & Noblet, C. T. (2009). *Childhood denied: Ending the nightmare of child abuse and neglect.* SAGE. https://doi.org/10.4135/9781483349534

Reiner, I., & Spangler, G. (2013). Representations of early attachment experiences and personality in adulthood. *Journal of Adult Development, 20*(1), 38–45. https://doi.org/10.1007/s10804-013-9154-x

Renaud, J. (2013, October). Rethinking the repressive hypothesis: Foucault's critique of Marcuse. *Symposium, 17*(2), 76–93. https://doi.org/10.5840/symposium201317221

Rheingold, J. C. (1967). *The mother, anxiety, and death: The catastrophic death complex.* Little, Brown.

Rholes, W. S., Simpson, J. A., Tran, S., Martin, A. M., III, & Friedman, M. (2007). Attachment and information seeking in romantic relationships. *Personality and Social Psychology Bulletin, 33*(3), 422–438. https://doi.org/10.1177/0146167206296302

Richardson, D., & Monro, S. (2012). *Sexuality, equality and diversity.* Macmillan International Higher Education. https://doi.org/10.1007/978-0-230-36423-3

Roberts, R., O'Connor, T., Dunn, J., Golding, J., & the ALSPAC Study Team. (2004). The effects of child sexual abuse in later family life; mental health, parenting and adjustment of offspring. *Child Abuse & Neglect, 28*(5), 525–545. https://doi.org/10.1016/j.chiabu.2003.07.006

Robinson, K. H., Smith, E., & Davies, C. (2017). Responsibilities, tensions and ways forward: Parents' perspectives on children's sexuality education. *Sex Education, 17*(3), 333–347. https://doi.org/10.1080/14681811.2017.1301904

Rohner, R. P. (1986a). *New perspectives on family. The warmth dimension: Foundations of parental acceptance-rejection theory.* SAGE.

Rohner, R. P. (1986b). *The warmth dimension: Foundations of parental acceptance-rejection theory.* SAGE.

Rohner, R. P. (1991). *Handbook for the study of parental acceptance and rejection.* University of Connecticut.

Rohner, R. P. (2008). Parental acceptance-rejection theory studies of intimate adult relationships. *Cross-Cultural Research: The Journal of Comparative Social Science, 42*(1), 5–12. https://doi.org/10.1177/1069397107309749

Rohner, R. P., & Khaleque, A. (2010). Testing central postulates of parental acceptance-rejection theory (PARTheory): A meta-analysis of cross-cultural studies. *Journal of Family Theory & Review, 2*(1), 73–87. https://doi.org/10.1111/j.1756-2589.2010.00040.x

Rohner, R. P., & Veneziano, R. A. (2001). The importance of father love: History and contemporary evidence. *Review of General Psychology, 5*(4), 382–405. https://doi.org/10.1037/1089-2680.5.4.382

Rosas, A. (2010). Beyond inclusive fitness? On a simple and general explanation for the evolution of altruism. *Philosophy, Theory, and Practice in Biology, 2*(4), e1–e9. https://doi.org/10.3998/ptb.6959004.0002.004

Rosenblatt, A., Greenberg, J., Solomon, S., Pyszczynski, T., & Lyon, D. (1989). Evidence for terror management theory: I. The effects of mortality salience on reactions to those who violate or uphold cultural values. *Journal of Personality and Social Psychology, 57*(4), 681–690. https://doi.org/10.1037/0022-3514.57.4.681

Rotenstein, O. H., McDermut, W., Bergman, A., Young, D., Zimmerman, M., & Chelminski, I. (2007). The validity of *DSM-IV* passive-aggressive (negativistic) personality disorder. *Journal of Personality Disorders, 21*(1), 28–41. https://doi.org/10.1521/pedi.2007.21.1.28

Ryan, R. M., & Deci, E. L. (2004). Autonomy is no illusion. In J. Greenberg, S. L. Koole, & T. A. Pyszczynski (Eds.), *Handbook of experimental existential psychology* (pp. 455–479). Guilford Press.

Ryan, R. M., Legate, N., Niemiec, C. P., & Deci, E. L. (2012). Beyond illusions and defense: Exploring the possibilities and limits of human autonomy and responsibility through self-determination theory. In P. R. Shaver & M. Mikulincer (Eds.), *Meaning, mortality, and choice: The social psychology of existential concerns* (pp. 215–233). American Psychological Association. https://doi.org/10.1037/13748-012

Ryan, R. M., Martin, A., & Brooks-Gunn, J. (2006). Is one good parent good enough? Patterns of mother and father parenting and child cognitive outcomes at 24 and 36 months. *Parenting, 6*(2–3), 211–228. https://doi.org/10.1080/15295192.2006.9681306

Sandfort, T. G., & Ehrhardt, A. A. (2004). Sexual health: A useful public health paradigm or a moral imperative? *Archives of Sexual Behavior, 33*(3), 181–187. https://doi.org/10.1023/B:ASEB.0000026618.16408.e0

Sarwer, D. B., & Durlak, J. A. (1996). Childhood sexual abuse as a predictor of adult female sexual dysfunction: A study of couples seeking sex therapy. *Child Abuse & Neglect, 20*(10), 963–972. https://doi.org/10.1016/0145-2134(96)00085-3

Schiffer, H. B. (2004). *First love: Remembrances*. Heartful Loving Press.

Schmemann, S. (1992, May 24). Ethnic battles flaring in former Soviet fringe. *The New York Times*, 7.

Schnarch, D. M. (1991). *Constructing the sexual crucible: An integration of sexual and marital therapy*. Norton.

Schneider, K. J. (2004). *Rediscovery of awe: Splendor, mystery, and the fluid center of life*. Paragon House.

Schneider, K. J. (2007). The experiential liberation strategy of the existential-integrative model of therapy. *Journal of Contemporary Psychotherapy, 37*(1), 33–39. https://doi.org/10.1007/s10879-006-9032-y

Schneider, K. J. (2013). *The polarized mind: Why it is killing us and what we can do about it*. University Professors Press.

Schneider, K. J., & Krug, O. T. (2010). *Existential-humanistic therapy*. American Psychological Association. https://doi.org/10.1037/12050-000

Schore, A. N. (2003). *Affect regulation and disorders of the self*. Norton.

Schore, A. N. (2005). Affect regulation and the repair of the self. *The Permanente Journal, 9*(2). https://pdfs.semanticscholar.org/9c91/74833c2a29a5e6afa933919e7814b8c66160.pdf

Schore, A. N. (2009). Relational trauma and the developing right brain: An interface of psychoanalytic self-psychology and neuroscience. *Annals of the New York Academy of Sciences, 1159*(1), 189–203. https://doi.org/10.1111/j.1749-6632.2009.04474.x

Schore, A. N. (2011). The right brain implicit self lies at the core of psychoanalysis. *Psychoanalytic Dialogues, 21*(1), 75–100. https://doi.org/10.1080/10481885.2011.545329

Schore, A. N. (2015). *Affect regulation and the origin of the self: The neurobiology of emotional development*. Routledge. https://doi.org/10.4324/9781315680019

Schore, A. N. (2018). The right brain implicit self: A central mechanism of the psychotherapy change process. In G. Craparo & C. Mucci (Eds.), *Unrepressed unconscious, implicit memory, and clinical work* (pp. 73–98). Routledge. https://doi.org/10.4324/9780429484629-4

Schore, A. N. (2019). *Right brain psychotherapy*. Norton.

Searles, H. F. (1961). Schizophrenia and the inevitability of death. *Psychiatric Quarterly, 35*(4), 631–665. https://doi.org/10.1007/BF01563716

Searles, H. F. (2013). Scorn, disillusionment and adoration in the psychotherapy of schizophrenia. *Psychoanalytic Review, 100*(2), 337–359. https://doi.org/10.1521/prev.2013.100.2.337

Sezer, S., & Gülleroğlu, H. D. (2017). The predictive power of life satisfaction and self-esteem in existential anxieties. *European Journal of Education Studies, 3*(7), 329–345. https://doi.org/10.5281/zenodo.818076

Shamir, B. (1995). Social distance and charisma: Theoretical notes and an exploratory study. *The Leadership Quarterly, 6*(1), 19–47. https://doi.org/10.1016/1048-9843(95)90003-9

Shaver, P. R., & Clark, C. L. (1994). The psychodynamics of adult romantic attachment. In J. M. Masling & R. F. Bornstein (Eds.), *Empirical perspectives on object relations theory* (pp. 105–156). American Psychological Association.

Shaver, P. R., & Mikulincer, M. E. (Eds.). (2012). *Meaning, mortality, and choice: The social psychology of existential concerns*. American Psychological Association. https://doi.org/10.1037/13748-000

Shaw, J. A. (2005, Fall). The cloak of invisibility over the New Orleans experience: Contributions to denial. *Out of Our Minds, 6*, 5.

Sheldon, J. (1997). 50,000 children are waiting: Permanency, planning and termination of parental rights under the Adoption Assistance and Child Welfare Act of 1980. *BC Third World Law Journal, 17*, 73.

Shirer, W. L. (1960). *The rise and fall of the Third Reich: A history of Nazi Germany.* Simon & Schuster.

Shneidman, E. S. (1966). Orientations toward death: A vital aspect of the study of lives. *International Journal of Psychiatry, 2,* 167–200. https://doi.org/10.1037/12238-009

Shtarkshall, R. A., Santelli, J. S., & Hirsch, J. S. (2007). Sex education and sexual socialization: Roles for educators and parents. *Perspectives on Sexual and Reproductive Health, 39*(2), 116–119. https://doi.org/10.1363/3911607

Siegel, D. J. (1999). *The developing mind: How relationships and the brain interact to shape who we are.* Guilford Press.

Siegel, D. J. (2001). Toward an interpersonal neurobiology of the developing mind: Attachment relationships, "mindsight," and neural integration. *Infant Mental Health Journal, 22*(1–2), 67–94. https://doi.org/10.1002/1097-0355(200101/04)22:1<67::AID-IMHJ3>3.0.CO;2-G

Siegel, D. J. (2007). *The mindful brain: Reflection and attunement in the cultivation of well-being.* Norton.

Siegel, D. J. (2010). *The mindful therapist.* Norton.

Siegel, D. J. (2012). *Pocket guide to interpersonal neurobiology: An integrative handbook of the mind.* Norton.

Siegel, D. J. (2020). *The developing mind: How relationships and the brain interact to shape who we are* (3rd ed.). Norton.

Siegel, D. J., & Hartzell, M. (2003). *Parenting from the inside out: How a deeper self-understanding can help you raise children who thrive.* J. P. Tarcher/Putnam.

Siegel, J. P., & Forero, R. M. (2012). Splitting and emotional regulation in partner violence. *Clinical Social Work Journal, 40*(2), 224–230. https://doi.org/10.1007/s10615-011-0352-3

Silverman, L. H., Lachmann, F. M., & Milich, R. H. (1982). *The search for oneness.* International Universities Press.

Simons, J. S., & Carey, M. P. (2001). Prevalence of sexual dysfunctions: Results from a decade of research. *Archives of Sexual Behavior, 30*(2), 177–219. https://doi.org/10.1023/A:1002729318254

Singer, I. (2001). *Sex: A philosophical primer.* Rowman & Littlefield.

Skowron, E. A., & Friedlander, M. L. (1998). The Differentiation of Self Inventory: Development and initial validation. *Journal of Counseling Psychology, 45*(3), 235–246. 10.1037/0022-0167.45.3.235

Skowron, E. A., & Schmitt, T. A. (2003). Assessing interpersonal fusion: Reliability and validity of a new DSI fusion with others subscale. *Journal of Marital and Family Therapy, 29*(2), 209–222. https://doi.org/10.1111/j.1752-0606.2003.tb01201.x

Skynner, R. (1991). One flesh: Separate persons. *The British Journal of Psychiatry, 158*(6), 868–880. https://doi.org/10.1192/S0007125000141728

Slaughter, V., & Griffiths, M. (2007). Death understanding and fear of death in young children. *Clinical Child Psychology and Psychiatry, 12*(4), 525–535. https://doi.org/10.1177/1359104507080980

Smailes, D., Alderson-Day, B., Fernyhough, C., McCarthy-Jones, S., & Dodgson, G. (2015). Tailoring cognitive behavioral therapy to subtypes of voice-hearing. *Frontiers in Psychology, 6*, 1933. https://doi.org/10.3389/fpsyg.2015.01933

Snyder, T. (2017). *On tyranny: Twenty lessons from the twentieth century.* Tim Duggan Books.

Snyder, T. (2018). *The road to unfreedom: Russia, Europe, America.* Tim Duggan Books.

Sober, E., & Wilson, D. S. (1999). *Unto others: The evolution and psychology of unselfish behavior.* Harvard University Press.

Sohlberg, S., Samuelberg, P., Sidén, Y., & Thörn, C. (1998). Caveat medicus— Let the subliminal healer beware: Two experiments suggesting conditions when the effects of Silverman's Mommy and I Are One phrase are negative. *Psychoanalytic Psychology, 15*(1), 93–114. https://doi.org/10.1037/0736-9735.15.1.93

Solomon, S. (2019). From cradle to grave: A terror management theory analysis of parenthood. In O. Taubman-Ben-Ari (Ed.), *Pathways and barriers to parenthood* (pp. 185–198). Springer. https://doi.org/10.1007/978-3-030-24864-2_11

Solomon, S., Greenberg, J., & Pyszczynski, T. (2000). Pride and prejudice: Fear of death and social behavior. *Current Directions in Psychological Science, 9*(6), 200–204. https://doi.org/10.1111/1467-8721.00094

Solomon, S., Greenberg, J., & Pyszczynski, T. (2004). The cultural animal: Twenty years of terror management theory and research. In J. Greenberg, S. L. Koole, & T. Pyszczynski (Eds.), *Handbook of experimental existential psychology* (pp. 13–34). Guilford Press.

Solomon, S., Greenberg, J., & Pyszczynski, T. A. (2015). *The worm at the core: On the role of death in life.* Random House.

Somer, E., & Herscu, O. (2017). Childhood trauma, social anxiety, absorption and fantasy dependence: Two potential mediated pathways to maladaptive daydreaming. *Journal of Addictive Behaviors, Therapy & Rehabilitation, 6*(4), 1–5. 10.4172/2324-9005.1000170

Soubrier, J. (1993). Definitions of suicide. In A. A. Leenaars (Ed.), *Suicidology: Essays in honor of Edwin S. Shneidman* (pp. 35–41). Jason Aronson.

Speece, M. W., & Brent, S. B. (1984). Children's understanding of death: A review of three components of a death concept. *Child Development, 55*(5), 1671–1686. https://doi.org/10.2307/1129915

Spiegel, J. (2013). *Sexual abuse of males: The SAM model of theory and practice.* Routledge.

Spinelli, E. (1997). *Tales of un-knowing: Therapeutic encounters from an existential perspective.* NYU Press. https://doi.org/10.4324/9780203890394

Spinelli, E. (2006). Existential psychotherapy: An introductory overview. *Análise Psicológica, 24*(3), 311–321. https://doi.org/10.14417/ap.170

Stern, D. N. (1985). *The interpersonal world of the infant: A view from psychoanalysis and developmental psychology.* Basic Books.

Stolorow, R. D. (2015). A phenomenological-contextual, existential, and ethical perspective on emotional trauma. *Psychoanalytic Review*, *102*(1), 123–138. https://doi.org/10.1521/prev.2015.102.1.123

Stone, L. (1985, October/November). The strange, secret history of sex. *Utne Reader*, 34–42.

Stone, H., & Stone, S. (1989). *Embracing ourselves: The voice dialogue manual.* New World Library.

Stritof, B. (2004). *Everything great marriage*. Everything.

Strong, B., DeVault, C., & Sayad, B. W. (1999). *Human sexuality: Diversity in contemporary America* (3rd ed.). Mayfield.

Suggs, D. N., & Miracle, A. W. (1993). *Culture and human sexuality: A reader.* Brooks/Cole.

Sullivan, H. S. (1953). *The interpersonal theory of psychiatry*. Norton.

Sutfin, E. L., Fulcher, M., Bowles, R. P., & Patterson, C. J. (2008). How lesbian and heterosexual parents convey attitudes about gender to their children: The role of gendered environments. *Sex Roles*, *58*(7–8), 501–513. https://doi.org/10.1007/s11199-007-9368-0

Tierney, S., & Fox, J. R. (2010). Living with the anorexic voice: A thematic analysis. *Psychology and Psychotherapy*, *83*(3), 243–254. https://doi.org/10.1348/147608309X480172

Tillich, P. (1952). *The courage to be*. Yale University Press.

Tomaszek, K., & Muchacka-Cymerman, A. (2020). Thinking about my existence during COVID-19, I feel anxiety and awe—The mediating role of existential anxiety and life satisfaction on the relationship between PTSD symptoms and post-traumatic growth. *International Journal of Environmental Research and Public Health*, *17*(19), 7062. https://doi.org/10.3390/ijerph17197062

Tomer, A., Eliason, G. T., & Wong, P. T. (2008). *Existentialism and spiritual issues in death attitudes*. Psychology Press.

Toynbee, A. (1976). *Choose life: A dialogue between Arnold Toynbee and Daisaku Ikeda*. Oxford University Press.

Tramonti, F. (2019). Steps to an ecology of psychotherapy: The legacy of Gregory Bateson. *Systems Research and Behavioral Science*, *36*(1), 128–139. https://doi.org/10.1002/sres.2549

Triandis, H. C. (2018). *Individualism and collectivism*. Routledge. https://doi.org/10.4324/9780429499845

Tronick, E. Z. (1989). Emotions and emotional communication in infants. *American Psychologist*, *44*(2), 112–119. https://doi.org/10.1037/0003-066X.44.2.112

Tronick, E. Z. (2007). *The neurobehavioral and social-emotional development of infants and children*. Norton.

Tronick, E., & Beeghly, M. (2011). Infants' meaning-making and the development of mental health problems. *American Psychologist*, *66*(2), 107–119. https://doi.org/10.1037/a0021631

Trower, P., & Harrop, C. E. (1999). *Self-construction in conflict episodes in schizophrenia* [Unpublished manuscript].

Tyler, S., Allison, K., & Winsler, A. (2006, February). Child neglect: Developmental consequences, intervention, and policy implications. *Child and Youth Care Forum, 35*(1), 1–20. https://doi.org/10.1007/s10566-005-9000-9

Ungar, M. (2009). Overprotective parenting: Helping parents provide children the right amount of risk and responsibility. *The American Journal of Family Therapy, 37*(3), 258–271. https://doi.org/10.1080/01926180802534247

Vahrmeyer, M., & Cassar, S. (2017). The paradox of finitude in the context of infinitude: Is death denial an essential aspect of being in the world? *Existential Analysis, 28*(1), 151–165.

Valle, R. S., & King, M. (1978). *Existential-phenomenological alternatives for psychology.* Oxford University Press.

van der Kolk, B. A. (2015). *The body keeps the score: Brain, mind, and body in the healing of trauma.* Penguin Books.

van Deurzen, E., & Arnold-Baker, C. (Eds.). (2005). *Existential perspectives on human issues: A handbook for therapeutic practice.* Macmillan International Higher Education. https://doi.org/10.1007/978-0-230-21624-2

Ventriglio, A., & Bhugra, D. (2019). Sexuality in the 21st century: Sexual fluidity. *East Asian Archives of Psychiatry, 29*(1), 30–34. https://doi.org/10.12809/eaap1736

Vergote, A., & Wood, M. H. (1988). *Guilt and desire: Religious attitudes and their pathological derivatives.* Yale University Press.

Videgard, T. (1984a). *The success and failure of primal therapy: Supplement (for professionals).* Author.

Videgård, T. (1984b). *The success and failure of primal therapy: 32 patients treated at the Primal Institute (Janov) viewed in the perspective of object relations theory.* Almqvist & Wiksell International.

Wang, X., Van der Werff, E., Bouman, T., Harder, M. K., & Steg, L. (2021, February 18). I am vs. we are: How biospheric values and environmental identity of individuals and groups can influence pro-environmental behaviour. *Frontiers in psychology, 12.* https://doi.org/10.3389/fpsyg.2021.618956

Ward, A., Ramsay, R., Turnbull, S., Steele, M., Steele, H., & Treasure, J. (2001). Attachment in anorexia nervosa: A transgenerational perspective. *The British Journal of Medical Psychology, 74*(4), 497–505. https://doi.org/10.1348/000711201161145

Watter, D. N. (2018). Existential issues in sexual medicine: The relation between death anxiety and hypersexuality. *Sexual Medicine Reviews, 6*(1), 3–10. https://doi.org/10.1016/j.sxmr.2017.10.004

Weinberger, J., & Smith, B. (2011). Investigating merger: Subliminal psychodynamic activation and oneness motivation research. *Journal of the American Psychoanalytic Association, 59*(3), 553–570. https://doi.org/10.1177/0003065111411481

Welldon, E. V. (2011). *Playing with dynamite: A personal approach to the psychoanalytic understanding of perversions, violence, and criminality.* Karnac Books.

Welling, H. (2012). Transformative emotional sequence: Towards a common principle of change. *Journal of Psychotherapy Integration, 22*(2), 109–136. https://doi.org/10.1037/a0027786

Wéry, A., & Billieux, J. (2017). Problematic cybersex: Conceptualization, assessment, and treatment. *Addictive Behaviors, 64*, 238–246. https://doi.org/10.1016/j.addbeh.2015.11.007

White, R. G., Larkin, P., McCluskey, J., Lloyd, J., & McLeod, H. J. (2020). The development of the 'Forms of Responding to Self-Critical Thoughts Scale'(FoReST). *Journal of Contextual Behavioral Science, 15*, 20–29. https://doi.org/10.1016/j.jcbs.2019.11.003

Wilkerson, I. (2020). *Caste: The origins of our discontents.* Random House.

Willi, J. (1982). *Couples in collusion: The unconscious dimension in partner relationships* (W. Inayat-Khan & M. Tchorek, Trans.). Hunter House. (Original work published 1975)

Williams, K. D., Cheung, C. K. T., & Choi, W. (2000). Cyberostracism: Effects of being ignored over the internet. *Journal of Personality and Social Psychology, 79*(5), 748–762. https://doi.org/10.1037/0022-3514.79.5.748

Wilson, E. O. (1998). The biological basis of morality. *Atlantic Monthly, 281*(4), 53–70. https://pdfs.semanticscholar.org/4598/d146387c326b19e9d050d34a22c1ab4b39e8.pdf

Winnicott, D. W. (1952). *Through paediatrics to psycho-analysis.* Routledge.

Winnicott, D. W. (1958). *Collected papers: Through paediatrics to psycho-analysis.* Tavistock Publications.

Winnicott, D. W. (1965). *The maturational processes and the facilitating environment: Studies in the theory of emotional development.* The Hogarth Press and the Institute of Psycho-Analysis.

Wirth, H. (2007). The roots of prejudice in family life and its political significance as discerned in a study of Slobodan Milosevic. In H. Parens, A. Mahfouz, S. W. Twemlow, & D. E. Scharff (Eds.), *The future of prejudice: Psychoanalysis and the prevention of prejudice* (pp. 111–127). Rowman & Littlefield.

Witty, S. K., & Khamsi, S. K. (1995). The seven stages of primal therapy. *Primal Renaissance: The Journal of Primal Psychology, 1*(2), 22–33.

Wong, P. T. (1998). *Implicit theories of meaningful life and the development of the personal meaning profile.* Erlbaum.

Wong, P. T. (2008). Meaning management theory and death acceptance. In A. Tome, G. T. Eliason, & P. T. Wong (Eds.), *Existential and spiritual issues in death attitudes* (pp. 65–87). Erlbaum.

Worley, N. K., & Melton, G. B. (2013). Mandated reporting laws and child maltreatment: The evolution of a flawed policy response. In R. Krugman & J. Korbin (Eds.), *C. Henry Kempe: A 50 year legacy to the field of child abuse and neglect* (pp. 103–118). Springer. https://doi.org/10.1007/978-94-007-4084-6_13

Yaakobi, E., Mikulincer, M., & Shaver, P. R. (2014). Parenthood as a terror management mechanism: The moderating role of attachment orientations.

Personality and Social Psychology Bulletin, 40(6), 762–774. https://doi.org/10.1177/0146167214525473

Yalom, I. D. (1980). *Existential psychotherapy*. Basic Books.

Young, J., & Flanagan, C. (1998). Schema-focused therapy for narcissistic patients. In E. F. Ronningstam (Ed.), *Disorders of narcissism: Diagnostic, clinical, and empirical implications* (pp. 239–268). Jason Aronson.

Young-Bruehl, E. (2002). On the origins of a new totalitarianism. *Social Research, 69*(2), 567–578.

Zeanah, C. H., & Zeanah, P. D. (1989). Intergenerational transmission of maltreatment: Insights from attachment theory and research. *Psychiatry, 52*(2), 177–196. https://doi.org/10.1080/00332747.1989.11024442

Zeig, J. K., & Munion, W. (1990). *What is psychotherapy? Contemporary perspectives*. Jossey-Bass.

Zhou, X., Liu, J., Chen, C., & Yu, Z. (2008). Do children transcend death? An examination of the terror management function of offspring. *Scandinavian Journal of Psychology, 49*(5), 413–418. https://doi.org/10.1111/j.1467-9450.2008.00665.x

Zoldbrod, A. P. (1998). *Sex smart: How your childhood shaped your sexual life and what to do about it*. New Harbinger.

Zull, J. E. (2004). The art of changing the brain. *Educational Leadership, 62*(1), 68–72. http://citeseerx.ist.psu.edu/viewdoc/download?doi=10.1.1.504.5667&rep=rep1&type=pdf

Index

A

Abstract reasoning, 6
Abuser, idealization of, 231n1
Acceptance
    of sexuality, 155
    of vulnerability, 198–199
Accomplishments, "feeding on" child's,
    37–38
Achievements, 61–62, 126–127
Addiction(s), 109–114, 243n1
    to another person, 114
    critical inner voice on, 115
    dulling pain with, 108
    and inwardness, 78
    to isolation, 114
    negative thoughts supporting, 89
    to physical substances, 110–111
    rationalization of, 116
    response to giving up, 109
    to routines, 111–114, 244n3
    sexual, 112–113, 138, 244n4
    treatment for, 116–118
    to work, 113–114
Adolescents
    idealization of parents by, 231–232n3
    individuation for, 122, 123, 245n2
Adult Attachment Interview, 231n2, 232n3
Adverse childhood experiences, 265n10
Affection
    from emotionally hungry parents, 37
    learning to accept, 106, 131
    between parents, 139–140
    withholding of, 101–102
Afterlife, 197, 267n3
Ageism, 207, 264n7

Aggression, 215–223
    and challenging fantasy bond, 23
    and origins of polarization, 216–220
    passive, 98–99, 103–105, 241n4
    psychodynamics of, 220–221
    separation theory on, 215–216
    terror management research on,
        221–222
    voice attacks leading to, 62
Aggressor, identifying with, 69–70
Ainsworth, M. D., 231n2
Alien self, 226n6, 234n5. *See also* Anti-self
    system
Allen, J. P., 231–232n3
Allen, K. L., 243–244n2
Alliance. *See* Therapeutic alliance
Aloneness, individuation and, 121, 122,
    126
Altruism, 61, 97, 106, 243n9
Ambivalent feelings, of parents, 40, 209
Analytic approach to voice therapy, 169
Anger
    motivational impact of, 239n5
    parental, 16, 57, 69–70
    as response to individuation, 123
    and self-attacks related to sexuality, 142
    withholding as alternative to, 99
Annihilation anxiety, 225–226n4
Annual Review of Gender Stereotypes, 206
Anorexia nervosa, 233n7, 235n7, 243n2
Antilibidinal self, 226n7
Anti-self system, 234–235n5
    in couple relationships, 34–35
    and critical inner voice, 16, 60

Morality
  and critical inner voice, 62–63
  cultural differences in views of,
    264–265n9
  and "normal" sexuality, 133
  and organized religion, 219–220
Mother. *See also* Parent(s)
  effect of insensitivity/withdrawal by,
    230n11
  good-enough mothering, 226n6
  idealization of, 47, 232n5
  shaping of infant's mind by, 239n5
Mother-Father-Peer Scale, 232n3
Motivational processes, 87, 239n5
Motivator, sex as, 131
Multidimensional psychotherapy to
    challenge fantasy bond, 151–162
  described, 151–152
  historical development of, 152–154
  principles underlying, 154–156
  resistance in, 158–160
  therapeutic process, 156–158
  therapist factors in, 160–161
Munion, W., 151
Murdoch, Iris, 9
Mystery of life, 6, 199–200

N

Narcissism, 193, 217, 218, 267n3
Nationalism, 196–197, 217–219, 221,
    267n3
Natural sexual behavior, 133
Neff, Kristin, 244n6
Negative distortions, 32–33
Negative parental traits, 65–73
  differentiation from, 180
  and idealization of parents, 65–66
  incorporation of, 69–72
  projection of, onto others, 66–68
Negative self-concept, 55–64
  challenging, in therapy, 48, 49
  and critical inner voice, 60–63
  described, 55–56
  and division of the mind, 58–60
  in formation of fantasy bond, 9–10, 20
  and incorporation process, 15
  and inwardness, 77
  origins of, 4, 56–58
  resistance to changing, 63–64
Negative self-image, 85–86
Negative thought patterns, 88

Negative traits and behaviors, challenging.
    See Challenging negative traits and
    behaviors (technique)
Negy, C., 251n12
"Neurobiological Foundations of
    Psychotherapy" (Przybyła), 248n12
Neuronal basis of resistance, 253–254n6
Neurons
  mirror, 21–22, 69, 234n2
  strengthening, in voice therapy, 181
Newman, K. M., 226n6
Normal sexuality, 133–134, 142
Nudity, views about, 139, 252n15

O

Older adults, 207, 264n6
Olsen, L. L., 230n9
Online addictions, 244n3
Organized religion. *See* Religion
The Origins of Totalitarianism (Arendt),
    267n4
Ostracism, fear of, 204
Outward, personal sexuality, 134–135
Overcontrol of emotion, 92
Overprotectiveness, 38
Overt resistance, 159

P

Pain
  critical inner voice as source of, 115
  loss of feeling to suppress, 91–92
  pool of primal, 158
  self-nourishing habits to dull, 108, 110,
    111
PAPD (passive-aggressive personality
    disorder), 241n3
"Paranoia and Self-Consciousness"
    (Fenigstein and Vanable), 236n2
Paranoid thinking, 66–68, 236n2
Parent(s). *See also* Mother
  acknowledging shortcomings of, 209
  affection between, 139–140
  death of, 70–71
  and development of negative self-concept,
    55–57
  distress over child's individuation for, 124
  exploring views of, in voice therapy,
    178–180
  fantasy bonds with. *See* Fantasy bonds
    in families

About the Author

Robert W. Firestone, PhD, clinical psychologist, author, and artist, has established a comprehensive body of written work and films focused on understanding how defenses are formed and how they affect human behavior and personal relationships. The primary emphasis of his theory has centered on the study of resistance in psychotherapy. He was engaged in the private practice of psychotherapy from 1957 to 1979, working with a wide range of patients, expanding his original ideas on schizophrenia, and applying these concepts to a theory of neurosis. In 1979, he joined The Glendon Association as its consulting theorist.

His major publications include *The Fantasy Bond, Compassionate Child-Rearing, Voice Therapy, Combating Destructive Thought Processes, Suicide and the Inner Voice, Fear of Intimacy, Beyond Death Anxiety, The Self Under Siege,* and *The Enemy Within.* In collaboration with his daughter, Dr. Lisa Firestone, he has developed three assessment instruments: the Firestone Assessment of Self-Destructive Thoughts (2006), the Firestone Assessment of Suicide Intent (2006), and the Firestone Assessment of Violent Thoughts (2008; Adult and Adolescent versions, 2009).